Psychological Development of Deaf Children

PSYCHOLOGICAL
DEVELOPMENT
OF DEAF CHILDREN

MARC MARSCHARK
The University of North Carolina at Greensboro

New York Oxford
OXFORD UNIVERSITY PRESS

Oxford University Press

Oxford   New York   Toronto
Delhi   Bombay   Calcutta   Madras   Karachi
Kuala Lumpur   Singapore   Hong Kong   Tokyo
Nairobi   Dar es Salaam   Cape Town
Melbourne   Auckland   Madrid

and associated companies in
Berlin   Ibadan

Library of Congress Cataloging-in-Publication Data
Marschark, Marc.
Psychological development of deaf children/Marc Marschark.
p.   cm.   Includes bibliographical references and indexes.
ISBN 0-19-506899-8
ISBN 0-19-511575-9 (pbk.)
1. Children, Deaf—Psychology.   2. Children, Deaf—Language.
I. Title.
[DNLM: 1. Child Development.   2. Child Psychology.
3. Deafness—in infancy & childhood.   WV 271 M363]
RF291.5.C45M373   1993
305.9'08162—dc20
DNLM/DLC
for Library of Congress   92-16491

9 8 7 6 5 4 3 2 1

Printed in the United States of America
on acid-free paper

To Janie

The wild geese do not intend to cast their reflections.
The water has no mind to receive their image.

Preface

I do not remember her name. She was short, cute, with sandy brown hair; she was always smiling and clearly enjoyed my company. She was also deaf and about 4 years old. It was a rare combination of events that threw us together: I was doing postdoctoral work with Allan Paivio at the University of Western Ontario, investigating metaphor comprehension among other things. I also was working for Mary Wright as the research coordinator for the Psychology Laboratory Preschool and hanging around Doreen Kimura's laboratory trying to learn about neuropsychology, language, and deafness. In return for acting as the "unofficial laboratory psycholinguist," Doreen had included me in the American Sign Language (ASL) lessons she and her students were taking. The classes were aimed primarily at facilitating the Kimura laboratory research with deaf aphasics, and it was in this context that a deaf woman came in with her young granddaughter.

As the unofficial member of the team, I offered to take the girl down to the preschool observation room and keep her occupied for an hour or so while her mother and grandmother took part in a research project. My signing skills were just below beginner level then, and it did not take long for my companion to discover that fact. At one point, we were looking through the observation mirror at a dramatic play center that included a "kitchen." My companion pointed into the room, turned to me, and made a sign. When I failed to respond, she took it (quite correctly) as a lack of comprehension. She then pantomimed putting bread into a toaster, pushing it down, taking out the finished toast, and taking a bite. Then, she repeated the sign TOAST.

I was awestruck. From my reading about development and deafness, I had acquired the idea that deaf children (and many deaf adults) were supposed to be concrete, literal, and egocentric. Nevertheless, this deaf 4-year-old recognized the need for social editing solely from my failure to make a socially appropriate response to her signing. Even more amazing was that she spontaneously produced a creative alternative to her sign that seemed remarkably similar to the many verbal metaphors produced by hearing children. According to the literature, deaf children were lacking in figurative language abilities, and yet. . . .

As becomes evident in Chapter 10 (if the reader has not already figured it out), my earliest foray into research on deafness concerned the production of figurative language by deaf children. We started out with only the naive question of whether deaf children produced any nonliteral content in their signing, because it seemed fairly well documented that they did not understand English metaphors and idioms. In fact, the first sentence of the first child we tested showed us that they did (thanks, Adrian, wherever you are); and the rest, as they say, is history. We went on to examine the nonliteral content in deaf children's signing versus hearing children's speech; figurative productions produced by deaf and hearing children at different ages; their relative frequencies in signing versus writing and in the productions of deaf and hearing mothers. I suppose that my 4-year-old companion is now nearing the end of high school, and Adrian must be about 24. Although I now have moved on to research in other areas of development and deafness, it is still those two young children who provide much of my motivation.

The theoretical, empirical, and practical considerations that made the writing of this book so exciting will become clear throughout the chapters to come. There are several more specific factors, however, that actually made it happen. Most central, perhaps, was my receiving a Research Career Development Award from the National Institute for Neurological and Communicative Disorders and Stroke (now administered by the more recently formed National Institute of Deafness and Other Communicative Disorders). The support of Dr. Judith Cooper, my program chair, throughout the duration of the award has made this book possible. More directly involved was Professor Herb Crovitz. It was Herb who suggested that I seemed "intellectually bored" (his words, not mine) and needed to do something "so onerous and hateful" that it would focus me in all aspects of my work.

"What's that?" I queried.

"Write a book," he said.

"On what?"

"It doesn't matter, write one on anything."

Twenty-four hours later, I understood Herb's wisdom and realized that the answer to my second question was right in front of me. Herb, this is all your fault.

There are also several others to whom I owe acknowledgment and thanks. Perhaps the greatest debt is to Al Paivio. It was he who gave me my interests in language and its relation to cognition—the interest that led me to study deafness in the first place. Most important, it was he who taught me how to keep an eye on the forest while walking through the trees, to seek and believe in the data rather than "hand-wave" at what might appear to be most palatable. As a mentor in a variety of respects, I acknowledge his contribution to whatever is right about this book and absolve him from any blame for whatever might be wrong.

Throughout my research on deafness, both empirical and literary, the assistance of the administrations, teachers, and students at the Central North Carolina School for the Deaf (CNCSD) in Greensboro and the North Carolina School for the Deaf (NCSD) in Morganton has been invaluable. Together with the deaf community of Guilford County, I must thank them for constantly reminding me that I never can truly know what it means to be deaf. I also owe thanks for help and support to Ron Wilson the superintendent of CNCSD, Ed and Susan Shroyer (who also supplied some of the figures in the book), Tim Barkley (who drew most of the others), and several others who have discussed issues raised in this book and helped me to see things from alternative perspectives: Garrett Lange, David McNeill, Renzo Vianello, Vicki Everhart, Amy Lederberg, and George Baroff. Special thanks are due to those who read earlier versions of these chapters: John Bonvillian, Diane Clark, Tony DeCasper, Betty Ann Levy, Margaret Halas (who also endured the indexes and bibliography), and especially Lynn Liben. Joan Bossert at Oxford University Press deserves honorable mention, primarily for leaving me alone but also for her warm support throughout this project.

Finally, I now understand why authors always acknowledge so much gratitude to their spouses. How do they put up with it? Ever since she convinced me to learn to "touch-type," Janie Runion has been helping me to enjoy writing this book. She came up with some valuable references in the social and affective domains of development and helped me think through some tough questions in these areas. She has been patient with me as I monopolized our only computer, spending many long days (including weekends) happily tapping away. In addition to being a superb copy editor, she has put up with an office that looks like a paper recycling center and has understood that if I did not look up when she walked by, she was better off just to keep on going. I probably could have done it without her help, but it would not have been as much fun.

Summerfield, N.C.   M. M.
May 1992

Contents

Psychological
Development
of Deaf Children

1

Development of Deaf Children: Issues and Orientations

A sensory deprivation limits the world of experience. It deprives the organism of some of the material resources from which the mind develops. Because total experience is reduced, there is an imposition on the balance and equilibrium of all psychological processes. When one type of sensation is lacking, it alters the integration and function of all of the others. Experience is now constituted differently; the world of perception, conception, imagination, and thought has an altered foundation, a new configuration. Such alteration occurs naturally and unknowingly, because unless the individual is organized and attuned differently, survival itself may be in jeopardy. (Myklebust, 1960, p. 1)

This passage set the tone for one of the first comprehensive accounts of the development of deaf children, Helmer Myklebust's *The Psychology of Deafness*. The implications of the passage are broad and numerous, but precisely which ones are drawn depend on the theoretical orientation that one brings to its reading. Perhaps a first impulse is to dismiss it as an outmoded and decidedly negative approach to deafness, intended to focus attention on audiological and rehabilitation issues and to ignore the resilience of deaf children. On closer examination, however, Myklebust presented some self-evident truths: That most deaf children experience a more limited world than hearing children, that their interactions with the world involve somewhat different rules and constraints, and that these differences have a variety of significant implications for the children's psychological development.

The goal of this book is to review, evaluate, and integrate more than 30 years' worth of evidence relevant to these issues. Taking Myklebust's view as a starting point, the question is not *Are* deaf children different from hearing children? but *How* are deaf children different from hearing children? or In what functionally significant *ways* does deafness affect the course of child development? The words "functionally significant" are important here for two reasons. The first reason is simply that there may be superficial differences between deaf and hearing children that do not have important implications for development because of either the nature of the differences or the context in which they occur. Thus a deaf child's hearing loss may not affect early social interactions with its deaf mother because the two can share a common medium of communication and the mother is sensitive to the needs of her child. The same hearing loss may have significant impact, however, when the mother is hearing and, as is most often the case, she is unaware of her child's deafness.

The second important aspect of "functional significance" here concerns the interaction of deafness with other aspects of development, leading to what are often referred to as *secondary effects* of deafness. Theoretical and empirical discussions of deaf children's development, like developmental psychology in general, frequently focus on the nature of observed or hypothesized relations between pairs of closely related domains. That is, beyond the direct effects of deafness—those relating to hearing and to speech—there are a variety of consequences of children's hearing loss that affect the children's interactions with the environment. These interactions, in turn, feed back into other aspects of development, resulting in qualitative as well as quantitative differences in the developmental histories of hearing and deaf children, especially those deaf children who have hearing parents. The goal here is to understand the subtle and not-so-subtle interactions of deafness and developmental change in an effort not only to understand deaf children better but also to shed some light on the variables and invariants of development in general.

Admittedly, it is frequently difficult in contexts such as this one to separate facts from feelings and to remain objective when considering the available evidence. Such a lack of prejudice is particularly difficult in the area of deafness because of its long history of contradictory findings. In part, such discrepancies have resulted from the sensitivity and emotions associated with research on deaf children's development—passions that are likely to arise during any investigation into possible cognitive, social, and cultural differences between a minority group and the majority in which it is embedded. As in other, similar situations, it often seems that the hearing majority thinks (rightly or wrongly) that it knows what is best for the deaf minority, and the deaf minority believes (rightly or wrongly) that it is powerless to change the establishment.

At a more objective level—the scientific and educational one—these passions sometimes linger and can impede progress toward the common goal of understanding the normal development of deaf children. All too often, however, the empirical facts (or what we believe to be the facts) about deafness and development are clouded by methodological difficulties and contradiction. One such problem is that of matching deaf children with appropriate (usually hearing) control groups for the purpose of determining the effects of some deafness-related variable. Another problem is selecting experimental materials or contexts that are equally meaningful or familiar to both deaf and hearing samples. Such controls are essential if the assessments of interest are to be validly and reliably interpreted. Nevertheless, research into questions of considerable importance sometimes appears to have been conducted with little regard for controlling significant dimensions of the investigatory setting.

Much more common is the problem of defining the significant dimensions. Does one match deaf and hearing children for chronological age, IQ, grade level, or language ability? Do we employ nonverbal tests or simplified materials to prevent bias, or do such manipulations simply introduce biases of their own? How far can we generalize from orally trained deaf children to manually trained deaf children or from deaf children of deaf parents to deaf children of hearing parents?

In an attempt to integrate and better understand both the methodological and theoretical issues relating to deafness and development, this book considers these questions as they arise in several domains. Toward this end, comparisons are made between deaf and hearing children and between deaf children with deaf parents and those with hearing parents. About 90% of children with congenital or early onset deafness are born into families in which both parents are hearing. Another 7% of such children have one deaf parent, leaving only about 3% who have two deaf parents. Most deaf children therefore are raised almost entirely in the hearing world, at least during infancy. Furthermore, most hearing parents of deaf children have relatively poor, if any, signing skills, and parent–child communication in such families frequently remains impoverished throughout childhood. Understanding the implications of this setting for early development is a primary goal of this book.

Perspectives on Deafness

In attempting to provide an integrated overview of the empirical evidence relevant to deaf children's development, it must be recognized that the studies to be described here initially were motivated by particular theoretical questions or, at the very least, were the products of research programs designed by investigators with particular theoretical orientations. Despite all efforts to be objective, it also is true that the way in which the pieces of the puzzle are assembled here and the conclusions drawn from them are significantly affected by my own theoretical views. Recognizing that fact and believing that we are still some way from a complete understanding of deaf children's psychological development, I consider most of the conclusions drawn here to be tentative.

Consider the variety of investigators interested in the psychological study of deafness. We come from such diverse backgrounds as linguistics and psycholinguistics, cognitive psychology, perception, speech and hearing, education, and developmental psychology. Within developmental psychology, we have been drawn from the areas of language acquisition, social development, cognitive development, and developmental disabilities. Yet others come to the study of deafness with more specific interests: interests in neuropsychology, intelligence, or reading. Finally, there are those investigators whose backgrounds are originally and entirely within the field of deafness by virtue of their clinical, experimental, or personal interests.

In part, the diversity and apparent inconsistencies of many findings in the field of deafness research derive from the varied histories of the investigators who contribute to the field. Our terminologies, questions, methods, and goals are different; hence it should not be surprising that we sometimes disagree about our conclusions. At the same time, however, it must be remembered that the scientific, psychological study of deafness is a relatively young field. As an adolescent drawing on the wis-

dom of its better established, elder sister disciplines, perhaps it deserves some lee-
way.

True, investigations involving deaf children have been around for more than a
century: *The American Annals of the Deaf* has been in publication since 1886 (as
the *American Annals of the Deaf and Dumb* beginning in 1847) and *The Volta
Review* since 1899. Most of the earliest work relating to deafness, however, concerned issues of rehabilitation and education. The twentieth century brought with it
more of an empirical approach to deafness and development, from Pintner's studies
of intelligence and short-term memory during the 1920s, to Templin's and Oléron's
studies of memory and cognitive development during the 1950s, to Furth's studies
of conceptual development and conservation during the 1960s. During the 1970s,
systematic explorations of deaf children's language development and academic
achievement were begun by Conrad, Quigley, Vernon, and others; and deaf individuals themselves took up the mantle of investigating the social, linguistic, and cognitive concomitants of deafness.

With the cognitive revolution of the late 1960s and 1970s, experimental psychologists became interested in deafness and deaf children as a means to provide
insight into the normal processes of language, cognition, and development. Some of
us became captivated with the field and have shifted our focus from an initial comparative approach to an emphasis on deafness and its concomitants. In my own
case, training as a psycholinguist and cognitive psychologist brought me first to
developmental psychology and then to deafness in an attempt to understand the
relation of language and thought. Initially, I expected that studying children, especially deaf children, would provide me with a relatively "pure" understanding of my
subject matter before language and thought became too intertwined to distinguish
between them. It soon became clear, however, that even in young children the interactions of language and cognition are inextricably interwoven with each other and
with the children's histories of verbal and nonverbal experience.

The above description is not so much intended to explain how I came to study
deaf children as to provide some understanding of the orientation adopted in the
chapters to follow. Given this brief biographical sketch, it should not be surprising
that deaf and hearing children are viewed here as active problem solvers attempting
to make sense of a less than regular environment. In the domains of linguistic, cognitive, and social functioning, it is assumed that children both shape their worlds
and are shaped by them. Working from this perspective, considerable emphasis is
placed on the *bootstrapping* of social and cognitive functioning. That is, it is
assumed that when children are "switched on" only the "hardware" and some simple, prewired "software routines" are functional. Quickly, however, interactions of
deaf children with animate and inanimate aspects of their environments provide the
information necessary for the building of more complex behavior patterns, both
external and internal. The suggestion that these earliest interactions are critical for
determining the course of development is not intended to imply that the course cannot be altered or is in any way predetermined. Nevertheless, the quality and diversity of early experience are seen to have important influences on children's
approaches to the world and their abilities to deal with novel situations.

Throughout the book, there is an emphasis on communication—verbal and nonverbal, intended and unintended. Language plays a central role in the normal development of human children, and its importance cannot be overemphasized. If there is one thing that the study of deafness has taught us, however, it is that *language* is not synonymous with *speech*; and it is assumed here that American Sign Language (ASL) or any other regular, socially agreed-on means of communication can be just as effective for normal development as is speech. With this assumption, though, come two caveats.

The first caveat is that, all biases aside, it is the case that over the millennia humans have developed a specialization for communication through the vocal-auditory channel. Although it is now clear that manual communication can fulfill all of the essential functions of oral-aural communication, it also may create subtle differences in social and cognitive functioning. In the social domain, for example, manual communication places a premium on face-to-face interaction, on nuances of expression, and on sequential rather than simultaneous touching and "talking." In the cognitive domain, emphasis on the visual-spatial channel may have both positive and negative consequences on development, as some abilities may become more finely tuned than in hearing children, e.g., in visual perception (Spencer & Deyo, 1993), whereas others may be relatively less developed, e.g., sequential memory (see Chapters 7 and 8).

The second caveat is a less subtle one, and one that is central to the discussions of the foundations of social and language development in Chapters 3 and 5, respectively. It is now well established that deaf children of deaf parents generally exhibit normal patterns of development in social, linguistic, and cognitive domains relative to hearing peers. This normality appears to be largely a function of the quality of early interactions with parents who are sensitive to the needs of their children and make use of a common channel of communication. Fewer than 10% of deaf children are in this situation, however, and most parents are not aware of their children's deafness until the expected norms for development are not met. This fact means that many of the typical interactions between parents and their infants are absent or impoverished relative to both hearing children of hearing parents and deaf children of deaf parents.

To the extent that these earliest interactions influence development in other domains, it can be assumed that some components of the normal bootstrapping process are altered or missing for deaf children with hearing parents. Hearing parents presumably could compensate for their children's lack of hearing if they were aware of the children's hearing loss—but such awareness is an exception. The important issue therefore is how hearing parents normally interact with their deaf infants and the apparent consequences of those interactions relative to the interactions among parents and children who share the same hearing status.

For both practical and theoretical reasons, those deaf children who have the earliest and most severe hearing losses have been the most interesting to investigators concerned with deafness. The primary motivation for this focus involves the fact that as age of onset and residual hearing increase, oral-aural communication becomes increasingly available and part of children's language repertoires. The relative influences of hearing loss, language modality, and related factors thus become correspondingly obscure and experimental control becomes much more difficult. In

the present context, children with earlier and more severe hearing losses are of primary interest for two reasons: They provide the "purest" examples of the effects of
deafness, and most of the existing literature is about them.

Plan of Study

The issues raised above are considered as they become relevant in the discussions to
follow. Throughout these deliberations, the primary goal is objectivity without losing sight of the practicalities and realities of those who are most involved.
Unfortunately, the issues of importance rarely are clear, even when they concern
apparently straightforward matters such as definitions of deafness and the demographics of the deaf population in the United States. These preliminaries are essential for understanding the development of deaf children, however, and so they are
considered first, in Chapter 2. Chapter 2 also provides some characterization of the
sociocultural contexts of deaf children, depending initially on whether their parents
are deaf or hearing and later on the nature of their schooling (see Chapters 3 and 4).
Included are brief descriptions of deaf culture (see also Higgins, 1980; Jacobs,
1988; Luterman, 1987; Padden & Humphries, 1988), the "socioeconomic status of
deafness," and signing and the American Sign Language (ASL) (see also Klima &
Bellugi, 1979; Wilbur, 1987).

Although primarily intended as a descriptive treatise, Chapter 2 sets the stage
for some of the later chapters by pointing out potential sources of difficulty and mis-
understanding for deaf children, parents of deaf children, and educators and
researchers involved in deafness. The issue of *deficiencies* versus *differences* is
important here, as different approaches and interests in deafness can lead to different interpretations of existing data as well as different directions of investigation.
The perspectives of parents, teachers, researchers, and the deaf children themselves
may be diverse, but all have in common the goal of understanding what it means to
be deaf and ensuring that deaf children are optimally ready to take advantage of the
opportunities of childhood.

Chapters 3 and 4 begin substantive consideration of deaf children's development by examining the origins and course of social development. Chapter 3, in
which the foundations of social development are explored, provides some integration of what we know about the roles of biological, cognitive, and communicative
origins of social development. The goal is to outline the contributions of such factors to early social relationships and the ways in which these relationships might be
affected by the hearing status of mothers and children. In this context, deaf infants
and their hearing mothers (and deaf mothers and their hearing infants) are found to
have somewhat different interaction strategies than hearing dyads. The central question is whether these different strategies lead to different consequences.

Chapter 4 considers social development beyond the earliest interactions with
parents. Of particular interest are the effects of early peer interactions and the
effects of schooling among other deaf children and deaf adults. Consideration of
social and personality development includes such topics as dependence, autonomy,
impulsivity, and prosocial development. Academic performance also is of interest

as it relates to achievement motivation, mastery, and the development of self-esteem and self-image.

Chapters 5 and 6 examine the origins and course of language development. Although it is necessary to distinguish language from social and cognitive development for the purposes of providing coherent overviews of these domains, it must be recognized that they are all tightly intertwined. At the very core of interactions between the newborn and its caretakers is communication, both "verbal" and non-verbal. Such communication is clearly two-way, even if one side does not always understand the message of the other. Chapter 5 considers the effects of these interactions on language development. Parental hearing status and mode of communication are examined together with the relations between gesture and language in deaf children compared to hearing children. The chapter also considers biological, linguistic, and cognitive constraints on language development (see also Chapter 12). In that context, the possible relations between babbling and language are considered as they relate to the vocal and manual productions of deaf infants. Chapter 6 then surveys the emergence of the first signs and first words, the movement from single units to multiple-sign and multiple-word utterances, and the development of meaning. The relative rates of manual and vocal language acquisition also are examined in this context. Special attention is paid to the question of whether there is an advantage for learning sign language over spoken language, expressed in the first signs being produced 1 to 3 months prior to the first words.

Chapters 7 through 10 examine various aspects of cognitive development in deaf children, always with an eye to disentangling the primary and secondary effects of deafness. Chapter 7 deals explicitly with cognitive abilities and intelligence. Issues surrounding the use of verbal and nonverbal assessments in this area are elaborated by examining the results of a variety of investigations concerning deaf children's intelligence per se and their abilities in several cognitive domains. Both methodological and theoretical concerns are raised about possible biases in the existing literature and assumptions underlying the ways we ask questions about deaf children's intellectual and cognitive abilities. The results of that discussion lead directly to consideration of short-term memory and long-term memory, in Chapters 8 and 9, respectively.

A diverse body of literature exists on deaf children's short-term memory abilities, especially as they reflect the underlying codes of mental representation. Children who are raised and educated using manual communication might be expected to rely heavily on visual-spatial processing, whereas those who use primarily oral communication may be tied more to the temporal-sequential constraints inherent in spoken and written language. In fact, there is considerable evidence that some deaf children are more likely to employ visual-spatial memory strategies relative to hearing peers. Chapter 8 considers the evidence on both sides of the issue, together with several important variables that relate to the children and the materials involved in those assessments. Chapter 9 then explores evidence concerning long-term memory in deaf children, especially with regard to the structure of their knowledge, the availability of alternative (linguistic and nonlinguistic) memory codes, and the effects of strategies, structures, and codes on memory performance.

Chapters 10 and 11 primarily address the verbal fluency of deaf children compared to that of hearing age-mates. Chapter 10 examines verbal and nonverbal creativity and flexibility. Nonverbal creativity has been assessed by a variety of methods that appear appropriate for evaluating children with hearing impairments. Most often, however, verbal creativity in deaf children has been assessed via written language production or via their understanding of nonliteral English expressions. Findings indicating that deaf children typically interpret English metaphors and idioms as though they are literal statements (if at all) have been taken as indicators of cognitive inflexibility and concreteness. More recent assessments of deaf children's sign language productions give a much different picture.

Chapter 11 surveys the extensive educational and empirical literature on deaf children's reading and writing abilities. Deaf children's poor reading abilities are now well documented, and it has been estimated that perhaps one-third of all deaf students graduate from high school functionally illiterate. In view of the relative impoverishment of early language interactions experienced by many deaf children and the unavailability of most spoken language, it should not be surprising that they lag behind hearing peers in such areas as vocabulary and grammatical competence. There is also a variety of evidence, however, indicating similarities between deaf and hearing students in several components of reading ability. Most surprising in that respect are reports suggesting that deaf readers engage phonological decoding processes similar to those of hearing age-mates. Unfortunately, much of that evidence comes from studies with deaf college students, who might not be representative of deaf children in general. This chapter also considers the popular belief that deaf children of deaf parents are superior readers relative to deaf children with hearing parents because of their early language experience (see also Chapter 6).

Chapter 12 provides an integrative overview of the central issues raised in the book. Intentionally not a summary, the chapter returns to questions of constraints and causes in deaf children's development. Possible neurological differences between deaf and hearing children are considered in this context, together with a hypothesized set of heuristics with which deaf children go about parsing, understanding, and remembering knowledge of the world. Looking back over the previous chapters, consideration is given to the possibility that the ways in which parents and educators structure deaf children's environments (intentionally or unintentionally) may be responsible for many of the differences and deficits observed in their performance relative to hearing children. Finally, the chapter considers the possible relation of scientific and educational research to living with a deaf child in the real world.

2

The Nature and Scope of Deafness

This chapter is intended as a general introduction to deafness, deaf people, and sign language. Understanding the development of deaf children requires some "feel" for the environments in which they grow up. Before considering the details of their early development within either hearing or deaf families, however, it is helpful to consider what the adult deaf community is like. Although most deaf children do not truly enter the deaf community until they are adolescents or adults, that description provides some idea of the "endpoint" of development for the average deaf child. The overview of deaf culture also is designed to give some feel for deaf children of deaf parents. Insofar as the context and rate of development in those children appear much the same as for hearing children of hearing parents, deaf children of deaf parents provide an important standard of comparison for deaf children of hearing parents—those who comprise fully 90% of all deaf children.

At the outset, it should be acknowledged that any attempt to provide complete and accurate descriptions of *deafness* and *deaf people* is unlikely to succeed. Like any other population, deaf individuals in the United States vary widely and, in some ways perhaps even more widely than the population of normally hearing individuals. In the case of the deaf population, there is variability contributed by differences in whether deafness is hereditary or adventitious, by physiological factors related to their deafness (e.g., degree and quality of hearing loss, possible concomitant impairments), by whether deaf children are born into deaf or hearing families, by the extent of linguistic and nonlinguistic interpersonal experience, and by the quality and type of education they receive. Whether or not these variables are any more significant than the innumerable factors that affect hearing children, they are *in addition* to the normal sources of variability that can influence development and as such seem destined to produce a more diverse population.

As becomes clear through the rest of this book, it appears that several of the effects of deafness, both primary and secondary, have a greater (additional) impact on deaf children's development than anything experienced by (most) hearing children. The emphasis here—on the interactions of social, linguistic, and cognitive experience—is intended to enhance the understanding of these domains within the whole context of development. To the extent that deaf children begin their lives by heading down somewhat different roads than hearing children, it seems most appropriate that we evaluate their abilities and disabilities within those particular contexts and within the more typical contexts of evaluation used with hearing children. Of course, context-sensitive assessments of deaf children (e.g., tests that are nonverbal or involve manual communication) are essential for understanding the full scope of their capabilities and the range of their typical performance. At the same time, the use of assessment tasks different from those used with hearing children or different standards of evaluation for the results of established assessments cannot give us a complete picture of the psychological development of deaf children.

The next section provides a characterization of the deaf population in the United States. Even with relatively recent figures, such a portrayal is necessarily approximate, but it serves the purpose of giving the reader some understanding of deafness and some perspective on life as a deaf adult in America. Recognizing that any description of a group is more or less accurate with respect to any particular individual within the group, it is important to try to avoid unfounded stereotypes. At the same time, stereotypes are the result of how individuals within a group are perceived and thus are often rooted in fact, if not universally applicable. Thus the "average deaf person" most surely exists, just as the "average hearing person" exists, but there may be fewer of them.

Definitions and Demographics of Deafness

To understand the influences of individual differences among deaf children in terms of their social, cognitive, and language development, it is important to understand the character of the community in which they are immersed. The definition and the demographics of deafness must be considered together in this context for the simple reason that the number of people counted as hearing impaired or deaf depend on how those terms are defined. Most generally, *hearing impairment* is used to refer to the spectrum of hearing losses from mild to profound (Greenberg & Kusché, 1987). Armed with this definition, Rodda and Grove (1987) suggested that in "the United States alone there are an estimated 13.5 million adults (6.6% of the population) who have some degree of hearing impairment" (pp. 3–4). If we accept this number, deafness is perhaps the single most prevalent, chronic, physical disability in the United States.

Myklebust (1960) defined the term *deaf* as referring to a more restricted group: "those in whom the sense of hearing is nonfunctional for the ordinary purposes of life." Consistent with this definition, Schein and Delk (1974) reported that approximately 0.2% of the adults in the United States (more than 505,500 people according to 1990 estimates) are without the capacity to hear and understand speech by the time they reach age 19. Focusing on children, more recent estimates of the prevalence of hearing impairment and deafness during the school years (ages 6 to 17 years) can be derived from data presented by Ries (1986) and from available census information (*Statistical Abstract of the United States*, 1985). According to data for 1981–1983, more than 800,000 (1.9%) of the 42 million children attending school in the United States had some degree of hearing loss. Approximately 135,000 children (0.3%) had losses that could be considered a major source of limitation in the school setting, but only about half of them (68,000, or 0.16%, of school attendees) were enrolled in special-education programs designed for students with significant hearing loss. Of these 68,000 students, 23,000 would be considered deaf and 45,000 hearing impaired according to the definitions given here.

A frequently encountered alternative to the term deaf is *hard of hearing*. To most who encounter the expression, *hard of hearing* represent a larger group than *deaf*. To them, deaf people are those who fit into a definition such as that of Myklebust, that is, those who do not have sufficient hearing for it to play a role in day-to-day life. Hard-of-hearing people, in contrast, are thought to include such individuals as our parents or grandparents, who simply do not hear quite as much as they used to. Myklebust (1960), however, described *hard-of-hearing* people not as those with a broader range of auditory impairments but as "those having a hearing loss but in whom [spoken] language acquisition has not been precluded" (p. 4). This definition was maintained by Rodda and Grove (1987, p. 1), who used it to refer to children with impaired hearing but whose speech and oral language abilities develop according to the same pattern, if not at the same rate, as hearing children.

The most interesting aspect of this distinction is that, rightly or wrongly, it high-lights the frequent centrality of spoken language in deciding who is deaf and who is not. In most cases, of course, those children who show the greatest facility for language acquisition are those who have lesser hearing impairments. It seems odd, however, that two children with identical hearing impairments might be differentially identified as "deaf" and "hard of hearing" solely because one has parents who can afford the cost of extensive speech therapy. In the present context, therefore, the term hard of hearing is avoided, and the degree of deafness based on audiological data is stipulated where relevant.

Mechanisms of Deafness

The centrality of aural-oral language capabilities when assigning the attribute of deafness to an individual is essentially a practical matter: Speech is undoubtedly the single most important auditory input available to most of us. Impairments that create hearing losses for sounds in the ranges of 500, 1000, and 2000 Hz are those that most affect speech perception because they are the frequencies at which the distinctive features of spoken language are expressed. With age-related losses, perception of the higher frequencies typically are lost before perception of lower frequencies (explaining why my father can hear me better than he can hear my wife). With congenital and early adventitious hearing losses, however, the particular frequencies involved vary widely, with a comparably broad range of implications. Thus although most statistics and descriptions of the severity of hearing impairment cite decibel loss in the better ear, consideration of any individual child must focus on qualitative as well as quantitative aspects of auditory loss and residual auditory discrimination abilities. This caution is especially important with mild hearing losses, in which the patterns of frequency loss tend to vary most widely.

Impairments that can cause hearing loss generally are categorized as either *conductive* (involving the middle ear), *sensorineural* (involving the inner ear and the proximal connections to the brain), or *central* (involving auditory centers of the brain and distal connection of the auditory nerve).[1] In all three cases, the measurement of practical interest is the loss of pure tone receptivity in the better ear, specifying the limit of potential hearing. Hearing is considered normal with losses up to 25 dB in the better ear; losses of 26 to 40 dB are *mild*, those of 41 to 55 dB are *moderate*, those of 56 to 70 dB *moderately severe*, and those of 71 to 90 dB *severe*. Losses of more than 91 dB in the better ear are considered *profound* hearing impairments. Most frequently, conductive hearing losses are of lesser severity, ranging up to about 60 dB. Hearing impairments above that level typically are of the sensorineural variety.

Etiologies of the hearing impairments observed in young children vary widely. Whereas heredity has been assumed to account for about 20% of all childhood deafness (Meadow, 1972), it accounts for a full 50% or more of the cases with known origins; hence the estimate of 20% of all cases is likely too low (Vernon & Andrews, 1990). According to 1984 figures for deaf children enrolled in special-education programs (Meadow-Orlans, 1987), the most frequent pathological causes of deafness (among subjects with diagnosed etiology) are maternal rubella (24%); childhood illnesses such as measles, mumps, and meningitis (25%); and birth-related complications such as prematurity, complications of pregnancy, trauma, and Rh incompatibility (22%).

The important point here is that the diversity in causes of congenital or early onset deafness leads to diversity in their developmental consequences. Most notably, with the exception of about 50% of hereditary etiologies, many cases of deafness carry with them the possibility of damage to other sensory systems or of central neurological damage (Konigsmark, 1972). This relation means that the identification of psychological differences between deaf and hearing children must be approached with considerable methodological care and a healthy dose of caution in interpretation. Differences and deficits typically attributed to some generic condition called *deafness* may well be the result of a host of related factors in addition to hearing loss per se.

Schooling of Deaf Children

Over the past 150 years, education of the deaf has changed dramatically in its content and in the number of children it reaches (for reviews see Luetke-Stahlman & Luckner, 1991; Moores & Kluwin, 1986). From 1850 to 1950, for example, enrollment in special schools or classes for the deaf rose from just over 1100 to more than 20,000. When special classes in regular schools are included, current figures are closer to 82,000, according to Ries (1986).

Craig and Craig (1986) reported that approximately 29% of deaf children in the United States attend state-run residential schools for the deaf, and 68% attend public schools either in special classes for deaf students or in regular classes with an interpreter or special resource teacher. In fact, enrollment in residential schools, especially for children of elementary school age, has decreased since the 1977 passage of PL 94-142, which contained a clause requiring education in the "least restrictive environment" for all handicapped children. According to the Center of Assessment and Demographic Studies (1985), enrollment in public residential schools dropped 18.3% from 1974 to 1984 and enrollment in private residential schools dropped 69% during the same period. Meanwhile, enrollment in public day-school programs increased more than 30% during that decade, and fully 40% of the children attending programs in residential schools are actually day students (Calderon & Greenberg, 1993). For the most part, those children who remain in residential schools tend to be those with congenital or early-onset deafness that is severe to profound (Schildroth, 1986).

Although a full consideration of the virtues and criticisms of PL 94–142 are beyond the scope of the present discussion (see Calderon & Greenberg, 1993; Moores & Kluwin, 1986; Vernon & Andrews, 1990) there is no doubt that it has affected education of deaf children in the United States. Whether those changes are seen as being for the better or worse depends largely on the hearing status and knowledge of the individual making the judgment. It is clear, however, that although the U.S. Congress placed the obligation of deaf education squarely on parents and local school systems, it has never appropriated sufficient funds to implement the law fully (Lowenbraun & Thompson, 1987). The result has been that most hearing parents of deaf children have taken on more responsibility for their children's education, without added external support. In many cases, this situation has forced parents into greater dependence on relatives, inconsistent child-rearing practices, and the cumbersome shuffling of work schedules and residences (Calderon & Greenberg, 1993; Luterman, 1987). In the absence of full implementation of PL 94-142, it is difficult to determine its potential impact on education of the deaf and the deaf community. Meanwhile, many schools for the deaf are finding it difficult to maintain minimum enrollments, and it remains to be determined if regular public schools really represent less restrictive environments for deaf children than do residential schools.

Beyond the practical side of deaf education for parents and administrators, differences in school experience represent confounding factors when trying to understand the psychological development of deaf children. Day schools for deaf children can be housed in public schools or residential school campuses; or the children may have to commute between the two for different subjects during the school day. These programs typically employ some deaf teachers or teachers' aides and do expose the child to other deaf children. In the residential school, however, deaf children have the opportunity to live with other children who are like them and to have both deaf adults and older deaf children as role models in all areas of work and play. The residential school thus long has been seen by the deaf community as the bastion of deaf culture and is the preferred educational system for most deaf children of deaf parents as well as being preferred by deaf teachers as a place to work. It should not be surprising that there appear to be academic and social-emotional differences between deaf children who attend residential schools and those who do not. The question is the extent to which such differences reflect a priori differences between the two populations versus effects of the programs themselves (see Chapter 4).

Proponents of residential schools for the deaf point out that without such programs only the 10% of deaf children with at least one deaf parent would be expected to possess knowledge of American Sign Language (ASL), deaf culture, and deaf art. Only that small proportion of deaf children would have the opportunity to identify with adults and older children who are similar enough to provide models for social, cognitive, and linguistic functioning. Although special preschools for deaf children now provide some such stimulation, the concern is with maintaining a social, cultural, and academic context that provides older deaf children with a supportive learning environment. In support of such arguments, deaf children enrolled in public schools generally evidence less adjustment and emotional maturity than those enrolled in residential schools, although the evidence is not unequivocal (Lowenbraun & Thompson, 1987).

At first blush, then, deaf children who attend residential schools for the deaf, especially those with deaf parents, might be expected to display more social, cognitive, and linguistic advantages than their peers without such benefits. At the same time, however, there are arguments concerning possible negative effects of residential schools in terms of the limiting effects on social-emotional development and the quality of their curricula (Johnson, Lidell, & Erting, 1989; Marschark, 1990; Vernon & Andrews, 1990). These issues are evaluated, where appropriate, in the chapters that follow. In fact, a host of variables related to school placement make any general conclusions about the utility of residential versus day-school programs difficult. There are several particular domains, however, in which positive and negative consequences of residential schools appear fairly well delineated. The primary goal is to identify the aspects of such environments that produce those effects and to determine the extent to which they might provide broader insight into the psychology of deaf children.

Socioeconomic Status

Although deafness is not confined to any particular social class, there are some conductive hearing impairments that result from factors frequently associated with low socioeconomic status (SES), including proximity to environmental noise, poor nutrition, and particular occupations. At the same time, there is a history in the United States of deaf individuals making up a surprisingly large percentage of the work force in heavy industry, such as steel, automobiles, and printing, where noise levels would make work difficult for workers with (perhaps temporary) normal hearing. In this vein, one colleague has suggested that we are on the verge of a deafness boom, as the hearing teenagers now growing up with portable stereos clamped on their heads soon will swell the ranks of deaf adults. For the present, however, this discussion focuses on those individuals who are already deaf.

It frequently is argued that congenital or early onset deafness in children is distributed evenly over the social strata (e.g., Rodda & Grove, 1987). Such an assertion, however, is clearly at odds with the fact that deaf adults tend to be overrepresented in the lower SES groups, at least in the United States (Schein & Delk, 1974). The latter finding suggests that deaf (and hearing) children of deaf parents also are likely to have lower SES, thus perpetuating that standing for the deaf community in general. Deaf employees, in fact, tend to be overqualified for their jobs and earn significantly less than their hearing peers. Moreover, the deaf are disproportionately employed in the service and clerical sectors, so, like other minorities, they are more likely to lack job security in the face of mechanization and cheaper labor.

In their frequently cited demographic study, Schein and Delk (1974) reported that deaf individuals with congenital or early-onset deafness are the most disadvantaged in terms of SES, and those who become deaf after age 11 are best positioned. There are, of course, likely to be interactions involved here relating to the effects of hearing loss on personality, education, job capability and performance, and employer selection biases. At present, however, it appears that deaf individuals continue to suffer economically from indirect consequences of their handicap. This situation may well change in the near future, as a result of the passage of the 1990 *Americans with Disabilities Act* by the U.S. Congress. In theory, opportunities for deaf individuals should begin to increase dramatically. In practice, there are several other variables, such as literacy skills, that must be considered.

Beyond its direct effects on families, SES also has an impact on the makeup of the student body in schools for the deaf. Deaf children in rural areas are more likely to attend residential schools, whereas those in urban areas are more likely to attend day schools or to be mainstreamed. In part, this difference is related to the financial standing of the family, as many day schools are private, and those children whose language skills are good enough to allow them to benefit from more normal school environments are often those who were diagnosed early, have had all possible medical attention, and have received extensive speech therapy. As a result, children in state-funded residential schools tend to be from lower SES homes and to have less oral ability than peers in day schools (Schildroth, 1986).

Not surprisingly, females and racial minorities within the deaf population are at an even greater disadvantage, relative to hearing peers, than are deaf white males. Deafness is more prevalent in males than females (Ries, 1986), but deaf females suffer the most in terms of education and subsequent employment, income, and divorce (Schein & Delk, 1974). Black children, in particular, appear to be overrepresented among deaf school-age children, according to data provided by Ries in 1986 (from the U.S. National Center for Health Statistics) and U.S. census estimates. Approximately 15% of the children attending school in the United States are black, but black children represent 18% of those who have hearing loss as a major cause of limitation in school and 20.6% of those with hearing losses greater than 41 dB in the better ear. More significantly, perhaps, black children comprise more than 23% of those attending special schools or classes for the deaf. These data suggest that, for whatever reasons (some of which are considered below), black children may be at risk for greater hearing losses and are more likely to attend special programs for hearing-impaired children relative to white age-mates. Hairston and Smith (1983) provide a description of the traditional inferiority of education available to black deaf children, as well as differences in culture, language, and their impact on both black and white deaf communities. Lest this discussion seem like ancient history, it is worth noting that Gallaudet University (then Gallaudet College) was not integrated until 1952, and many clubs for the deaf remain segregated.

It is certainly true that hereditary and pathological causes of deafness occur across all segments of society. When considering pathological etiologies of deafness, however, one would expect that families that have better medical care—with mothers who take better care of themselves prenatally and provide good postnatal care to their children—might be less likely to have children with congenital or adventitious deafness (as well as other medical disorders). Relevant statistics are not readily available in this regard, but the prediction could be seen as consistent with the data concerning the overrepresentation of minorities among deaf individuals. Combining the generally lower SES of deaf children with deaf parents and the medical costs and socioeconomic factors affecting the resources of hearing parents of deaf children, it is not surprising that deaf children, on average, live in families at or below the middle-middle class level (Rawlings & Jensema, 1977). Viewed another way, childhood deafness may not be as socioeconomically unbiased as is often suggested.

Parents of Deaf Children

The above descriptions, of course, capture only *part* of the situation of *some* deaf children. Schein and Delk (1974) provided a wealth of information about deaf adults in the United States, and Ries's (1986) report provided important data concerning deaf children. Neither study, however, tells us much about the hearing parents of most deaf children. Given that fewer than one in ten deaf children have even one deaf parent, relatively few of them can be considered to have been raised within the deaf community.[2] Upon their entry into residential schools or other programs, many more deaf children discover that community, including its values, customs, and rules (see Chapter 4). Until that time, however, most young deaf children reside almost entirely in the hearing world.

One source of information about the parents of deaf children is a report by Rawlings and Jensema (1977). Consistent with the assumptions made above, they found that the parents of hearing-impaired students tended to be disproportionally represented in lower income categories relative to national norms. In addition, these authors reported several findings consistent with the suggestion of indirect effects of parental SES on the incidence of childhood deafness. For example, 49% of the deaf children from families with the lowest incomes became deaf after birth, compared to only 17% of those from families with the highest incomes. "This could mean either that higher income children are deafened less often after birth—due perhaps to better medical care—or it may reflect later detection of hearing loss in lower income families, in which case it becomes difficult to know whether the child was perhaps actually hearing impaired at birth, though undetected" (Jensema & Rawlings, 1977, p. 9).

Rawlings and Jensema found that deaf children from high income families were relatively less likely to be enrolled in residential schools but more likely to be in special education classes and more likely to have begun attending special preschool programs prior to their first birthday (cf. Brasel & Quigley, 1977). At the same time, parental income was positively associated with academic achievement, frequency of speech usage, and speech intelligibility. Although these findings are no doubt interrelated, the precise nature of their relations remains unclear. The birth of a deaf (or otherwise handicapped) child can have profound effects on family life, and the academic success of such children depends on a variety of factors beyond parental income (e.g., parental education).[3]

The adjustment of hearing families to the arrival of a deaf child has a variety of ramifications, which are considered later in this chapter as well as in Chapters 3 and

4. The important point to keep in mind is that the entire family is affected by having a deaf child (Calderon & Greenberg, 1993). Although mothers do tend to take the greater responsibility for dealing with the added needs of a deaf or otherwise handicapped child, the effects of such changes are felt by each member of the family, perhaps especially by older children who may receive relatively less attention than they did prior to their sibling's diagnosis. Ultimately, placing a deaf child in a residential school may be motivated not just by the special programs available but also by the parents' striving (perhaps unintentionally) to regain some day-to-day normality in family life (Luterman, 1987).

Although there is no evidence that having a deaf child impacts on hearing marriages in any way that affects their success or failure, Lederberg and Mobley (1990) found that hearing mothers of deaf children tend to report more stress and are less satisfied with their lives (Luterman, 1987) than do mothers without deaf children. Calderon and Greenberg (1993) suggested that at the very least such families should be considered *at risk* as a result of having a continuous source of potential stress. Interestingly, Calderon and Greenberg found that social support was the single most important predictor of stress and adjustment within the family. Insofar as maternal functioning and coping have significant effects on deaf children's academic achievement and social-emotional development, such findings clearly indicate the need for greater support and training for hearing parents *throughout* their deaf children's childhood.

The Sociocultural Context of Deafness

It will not come as a surprise to most readers that deaf adults and their children are part of a social group that is relatively more restricted or at least well bounded than other groups defined by, for example, religious affiliation, political interests, occupation, or even their neighborhoods. As Vernon (1969, p. 552) asked, "Why would anyone choose to be with people with whom they could communicate only with great difficulty?" Indeed, for most people, their only knowledge of deafness, unless they live near a school for the deaf or have a deaf relative, comes from movies such as *The Miracle Worker* or *Children of a Lesser God*.

In recent years, however, there have been several books published about the deaf community, some written by deaf individuals and others by hearing people within the community or close to it (e.g., Higgins, 1980; Higgins & Nash, 1987; Jacobs, 1988; Luterman, 1987; Padden & Humphries, 1988). Although largely anecdotal, these works provide new and valuable insights into a subculture that otherwise might be inaccessible to hearing people. Indeed, Higgins (1980, p. 46) suggested that "deaf people are skeptical of hearing people's intentions" as well as being wary of other deaf people with whom they are not familiar or who do not play sufficiently active roles in the deaf community. In portraying deaf people as "outsiders" in a hearing world, Higgins gives the impression of an insular, even paranoid group that is less tolerant than other minorities—even of their own. It is thus well worth taking a closer look at the cultural and social contexts in which most deaf children eventually find themselves.

The Ethnic Status of Deafness

A *subculture* is typically defined in terms of its language, geographic location, technology, social relations, and ideology. Consistent with this definition, Rodda and Grove (1987) pointed out that deaf people have their own social structures, organizations, attitudes, values, and cultural history. In recent times, we also have seen the emergence of a deaf political structure, centered primarily around Gallaudet University in Washington, D.C. Among the other results of such changes are the Americans with Disabilities Act of 1990 and the creation of a new institute within the National Institutes of Health: The National Institute for Deafness and Other Communication Disorders, which will have a long-range impact on the quality and extent of research on both scientific and applied aspects of deafness.

In the same spirit as calling the deaf community a subculture, several authors have referred to deafness as an "ethnic concept" that applies not only to deaf people but to all participants in the deaf subculture (Nash & Nash, 1981; Rodda & Grove, 1987; Stokoe & Battison, 1981). Rodda and Grove (1987), for example, suggested that the ethnicity of deafness is a "preeminent" distinction—necessary if one is to understand the social structure and processes of the deaf community. Such broad definitions might be useful for sociological and political purposes, but it is difficult to see the utility of labeling hearing individuals with strong ties to the deaf community as *deaf*. More centrally for the present purposes, the deaf subculture and deaf ethnicity may be important for deaf adults, but they have relatively little impact on most deaf children, at least during the early years when their personalities and identities are emerging.

For deaf children of deaf parents, development in the context of this relatively closed social group likely has some rather specific consequences (see Chapters 3 and 4). Not only are deaf adults not fully assimilated into the larger, ethnically mixed society, but neither will be their (deaf or hearing) children. True, there is the support of the deaf community, and later chapters consider the evidence suggesting that deaf children of deaf parents may have a variety of advantages over deaf children of hearing parents in both social and academic domains. At the same time, however, one would expect that the potential for frustration, lack of self-esteem, external locus of control, and impulsivity characteristic of many deaf adults (see following section) could impact negatively on their relations with their children.

Emotional Stability and Deafness

Several factors noted above have the potential to affect the social and emotional lives of deaf individuals, just as they might affect members of any other ethnic minority. Unfortunately, most of the available data regarding the emotional status of deaf adults are from the 1960s and early 1970s, and many investigators consider these data no longer valid. There are some newer direct and indirect sources of evidence, however, coupled with anecdotal reports (e.g., Higgins, 1980), still suggesting that deaf adults on average may be more fragile emotionally than hearing adults.

In addition, there are more recent data indicating that many deaf children from hearing families carry emotional difficulties into adulthood (e.g., Leigh, Robins, Welkowitz, & Bond, 1989) (see Chapter 3).

The apparent burdens imposed on deaf individuals as both primary and secondary consequences of their deafness certainly appear to place them at risk for psychological distress. High rates of divorce and underemployment coupled with limited educational backgrounds, for example, seem likely to create a milieu conducive to depression, anxiety, frustration, and lack of self-esteem (Altshuler, Deming, Vollenweider, Rainer, & Tendler, 1976). Regrettably, accessibility of social services for the deaf is notoriously poor, and psychologists or psychiatrists who can sign are rare.

It is difficult to know precisely what toll is exacted from deaf children and adults by these disadvantages and to what extent those individuals who are fully supported by the deaf community (e.g., deaf children of deaf parents) are better adjusted. Part of this difficulty arises from the fact that most personality and social-adjustment tests are standardized on hearing individuals. Just as in the case of intelligence and achievement tests, there might well be cultural biases in such tests that give a distorted view of any particular deaf individual.

A second confounding factor is seen in the forms of the tests themselves, as they typically involve a "pencil-and-paper" format that demands some facility with English (see Chapter 3). Research conducted with my students and colleagues has shown that even apparently simple standardized tests and demographic questionnaires are sometimes misinterpreted by our deaf informants. Changing such tests or interpreting them for deaf individuals might seem an adequate solution, but generalization from original norms would be tentative at best. In fact, when relations (especially negative ones) are found between hearing loss and emotional self-report measures, investigators appear more likely to interpret them as indicating test bias than to take them as indicators of any emotional difficulty (e.g., Garrison, Tesch, & DeCara, 1978). Which position is correct and which does more service to the needs of the deaf individual remains unclear.

The fact that some findings obtained with standardized psychological tests may not be accurate with respect to the cultural experience and emotional makeup of many deaf individuals does not mean that deaf children or adults are necessarily any more emotionally stable than those tests indicate. It is likely, however, that the tests are somewhat less valid and less reliable when administered to deaf than to hearing populations. For example, to the extent that the (English) language requirements of such a test are more demanding for a deaf individual than a hearing individual and the intentions of the questions less clear, there may well be a bias against the deaf respondent. Finally, the fact that deaf individuals typically show far greater variability in psychological testing than hearing populations adds to the difficulty of applying hearing norms to the deaf population.

The most comprehensive survey of emotional problems in deaf adults was the "New York Project" of Rainer, Altshuler, Kallman, and Deming (1963). That study and subsequent evidence from follow-up studies in other locales indicated that, in general, deaf and hearing individuals are equally likely to suffer from severe mental illnesses. Meanwhile, deaf individuals typically are reported disproportionately more likely to suffer from some specific disorders, such as attention deficit disorder (Levine & Wagner, 1974; Vernon, 1969). Vernon and Andrews (1990) reported that in terms of the frequencies of severe depression and mental retardation, deaf individuals typically have lower rates than the general population. A study by Leigh et al. (1989), however, found that deaf college students were significantly more depressed, as a group, than hearing peers. More than 50% of the deaf students in that study reported being at least mildly depressed (on the Beck Depression Inventory), compared to 33% of the hearing students. Interestingly, for both deaf and hearing students, reports of greater maternal overprotection and lower maternal care were associated with a greater incidence of depression. "This argues anew for the relevance of maternal factors in molding the affective adaptability of young deaf adults and reemphasizes the value of appropriate maternal support and guidance in rearing deaf children" (Leigh et al., 1989, p. 253; see also Calderon & Greenberg, 1993).

When considering the emotional context of deaf children's development, it is important to avoid overgeneralizing from the relatively sparse data that are available. There are, however, some fairly well documented social-emotional problems of deaf children and adults that appear to be rooted in early socialization and intertwined with impairments in hearing and language competence. For example, there is some evidence indicating that deaf children are relatively passive and immature emotionally relative to their hearing peers (e.g., Lederberg, 1993; Schlesinger & Meadow, 1972), and they are frequently reported more likely than hearing children to be aggressive, to have tantrums, to be easily distracted and angered, and to have poorer self-images (for a variety of relevant findings see Altshuler, 1974; Meadow, 1976; Rodda & Grove, 1987; Stokoe & Battison, 1981). Some of these characteristics, such as the possibility of shorter attention spans, may be linked to other handicaps, genetic influences, or environmental factors independent of the effects of deafness. In general, however, many of these attributes may be considered secondary effects of deafness to the extent that they have their origins in, or are exacerbated by the context and content of early social development.

Several investigators have suggested that the differences in temperament observed between deaf and hearing individuals derive at least in part from differences in their social and educational experience growing up with a signed versus a spoken language (e.g., Cicourel & Boese, 1972) (see Chapter 3). This proposal does not mean that manual communication per se has any direct effect on temperament (cf. Sharpe, 1985) but that there are concomitants of having sign as the primary means of communication that affect other aspects of social-emotional development. For example, the switching of visual attention from the speaker to a referent can disrupt the "flow" of interpersonal communication. Erting, Prezioso, and O'Grady Hynes (1990) reported that deaf mothers of deaf 3- to 6-month-olds frequently move objects of interest to within the mother–infant line of sight and tend to maintain a positive facial expression 70 to 80% of the time when interacting with their infants (compared to about 50% of the time for hearing mothers interacting with their hearing infants). Specialized behaviors of this sort improve the efficacy and quality of early interactions, but these behaviors will occur only when mothers are aware of their necessity.

Such findings suggest that in order to unravel the effects of sign language from social and emotional aspects of deafness, we may need to distinguish among subgroups of deaf individuals differing in etiologies of hearing loss as well as early socialization contexts. At present, however, definitive clarification of the clinical/psychological implications of deafness is still some way off, and it seems safest to conclude only that deaf individuals, on average, may be at some greater risk for psychological distress than hearing individuals.

The Linguistic Context of Development

Language development is extensively considered in Chapters 5 and 6. In that context, deaf children's acquisition of manual and oral language abilities is discussed together with the implications of communication within these modalities for other aspects of psychological functioning. Language, however, pervades all aspects of development, including the various aspects of social development and social functioning that are considered in the next two chapters. It is therefore worthwhile to consider briefly the linguistic contexts in which deaf children are immersed, be they the oral environments of most children with hearing parents or the manual environments of those with deaf parents.

Language Availability for Deaf Children

Many quantitative and qualitative differences observed among deaf children with deaf parents and those with hearing parents can be linked to the effectiveness of early communication. From the outset, deaf children born to deaf parents have a channel of communication that serves cognitive, linguistic, and social functions. The advantage of this availability can be seen in findings from several psychological and academic domains suggesting that deaf children of deaf parents are more competent than deaf peers who have hearing parents (but see Chapters 4 and 11). Certainly, such differences have complex origins and cannot be attributed to any single cause. The importance of early communication, however, is reflected in the fact that children (of hearing parents) who lose their hearing postlingually tend to demonstrate superior abilities and adjustment in the same domains as deaf children of deaf parents relative to children of hearing parents with congenital or early-onset deafness. The relative availability of language also affects the quality and quantity of interpersonal interactions that form the social-cognitive matrix of development (see Chapter 3). Lack of a coherent parent–child communicative channel is, by definition, atypical; subsequent atypical development should not be surprising.

During the 1960s several investigators reported that only about 10 to 12% of hearing parents used manual communication with their deaf children. Diagnoses of deafness (or acceptance of those diagnoses) and commencement of oral language training typically was delayed until children (particularly boys) were 2 to 3 years old; and resultant quantitative and qualitative deficits in development were the rule. Since that time, however, the use of manual communication has been on the rise.

Jordan and Karchmer (1986) reported that 64.5% of the deaf students they surveyed used some form of sign language, and 66% of their school programs incorporated at least some signing in their curricula. Still, only about 35% of the students surveyed reported that they used sign language with their families, and the fact that 28% of those surveyed did not answer that question suggests that the true proportion might be much smaller. Jordan and Karchmer also found that minority children were more likely to use sign than were their white peers, probably because relatively fewer of the minority students were enrolled in mainstream settings (p. 130).

Despite apparent claims to the contrary (e.g., Schiff & Ventry, 1976; Todd, 1976), the available evidence suggests that the early use of manual communication does not hamper development of oral language skills (e.g., Jones & Quigley, 1979). Several studies have demonstrated that children who receive early manual training are actually more advanced in terms of early cognitive, social, and academic achievement and that these gains are maintained over the school years (Vernon, 1969) (see Chapters 4, 6, 11). Also contrary to popular claims, however, oral training of deaf children generally does not result in their assimilation into hearing society. It is important to distinguish here between deaf children who have severe to profound hearing losses and those with sufficient residual hearing to benefit from oral training and to carry on oral-aural communication. The latter group is not deaf by the "ordinary purposes of life" definition adopted above. Most children who are truly deaf eventually find themselves with friends, dates, and spouses who are deaf. They become involved in the deaf social clubs and other deaf organizations that play an important role in deaf social interactions and deaf culture. For the purposes of understanding both cognitive and social development, therefore, it is essential to have some understanding of the primary communication medium available to deaf children.

About Signing and Manual Communication

According to Karchmer (1985), 87% of profoundly deaf children and 75% of severely deaf children in the United States receive some kind sign language education during the school years. The term *manual communication* typically is used in a general sense to refer to all forms of interpersonal communication that depend on visual-spatial use of the body, head, and hands (Feyereisen & de Lannoy, 1991; McNeill, 1992, 1993). For the present purposes, *sign language* refers only to those standardized or lexicalized languages (e.g., ASL) that parallel the functions of spoken language but that depend on the hands as articulators, supplemented by facial expression, bodily movement, and orientation. Embedded within most such systems is some form of letter-by-letter *finger spelling*, used primarily in cases where there are no conventional signs for particular ideas, where a sign may be obscure or idiosyncratic, or where a receiver expresses doubt over the meaning of a sign. Finger spelling also is used by children and adults when a new sign is being introduced or created in a particular context, after which the finger spelling is abandoned (Marschark, Everhart, Martin, & West, 1987) (see Chapter 10).

Linkage of a sign language such as ASL to finger spelling is an interesting situation because it binds a language that is explicitly not English to an English "backup" system.[4] Paradoxically, that linkage assumes some degree of English fluency in a linguistic system that developed explicitly to take its place. This unique relation is worthy of consideration by both linguistic and psycholinguistic circles, but it has gone largely unexplored. A description of the status and role of fingerspelling in British Sign Language (BSL), however, has been provided by Spence-Sutton and Woll (1993).

For purposes of clarity in later descriptions of ASL signs and gestures, the North American manual alphabet and the numbers 1 to 10 are presented in Figure 2-1. Interestingly, the alphabet cannot correctly be called "English" because the British alphabet (like BSL itself) is different.

Identifying Sign Language Use

As a prelude to a description of signing as it might be available to deaf children, three distinctions should be noted. The first is that between pure manual communication and the language actually experienced by deaf children. It is rare that deaf children are exposed *exclusively* to sign language. Although some profoundly deaf adults rely solely on ASL for communication among themselves, their communication with deaf children and hearing individuals frequently includes oral movements and vocalization, which function to increase the number of cues available to the receiver. In educational settings, the multiplicity of language cues is explicit; and most "manually oriented" schools for the deaf employ either *Simultaneous Communication* (SC) or *Total Communication* (TC) in their curricula. SC refers to the simultaneous production of sign and speech and is the most common means of communication between deaf children and hearing individuals who can sign. Within the classroom, many schools utilize TC, a method that makes use of all potentially available sources of linguistic communication, including sign, speech, and amplification through the use of hearing aids.

A second important distinction is the one between formalized languages, such as ASL (or Ameslan), and the pidgin forms of sign language and Sign English used in most contexts other than social conversations among deaf adults.[5] Vernon and Andrews (1990) suggested that approximately 500,000 people in the North America use ASL on a regular basis. This figure seems likely to be an overestimate, however, based on the fact that roughly that number of adults lack sufficient hearing for aural-oral communication. Although most deaf adults know how to sign, not all of them know ASL. In fact, some hearing children of deaf parents argue that ASL cannot be taught explicitly postlingually. Rather, they argue, most deaf adults (of hearing parents) use some pidgin form of signing that combines the ASL they encounter in their interactions with deaf peers (of deaf parents) and other forms of signing and Sign English they learned in school.

Sign English is the form of signing most frequently taught to deaf children, a contrived combination of the morphological (word) structure of ASL and the syntactic (grammatical) structure and inflectional (number, tense, and mood) system of English. The goal of such a system is clear enough: It seeks to foster effective manual communication while facilitating the acquisition of English necessary for reading and many forms of functioning in a hearing society. Just as the oral versus man-

FIGURE 2-1. Manual alphabet and signs for the numbers 1 to 10 of American Sign Language. (Copyright © 1988 by Sugar Sign Press; reprinted by permission.)

ual debate raged for many years (Rodda & Grove, 1987; Vernon & Andrews, 1990), there is now an ongoing debate concerning whether deaf students should continue to be taught using systems such as Sign English or should learn entirely in ASL, one goal of which would be the preservation and extension of deaf culture (Johnson et al., 1989; Moores, 1990).

For the present purposes, the description of the signing available to and adopted by deaf children is restricted primarily to ASL in order to highlight the linguistic status and some psycholinguistic implications of manual communication prior to considering language development. The structural changes to ASL that accompany its "conversion" to Sign English are not considered here. It should be understood, however, that the imposition of English grammar on a sign system and even the use of particular initial-letter handshapes in otherwise identical signs (e.g., *D*-EPART-MENT, *C*-LASS, *G*-ROUP) are only concessions to educational pursuits and are not in any sense fundamental to sign language in the generic sense or to ASL in particular.

At the same time, one could mount a theoretical argument concerning the inevitability of ASL becoming more English-like with time, as the users of ASL remain in an English-speaking culture and deaf children receive increasingly more successful instruction on reading and writing. To get some idea of how such modification of ASL might come about in the context of biological and social pressures on deaf children to develop language, interested readers are referred to Bickerton's (1984) consideration of the emergence of Hawaiian Pidgin and Hawaiian Creole, as well as Fischer's (1978) consideration of creoles and ASL. The third introductory distinction to be raised here is that between sign language and gesture (McNeill, 1993). This issue is considered in depth in the context of the foundations of language acquisition in Chapter 5. At this point, the purpose of such a restriction is simply to distinguish linguistic, rule-governed forms of communication such as speech and sign language from the gestures and "body language" that accompany them both. McNeill (1985, 1992) argued convincingly that both language and gesture derive from the same underlying *verbal* system, and Marschark (1992) has described the role of gesture within sign language production. When attempting to understand development, however, it is necessary to distinguish the acquisition of conventional forms of *language* from more idiosyncratic forms of communication used by prelingual children. Toward this end, the focus here is on those forms of sign language that are used for the "ordinary purpose of life."

On the Status of Sign Language

In both practical and scientific terms, it is difficult to understand how any informed observer could claim that a sign language such as ASL is not a "true" language. From its early uses as a mnemonic and a specialized, if simple, means of silent (usually secret) communication (Hough, 1983), signing emerged during the late eighteenth and early nineteenth centuries as a systematic means of communication with and among the deaf. Primarily developed in its conventional forms by hearing educators and deaf individuals, the early use of manual communication in classrooms and less frequently between deaf children and their parents must have opened new horizons of interpersonal contact not much less dramatic than the classic scene in *The Miracle Worker* in which the deaf and blind Helen Keller first grasps the meaningfulness of fingerspelling.

Although several authors have made reference to American Indian "sign languages" in their discussions of the ASL (e.g., Hough, 1983; Rodda & Grove, 1987), those manual systems did not *replace* spoken language; insofar as we know, there were no silent tribes. Instead, Amerind signs were used primarily as part of an *interlingua* when different tribes having different spoken languages gathered for festive, political, or commercial purposes. Interestingly, many of the more functionally based and iconic Amerind signs have near-identical analogues in ASL, e.g., COFFEE, DRAW, BOAT (Tomkins, 1969).

Over the last 200 years, signed languages have become both more conventional and more rule-governed in their use by deaf people and more accepted by hearing people as a viable means of communication and education. Most recently, the naturalistic use of ASL and other sign languages has become an object of study in its own right as a means of extending our linguistic and psycholinguistic understanding of language and language development. The linguistics of ASL were well described by Klima and Bellugi (1979) and Wilbur (1987), so little detail is presented here. Because there are still sufficient doubters who think otherwise (especially among European audiences), however, it is worth emphasizing that such examinations are in no danger of reifying an otherwise "informal" and "concrete" gestural system. Sign language conforms to the definition of *language* in essentially all senses that are held holy by linguists.

Perhaps the most thorough analysis of what it would take to define a language was provided by Hockett (1963) and Hockett and Altmann (1968). Hockett's (1963) examination of *linguistic universals* (i.e., characteristics shared by all human languages) led him to propose a set of "design features" that distinguish language from various forms of animal communication. Some of these features are shared by various communication systems other than human language, but only mature language posesses them all. Design features are briefly considered here as they relate to sign language and deaf individuals so as to clarify the objective status of sign languages, such as ASL, as formal languages. It might be argued that the conforming of ASL to external definitions of language is beside the point—that the functional, pragmatic role of ASL in communication by deaf and hearing individuals is sufficient for the attribution of "linguistic status." Such an argument may have intuitive appeal, but it avoids, rather than eliminates, the need for scientific evaluation of sign language and in the long run can only hurt the chances for a comprehensive understanding of the role of manual communication in psychological functioning. For this reason, it is worth considering Hockett and Altmann's 16 design features in some detail.

1. *Channel.*   Languages, in part, are defined by the channel of their expression. Unlike Hockett's (1963) original description of design features, which limited language to the vocal-auditory channel, Hockett and Altmann (1968) explicitly included the manual and visual channels as potential modes for language. Chemical senses (e.g., taste and smell) are never involved in language.

2. *Broadcast transmission and directional reception.*   Like speech, signs fundamentally are broadcast in all directions at once, so long as there are no modality-specific blockages (e.g., walls) between producer and receiver. Sound and most

human languages, via the vocal-auditory channel, however, provide for directional reception, such that the receiver can identify the relative location of the producer via the wonders of binaural hearing and the movement of sound through the air. As Paivio and Begg (1981, p. 22) noted, "This feature has important psycholinguistic consequences when contrasted . . . with visual stimuli, including the sign language of the deaf, since broadcast transmission to some extent frees the receiver from being locked in to the source . . . one is more free to do other things while listening to a message than while looking at one." With regard to social and cognitive development, directional reception, or more precisely the lack of it, may have significant implications for deaf children (see Chapters 3 and 7).

3. *Rapid fading.* Signs, like speech, are evanescent. Unlike other means of communication—such as writing or leaving a scent behind—when a sign or word is finished it is gone. Language producers can certainly replicate linguistic signals, and mothers seem to do so often, but there are particular consequences of the rapid fading of such signals for social interaction, learning, and the course of development (correlated to some extent with the development of memory).

4. *Interchangeability* and 5. *Complete feedback.* The first of these two features refers to the fact that all competent users of a language are both producers and receivers of linguistic signals, barring special pathological circumstances. Interchangeability thus distinguishes human language from several types of animal communication in which one sex produces particular signals that the other cannot. Similarly (and again barring pathological limitations such as blindness and deafness, respectively), both signers and speakers receive their linguistic messages as they produce them; that is, they have complete feedback.

6. *Specialization.* An essential aspect of both sign and speech is that they are specialized for communication and have essentially no effect on the world by physical production. The hands and vocal tract may at times be involved in functions other than communication, but when they are marshaled for language they do not fill any other roles.

7. *Semanticity* and 8. *Arbitrariness.* Signs and speech have meaning only by social contract. Although there are iconic and indexical signs that "look like" what they represent (e.g., TENNIS, HAIR) and onomatopoetic words that sound like what they represent (e.g., "swish," "plop"), most linguistic units are arbitrarily linked only by convention to the things they represent. This feature is readily apparent to hearing speakers when it is noted that the word "whale" is smaller than "microorganism," although the things they represent have the opposite relation. With regard to sign, naive hearing speakers often have doubts about its arbitrariness, seeing an occasional iconic sign and overgeneralizing in a way that reveals a previous bias (cf. Page, 1985). Heaving sighs of relief at the special status of speech, they can slam the door on sign language, flop into their easy chairs, and click on their (not closed-captioned) television sets. In fact, aside from some possible minor variations, the semanticity and arbitrariness of sign language mean that deaf children may not learn to sign any faster than their hearing peers may learn English (cf. Orlansky & Bonvillian, 1984); but they are able to discuss things that are abstract as well as concrete, rather than being "context-bound" in a "concrete" world of "gaps" and "blanks" (cf. Evans, 1988).

9. *Discreteness* and 10. *Duality of Patterning.* Both speech and sign permit

the manner in which some units are produced to communicate affect or magnitude (e.g., through loudness, voice, or violations of the signing space). Signs and words, as well as their component parts, however, are discrete rather than continuous, which means that a pair of words or signs with different meanings differ in at least one phonological, or *cheremic*, feature. These distinctive features of both signs and words eventually come to be discriminated by the young child, and a potentially infinite vocabulary develops from a limited number of constituent elements. That is, the components of linguistic messages and the messages themselves represent two levels of structure, or dual patterns.

11. *Openness* or *productivity*.   Via duality of patterning at both the syntactic and semantic levels, human languages are creative, productive communication systems. We can sign things that have never been signed before; and, in principle at least, there is nothing about which we cannot construct a signed or spoken description.

12. *Displacement*.   Linguistic messages, be they signed or spoken, may refer to things that are not immediately present. Although it frequently has been argued that sign language can refer only to the concrete "here and now," anyone who has ever taken the time to learn to sign knows otherwise. Together with discreteness, arbitrariness, and semanticity, displacement appears to capture the essence of human languages, placing demands on a complex cognitive system within each language user as well as defining the linguistic status of that which they produce.

13. *Prevarication*.   When we say that human languages allow the reference of things that are not immediately present, there is the assumption that those not-present things nonetheless exist. True language, however, also allows the communication of false, meaningless, and imaginary messages. Alas, deaf children appear to lie just as well and just as often as their hearing peers (although this topic apparently has not been studied).

14. *Reflexiveness*.   In addition to the freedom to lie and refer to things that are not, language also confers the ability to refer to itself. Birds cannot sing about the beauty of their songs, nor can dogs bark about other dogs' barking. Thanks to its reflexive or metalinguistic character, language allows signed or spoken messages about signed or spoken messages. Without this feature, books and meetings on language and linguistics would prove difficult indeed.

15. *Learnability* and 16. *Traditional transmission*.   Unlike animal communication systems, humans who know one language typically have all of the necessary equipment to learn another. Deafness confers some difficulty on the learning of spoken (but not other signed) languages, but certainly no more than does blindness on the learning of sign language. Other than in such special, pathological situations, however, all languages are learnable. Moreover, they are traditionally passed from generation to generation, most frequently through the direct and indirect tutelage of parent to child. Animal communication, in contrast, is passed along genetically, although there are some cases (e.g., songbirds) in which juveniles must be exposed to "competent" models if they are to develop normal song. There is no sense, however, in which speech is transmitted in any more fundamental manner than sign.

It is important to remember in this context that most deaf children have hearing parents, and that many if not most have parents who do not sign. Those parents who do sign are rarely competent signers, and it is rarer yet that they know ASL. Therefore, although sign language can and sometimes is passed from parents to child, ASL and related languages may be the only human languages that children are more likely to learn outside than inside the home. Deaf children of deaf parents are the beneficiaries of direct, parental traditional transmission; but those with hearing parents may have to rely on later, sometimes less competent models. In fact, there is now considerable evidence that in the absence of traditional transmission, children may develop regularized and rule-governed communication systems on their own (e.g., Goldin-Meadow & Mylander, 1984). The extent to which these nonconventional systems conform to linguistic definitions of language is a separate issue but one that is sure to attract scrutiny in the near future.

It is also important to keep in mind that Hockett and Altmann's (1968) design features are characteristics of languages, not of language users. They described universal features of the vessels of human communication but not the nature of that communication per se. To understand the acquisition and use of language requires the consideration of psychological and social factors, factors that are dealt with later. Taken together, design features describe universal features of natural human languages. Regardless of whether sign systems such as ASL would qualify as "natural" languages, they clearly conform to the essential features of language as defined in these linguistic terms. ASL carries all of the structural, semantic, and pragmatic qualities and constraints of spoken language.

In the absence of any linguistic or psychological data indicating that sign languages are inferior to spoken languages as a means of learning or communication, the only possible explanations for the failure of many programs (and entire countries) to adopt manual communication systems for the deaf are concerns over social integration and oral chauvinism. Both of these issues are considered at several places in this book in the context of deaf children's development. Now, we turn to some of the structural characteristics of sign language and their relevance for later considerations of the acquisition of language by deaf children.

Sign Language Structure and Sign Language Users

Rodda and Grove (1987, p. 101) noted that "Until 1970 . . . visual gestural systems were thought to be linguistically primitive, lacking in vocabulary, grammatically confused, and incapable of expressing subtle and abstract concepts." In fact, one need only attend an international conference on handicapped children (versus one on deafness, which attracts a select audience) to discover how widespread these impressions remain. Contrary to such beliefs (held even among teachers of the deaf in some places), established sign languages such as ASL are intact linguistically. As indicated in the previous section, ASL has its own combinatorial, morphological, syntactic, and semantic rules. Other than in educational concessions, such as those of Sign English, the arbitrariness of sign language extends to the vernacular of the country in which it is found as well as the physical world itself. If sign language appears to the naive observer to be related to English, it is only because the signer is using a modified form of sign in order to improve communication with English-dominant receivers.

"PHONOLOGY" AND MORPHOLOGY

Signs themselves can be described in terms of three to five classes of phoneme-like features, or *cheremes* (Stokoe, Casterline, & Croneberg, 1965). (*Phono-*, from Greek, meaning sound or voice, seems somewhat inappropriate here.) Of these, chereme classes, *hand configuration*, *place of articulation*, and *movement* are the primary three descriptors, described by Stokoe and his colleagues in the first comprehensive morphological analysis of ASL. Within each class of cheremes are several *primes* that serve to distinguish "minimal pairs" of signs. In English, minimal contrasts are those in which different words differ in only a single phoneme, as in /duk/ and /tuk/. With ASL, a minimal contrast involves two signs that differ by a single chereme prime, such as APPLE and ONION, which differ only in their place of articulation, or EGG and NAME, which differ only in their movement (see Figure 2-2).

Stokoe et al. (1965) identified a set of 55 primes: 18 handshapes, 12 places of articulation, and 25 movements, which carry most of the load of sign contrasts. Other parameters include whether a sign is made with one or two hands (*hand arrangement*) and the *orientation* of the hand(s) relative to the signer during production of a sign. During sign movements the place of articulation and, less frequently, the handshape may change from their normal, canonical or *citation* forms. Movements also may be modified as a means of inflecting verbs (e.g., when COMPLAIN becomes COMPLAIN CONSTANTLY), and a variety of such modifications can be incorporated into signs to create figurative and other nonliteral constructions (Klima & Bellugi, 1979; Marschark et al., 1987). Newport (1981) referred to a related distinction: that between the conventional *frozen lexicon* and *sign mime*, the latter consisting of "analogue" or "mimetic" signs that "reflect aspects of the world in form" (p. 97) by their shapes, movements, or manner. Sign mime in this sense includes both conventional and nonconventional productions and is thus broader than the "nonliteral" signs examined in studies of deaf children's creative use of signs (see Chapter 10).

One central component in the conventional modifications described by Newport is the use of *classifiers*. Classifiers are one component of sign language that does not appear to have a direct analogue in English. There are actually two senses in which "classifier" is used. The more general of the two, used by Wilbur (1987) and others, refers to any handshape that changes position during execution of a sign. Thus all signs that include movement can be said to incorporate a classifier.

The psycholinguistically more interesting use of "classifier" concerns the use of several handshape primes that conventionally have particular referents. Examples include an upright D-hand or a G-hand to denote a person; a bent, downward V-hand to denote an animal; and a thumb-up 3-hand to denote a vehicle (see Figure 2-1). Classifiers typically are first assigned an explicit referent (e.g., a particular person) and then are used to denote action or manner of action. In Figure 2-3, for example, the person classifier is used in the sign MEET, and the vehicle classifier is used in the sign PARK. More complex uses of classifiers occur outside of specific signs, frequently in iconic movements. Wilbur (1987, p. 59), for example, noted that two classifiers can be used simultaneously, as "3 on the right and G on the left for a vehicle chasing a person, or a bent V on the right hand and 3 on the left hand for an animal chasing a vehicle."

apple   onion

egg   name

FIGURE 2-2. ASL minimal contrast pairs differing in location (APPLE and ONION) and movement (EGG and NAME). (Copyright © 1988 by Sugar Sign Press; reprinted by permission.)

There is also a class of less specific classifiers that typically function more like adjectives than nouns. Most often, these classifiers denote shape or extent. For example, F-hands or C-hands (see Figure 2-1), moved vertically or horizontally can denote widths of cylindrical objects, and I-hands can denote thin filaments or lines (and indeed are involved in signs such as DRAW and SPAGHETTI). Note that although both these and the more specific noun-like classifiers make use of alphabetical and numerical primes, their meanings are completely arbitrary and are not

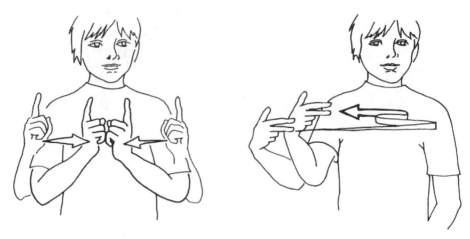

Figure 2-3. ASL sign MEET incorporates the "person" classifier, and the sign PARK incorporates the "vehicle" classifier.

tied to the designation of the handshape. Classifiers thus are distinct from the use of initial-letter handshapes in Sign English to distinguish semantic alternatives of signs such as *S*-ITUATION, *C*-ONTEXT, and *E*-NVIRONMENT. With ASL, all three are made with the same canonical sign (SITUATION), the precise meaning being derived from the context (for further discussion of classifier flexibility and morphological derivation see Klima & Bellugi, 1979; Newport, 1981).

Precisely because of the lack of correspondence with any structure in English, the acquisition and psycholinguistic use of classifiers present a fascinating topic of study. The closest similar device in English seems the occasional relation of particular phonetic combinations to semantic domains. For example, the initial sound /sn-/ seems to be associated with a variety of nose- or (metaphorically) nosey-related words: snoop, Snoopy, snooty, snore, sneeze, sneak, sniffle, snuffle, snot, and snotty; and initial /cr-/ sounds seen to be associated with immediate (typically nonbeneficial) contact between two things: crunch, creak, crumble, crack, crash, cram, and crop (as in cutting or a riding crop). These constructions may have some connotative effects (e.g., is the Canadian term "snarky" positive or negative?), but they have little if any denotative semantic significance. In comparison to ASL classifiers, they appear to be something to sniff at.

Handshapes, their movements, and their points of articulation conform to a variety of combinatorial, morphological rules. These rules involve such features as the nature of the signing space, symmetry in movement, the use of "base" hands, and the ways in which signs and classifiers are combined (Wilbur, 1987). At the level of cheriology and morphology, sign language has its own accents, dialects, and *home signs*. Dialectical differences can produce some difficulty in communication as well as some lighter moments, as when I first discovered that one of the signs I originally learned in Canada was indistinguishable from a common "four-letter" sign profanity in North Carolina. An interesting and enlightening survey of accents and dialects in ASL can be found in Shroyer and Shroyer's (1985) *Signs Across America*.

Home signs are those idiosyncratic signs used within particular families or other small groups in much the same way as particular words and names are used in hearing families. Both are most common in homes with small children (often originating in youthful mispronunciations or missigns), but some seem to live on into adulthood. These signs often are obscure to those outside the family, just as, presumably, are my family's "grabbers" and "bazuter." Relatively little research has been conducted concerning the characteristics and contexts of such signs, but there seems little doubt that they conform almost universally to all of the cheriological constraints of conventional signs, just as one would not expect "home words" to violate pronounceability requirements of English. Morphological violations may be more common in both home signs and home words, but that remains to be determined [but see Mylander and Goldin-Meadow's (1991) description of the home signs of a child without sign language models; and Vernon and Andrews's (1990) description of the manual gestures developed by deaf individuals isolated from conventional sign language].

SYNTACTIC STRUCTURES

Linked to constraints on the formation of sign components and their combination, akin to phonology and morphology, ASL has a rich variety of syntactic regularities that had gone unnoticed until relatively recently. Unfortunately, much of the excellent research relating to the grammar of ASL by authors such as Kegl, Newkirk, and Padden is unavailable to most readers, frequently being in the form of conference presentations, unpublished manuscripts, or internally circulated bulletins at institutions with large ASL or deafness research programs. Wilbur (1987, Ch. 6) provides excellent coverage of ASL syntax, including many references to such papers. Rather than duplicate that analysis here, several brief points about sign syntax are made as they relate to broad developmental issues.

Perhaps the most important issue to consider with regard to the syntax of signed languages, especially ASL, is the linguistic chauvinism imposed by the host language. Those familiar with more than one spoken language can recognize that languages vary in the extent to which particular morphological and syntactic constraints are operative. English, for example, happens to be one of the most word-order-"conscious" languages in the world. Thus when naive English-speaking observers see the relative flexibility of sign order in ASL, the first response frequently is to assume that it has little or no syntax—another perceived strike against sign language as a true language.

However, duality of patterning in no way requires a particular mechanism for the recombination of linguistic units into higher-order structures. Within the broad spectrum of human languages, it turns out that the rigidity of word order in a language is inversely related to the degree to which it can be inflected. English and French are languages with relatively strict word-order constraints and relatively little inflection. Japanese and ASL are languages with relatively free "word"-order constraints and quite a lot of inflection. The richness of the morphological possibilities and the frequent, if infrequently acknowledged, inflections of nouns and verbs in ASL provide for sufficient grammatical complexity to satisfy any linguist (Klima

& Bellugi, 1979); but then, linguists are better at shedding their linguistic chauvinisms than the rest of us, and deaf linguists may be the best of all.

The emphasis on the inflectability of ASL should not be taken as implying that it lacks ordering constraints. A variety of studies have indicated that ASL has a preferred, underlying subject–verb–object (SVO) ordering, as indicated by grammatical judgments and the "prosodic" features of signing (Lidell, 1980). The extent to which the SVO preference in ASL is the result of contamination by the SVO requirement in English has been a matter of some debate (Wilbur, 1987, pp. 141–148). Although there now appears to be a preference for assigning that structure to ASL on the basis of empirical measures, the issue seems to be related to the finger-spelling issue raised earlier (the mixing of English and an explicitly non-English language) and is hopelessly confounded. The important point is clear: ASL users do exhibit production and comprehension tendencies for the SVO order. There is no obvious reason, however, to assume a source for this preference outside the contribution of English as a host language (cf. Lillo-Martin, 1993). Perhaps the most fruitful approach would be to make comparisons across several sign languages and their respective hosts. More than likely, the manual ones reflect underlying patterns similar to those of their vocal hosts. If not, similarities across sign languages would demonstrate a qualitative independence from vocal languages and would suggest the possibility that deaf (i.e., ASL-using) and hearing individuals might well structure their conceptions of the world somewhat differently.

In summary, ASL has a complex syntactic structure including all of the hallmarks of linguistic status: a "phonology," morphological rules, and a complex syntax including hierarchical structures (i.e., embeddings and subordination), inflection, and preferred orderings. The fact that all rules and structures of ASL and other signed languages do not necessarily conform to those of their host languages is not surprising. Such findings would be worthy of wonder only if one assumed that signed languages mapped directly onto their host vocal languages. That it is not the case only adds to the psychological and linguistic reality of sign as a qualitatively different mode of communication. We therefore should be on alert for corresponding qualitative differences in the interactions of deaf and hearing children within their social, cognitive, and academic environments. The extent to which those differences might have significant rather than superficial impact seems one of the most interesting questions concerning the psychological development of deaf children. Not surprisingly, it forms a recurring theme throughout this book.

Summary

Deaf people comprise a surprisingly large minority in the United States. It is a group with its own culture, art, social organizations, and language. Deaf children who have deaf parents are brought up within that culture and learn and absorb the values and proclivities of the community naturally. Deaf children of hearing parents, however, comprise 90% of the deaf population. For them, it frequently is not until they attend a residential school for the deaf that they encounter deaf adults and deaf children with deaf parents, who serve as role models and social educators. The social consequences of this situation, for both groups of children, are considered in the next two chapters. Linguistic, cognitive, and academic consequences are considered later.

Because of the nature of the invisibility of their handicap, deaf individuals tend to be underemployed and over-represented among low SES families. Together with the potential for related stress and familial instability, these factors affect a variety of dimensions on which deaf children differ from hearing children and deaf children with deaf parents differ from those with hearing parents. As is seen in the next chapter, there are a variety of "advantages" to having deaf parents if a child is deaf. Despite the many goals and aspirations of deaf children, their parents, and their teachers, most deaf children are still handicapped relative to their hearing peers, and it should not be surprising if such a profound handicap affects their development in a variety of ways. It is the nature of those developmental differences and the means by which deaf children cope with them that comprise the substance of the remaining chapters.

Notes

1. *Sensory-neural* is sometimes alternatively divided into sensory (peripheral) and neural (central) components or sensorineural and central components, eliminating the separate *central* classification.

2. There is also a potentially fascinating and relatively large group of hearing children who were raised by deaf parents. These individuals appear to have cognitive and linguistic abilities as well as neuropsychological organizations that differ from hearing children of hearing parents. One also would expect that the course of their social development would differ from hearing children of hearing parents. This impression is shared by many of those who have hearing friends whose parents are deaf, as well as (sometimes) by those children themselves. With few exceptions, however, this group has not been investigated.

3. It should also be acknowledged that Rawlings and Jensema's (1977) results might have been affected by sampling bias, as only 60 percent of the parents contacted completed the surveys. Those particular parents might have tended to be those with higher- or lower-than-average incomes, more involvement in their children's education, or with greater concerns or knowledge about deafness. Parental education levels were not reported.

4. Throughout this book, "English" is used in a generic sense to refer to the oral vernacular of the deaf child's larger social context. Most of the research described involves children who use either ASL or English (or some combination of the two); there is no reason to believe that these differ from other manual and oral languages.

5. There are a variety of other manual + oral communication systems taught to deaf children in various settings, including Seeing Essential English (SEE1), Signing Exact English (SEE2), and Cued Speech. These systems are less commonly used in academic settings than Sign English (or *Siglish*) and its various pidgins, and they practically never occur in naturalistic communication contexts. For descriptions of these restricted, educational language systems see Wilbur (1987).

3

The Early Years: The Social-Emotional Context of Development

This chapter considers the context of deaf children's early social and emotional development (which of course also is the context of early cognitive and language development). Early research in this area provided a rather bleak picture of deaf children living isolated lives filled with emotional distress and psychological disorders (for a review see Myklebust, 1960). More recent studies, in contrast, have suggested that deaf and hearing children appear similar on several dimensions relevant to social interactions with their mothers and their peers (for a review see Lederberg, 1993). This discrepancy can be explained in part by differences then and now in the social environments of deaf children and by attitudes toward deafness and development. At the same time, several methodological aspects of both the early and more recent research limit the conclusions that can be drawn from those studies.

Looking ahead, it is suggested that the social correlates and implications of deafness begin earlier, have more far-reaching direct and indirect consequences, and are far less understood than is generally assumed, which is not to suggest that such consequences are necessarily negative. It would be surprising, however, to find that environments that lead to marked cognitive, academic, and linguistic differences between deaf and hearing children do not also lead to some differences in personality and social behavior. Furthermore, in those cases in which deafness is not hereditary, deaf children already may be at risk when they are born, the result of those maternal or fetal/neonatal medical problems that led to their deafness in the first place.

Suggestions of any real differences in the patterns of social and emotional development in deaf and hearing children may sound somewhat rash when considered in the context of recent literature about deafness and against the backdrop of the current politics surrounding deafness in America (see various chapters in Marschark & Clark, 1993; Moores & Meadow-Orlans, 1990; Volterra & Erting, 1990). Nonetheless, such conclusions are fully in accord with the intuitions of most parents of deaf children (e.g., Calderon & Greenberg, 1993; Luterman, 1987) and will become more apparent after consideration of the relevant literature. In particular, examination of consistent findings in several areas relevant to the developmental contexts of deaf children reveals a thread that connects a variety of studies of early mother–deaf child interactions with other studies concerning early language development, attachment, and child-rearing practices. Although there is a notable gap in relevant research between the early school years and adolescence, the available studies provide a new and exciting perspective on the social growth of deaf children.

Origins of Social Development

The goal of this section is to fit the early interactions of deaf children and their parents into the larger context of social development. Toward this end, the focus is on the beginnings of social interchange between deaf children and their mothers. These earliest foundations have ever-widening implications for cognitive, language, and social development: They set the stage for (but do not *determine*) exploration, learning, and further social interactions as the child ventures beyond the mother–infant relationship and eventually beyond the familial context to deal with the rest of the world.

Normal babies come into the world with the potential for hearing a universal set of language sounds and contrasts, some of which are maintained and some of which disappear as the child matures and experiences language input (see Chapter 5). Even before birth, however, it appears that the sounds in a hearing child's prenatal environment may indirectly affect the course of development. During the last trimester of pregnancy, the fetus turns from its former position and now rests with its head against the mother's pelvis. At this point in development, normal fetuses already have considerable responsiveness to sound, especially human speech (Eisenberg, 1976). For those mothers who speak and are carrying babies who can hear, this period presents the opportunity for the fetus to hear its mother's voice and heartbeat through bone conduction (Als, Lester, & Brazelton, 1979). That the fetus experiences its mother's voice before birth is not a matter of dispute. How the effects of that experience are interpreted, however, has important implications for our understanding of children who are born deaf and those hearing infants who are born to deaf parents.

A variety of studies have shown that prenatal auditory experience can exert powerful effects on postnatal learning and perception in humans and animals. DeCasper and Sigafoos (1983), for example, showed that infants less than 3 days old can be trained to suck on a nonnutritive nipple in a particular pattern in order to obtain auditory exposure to the sound of a maternal, intrauterine heartbeat. DeCasper and Fifer (1980) reasoned that early auditory competence would support a variety of biologically adaptive functions, including language development and mother–infant bonding. Furthermore, they suggested that "Mother–infant bonding would be best served by (and may even require) the ability of a newborn to discriminate its mother's voice from that of other females" (p. 1174).

DeCasper and Fifer fitted 1- to 3-day-old babies with stereo headphones and a nipple attached to a pair of tape recorders. After establishing the baseline for spontaneous sucking in each infant, they presented infants with a two-choice task in which they could "select" one of two tape recordings by sucking at a rate either faster or slower than their baseline rates. One recording contained the infant's mother, and the other contained the voice of an unfamiliar woman, both reading the same story. The results indicated that DeCasper and Fifer's babies, who had had less than 12 hours postnatal experience with their mothers, were willing and able to work to hear their mothers' voices by adjusting their sucking patterns. DeCasper and Spence (1986) even showed that when mothers read a particular passage aloud (viz., to their fetuses) daily during the last 6 weeks of pregnancy their newborns showed a preference for the familiar passage over a novel one 2 to 3 days after birth. Interestingly and importantly for the present purposes, fathers' voices, which are not available to the fetus until after birth, do not show any sign of being reinforcing to the neonate (DeCasper & Prescott, 1984).

These results suggest that for normal mother–infant dyads prenatal and early postnatal maternal speech can play a role in initial mother–child bonding. This conclusion does not mean that there are no other cues that would be available to deaf babies or hearing babies of deaf mothers. Balogh and Porter (1986), for example, have shown that maternal odors are preferred stimuli for day-old infants who are breast-fed, although they apparently are not preferred by those infants who are bottle-fed (like those tested by DeCasper and Fifer). Moreover, both deaf and hearing infants probably engage in *additive cue strategies* using diverse sources of information for identifying familiar people. As Hofer (1987) suggested, it is likely that the components of mother–infant interaction in each sense modality have their own dynamics and transduction mechanisms.

What is important here is that the early, physiologically based "regulators" of interaction can influence developing systems *throughout their formative stages* and contribute to attachment and early mother–child relationships. These relationships, in turn, affect and are affected by other aspects of development as the infant enters into a symbiotic relationship with its environment (Main, Kaplan, & Cassidy, 1985). In human society, deaf children may not be at any particular disadvantage due to their failure to recognize their mothers' voices at birth. Compared to hearing dyads, however, deaf infants and their hearing mothers may have different interaction strategies that have different consequences (e.g., Koester & Trimm, 1991; Lederberg, 1993).

Spelke and Cortelyou (1981) reviewed a variety of findings indicating that voices and faces are the most effective attractors of attention for hearing newborns. Normally hearing babies are able to link maternal mood with expression and faces with voices as early as 2 months of age (with respect to older deaf children see Odom, Blanton, & Laukhuf, 1973), and they can decipher the affective tone of maternal speech by 9 months. Spelke and Cortelyou concluded that (for hearing babies) speech maintains adult–child interactions better than visual contact alone. Clearly, these linkages are based largely on the extensive postbirth interactions of mother and infant, and both deaf mothers and hearing mothers of deaf infants spend considerable time interacting with their newborns in a variety of modalities (Koester & Trimm, 1991; Maestas y Moores, 1980; Rea, Bonvillian, & Richards, 1988; Spencer, 1991). The interesting question is whether the absence of vocal-auditory cues to emotional states have any particular consequences or are compensated for by alternatives in other sense modalities.

Snitzer Reilly, McIntire, and Bellugi (1990) reported that facial expressions associated with the basic emotions are produced consistently by both deaf and hearing children by 12 months of age. They examined the naturalistic interactions of five deaf infants, all of whom had deaf parents. At 12 months the children all appeared to have command of the basic affective displays and used "culturally appropriate" (i.e., nonvocal) attention-getting devices. Findings of this sort suggest that many of the earliest interactions between mothers and their deaf infants proceed naturally and normally, at least when the mothers are also deaf. In the case of hearing mothers, it is difficult to assess the full impact of the lack of vocal-auditory communication on early interactions with their infants. The following sections suggest that such a want during the first year of life may well have some influence on subsequent development. One would expect, however, that such effects would be less pronounced when parents are aware of their infant's hearing loss (e.g., when there is a history of deafness in the family) than when they are unaware of the hearing loss. In the former case, parents can engage in a variety of strategies intended to enhance interactions in nonauditory domains (e.g., Erting et al., 1990). Although it is by no means certain that such compensation is necessary, it certainly seems likely to be beneficial.

Early Mother–Child Interactions

The evolution of any parent–child relationship is a combination of the initial states of the parents and child, and fast learning by both. During the earliest stages of mother–child interaction, it is essential that the mother and child become attuned to each other through the development of synchrony and reciprocity. *Synchrony* here refers to the contemporaneous intertwining of the behavior patterns of mother and infant as they converge on a common routine of interaction. *Reciprocity* refers to the development of mutual cuing systems that result in complementary behaviors— a kind of symbiosis between mother and child. Mothers and infants stimulate and respond to each other, developing reciprocal patterns of interchange that usually are different from those that pass between the infant and other individuals. These early interactions provide the roots for later attachment and emotional bonding between mother and child.

Brazelton (1982) suggested that vocalization can be replaced as an element of this early symbiotic relationship by smiles, particular postures, and tactile cues, so long as they are rhythmically patterned. Several other investigators have argued that maternal touch can have powerful effects on newborns, both deaf and hearing, and have shown that deaf mothers are likely to engage in more touching behavior with their infants than are hearing mothers (e.g., Rea et al., 1988). Spencer (1991) also showed that hearing mothers of deaf 12- and 18-month-olds (enrolled in an early intervention program) engage in more tactile and visual interactions with their children than hearing mothers of hearing children. None of these findings, however, speak to most deaf infants, whose hearing parents have no idea of their deafness and thus do not attempt to compensate for the lack of hearing with increased touching. Successful "replacement" of maternal vocal cues seems unlikely if the mother does not recognize the need for such alternatives.

Consider a typical and almost universal routine: The infant cries or fusses; the mother attends to it, touching and caressing it, talking to it, and perhaps picking it up. The infant temporarily ceases to fuss; looks at the mother, who is now speaking or smiling; produces some vocalization; and is "answered" by the mother with more vocalization, more handling, and so on. It is important to note here that, although relatively inexperienced at such things, the infant is playing a vital, reciprocal role in this interaction. Unwittingly, the child is giving mother cues that in part determine her behavior, including the passing of cues back to the child. Over time, both sides become better at the socialization game, and these reciprocal patterns of interaction develop greater synchrony and complexity (e.g., Bell & Ainsworth, 1972). True linguistic conversation is still a long way off, but in the meantime the child is learning about taking turns vocally and behaviorally and about being part of a complex social unit.

Consider now the situation when the mother or infant (or both) are deaf. For deaf mothers there are now electronic devices available to signal when the child is crying or making other noises, so the mother can initiate her part of the social dance—if she can afford the technology and is able to monitor its output. From that point, the interaction can follow a near-normal course, with sign language playing the predominant linguistic role, sometimes accompanied by vocalization. Ultimately, manual communication allows the two to interact at a distance, permitting the mother to return to other duties while maintaining at least some contact with her child.

The situation is probably different in the case of deaf infants, especially in those cases (the majority) in which the hearing mother does not recognize (or even imagine) her child's deafness. As noted above, one potential source of difference stems from the medical bases for children's nonhereditary deafness. Even if there are no direct consequences of such conditions beyond hearing loss, there may be secondary effects, such as maternal stress or temperament differences, that affect the way in which mother–child interaction patterns develop.

Also relevant to the early bonding of deaf infants and their mothers is the finding that species-specific and especially maternal vocalizations play an important role in soothing the infant across a wide spectrum of animals, including humans (e.g., Eisenberg, 1978; Gottlieb, 1980). High-frequency vocalization typically causes distress in young infants (as it does later), whereas low-frequency vocalizations have the dual effects of quieting the infant and eliciting gross motor movement. In the latter case, the infant is responding to a stimulus complex in which vocalization typically is associated with physical satisfaction at touching, feeding, and soothing (Eisenberg, 1978).

For human children born with severe hearing impairments, this prewired adaptive mechanism is unavailable. The extensive touching of their deaf infants by both deaf and hearing parents (Rea et al., 1988; Spencer, 1991) may serve a soothing function comparable to that of parental vocalization. In fact, it may turn out to be the case that oral and manual communication (broadly defined) have functionally equivalent effects on early social-emotional development. At present, however, we know the effects of vocal stimulation on infants, whereas the effects of "substituting" manual stimulation remain to be determined.

The Growth of Social Interaction

The impact of an infant's deafness on early socialization with hearing parents is not limited to the relative importance of maternal vocalization or touching as tools for quieting a fussy newborn. For example, hearing parents of hearing infants spend considerable time attending to their infants' varied responses to adult vocalizations. When an infant is deaf, such interactions are different and depend on the linkage of parental vocalizations to nonvocal behaviors. Deaf infants do not orient to the sound of the mother's voice, nor do they become quiet at the sound of her approach. As the months go by, hearing parents realize that their deaf infant's behavior is deviating more and more from what is considered normal. Some parents come to feel rejected, deprived, and anxious about the lack of reciprocity (R. I. Harris, 1978; Luterman, 1987). Eventually, of course, their social behavior changes to accommodate the unexpected responses (or lack responses) from their young partners. The resulting social interaction strategies acquired by children, however, may be relatively idiosyncratic and restricted in their generalizability to persons outside the immediate family.

The Emergence of Attachment

Psychological attachment is not something that can be seen but is inferred from particular behaviors of the infant. In a variety of mammalian species, infants attempt to maintain proximity or contact with their mothers and other familiar social companions and show aimless locomotion and withdrawal at separation from those individuals. The most consistent indicator of attachment across species, however, is the demonstration of distress through vocalization (Hofer, 1987).

In human infants, the first phases of attachment occur during early infancy and are indicated simply by the selective responsiveness of the infant to one or two significant adults. By 8 months of age, the infant is seen to attempt to maintain proximity to the mother or other caregiver in an obvious and intentional manner. At this point, attachment is often assessed using Ainsworth's *Strange Situation*. In this paradigm, an 8- to 18-month-old child is occupied in a play room, accompanied by the mother and a stranger, and is subjected to several episodes in which one of the adults leaves the room and returns after a brief absence. Those infants who positively greet their mothers at reunion or who approach them to seek comfort if they have shown signs of distress are classified as *securely* attached. Those who fail to greet or approach the mother or who begin to do so but turn away are classified as *avoidant*; and those who approach mother but cannot (or will not) be comforted, have temper tantrums, or react negatively toward the mother are classified as *resistant* in their attachment relationship (Ainsworth, 1973).[1]

In the case of babies of deaf mothers, it is important to recognize at the outset that there may be cultural factors in the deaf community, relative to the hearing community, that shape maternal attitudes toward mother–child interactions. There is considerable evidence that hearing mothers' conceptions of attachment depend on societal norms as well as the nature of their relationships with their own mothers (e.g., Ricks, 1985). In Northern Germany, for example, there are strong demands for children to be self-reliant, and proximity-seeking is discouraged. At the same time, there is a greater frequency of avoidant behavior in infants by North American standards, as German babies cry less when their mothers leave and are less likely to approach them on their return in the Strange Situation (Grossmann, Fremmer-Bombik, Rudolph, & Grossmann, 1988). Nevertheless, those dyads are well adjusted in terms of patterns of infant interactive behaviors and maternal sensitivity to their children's needs.

In contrast, the encouraging of emotional dependence in Japanese babies has the result that patterns of secure attachment (again by North American standards) are rare, with a much greater proportion of resistantly attached babies than are found in U.S. or German studies (Miyake, Chen, & Campos, 1985). Although the differences in the precursors of attachment behaviors between deaf and hearing mothers within any particular country may be smaller than those between hearing mothers in two different countries, it is not at all necessary that deaf and hearing communities would have identical standards for mother–child attachment behaviors (Lederberg & Mobley, 1990).

Considering the social development of deaf children, Schlesinger (1978) suggested that, "During the attachment phase of infancy, communication between parent and [hearing] child occurs primarily through such nonverbal means as voice quality, touch, and smile" (p. 160). Schlesinger's statement emphasizes her goal of contrasting early aspects of attachment in deaf children with its more sophisticated component of linguistic communication. At the same time, however, the foregoing discussion indicates that maternal vocalization may play a larger role in early development than Schlesinger appears to have imagined. The role of maternal language in later mother–child interaction is considered in detail in the next section. For the present, it is sufficient to point out several aspects of early attachment that appear linked to verbal communication, even if these possibilities have not been investigated explicitly.

First, although hearing infants may understand relatively little of the content of mothers' speech at first, by the time they reach 8 to 9 months of age (the point at which studies of attachment in the Strange Situation begin) they typically have acquired a considerable comprehension vocabulary. According to Gregory (1976), this vocabulary includes a variety of words and phrases that mothers of hearing children—but not mothers of deaf children—use to indicate that they are taking temporary leave of the child and to elicit the child's acknowledgement of that fact (but see Greenberg & Marvin, 1979, described below). Moreover, while mother is gone, the hearing child is able to "keep tabs on her" from a distance by following her auditorally through the house, a monitoring that is not available to the deaf child.

Second, to a considerable extent, young hearing children's abilities to interpret parental emotional states appear to come from the observed correlation of those states with particular verbal and nonverbal behaviors (Spelke & Cortelyou, 1981) and later via verbal explanations and analyses (Snitzer Reilly et al., 1990). In the case of deaf children with hearing parents, that correlation is likely to be somewhat lower, and later explanations concerning the emotional situations experienced by both parties are less frequent and less competent owing to the typical inefficiency of their parent–child communication. This relative lack of coordination seems likely to be responsible in part for the finding that deaf children may be unable to match facial expressions to pictures of emotion-arousing situations as late as 7 to 8 years of age (Odom et al., 1973) despite their recognition of emotions when actually involved in interpersonal interactions (Snitzer Reilly et al., 1990). It thus appears that even if the *content* of language does not play a primary role in attachment, it may have secondary effects on the emotional development of the child during the time the attachment bond and other components of social interaction (e.g., locus of control) are developing.

Third, there is a long but primarily anecdotal history of describing deaf children as less likely to be securely attached to their mothers than are hearing peers (e.g., Gregory, 1976; Schlesinger & Meadow, 1972). This conclusion might seem reasonable, at least if restricted to deaf children of hearing parents, given the apparent role of speech and hearing in the development of normal reciprocal, mother–child relationships. However, *the empirical case has not yet been made.* In the case of mother–child dyads with low communication efficiency, for example, deaf children's apparent indifference to the mother's leaving could be due to their not being aware of or understanding the departure (Greenberg & Marvin, 1979). Subsequent distress at her return thus could well be the result of generalized surprise or fear rather than (primarily) any mother-directed reaction. At the same time, other sources of temporary stress in the relationship of deaf children and their hearing mothers (e.g., recent discovery of their child's hearing loss) may lead to incorrect interpretations of attachment behaviors that appear different from those in hearing dyads. Finally, it may well be that deaf children and their hearing mothers simply develop behavioral patterns of reciprocity that are somewhat different than those of hearing mother–child dyads and thus not accurately captured using standard techniques.

Beyond examining how deaf toddlers respond to laboratory assessments of attachment, it is possible to observe both similarities and differences in the behavior patterns of dyads consisting of hearing mothers and deaf versus hearing children. For example, hearing mothers of deaf children frequently are described as playing a far more active, perhaps intrusive, role in their children's day-to-day behaviors than mothers of hearing children (but see Lederberg, 1993). As a result, when the mother's attention to her deaf child is withdrawn (whether in a laboratory situation or the real world), the change is greater from the child's perspective than it is in the case of a hearing child. At the same time, it also may be more welcomed.

Early Language and the Attachment Bond

A variety of studies have described the communicative interactions of hearing mother-deaf child dyads (e.g, MacKay-Saroka, Trehub, & Thorpe, 1987, 1988; Meadow, Greenberg, Erting, & Carmichael, 1981; Swisher, 1984). Evidence from studies with preschool and early school-age children reveals that relative to mothers in either hearing or deaf dyads, hearing mothers of deaf children are more likely to be intrusive, tense, and directing in their verbal and nonverbal interactions (Gregory, 1976; Henggeler, Watson, & Cooper, 1984). Hearing mothers who have not had the benefit of early intervention programs, especially those who have not received manual communication training, also appear to be more controlling of their deaf children's behavior compared to those mothers who have had such training (e.g., Brasel & Quigley, 1977; Goss, 1970; Greenberg, Calderon, & Kusché, 1984; Henggeler et al., 1984; Lederberg, 1993; Meadow et al., 1981; Wedell-Monnig & Lumley, 1980). One would suspect that this pattern of maternal control has its basis in earlier interactions, in which the mother might have felt herself to be the only player in the supposedly reciprocal mother-child relationship (for a variety of convergent evidence see Ainsworth, 1973). Mothers who have established an effective channel of communication with their deaf children presumably would have less need for such control, especially the physical manifestations of it (Erting et al., 1990; Greenberg et al., 1984; Gregory, 1976; Lederberg, 1993; Rea et al., 1988).

Regardless of its origins, differences in maternal intrusiveness and directiveness in interactions would be expected to influence the development of reflective (versus impulsive) cognitive styles and internal (versus external) loci of control (see Chapter 4). The establishment of an effective, reciprocal, mother-child communication system thus should help not only to promote a secure attachment bond but also to facilitate later social development by making the mother more "available" to the child (Ainsworth, 1973) and by providing for the explicit transmission of social information.

Surprisingly, there have been relatively few investigations comparing the development and patterns of attachment in deaf children compared to hearing children. There has been somewhat more research concerning differences between deaf children raised in oral only versus manual + oral environments. Focusing on the role of communication in mother–child interaction, Greenberg and Marvin (1979), for example, hypothesized that communication competence should be positively related to mature mother–child bonds. In particular, they suggested that effective mother–child communication would be linked to the transition from *proximity-seeking* attachment to a *goal-corrected* relationship in which parting is characterized by mutual consent. They therefore predicted that profoundly deaf preschool children whose mothers used total communication would evidence more mature and sociable attachments than those whose mothers used a less effective, oral-only mode of communication.

Greenberg and Marvin employed the Strange Situation paradigm in a study involving 28 hearing mother–deaf child dyads. For the purposes of testing their prediction, but unlike the standard paradigm, the children were between the ages of 3 and 5 years (versus 8 to 18 months). Mothers also were allowed to communicate with their children prior to departure, explaining their leaving if they so desired (cf. Sroufe, 1990). Interestingly, this availability of "exiting communication" resulted in five of the seven mothers in the oral subgroup using a form of STAY or WAIT gesture prior to departure (cf. Gregory, 1976). It was apparently the only sign-like gesture in any of their interactions, and it appeared to be effective as a consensual signal indicating a brief departure.

Perhaps the most surprising result of Greenberg and Marvin's study was their finding that most of the children did not object to their mothers' departure. Unfortunately, this result cannot be taken as strong evidence of secure attachments in hearing mother–deaf child dyads because of the age of the children and the allowance of maternal explanations of their departures. Greenberg and Marvin (1979), in fact, suggested that the use of temporary-departure gestures by the mothers in low-communication dyads might have been the best explanation of the low distress of children in that group—the one that had been expected to show the most separation anxiety.

Overall, Greenberg and Marvin reported that high-communication dyads showed more mature and secure attachment relationships than low-communication dyads, regardless of the mode of their communication. It remains unclear, however, whether this pattern of results was a consequence of the counseling received by the total communication mothers as part of the early intervention program, a product of communication fluency per se, or some combination of factors. Children classified as high communicators in this study tended to be older, were diagnosed as deaf and entered parent–infant intervention programs at earlier ages, and had more school experience than low-communication children. On the basis of their data analyses, Greenberg and Marvin (1979, p. 273) concluded that "only age of diagnosis . . . and amount of school experience . . . truly differentiated high and low communicators." More generally, however, there is likely a host of other child-related and parent-related variables that contributed to the observed differences.

Lederberg and Mobley (1990) compared the quality of mother–child interactions and attachment behaviors of 41 hearing-impaired toddlers and 41 hearing agemates, all of whom had hearing mothers. The hearing-impaired children had hearing losses ranging from mild to profound. They were all between 18 and 25 months of age and had been diagnosed as hearing-impaired at 1 to 21 months of age (mean 10 months). The children and their mothers were observed during a free play session and in the Strange Situation. Lederberg and Mobley found that 56% of the hearing-impaired toddlers and 61% of the hearing toddlers were securely attached, according to their responses to the Strange Situation. They concluded that the development of secure attachment and the maintenance of a good mother–child relationship does not depend on normal language development during the toddler years.

Lederberg and Mobley's results, however, should not be taken to indicate that the deaf and hearing toddlers show equivalent patterns of social interaction. In fact, they found that hearing status affected the quality of mother–child interaction in at least three important ways: (1) the hearing-impaired children and their mothers spent significantly less time interacting than did the hearing dyads; (2) mothers of hearing-impaired children initiated interactions with their toddlers significantly more often than did mothers of hearing children; and (3) the hearing-impaired children were much more likely to terminate interactions with their mothers because they did not see or hear a communication. Despite the finding of these quantitative differences, Lederberg and Mobley reported that ratings of the quality of mother–child play indicated no significant differences between the hearing-impaired and the hearing dyads. Although the mothers of the hearing-impaired toddlers reported being more stressed and less satisfied with their lives and their maternal roles relative to the mothers of hearing toddlers, the two groups did not differ on observer ratings of their dominance, sensitivity, or affect toward their children.

Lederberg and Mobley's (1990) study augurs well for deaf children's relationships with their mothers, but there are two aspects of it that potentially limit its implications. The first is a methodological limitation. As Sroufe (1990, p. 1) pointed out, if the goal of any particular study is to claim that a laboratory assessment of attachment reflects "real-world" attachment behaviors, administration of the paradigm must be comparable to its validated form. Just because the procedure "relates to home behavior does not give license . . . for using the strange situation beyond 18 months." In other words, it is not entirely clear what conclusions can be drawn about attachment from Strange Situation results obtained with older children (cf. Greenberg & Marvin, 1979).

The second limitation concerns the generality of Lederberg and Mobley's findings. The dyads in their study had been participating in an intervention program for deaf children for a minimum of 8 months. As the authors acknowledged, "There may be more insecure attachments and worse social interaction patterns between hearing impaired toddlers and parents who are not sensitive enough to notice or to seek help for a hearing problem until that child is older" (Lederberg & Mobley, 1990, p. 1603). Furthermore, although Lederberg and Mobley did not discuss the nature of the intervention program, it undoubtedly included training for the mothers designed to increase the efficiency and fluency of linguistic interaction. Eight months of such enhanced interaction, representing at least one-third of the child's life, likely would have significantly ameliorated any more pronounced mother–child dysfunction that might be observed in dyads that did not have the benefit of such interaction. Unfortunately, "before" and "after" measures are not available.

Interestingly, in a follow-up of the Lederberg and Mobley (1990) study, when the same children were 3 years old, Lederberg, Willis, and Frankel (1991) found that the deaf children showed less social initiative, compliance, creativity, and enjoyment in interactions with their mothers, as well as more misbehavior than they had earlier. Unlike the findings at 22 months, the deaf dyads at 3 years were found to be more mother-dominated and less harmonious than were the hearing dyads. Although Lederberg and her colleagues did not speculate on the reason for the changes over the course of 1 year, they attributed them to the deaf children because ratings of the mothers of the deaf and hearing preschoolers remained roughly equal on dominance, sensitivity, and affect. (It is unclear if the children had remained in an intervention program through their testing at 3 years of age.)

A Prognosis for Deafness and Attachment

During the period between the Greenberg and Marvin (1979) study and the Lederberg and Mobley (1990) study, considerably more public awareness emerged with regard to the nature of deafness and opportunities for intervention with deaf children (e.g., Meadow-Orlans, 1987; Moores & Meadow-Orlans, 1990). More complete studies of the relation between deafness and early attachment, however, remain relatively rare. On the basis of the findings described thus far, it appears safe to conclude that emotional development is facilitated in deaf children whose hearing mothers are sensitive enough to their needs to pursue early diagnosis, intervention, and communication training. They also strongly support the hypothesized link between mother–child communication and security of early attachment, regardless of maternal hearing status. Until direct comparisons of emotional development are made among all possible combinations of deaf and hearing mothers and children, however, several issues will remain unclear: (1) the relative benefits of vocalization versus other modes of communication in the establishment of early mother–child bonds; (2) the timing of possible *sensitive periods* for maternal vocalization and language in the development of synchrony, reciprocity, and early affective bonds; (3) the importance of hearing per se in the establishment of attachment bonds; and (4) the implications of items (1) to (3) for subsequent social-emotional development.

At this point, we can be sure of two general points: First, any factor that decreases the availability of mothers to meet their infants' needs has the potential to result in underlying "mistrust" or "doubt" on the part of the infant as reflected in the attachment bond (Belsky, 1986). Second, in hearing dyads, the quality of the attachment bond is predictive of later individual differences in social ability, as those children with secure attachments tend to be more socially competent than those with insecure attachments (Belsky, 1986; Lamb, Thompson, Gardner, & Charnov, 1985). At face value, the Lederberg et al. (1991) results suggest that this relationship may not be as clear for deaf children as it is for hearing children. Nevertheless, to the extent that communication abilities or any other factor(s) disrupt the development of secure attachment in deaf children, one would expect that there will be some consequences for social and emotional development. Unfortunately, we still do not have sufficient data from which to draw any general conclusions concerning attachment in deaf children or to estimate the relative frequency of their secure versus their insecure attachments.

Looking Beyond the Mother-Infant Bond

One approach to understanding the roots of social and emotional development in deaf children would be to work back from the social behaviors and personality characteristics observed in older deaf children. Toward that end, the remainder of this chapter considers several later-emerging components of personality and emotional development in deaf children. Keeping in mind the underlying continuity and interconnectedness of various aspects of social development, we should be able to gain some insight into the correlations of earlier and later social functioning and perhaps even be able to make some causal connections.

In this context, it is important to note that the above discussion did not claim that young children's social behavior with peers is *determined* by the nature and quality of their attachment with mother or any other specific aspect of the mother–child relationship. Although this *maternal precursor hypothesis* has been explicitly or implicitly espoused in the developmental literature for some time, it is not unequivocally supported by the available data (for a review see Lamb & Nash, 1989). Despite the lack of a strong *causal* relation between security of attachment and subsequent prosocial behavior, there is nonetheless strong support for the claim that children who tend to have better social relationships with their primary caretakers are also those who tend to develop good social relations with peers (e.g., Sroufe, 1983). Still at issue is whether this correlation is the result of some other factor common to both, such as general sociability, social problem-solving ability, or sensitivity to reciprocal social cues. Research in this area proceeds apace with hearing children, but the topic apparently has not been addressed with regard to deaf children.

The preceding discussions have emphasized the bidirectional nature of early mother–deaf infant interaction, and it is important to keep this perspective when considering later social relations. In fact, many of the skills involved in peer–peer interactions are different from those involved in mother–child interactions, and a variety of individual differences in both types of situation make for some difficulty when drawing any direct connections between the two (Lamb et al., 1985). Just as attachment is more of a mutual process than one controlled by the child alone, so the successors and products of attachment depend on the quality of affective bonds and social interactions between the child and significant others. For the deaf child whose deafness has gone undiagnosed until the preschool years, those interactions likely would be atypical. Even for deaf children who are diagnosed early, the breadth of their social experience may be relatively limited in terms of both the number of other children and (more importantly, it may turn out) the number of adults with whom the child interacts (Athey, 1985; Liben, 1978; Nelson, 1973).[2] In either case, it would not be surprising if subsequent behavior and emotional stability are colored by the quality of the mother–child bond. Rather, it would be surprising if they were not.

Implications of Insecure Attachment for Later Social Interaction

When considering the social (or antisocial) behaviors of young deaf children that one might want to link to attachment, it is important to keep in mind the consistent characterization of their hearing mothers described above. That is, when evaluating the ways in which deaf children's behavior may differ from that of hearing age-mates, remember that their mothers tend to be relatively controlling, directive, over-protective, and intrusive (Henggeler et al., 1984). These factors alone might be expected to affect children's interactions with peers and other adults beyond their being related to the quality of the mother–child attachment bond. At the same time, however, it should be recognized that some of these maternal behaviors might be justified, insofar as they are necessary for ensuring the safety, cooperation, or obedience of deaf children to a greater extent than hearing children (Gregory, 1976). Schlesinger and Meadow (1972, p. 108), for example, suggested that to a large extent the intrusiveness of mothers of deaf children may be part of getting the child's attention and may not be experienced negatively by the child. Lederberg (1993) similarly argued that some of hearing mothers' directiveness might reflect attempts to overcome communication barriers rather than being a reflection of their disappointment with their children's levels of responding.

Among hearing children, the avoidant behavior patterns associated with insecure attachment are highly related to subsequent display of a behavioral "syndrome" that includes having a low frustration threshold, noncompliance with mother and other authority figures, aggressive behavior toward peers and adults, and emotional distancing from parents (Lamb et al., 1985). Belsky (1986) has described this pattern of behavior as also characterizing both high- and low-SES infants who spent considerable time in day-care centers during their first year (see also Meadow-Orlans, 1987). The likelihood that a greater than average proportion of families with deaf children also tend to have low SES (see Chapter 2), and have mothers who must work, and thus may place their children in day care from an early age, creates an additional confound for understanding the link between early attachment and subsequent behavior in young deaf children. Nonetheless, the characteristics ascribed to insecurely attached hearing children are remarkably similar to those frequently used to describe young deaf children of hearing parents, even if this similarity is coincidental. That the link may not be coincidental is suggested by the fact that both deaf infants and "day-care reared" infants experience disturbances in the availability and responsiveness of the mother.

Preschool Behavior of Deaf Children

Before moving on to consider the social development and social behaviors of deaf children during the school years, it is worth emphasizing the impact of preschool experience on young deaf children. The growth of state-funded preschools over recent years has provided important, "educational" experiences for both deaf children and their parents. These intervention programs tend to be more numerous than schools for the deaf and thus are more readily available. In this setting, deaf children are exposed to considerable environmental diversity as well as social and linguistic interactions with other children and adults.

A recent and continuing research program by Amy Lederberg, Victoria Everhart, and their associates has indicated several marked effects of early preschool experience of deaf children's social behavior. Lederberg, Rosenblatt, Vandell, and Chapin (1987), for example, found that the stability of friendships among deaf preschool children was comparable to that of hearing children; moreover, the two groups showed similar patterns of playmate preference. With regard to language interactions, Lederberg, Ryan, and Robbins (1986) observed that, although deaf preschoolers did not use much formal language in interactions with either deaf or hearing preschool peers, they did use a variety of nonlinguistic communication devices during those interactions. Deaf children were more likely to use linguistic and nonlinguistic visual communication with deaf than with hearing peers, and such interactions tended to be less object-centered than were the communications between deaf and hearing playmates.

Lederberg (1991) further found that within the preschool setting, deaf children who were high in language ability were more likely than children with poor language ability to play with multiple peers at one time, to interact with teachers, and to produce and receive more language in interactions with their play partners (see also Cornelius & Hornett, 1990; Spencer & Deyo, 1993). Nevertheless, because language was not significantly related to the quantity of peer interaction overall (despite a large difference in favor of children with better language skills) or to children's preferences for playing with particular peers Lederberg concluded that language and social skills develop, for the most part, independently of each other.

Spencer and Deyo (1993) examined the play of fifteen 2-year-olds playing in a controlled setting with their mothers present. Ten of the children were congenitally deaf: five had deaf mothers who used manual communication with them, and five had hearing mothers who used primarily aural-oral methods of communication. The remaining five children were hearing and had hearing mothers. Spencer and Deyo found that, although children with lower language levels spent less time in higher levels of symbolic play, the time spent in lower levels of play equaled or exceeded that of children with more advanced language. Most importantly, and consistent with the trend noted in Lederberg's (1991) results, they suggested that previously observed differences between deaf and hearing children's play behaviors may be largely the consequence of differences in language ability. Spencer and Deyo found that deafness without delayed language development did not result in lower levels of play behavior.

Schirmer (1989) also reported an apparent relation between deaf children's language development and their style of play. Examining imaginative play in a group of twenty, 3- to 5-year-old preschoolers who had severe hearing impairments, Schirmer found no relation between age and either the quality or the quantity of play. There was a significant relation, however, between language ability and play such that those children with better language skills spent more time in imaginative play and were more likely to use a planned story line and pretend behaviors than were peers with lesser language skills. Schirmer did not statistically separate the effects of age and language development in her sample, and the effects of those two variables are likely to be confounded in deaf children at this age. Nevertheless, the findings are consistent with other results indicating that, although deaf and hearing children may have some similar patterns of friendships and playground behaviors, language fluency may be related to deaf children's abilities to engage in types of play that reflect cognitive decentering and imagination.

Consistent with this suggestion, Cornelius and Hornett (1990) reported that within a sample of kindergartners with congenital or early-onset deafness social play behaviors were related to both communication mode and communication strategies. They observed groups of hearing-impaired 5- and 6-year-olds, of whom half were enrolled in an oral-only program and the other half in a program that utilized both signing and oral communication. Cornelius and Hornett found that relative to the oral-only children, the children in the classroom using manual + oral communication showed higher levels of social play and more frequent dramatic play. The children in the oral-only classroom, meanwhile, were found to be far more disruptive in their play, exhibiting more than eight times as many aggressive acts (e.g., pushing, hitting, and pinching) as those in the manual + oral classroom. Unfortunately, because Cornelius and Hornett's data were collected in two different settings, it is possible that the results were affected by other contextual dynamics.

The available data thus indicate that special preschool and kindergarten programs provide a variety of linguistic and nonlinguistic opportunities for interactions among deaf children (and between deaf and hearing children) that would not be otherwise available. Although comparisons of older children with and without preschool social experience lie ahead, it seems likely that the availability of more diverse social, linguistic, and cognitive experiences can only enhance the flexibility of young deaf children for dealing with later social interactions and the necessity of growing up in a largely hearing world.

Summary

The behavioral problems of deaf children at school and at home are a familiar theme of parents, teachers, and researchers interested in these children's development (see Chapter 4). Although the traditional assumption that much of social development is *determined* by the earliest interactions between mother and child is now frequently questioned, there seems little doubt that the mother–child bond is fertile ground for the acquisition of interpersonal behaviors. It has been argued here that normal social development may actually begin before birth, in more ways than just the metaphorical one of the family preparing for the arrival of a new child. While still in the womb, hearing fetuses are able to hear their mothers' voices, and mother–child relationships begin to develop. After birth, the maternal voice is a familiar and soothing stimulus, with far more attractiveness than other human voices.

The deaf neonate thus lacks at least one component of the earliest social context available to hearing neonates. Evidence available from work with other species suggests that the absence of the vocal-auditory linkage between mother and infant may be a significant one with distinct behavioral and emotional consequences. In the case of children with parents who are deaf or who are aware of their child's deafness, it may be that increased rates of touching, visual stimulation, and facial expression can compensate for the absence of auditory stimulation in mother–child interactions. In other cases, where parents do not realize that their child is deaf, such compensation may not occur, and there could well be a disruption or lag in the establishment of behavioral synchrony between mother and child. This anomaly is likely to increase with the passage of time until the infant's handicap is discovered and parental child-oriented behavior patterns are adjusted. In the meantime, the infant not only receives less of the social experience available to hearing infants, but what experience is available may be less than ideal. At the extreme, one can imagine a scenario in which the only time a hearing-impaired child hears the mother's voice is when she raises it in anger or frustration.

After surmounting the immediate emotional and practical problems related to their child's diagnosis as hearing-impaired, parents who participate in early intervention programs have the opportunity to begin a "remodeled" social relationship with their infant. The use of Total Communication methods, combined with counseling to better understand their child's and their own situation, appears to produce significantly better social adjustment in those deaf children as compared to deaf peers without such intervention. Such benefits are observed in both parent–child relations and in the patterns of social interactions within preschool settings. Without yet understanding fully the relative contributions of the linguistic and psychological components of such programs, it is clear that secure mother-child attachment is more likely in those children whose parents have undertaken such remediation. The extent to which the eventual social successes of those children are a consequence of a priori characteristics of their parents (who took the step), specialized parenting styles, or particular attributes of the child is yet to be determined.

Notes

1. Sroufe (1990) pointed out the importance of standardized procedures for drawing valid conclusions from studies employing the *Strange Situation*. In the absence of detailed

information from the original studies, findings described here should be accepted with some caution. Results based on obvious variations of the paradigm should be viewed as tentative.

2. When examining hearing children's language development, Nelson (1973) found that the diversity of children's experience with adults was a better predictor of vocabulary growth than diversity of experience with peers (see Chapter 5). This finding reflects the fact that adults are better language models than children, a parallel also likely to be found in some other behavioral domains. This possibility, with regard to both deaf and hearing children, awaits empirical investigation.

4

Social and Personality Development During the School Years

The beginnings of social development in deaf children were explored in Chapter 3. The primary focus in that context was on the early interactions and relationships between mothers and infants because of, first, their preeminence as the infant's initial foray into the social world, and second, the role of mother–infant social interactions as the foundation for the child's later interactions with others. The course of these earliest social interactions, however, was shown to depend on the reciprocal interchanges of deaf children with their mothers and with other significant individuals in the environment.

The present chapter moves beyond infancy and the influences of particular individuals to consider more broadly the effects on subsequent development of those earliest social behavior patterns and children's acquired skills and preferences. What might we expect? It is important to recognize here that in the case of deaf children, particularly those of hearing parents, the rules, customs, and social behaviors learned in the home may not generalize to social situations outside the home. In part, this situation results from deaf children's emerging from hearing homes having had a relatively more restricted range of interpersonal interactions than either hearing peers or deaf peers who have deaf parents. Furthermore, interaction patterns that such children acquire at home frequently differ from those of children raised in homes in which children and parents share a common hearing status and a common mode of communication.

For deaf children coming from deaf families, the transfer of social processes to a broader audience is likely to be somewhat easier. Not only are those children likely to have had a wider range of social interactions, but they will have experienced greater understanding and acceptance from others in the family and the community relative to children who might be the only deaf individual with whom the family has ever had experience. Social interactions with individuals outside the immediate family thus are more likely to be similar to those within the family. Deaf children of deaf parents also are more likely than those with hearing parents to have experienced consistent parenting behaviors, effective communication, and more tolerant (less stressed) social environments (Greenberg & Kusché, 1987). Consequently, they generally would be expected to have relatively greater social confidence and self-esteem, as well as a greater likelihood of having an internal locus of control relative to children from less consistent, less tolerant, or less understanding environments (Luterman, 1987; Padden & Humphries, 1988; Schlesinger & Meadow, 1972). Deaf children of deaf parents also are at an advantage in that they have better linguistic means with which to deal with new social settings.

Regardless of parental hearing status, patterns of social interaction laid down in the home will form the bases for deaf children's social interchange outside the home. The success or failure of those interactions depends on children's flexibility, the individuals with whom they are interacting, and the contexts of social interchange. Eventually, the school setting plays a vital role in the acquisition of mature social skills. In that venue, language ability and cognitive functioning play an increasingly important role as children confront novel social situations and attempt to adapt to them. Out of these new social and academic experiences comes academic, personal, and interpersonal growth.

Dependence, Independence, and Social Change During the Early School Years

Social Dependence and Social Independence

As young children develop into more social organisms, the variety of their relationships with family, peers, and other adults (e.g., teachers) increases far beyond that established with the mother and other caregivers within the home. Most children exhibit an affinity toward others, displaying both instrumental and emotional (or person-oriented) dependence. *Instrumental dependence* refers to seeking attention from others to satisfy needs or wants, whereas *emotional dependence* refers to the extension of attachment-like bonds as children strive for proximity, approval, and affection from others. The child who is *independent* still displays appropriate instrumental and emotional dependence but blends such behavior with self-reliance, assertiveness, and a need for achievement.

Handicapped children, in general, are likely to encounter difficulty establishing their independence. In part, the relatively greater need for instrumental assistance is a real one, the qualities and extent of which vary with the nature of the child's handicap. However, the frequent overprotection of handicapped children by their parents creates further impediments to social independence, as those children are often *able* to perform a variety of tasks that others typically do for them. As Meadow (1976, p. 3) noted:

> This suggests that parents generalize from the narrow range of tasks that the handicapped child actually cannot do, and assume that there is a much larger spectrum of tasks of which he is incapable. Eventually, the assumed inability becomes a real inability because the child does not have the opportunity to practice tasks and develop new levels of expertise. In addition, it takes more patience and time for handicapped children to perform the trial-and-error process of skill acquisition—time and patience that parents may not have or be unwilling to give. For deaf children with deficient communication skills, it takes additional time and patience merely to communicate what is expected, required, and necessary for the performance of even a simple task.

Unfortunately, there has been little research concerning the development of personality characteristics such as independence and self-esteem in school-age deaf children. What data are available largely concern the effects on such variables of residential versus public school education (described below).

A. E. Harris (1978), among others, has suggested that the lack of effective communication with parents and peers is frequently a major impediment to social adjustment for deaf children. Because they typically receive fewer explanations for the causes of social and emotional behaviors in others, deaf children experience more difficulty in self-regulation and a reduced ability to learn from social interactions (Rodda, 1966). Less understanding of others' reactions to their behaviors results in less accurate self-images and, possibly, low self-esteem. Ultimately, these qualities can lead to less social independence and may negatively impact on the quality of relationships in the school setting. Consistent with this view, Schlesinger and Meadow (1972) reported a strong relation between the degree to which parents promoted social independence in their deaf preschoolers and the extent to which the children were socially outgoing, spontaneous, and motivated.

Greenberg and Kusché (1987) argued that although many deaf children are relatively impulsive and egocentric, these characteristics can be attributed only partially to linguistic or sociocultural sources. More centrally, deaf children and adolescents frequently have significant deficits in knowledge and skills that impede their independence in both social and academic domains. Pointing out the dangers of generalizing to deaf children as a group, Greenberg and Kusché suggested that, given the numerous impediments to development experienced by many deaf children, their resilience is remarkable. Nevertheless, "as with other individuals who share a combination of poor communication (especially in their early family/developmental environments) and minority/subcultural group status, many deaf persons manifest similar competencies and deficits in the social/affective domain" (p. 117).

Autonomy and the Emergence of Self

Greenberg and Kusché (1987), like Schlesinger and Meadow (1972) and others, observed that deaf children and deaf adults tend to be more emotionally immature than hearing peers. In the case of deaf children of hearing parents, one could argue that lags in social and emotional development result in part from the lack of appropriate social models with whom they can identify and communicate. Clearly, the lack of communication between parents and children leaves both sides unclear about the needs, wants, and capabilities of the other (A. E. Harris, 1978; Kusché & Greenberg, 1983; Young & Brown, 1981). Luterman (1987) suggested further that hearing parents of deaf children often become emotionally "stiff" in their interactions with their children after a hearing loss is diagnosed. In his view, such behaviors derive at least in part from the unresolved guilt and vulnerability felt by parents, and they lead children to develop external loci of control and a lack of autonomy.

Lags in the development of autonomy in young deaf children are reflected in observed delays in toilet training, self-feeding, and "safety" behavior. As indicated by the earlier quote from Meadow (1986), however, such delays frequently may be just as much the result of parents' doubts about the competencies of their children as the consequence of any true, extraordinary incompetencies. The lack of social and personal initiatives by deaf children thus may both cause and be caused by parental overprotection, leading eventually to the high instrumental dependence seen in deaf children relative to their hearing age-mates (Schlesinger & Meadow, 1972). The important point is that rather than ascribing the lack of autonomy solely to the deaf child we need to consider possible differences in the development of early mother–infant reciprocity, the lack of deaf models, and the limited diversity of social partners during infancy and early childhood.

The observed pattern of developing personal and social behaviors exhibited by many deaf children appears consistent with their relatively restricted communicative and social interactions within the hearing community. Although preschool day programs for deaf children have provided a setting in which deaf and hearing children may display many similar peer interactive behaviors (e.g., Lederberg et al., 1987), researchers have yet to consider fully the impact of these programs on the emotional and personality development of the children. Greenberg and Kusché (1987), however, described the successes of one such program, Providing Alternative Thinking Strategies, or (PATHS). PATHS attempts to remedy some of the social delays of deaf children by explicitly helping them acquire appropriate social problem-solving skills, self-control, and emotional role-taking abilities. Not only has that program been shown to lead to significantly improved social and emotional functioning, it also has provided beneficial transfer effects to classroom academic performance, at least as assessed by evaluating reading achievement scores. Unfortunately, such programs are not yet widely available and utilized. For the present, therefore, we will focus on the family's contributions to deaf children's emerging personalities.

The general qualities of that familial context were summarized by Gregory's (1976) interviews with 122 British mothers of young deaf children and Schlesinger and Meadow's (1972) study of mother–child interactions of 40 deaf children and 20 age-matched hearing children, all of whom had hearing mothers. Although both of these studies are somewhat dated, no newer information with such breadth is available (but see related findings by Henggeler et al., 1984; Lederberg, 1993; Luterman, 1987).

The Gregory (1976) and Schlesinger and Meadow (1972) studies painted a picture of deaf children learning about social interactions in contexts characterized by maternal behaviors that, compared to mothers of hearing children, are less flexible, less imaginative, less encouraging, and less permissive while being more didactic, more intrusive, and more physically punishing. At the same time, those mothers are more responsive in some ways. The latter finding may be somewhat surprising because of the expectation that hearing mothers would tend to be less synchronized with their deaf infants than would be the case with hearing infants. By the time deaf children are in preschool, however, there is a marked tendency for hearing mothers to be more responsive, perhaps even overly responsive, to them. For example, hearing mothers of deaf children are approximately six times more likely than mothers of hearing children to "invariably respond to demands for attention" (Gregory, 1976; see also Lederberg, 1993). This behavior appears to be a joint product of mothers' inability to explain the need to wait to their young deaf children and the (probably not unrelated) tendency toward impulsivity in deaf children (R. I. Harris, 1978).

Investigating the interactions of deaf preschoolers and their mothers, Schlesinger and Meadow (1972) engaged dyads in several semistructured situations: free play, copying designs from a blackboard, looking at pictures, and sharing refreshments. The children's behaviors then were compared to norms from unspecified "standardized tests." Keeping in mind the earlier caution that social norms derived from observations of hearing children may not be appropriate for deaf children, Schlesinger and Meadow's findings revealed marked and consistent differences in the observed behaviors of the two groups. In general, the deaf children in their study were reported to be significantly less happy and buoyant in interactions with their mothers, as well as less enjoying of the interaction, less likely to take pride in mastery, and less flexible in their interactions. Interestingly, although children's levels of language competence did not affect their mothers' behaviors to any great extent (likely because alternative modes of communication had developed), it was positively related to the above qualities of the children's interactions. Children's communication competence also was related to the quality of peer–peer interactions in Gregory's (1976) study and to peer–peer and child–teacher interactions in the Lederberg (1991) study described earlier.

Finally, Schlesinger and Meadow observed that mothers of deaf children were almost three times more likely than mothers of hearing children to report being comfortable spanking their children (71% versus 25%). Gregory (1976) reported a similar finding and concluded that many mothers of deaf children find physical punishment simpler than a verbal explanation when linguistic communication ability is low. Most likely, maternal frustration also plays a role there, as deaf children are likely to be less responsive and more disruptive than hearing siblings.

Identifying the Loci of Social Change

It is disappointing that observations such as those obtained by Schlesinger and Meadow (1972) and Gregory (1976) have not yet been analyzed using available methods that would allow separation of child-related versus parent-related variables (for discussion see Lederberg, 1993). Although deaf children frequently are observed to be less competent than hearing peers in semistructured tasks requiring maternal involvement, they also are seen to be more involved in the family, as any handicapped child is likely to be (Luterman, 1987). However, the quality of such social interactions is difficult to assess.

In general, the nature of family interaction is probably even more important for deaf children than for hearing peers because the family represents a much larger proportion of their social experience. This situation places the family in a much more central role with regard to social modeling for the deaf child. Identification and modeling, however, largely depend on children's assessments of similarity to models and feedback about that similarity and the models' evaluations of child behaviors. The adult models most frequently available to deaf children lack hearing impairments and a common system of efficient communication. They therefore would be expected to contribute less to children's acquisition of well-defined social roles and internalized social expectations than would otherwise be the case. The availability of deaf adults and older deaf children in school settings provides some of the necessary social input, but it is unclear if they can fully replace parents and siblings as the major source of social training.

Both Rodda (1966) and Gregory (1976) have pointed out that deaf children are less likely than hearing children to receive explanations from parents concerning emotions, reasons for actions, expected roles, and the consequences of various behaviors (see also, A. E. Harris, 1978; Odom et al., 1973). Findings of less advanced understanding of social-emotional functioning in deaf children than in hearing children thus might not seem surprising. Rodda and Gregory, however, dealt primarily with British schoolchildren trained exclusively in oral programs. In fact, studies in the United States have indicated that deaf children with deaf parents (who communicate via American Sign Language, or ASL) show greater social maturity than deaf children with hearing parents (who also have less fluency in parent–child communication) (e.g., Schlesinger & Meadow, 1972). Still unclear is the extent to which that maturity derives directly from effective communication between parents and children or the variety of other factors involved in having parents of the same or different hearing status.

One would expect that this issue would be well served by a study involving deaf children who have effective sign language communication with their hearing parents. Evidence presented in Chapter 3, for example, indicated that, among deaf children enrolled in communication-supportive preschool settings, those with better communication skills eventually are more competent in several peer-related social domains (e.g., Greenberg & Kusché, 1987; Henggeler et al., 1984). Does early sign language experience between deaf children and their hearing parents also have significant impact on children's personality and emotional development?

A study by Greenberg, Calderon, and Kusché (1984) suggested that the answer is "yes." Greenberg et al. compared deaf children from 12 hearing families involved in a preschool intervention program (utilizing Total Communication) with children in 12 families that had not had such experience. They found that intervention was associated with a greater likelihood of compliance with maternal requests, more mother–child communication during free play, and a greater likelihood that initiated mother–child interactions subsequently would be elaborated. In general, interactions of those dyads that had the benefit of an intervention program were longer, more relaxed, and more gratifying on both sides (cf. Schlesinger & Meadow, 1972).

Perhaps of greatest significance, was the finding of Greenberg et al. that those children in the intervention group were at least three times more likely to communicate spontaneously in social interactions and asked four times as many questions as the children in the nonintervention group. These differences probably derived in part from the fact that relative to the non-intervention mothers the mothers of children in the intervention group were found to be less controlling, more reinforcing, better able to gain their children's attention, and better able to time their interactions so as to be less interrupting. It thus seems that children who have established good communicative/social relationships within the family are better equipped to venture out into the social world. Yet to be determined is the impact of such skills on academic achievement and social adjustment during the later school years.

Parents Versus Peers: Social Implications of Schooling for Deaf Children

It is not the goal of this section to provide a full description of residential school and day-school programs for hearing-impaired children or even to summarize the differences between them. Instead, the focus of this discussion is on the movement of social interaction from the family context to one involving significant other adults (e.g., teachers) and, perhaps for the first time, deaf peers.

According to Schildroth (1986), more than 16,000 children were enrolled in residential school programs for hearing-impaired children during the 1982–1983 school year, 97% of whom had congenital or early-onset deafness (i.e., before age 3 years) and 91% of whom had severe to profound hearing losses. Considered in terms of the total number of hearing-impaired children in the United States (see Chapter 2), this figure indicates that only 25% of those in special programs for hearing-impaired children attend programs run by residential schools.

In contrast to the views of most deaf adults (Higgins & Nash, 1987; Padden & Humphries, 1988), who see the residential school as a vital source of social and cultural growth for deaf children, Meadow (1976) and several other investigators have argued that living in residential schools might impede the development of social maturity in deaf children. Meadow (1976, p. 3), for example, suggested that "the limited social opportunities of the deaf adolescent in the residential school can add to an already underdeveloped sense of self-responsibility and social immaturity." Evidence for such claims is scarce, however, and it is unclear what the comparison group should be. Schlesinger and Meadow (1972) and Meadow (1976), for example, suggested that any time children live in groups rather than in individual homes, the needs of "normal," individual development suffer because of the needs of group living: allocation of responsibility differs, there are fewer opportunities for privacy, and administrative and parental fears concerning boy–girl relationships lead to more restrictive rules than would be experienced at home.

Although the social structure of the residential school for the deaf is different from the hearing home of a hearing child, the case has not been made that residential schools lead to any social maladjustment of deaf children or that their atmosphere is any less conducive to social development than is growing up "full-time" in a hearing household. In fact, one might well expect the opposite. Given the relative lack of communication between most hearing parents and their deaf children and the overprotective maternal behavior patterns frequently exhibited toward deaf (and other handicapped) children, it would be difficult for even a supportive and accepting family to provide a deaf child the full range of interactions available to hearing children during the school years.

At the same time, empirical determination of the impact of residential school training is difficult. For example, it could be argued that living at a residential school during the week would be likely to result in a reduction in parent-to-child transmission of cultural values (e.g., religious, ethnic, familial), sex roles, and social roles. Keep in mind, however, that it is the children with the most severe hearing losses who attend such programs. It thus seems likely that any relevant differences observed between residential students and day school students would be hopelessly confounded with parental sign language ability (cultural values and social roles are abstract concepts) and the degree of children's hearing losses. In fact, for deaf children of deaf parents, the values communicated within the school setting appear to be largely congruent with those held within the family. Deaf parents thus often send their deaf children to residential schools explicitly to help them acquire some of their cultural training.

The odd group out, again, is deaf children with hearing parents. When parent–child communication is high, those children may adapt well to attending regular public schools either full- or part-time (Calderon & Greenberg, 1993; Moores & Kluwin, 1986). Even when their children are in residential schools, parents of such children tend to take an active part in their children's educations. Warmth, communication, and transmission of values when the child is at home, then, can serve much the same functions as in fully hearing households. In contrast, those hearing families that lack effective communication with their deaf children and within which the social interactions are less fluent may well benefit from their children attending residential schools. In that setting, children may gain personal and interactive skills that simply are not available within the home.

It is important to acknowledge here that advocating residential school living for deaf children does not deny their need for a secure family life. Residential schools simply represent a fertile ground for social interactions with peers and deaf adults that go beyond what is available in most homes and special preschool programs. Residential schools also would be expected to lead to an enhanced sense of identity from being among others with whom the child is similar. In that setting, deaf children are likely to have more playmates and more collaborative play than in public school settings and are less overprotected and intruded upon by well-meaning adults. Although in some ways the residential school may limit children's range of experience with "normal" aspects of social development, in other ways they are afforded opportunities of social interaction that would be missing, or at least impoverished, in a public school setting. Some of the possibilities—on both sides of the coin—may seem trivial to some investigators: hanging around at the mall, riding a bicycle to school, telling dirty jokes, and flirting on the playground. However, the implications of such behaviors for coherent social and personality development during the school years cannot be ignored. Such experiences lead directly to children's acquisition of an internal locus of control, an accurate self-image, and positive self-esteem. These characteristics, in turn, play an important role in children's desire for achievement and eventual success in academic and social settings (Janos & Robinson, 1985).

Striving for Achievement and Success

Achievement refers to behaviors intended to gain approval or avoid disapproval with regard to the competence of performance. *Autonomous achievement* specifically refers to performance in which the individual strives to match some internalized standard of excellence, a standard usually derived from significant others in the family or from other social contexts (e.g., peers in school). Children's seeking of success in school, bicycle riding, dating, and interpersonal communication thus all can be seen as achievement-related, at least within most of North American culture.

Not all cultures, or even subcultures within a particular society, however, have identical values. Those goals that are seen as worth achieving therefore vary to a greater or lesser extent across cultural and ethnic groups and even within those groups. The differences in cultural values and attitudes between deaf and hearing populations, for example, might result in deaf children having somewhat different goals and desires than hearing peers. In particular, the two groups could have different emphases in their achievement-related behaviors (e.g., Padden & Humphries, 1988; Sisco & Anderson, 1980). Differences in the early socialization of deaf and hearing children also might contribute to the two groups having some distinctive achievement-worthy ambitions. When considering the possibility of divergence in the achievement orientations of deaf and hearing children, we therefore must consider differences in values, differences in standards, and differences in who are seen as the "significant others" worth pleasing. Of course, there is a continuum of similarity in these areas depending on the extent to which particular children are oriented toward the deaf or hearing communities. Accordingly, achievement-related differences would be expected to vary with children's degree of hearing loss, parental hearing status, and early social experience. In addition, the educational context, where both academic and social achievement are influenced by peer attitudes, play a major role in determining the goals of achievement and the standards by which it is measured.

Having suggested several contributors to deaf children's school achievement, any general summary of their academic performance would be decidedly negative. Relative to hearing peers, deaf children have been described as having difficulty in understanding and using abstract relationships (Conrad, 1979; Furth, 1973; Myklebust, 1960; Watts, 1979), conceptual categorization (Liben, 1978, 1979; Ottem, 1980), mathematics (DiFrancesca, 1972; Karchmer, 1985), reading (King & Quigley, 1985), and writing (DiFrancesca, 1972; Greenberg & Kusché, 1987)[1] Importantly, lack of competence in these areas not only has direct impact on functioning within particular academic courses but also exerts indirect influence on the general ability to learn both inside the classroom and outside, in the "real world."

Importantly, observations of deaf children's relative lack of school achievement do not depend on differences in manual versus oral education, at least not in the direction that many (e.g., Johnson et al., 1989) would expect. Deaf children exposed to manual or manual + oral methods during the early school years typically show superior performance and are at least equal to orally trained peers in academic performance, linguistic development, speech-reading (i.e., lip-reading), and psychosocial adjustment (Brasel & Quigley, 1977; Moores, 1990; Vernon & Koh, 1970).

When achievement of deaf children with deaf parents is compared to those with hearing parents, the apparent benefits of an effective early communication medium, more normal social development, and broader experience appear to emerge, as those children with deaf parents evidence uniformly better academic performance in several areas (e.g., Balow & Brill, 1975; Brasel & Quigley, 1977; Meadow, 1968; Quigley & Paul, 1984; Vernon & Koh, 1970, Vernon et al., 1971) (but see Chapter 11). Contrary to popular belief, however, even deaf children of deaf parents do not exhibit academic achievement comparable to that of hearing peers. Vernon and Koh (1970), for example, compared 32 manually trained deaf children of deaf parents with 32 orally trained deaf children of hearing parents. The children were matched on Stanford Achievement Test (SAT) performance and evaluated on several variables related to communication skill, educational achievement, and psychological adjustment. As expected, Vernon and Koh found that the children of deaf parents surpassed those with hearing parents on all dimensions. Nevertheless, the performance of the manually trained children was just as far below hearing norms as it was above the performance of their orally trained peers. In their overall averages, for example, scores obtained by manual and oral students at age 12 were approximately 75% and 47%, respectively, of those achieved by hearing peers. Those differences were almost exactly the same for subjects at age 20 years.

Balow and Brill (1975) evaluated the academic achievement of 16 graduating classes from a single school for the deaf, creating a sample of 455 students, 34 of whom had two deaf parents. They found that, on average, the students with deaf parents had SAT scores that placed them almost 1.5 years ahead of their classmates who had hearing parents. However, it still left them only at grade level 8.4, when they were graduating from grade 12.

Admittedly, many of the data concerning scholastic achievement of deaf children come from studies now more than 10 years old (see Chapter 11 for more recent research on reading and writing). More recently, the Center for Assessment and Demographic Studies (CADS) at Gallaudet University has been examining the achievement levels of hearing-impaired students based on SAT and other data. Using CADS data obtained when determining norms for the SAT in 1974 and 1983, Allen (1986) compared mathematics and reading scores of deaf children aged 8 to 18 years who were receiving special education services. Some of those data are presented in Table 4-1, where it can be seen that deaf children's SAT performance

TABLE 4-1. Reading and Mathematics SAT Performance by Deaf Students for Two Years Compared to 1982 Median Scores for Hearing Students

Age (years)	Mathematics Scores			Reading Scores		
	Deaf Students			Deaf Students		
	1974	1983	Hearing Students[a]	1974	1983	Hearing Students[a]
8	503	546	533 (2)	467	507	530 (2)
10	544	590	590 (4)	493	539	615 (4)
12	582	622	645 (6)	522	558	645 (6)
14	607	651	680 (8)	533	581	670 (8)
16	628	662	710 (10)	556	586	690 (10)
18	643	662	NA (12)	572	579	NA (12)

Source: Based on Allen, 1986.

Note: NA = Not available. The SAT scores are approximate scaled scores.

[a]The numbers in parentheses represent the grade level.

increased for both reading and mathematics during that decade, with the largest increases being observed for younger children.

Allen (1986) observed two other important trends that are evident in Table 4-1. First, he found that math computation abilities appeared to plateau for deaf students at about a seventh grade level (scaled score 665), even when differences in screening procedures in 1974 and 1983 were taken into account. Second, although both mathematics and reading scores showed improvements over the decade, deaf children's reading abilities continued to lag behind those of hearing age-mates. The scaled scores from 1974 indicated that whereas deaf 8-year-olds were reading just one and one-half grade levels behind hearing age-mates, the 12-year-olds were more than five grade levels behind, and the 16-year-olds were almost seven grade levels behind. In 1983 the 8-year-olds were reading a bit more than one grade level behind, whereas the 12-year-olds were still more than four grade levels behind, and the 16-year-olds were seven grade levels behind, i.e., reading at a third grade level (Allen 1986, p. 164).

Johnson et al. (1989) and others have suggested that the relative inefficiency of teacher-child communication in the classroom, the lack of clear-cut educational goals, and insufficient parental involvement in deaf education contribute to deaf children's relatively poor academic achievement. Academic success is multifaceted, however, and is not predictable from any single variable or combination of variables (Brasel & Quigley, 1977; Moores, 1990). Achievement differences observed between deaf and hearing children and between different groups of deaf children also are affected by the children's age of language acquisition, their relative abilities to take advantage of classroom instruction, and their motivation to succeed.

Surprisingly, it appears that no investigators have directly evaluated deaf children's *achievement motivation* or *need achievement* (nAch) in relation to their actual academic performance. The standardized assessment tools for nAch, the Thematic Apperception Test for adults and the Roberts Apperception Test for children, involve verbal productions in response to several pictures, and they seem well suited to testing of deaf children. Deaf children's achievement motivation in school currently is being investigated in my laboratory, but the results are not yet available.

Impulsivity and Deafness

Although its possible causal role has yet to be extricated from other factors, deaf children's poor scholastic performance seems likely to be linked, at least in part, with their reported tendency toward impulsive behavior (e.g., Altshuler et al., 1976; Chess & Fernandez, 1980; R. I. Harris, 1978; Schlesinger & Meadow, 1972a, 1972b). *Impulsivity* has a generic definition that frequently is applied to deaf individuals who are perceived as not behaving in a way that indicates "careful, coherent, advance planning . . . [who are] unable to plan a course of action and adhere to it . . . [or who] may make rash choices based on a desire for immediate gratification rather than on the expectation of long-term goals" (Meadow, 1976; p. 4). When empirically evaluated in deaf and hearing children, however, the impulsivity-reflectivity dimension refers to a *cognitive style* that is expressed in a speed-accuracy tradeoff in decision making, usually in choosing the "same" or "different" stimulus from a set of alternatives. Children who make decisions quickly and with frequent errors fall into an impulsive range, whereas those who take more time to consider the alternatives before making (more often correct) decisions fall into a reflective range.

Considering the generic brand of impulsivity, several investigators have attributed deaf individual's "rash" behavior to the lack of early language interaction with parents, who are generally unable to explain delays in gratification (e.g., Gregory, 1976). Hearing parents of deaf children frequently yield to demands for attention, assistance, and objects rather than risk the possibility of temper tantrums, which also cannot be stopped with linguistic intervention. Without sufficient communicative fluency to relate the present to the past and the future, these parents unwittingly may be teaching their children that emotional and instrumental dependence is immediately rewarded. This attitude is then carried over into the school setting, where deaf children are three times more likely to demonstrate emotional difficulties than are their hearing peers (R. I. Harris, 1978).

Relatively few studies have utilized the standard, nonverbal tests of impulsivity—the Kansas Reflectivity-Impulsivity Scale for Preschoolers (KRISP), the Matching Familiar Figures Test (MFF)—to compare deaf and hearing children or to compare deaf children who have deaf parent versus those who have hearing parents. In one such investigation, Moores, Weiss, and Goodwin (1973) examined 22 impulsive and 22 reflective deaf children (selected on the basis of MFF test scores), all between 5 and 7 years of age. The children were compared on several subtests of the Metropolitan Readiness test, the Receptive Communication Scale (both prereading tests), and the Illinois Test of Syntactic Abilities (TSA) (see Chapter 11). The expectation was that reflective children would appear more "ready" for reading than the more impulsive children. In fact, the reflective deaf children performed significantly better than the impulsive children only on those tests that had time limits. Moores and his colleagues thus concluded that prereading skills were unrelated to the impulsivity-reflectivity dimension.

R. I. Harris (1976; cited by R. I. Harris, 1978) used the MFF and the Draw-A-Man test to evaluate the relation of impulsivity to parental hearing status, manual communication ability, and academic achievement in a group of 324 six- to ten-year-old deaf children. His results indicated that the 50 deaf children of deaf parents in his sample obtained greater impulse control scores on all measures (i.e., they were more reflective), relative to the deaf children with hearing parents. Harris also found that the more reflective children had acquired manual communication earlier than the more impulsive children, although this relation is confounded by parental hearing status. Finally, the reflective children in Harris's study tended to have higher achievement scores than the impulsive children in the reading and other domains tapped by the SAT, the Metropolitan Achievement test, and the Gates Primary Reading test.

Harris apparently did not compare his deaf sample to a hearing sample, and he did not report where the children fell with respect to the hearing MFF norms. On the basis of his finding a link between early manual communication abilities and language achievement, however, he argued that impulsivity is independent of early auditory experience. "What is needed is two-way communication between child and parents and a loving and caring relationship. Absence of either impedes the development of impulse control and results in a personality in which impulsive satisfaction is the guiding rule" (R. I. Harris, 1978, p. 151). In addition, if deaf children are exposed to "successful" impulsive models who are similar to them (i.e., deaf peers or adults), that behavior pattern is readily acquired.

The finding that deaf children of deaf parents display better impulse control, as well as better academic and linguistic competence relative to deaf children of hearing parents suggests that early parenting that is consistent, rational, and supportive might reduce the likelihood of impulsivity in deaf children (cf. Janos & Robinson, 1985). Further studies are needed, however, examining impulsivity in deaf children in residential versus mainstream classrooms and in combination with the variety of other variables that affect deaf children's social and academic development.

Morality and Social Perspective-Taking

The ability to consider the world from alternative perspectives is intertwined with both cognitive and social development. With respect to social interaction, the focus is on children's abilities to consider social roles, the feelings and goals of others, and the moral values of their family and subculture. To the extent that appropriate behavior depends on the ability to take alternative perspectives in social situations, role-taking is an essential component of mature social cognition.

A variety of investigators have described deaf individuals (and deaf children in particular) as unable to take the affective perspective of others, thus making them emotionally egocentric, lacking in empathy, and insensitive to the needs of those around them (e.g., Altshuler, 1974; Altshuler et al., 1976; Bachara, Raphael, & Phelan, 1980; Myklebust, 1960). Meadow (1976) and others have suggested that the relatively limited social interactions available to deaf children living in residential schools might be an important contributor to such emotional egocentrism. Alternatively, one could argue that for most deaf children being in an environment in which they can communicate with many children and adults would improve the range of social interactions over that accomplished in a communication-impoverished home or school setting (Kusché, Garfield, & Greenberg, cited in Kusché & Greenberg, 1983; Rodda, 1966; cf. Lederberg, 1991). Several studies bear on this issue.

Bachara et al. (1980) found that deaf 9- to 14-year-olds were more egocentric than hearing age-mates, lagging behind as much as 5 years, as assessed by a role-taking task. Young and Brown's (1981) report that role-taking and language competence are significantly ($r = .45$) related in preschoolers, however, suggests that the Bachara et al. findings with older children might be interpreted in two ways. One possibility is that language flexibility is intimately related to social and cognitive maturity, so that children who have the benefits of early linguistic interactions with parents and others are better able to consider the perspectives of others in social situations. Another possibility is that deaf children generally might be able to assume the perspectives of others but be unable to interpret or evaluate the consequences of those perspectives with regard to their own actions.

The latter alternative is supported by findings obtained by Kusché and

Greenberg (1983) and Cates and Shontz (1990). Kusché and Greenberg explicitly evaluated the role of language in deaf children's perspective-taking skill as part of a larger study on evaluative understanding and role-taking ability during the early and middle school years. They examined the abilities of deaf and hearing 4-, 6-, and 10-year-olds to distinguish *good* versus *bad* behaviors (depicted in pictures) and their abilities to consider the goals of others. The results from the evaluation task indicated that the hearing children were better able to make correct good/bad judgments, doing so as early as 6 years old, whereas the deaf children did not do so until age 10 (see also Odom et al., 1973).

Kusché and Greenberg's (1983) role-taking task involved a guessing game in which the experimenter hid a penny in one hand and had the child guess where it was on 11 trials. According to Kusché and Greenberg, children at an immature stage of social cognition perseverate in this task, always taking the same hand, whereas children at a more advanced, intermediate stage alternate their hand choices. Only at a "mature" stage do children understand the other's desire to outwit them and adopt a random guessing strategy. Kusché and Greenberg found that the 4-year-old deaf children were more likely than their hearing age-mates to perseverate on this task, but there were no significant differences between the deaf and hearing 6- or 10-year-olds. These results suggest that, although deaf preschoolers might lag behind hearing peers in role-taking ability, that difference disappears by the early school years.

Relevant to these results are others reported by Cates and Shontz (1990). They examined the relation of role-taking skill and social-emotional adjustment in twenty-three 7- to 14-year-olds, all of whom had moderate to profound, congenital or early-onset deafness. Cates and Shontz found that role-taking ability was positively and reliably related to social adjustment, self-image, and communication effectiveness. Children's abilities to consider another's position, however, was not related to measures of their actual social behavior, such as altruism and helping. Unfortunately, Cates and Shontz did not include a hearing control group in their study, and it therefore is unclear if their results are specific to deaf children. In any event, their findings and those of Kusché and Greenberg (1983) suggest that, although role taking ability may be a precursor of social attribution and prosocial behavior of deaf children, it clearly is not sufficient for their display.

The relation of role taking and social behavior in deaf children clearly warrants further investigation. In particular, it would be interesting to compare deaf children's perspective-taking abilities in the cognitive domain (e.g., with Piaget's three-mountain problem) with those in the social domain (see Chapter 7). In the meantime, some aspects of this issue are revealed by studies of the development of moral reasoning by deaf children and its possible reliance on role-taking and other cognitive abilities.

Moral Reasoning and Moral Judgment

The two most popular theories of moral development in children are those of Jean Piaget (1932) and Lawrence Kohlberg (1969). Both of these approaches are aimed at identifying the bases of children's judgments of right and wrong, and both assume that sophistication in moral reasoning is directly related to cognitive development. According to Piaget and Kohlberg, each child passes through a series of stages, characterized by increasing understanding and internalization of parental and societal norms. Children thus can be classified according to the mental structures that underlie moral reasoning. Early on, for example, children are more concerned with observable outcomes and the likelihood of reward or punishment than the possible causes of such an incident.

In an early study of moral development in deaf children, Nass (1964) examined moral judgments made by 30 children, six each at the ages of 8 through 12 years. Other than noting that the children were congenitally deaf, Nass gave no information on the children's normal mode of communication or the extent of their hearing losses. Each deaf child was *orally* told four stories, however, and then interviewed on their interpretation of the events. Children's responses to questions posed by the interviewer were compared to judgments provided by matched hearing children who had participated in an earlier study.

Nass found that following one story about a play fight in which a child was accidentally injured, deaf children were significantly more likely than hearing students, across all ages, to excuse the responsible child from blame (e.g., by noting that the injury was accidental). In contrast, after hearing stories about unintentionally breaking some dishes and accidentally giving erroneous directions, the hearing children were far more likely than the deaf children to excuse the protagonists from blame (e.g., by noting that the child thought the directions were correct). There were no differences between the deaf and hearing children on a fourth story.

Nass interpreted the results from the fight story as indicating that "the deaf are less concerned about pleasing authority for its own sake . . . and respond more to the reality qualities of the situation" (p. 1079). That is, he suggested that the common experiences of deaf children might make them more sensitive to each other's needs. Alternatively, that story simply might have been closer to the experiences of deaf children and thus more amenable to reasoned responses. Unfortunately, we do not know enough about the early socialization or schooling of the deaf subjects to be able to evaluate these two possibilities. In any event, despite the inconsistency of his results, Nass argued that deaf children lag behind hearing children in their abilities to judge behavior based on motive rather than perceived outcome.

Nass's conclusion later was supported by a study reported by DeCaro and Emerton (1978) involving entering (deaf) freshmen at the National Technical Institute for the Deaf (NTID). Based on Kohlberg's (1969) theory of moral development, the DeCaro and Emerton study indicated that the moral reasoning of 80% of the deaf freshmen was based on fear of punishment rather than an understanding of the principles underlying morality. This proportion compares to approximately 25% of 18-year-olds in a hearing population who would be expected to display such *preconventional* moral reasoning (Kohlberg, 1969). DeCaro and Emerton concluded that deaf children's relatively restricted range of social interaction might lead to deficits in role-taking ability, but no assessments of cognitive or social role-taking abilities were reported. Given the emphasis of Kohlberg on the cognitive and social underpinnings of moral development and the potential for language confounds within his judgment-explanation paradigm, such evidence seems necessary if we are to have confidence in DeCaro and Emerton's conclusions.

A study by Couch (1985) attempted to provide this kind of comprehensive evaluation of moral reasoning in deaf children. To ensure comprehension of the stories by his 10- and 15-year-old deaf subjects, Couch modified Kohlberg's (1969) paradigm by using signed stories that were relevant to deaf children's experience (e.g., saving money for a summer holiday). Couch also evaluated cognitive and social role-taking abilities in deaf and hearing subjects using picture stimuli, sign language, and familiar contexts.[2] On tests of cognitive perspective-taking ability (i.e., what something would look like from another vantage point), Couch found that the deaf children (as well as a group of deaf adults) lagged significantly behind hearing peers. Nevertheless, his tasks also showed higher levels of moral reasoning than had been obtained in earlier studies of deaf students, as most of the subjects appeared to have reached *conventional* (internalized) levels of moral reasoning. These results suggested to Couch that when linguistic and experiential confounds are removed deaf children as a group show evidence of sophisticated moral reasoning. At the same time, however, deaf subjects still lagged behind hearing peers on Couch's moral reasoning task when the two groups were matched on their performance on the cognitive task. The safest conclusion from this study therefore seems to be that to the extent that moral reasoning depends on social cognition deaf children remain behind hearing peers in their development of moral reasoning ability.

Moral Reasoning in Perspective

Any interpretation of findings concerning moral reasoning in deaf children must be made keeping in mind the sociocultural context of their social development. At one level, it would not be at all surprising if deaf children perform at more concrete or superficial levels in moral reasoning tasks—if they have been raised in situations in which their parents and other adult figures have not communicated affective responses, goals, and desires (A. E. Harris, 1978; Odom et al., 1973) and have provided immediate gratification rather than rational explanations for behavior (Gregory, 1976). Many deaf children find that it is the consequence of their behavior and not its initial goal that is praised or punished. Moreover, for deaf children with hearing parents, the inconsistency of social feedback and alternating permissiveness and physical punishment frequently has led to a resistance to parental values as early as the middle school years (Luterman, 1987). In the case of deaf children with deaf parents, one would expect that the consistency of early social interaction and moral training would lead to higher levels of moral reasoning in context-appropriate settings, but comparisons of the moral reasoning abilities of deaf children with deaf versus hearing parents apparently have not been made.

To some extent, deaf children may be able to infer moral values by observing the consequences of their own and others' behavior. However, this process is far slower and less efficient for the communication of moral values than is the use of language (see Chapter 12). For those deaf children who lack effective *abstract* communication within the home, the major portion of moral training does not begin until they enter a special deaf preschool or classroom. In those contexts, morality is learned in part from teachers and other adults who also have a variety of more explicit responsibilities. Most moral training, one suspects, comes from peers—who may have been raised in similar circumstances and thus also have relatively limited exposure to alternative bases for moral reasoning. Furthermore, the morality and cultural values acquired from residential schools, by and for deaf children of deaf parents as well as those with hearing parents, are not necessarily equivalent to those "expected" within the standard moral reasoning paradigms. Such situations emphasize the importance of bilingual/bicultural methods in research as well as in education.

Summary

The average deaf child of hearing parents enters school with a relatively impoverished social repertoire and breadth of social experience relative to hearing peers. Patterns of social interaction that develop in the home are not always appropriate for social interactions with other adults and peers. Some frequent, well-established behavior patterns, such as impulsivity, aggression, and egocentrism, therefore influence early school experience with teachers and with other children.

Children involved with their parents in early family intervention programs generally fare better in the social domain than do those who do not have the benefit of such experience. In part, such programs facilitate the adjustment of parents to the practical and emotional aspects of having a deaf child. Participation in such a program in the first place also indicates significant parental involvement in their deaf child's education and "rehabilitation." At the same time, language training for parents and children within family intervention programs provides a means of parent–child communication that carries over into linguistic and cognitive development as well as social development. Other intervention programs for deaf children focus more specifically on the social and cognitive skills necessary for normal social and personality development (e.g., the PATHS program described by Greenberg & Kusché, 1987).

In residential schools and special day-school settings, deaf children come into contact with other deaf children, deaf adults, and, perhaps for the first time, a subculture in which the child is a natural and welcomed member. Within this setting, the normal demands for achievement, prosocial behavior, cooperation, and morality are communicated by a somewhat different means than previously available: via identification and modeling of similar peers. The desire to integrate deaf children into hearing society notwithstanding, the residential school for the deaf thus appears to fulfill several social functions frequently unavailable to deaf children.

The apparent social importance of schooling with other deaf children is not matched by success in the academic domain. Deaf schoolchildren typically perform more poorly than hearing age-mates in most scholastic domains. Although not all the academic subjects are directly language-related in the same way as reading and writing, they share the fact that they are taught through the written word and some form of interpersonal communication—all too frequently by or with individuals who are less than fluent in the medium of the message. Data indicate that deaf children's scores on standardized tests are improving but at a rate that seems agonizingly slow. Meanwhile, the arguments concerning the most appropriate sites and communication styles for deaf education continue as they have for more than 100 years (Schildroth, 1986).

Notes

1. Many of the findings in these domains have involved the Stanford Achievement Test (SAT), originally developed for hearing children. As with most "hearing" intelligence tests (see Chapter 7), the validity of the SAT for assessing deaf children has been debated for years. At present, however, it remains the only viable measure of academic achievement available in the field.

2. It should be noted that scoring in Kohlberg's paradigm is so complex that prior to his death investigators had to travel to his laboratory for training in its correct use. Most investigators, such as Couch and perhaps DeCaro and Emerton, did not receive such training, and thus the reliability and validity of their results is open to question.

5

Foundations of Language Development in Deaf Children

For psychologists interested in language development of deaf or hearing children, there are two basic questions: How do children learn language? and Do children acquire language in the same ways as they acquire other abilities? Both questions are associated with a variety of obvious and not so obvious "subquestions" (although they can hardly be considered small). These related questions concern such issues as: (1) whether language is a uniquely human ability, i.e., distinct from communication and whatever it is that "language-trained" chimpanzees do (Greenfield, 1991; Hockett & Altmann, 1968); (2) the extent to which language learning involves an innate language acquisition device (McNeill, 1966), biopro-gram (Bickerton, 1984), or predisposition toward symbolic communication (Macnamara, 1972); (3) the extent to which language learning, especially the earli-est language learning, can be accounted for in terms of maturation or behavioral principles, in contrast to the obvious cognitive underpinnings of later language, problem-solving, and information-processing abilities (Lenneberg, 1967; Meier & Newport, 1990); and (4) the interaction of language learning with the complexity of the vernacular (Slobin, 1973) and the richness of the linguistic corpus available to the child (Abrahamsen, Cavallo, & McCluer, 1985; Chomsky, 1965).

Such issues define the biological, cognitive, and linguistic constraints on lan-guage development—factors that not only determine the *whens* and *whats* of lan-guage development but also the character of the language being observed. In addi-tion, these constraints—and the language to which they give rise—subtly influence the subsequent courses of cognitive and social development. In this chapter, several precursors, concomitants, and constraints on language development are considered in terms of their expression in deaf children. The cognitive and social skills that deaf children bring to the language-learning situation also are examined, together with the requirements for learning language in the absence of aural-oral communi-cation. Throughout these discussions, interactions of language-learning abilities and the contents and context of language learning are of central interest. (Chapter 6 then goes on to consider language acquisition proper.)

When attempting to understand the bases and products of language development in deaf children, the four broad issues noted above are relevant in several respects. Clearly, however, complete consideration of them all would be beyond the scope and page limitations of this book. Instead, this discussion focuses on several issues that bear on language development in children who are deaf compared to children who have normal hearing. Of central concern here are the implications of acquiring a manual, visual-spatial language rather than an aural-oral one, the absence of the auditory modality and consequent effects on the phonological component of language, and the place of deaf children as special individuals within a hearing society and within hearing families.

For the most part, the substance of this chapter is the *psychology of language development* rather than developmental psycholinguistics. That is, it focuses primarily on the processes of language growth rather than the structure of its products. Detailed discussion of the form of deaf children's language can be found in Wilbur (1987) and other references noted below (see also Chapters 2, 6, and 11). In the tradition of psychological treatments of language acquisition, it is especially important to the present discussion to keep in mind the difference between the presumed knowledge underlying language use and language production per se. "Knowledge" here is not meant in the sense of the semantic content of language but in the sense of its rules and structure. The distinction is thus one of competence versus performance.

Competence Versus Performance

The competence-performance distinction originally was raised by Noam Chomsky (1957, 1965) in his presentation of transformational generative grammar as a model of the structure of language. Chomsky did not intend transformational grammar as a model of the language user but of language itself. Nonetheless, a variety of psychologists and educators attempted to map his linguistic theory directly onto adults' and children's language and even to use training in transformational grammar as an avenue toward improving language performance in deaf children. The latter exercise, in fact, is still popular in some deaf education curricula (Quigley & Paul, 1984).

Chomsky's (1965) competence-performance distinction separated observed linguistic data (i.e., the finite set of utterances produced) from the underlying linguistic knowledge inferred from those data. That is, by observing the fluencies and disfluencies of language performance in children or other language users, one should be able to construct a model of the knowledge that would allow the individual to produce an infinite number of valid sentences and to make judgments as to what is and is not acceptable within the language. This model, or *grammar*, is not always correctly expressed by the language user because there are a variety of psychological and environmental variables that contribute to production disfluency. Nonetheless, a sufficiently rich corpus provides a good working model of the structure of the language and to a more remote degree of the knowledge of the language user.[1]

Given the importance of the competence-performance distinction and the use of descriptive grammars since the 1960s, it is surprising that they have not been more fully considered with regard to deaf children's knowledge of sign language. Rather than attempting to construct a model of their linguistic knowledge and its reflection in sign language or speech, the primary focus in this area has been on relatively direct descriptions of deaf children's language performance (e.g., Goldin-Meadow & Mylander, 1984; Petitto, 1987; Wilbur, 1987) or attempts to map deaf children's language onto English grammatical structure (King & Quigley, 1985). Meanwhile, great strides have been made in understanding the linguistics of American Sign Language (ASL) (e.g., Klima & Bellugi, 1979) (see Chapter 2), but the extension of that work to deaf children is still in its infancy (e.g., Newport & Ashbrook, 1977).

Research in this domain seems imperative because of the heterogeneity (and frequent deficiency) of deaf children's language environments and the still unresolved issues concerning the use of ASL, Sign English, and other forms of manual communication in deaf education. The competence–performance distinction emphasizes that deaf children's linguistic competence is not equivalent to their performance within a particular language. Knowledge of *language* is distinct from knowledge of English or knowledge of ASL. This differentiation becomes more important as a greater degree of innate, presumably modality-independent language competence is granted to the child (e.g., Petitto & Marentette, 1991). Schlesinger and Meadow (1972a) went so far as to suggest that if language capacity is genetic no important differences should be seen between acquisition of manual and oral languages (cf. Meier & Newport, 1990).

The competence–performance issue arises again later as it concerns the emergence of regularized gestural systems in deaf children who have not been exposed to effective language models. It also is relevant to the issue of whether there is a *sign advantage*, wherein signs are acquired before words (e.g., Bonvillian & Folven, 1993; Goodwyn & Acredolo, 1991; Meier & Newport, 1990). Finally, the distinction is considered in the context of evaluating the status of early gestures as a specific precursor of sign language versus its predating and possible structuring role for linguistic communication. The extent to which gestures are a fundamental component of social and linguistic functioning in hearing children has a bearing on how we interpret their appearance in the behavioral repertoires of deaf children. Gestures and other nonlinguistic or nonliteral devices also provide insight into the cognitive underpinnings of language development as distinct from the contributions of any innate linguistic endowment and of apparently nonlinguistic cognitive abilities (Marschark, 1992).

The following discussions highlight the competence–performance distinction as it relates to relations between language and other cognitive abilities, language production versus comprehension, and oral versus manual modes of production. While following the course of deaf children's language development, these issues help to guide the search for an integrated understanding of the interaction of language, cognitive, and social development (for elaboration see Marschark, 1993).

As a beginning point, let us consider the emergence of functional communication (defined in terms of its effect on the receiver) and symbolic communication (defined in terms of related cognitive functioning of the child and the contexts in which apparent communication is evident). It is at this point, during the first year of life, that both deaf and hearing children show the rudiments of vocal and manual communication, as both are vocalizing and using simple gestures.

Do Deaf Children Babble?

The availability of both manual and articulatory apparatuses at the outset of life and their apparent exercise during the first year suggest an equipotentiality for children to develop signed or spoken language (Bates, 1979; Schlesinger & Meadow, 1972). Whether having the necessary production equipment is a true reflection of a biological equality of speech and sign or simply a consequence of the vocal tract and hands being the two most flexible and precise motor systems available to us is an issue worthy of elaboration but outside the scope of the present discussion. [See Abrahamsen et al. (1985), concerning the greater robustness of the manual system, and Kimura (1975) and Tzeng & Wang (1984) for discussions of the similarities in the neuromotor mechanisms involved in speech and sign.] The issue of deaf children's manual and vocal babbling, in contrast, is both closer to the present focus on the foundations of language acquisition by deaf children and central to the larger understanding of psychological and biological bases of language development in general. Observation of the vocal babbling of deaf infants could help to decipher the extent of the innate endowment or potential for oral language (if not *language* in the more abstract sense) as well as the importance of auditory feedback from the self and others as a precursor of normal phonological development.

As Oller and Eilers (1988; p. 441) noted: "If deaf infants babble in the same way and at the same age as their hearing counterparts, it would suggest that humans are born with a phonetic inheritance that unfolds without extensive auditory experience. On the other hand, if deaf infants' vocalizations differ from those of hearing infants, it would suggest that auditory experience plays an important role in the timely emergence of speech-like sounds" (for consideration of parallel questions with regard to speech perception see Burnham, 1986). At face value, babbling could represent either an exercising of the articulatory apparatus that has implications for subsequent language or spontaneous use or play with the articulators (e.g., as self-stimulation) with only a coincidental relation to subsequent language (Jakobson, 1968; Piaget, 1962). Which of these positions one adopts appears to depend largely on the literalness of the definitions imposed. Bates (1979), for example, suggested that babbling has the form of language but not its function. She found it only weakly related to other aspects of language development and suggested that babbling is outside the "language complex." Lenneberg (1967; p. 140) provided some evidence consistent with this view. He observed a child who did not have the opportunity for babbling from 10 to 14 months of age because of a tracheotomy. When the tracheotomy was reversed, babbling was age-consistent rather than taking up where it left off. Lenneberg therefore concluded that babbling was largely a prewired behavior, with little relation to the development of real speech and language.

More recently, Oller, Wieman, Doyle, and Ross (1976) analyzed the babbling and early speech of 10 children, half of whom were between 6 and 8 months and the others between 12 and 13 months. In contrast to the position of Jakobson, Lenneberg, and others, Oller et al. found that the phonological characteristics observed in the meaningful speech of the older children were all present in the babbling of the younger ones. This continuity in the content of babbling and the first words leads to the conclusion that the two are more than just randomly related. Rather, it appears that there is a *babbling drift* (Brown, 1973) from less well formed vocalizations through ones that approximate the structure and the function of spoken language and so on, eventually, to speech.

In the existing literature, consideration of the babbling produced by deaf infants largely has involved vocal babbling. This topic is dealt with below. First, however, consider the question of whether deaf children might produce manual babbling that could serve a function similar to that of vocal babbling for hearing infants and also be informative with regard to the underlying issues concerning language development.

Manual Babbling?

Whereas vocal babbling consists in phonological segments of consonants or consonants plus vowels, manual babbling (mabbling?) has the potential to include either cheremic components of signs (e.g., handshapes or movements) or complete signs that require only canonical reduplication of handshape and movement (e.g., MILK—an opening and closing of the hand into a fist) or handshape and place of articulation, e.g., MAMA—movement of an open hand toward the chin (see Figure 6-1). At a basic level, such babblings likely have social implications when "uttered" to deaf parents, regardless of their status as practice or play. Just as particular vocal productions of hearing infants (e.g., "ma") might selectively elicit potentially language-shaping responses from hearing parents, so such manual productions of deaf children might be interpreted by deaf or sign-sensitive hearing parents (Moerk, 1983). Researchers interested in vocal babbling generally have not considered its social implications, however, and the social implications of manual babbling are similarly untouched.

One description of manual babbling in a native signing child was supplied by Prinz and Prinz (1979), involving their hearing daughter Anya. It should be emphasized that at the outset that as language teachers and researchers, Prinz and Prinz may have provided Anya with a context for language development not truly representative of the naturalistic language-learning situations encountered by most children. This criticism can also be applied to other language development studies, involving both signing (e.g., Holmes & Holmes, 1980) and speaking (e.g., Halliday, 1975) children, in which the parents are language investigators. Furthermore, many of the now classic studies of child language have been conducted with children of university faculty and staff (e.g., Brown, 1973), who also are not known for being typical with regard to their interest and involvement in their children's development. It thus is incumbent on researchers who use small, nonrepresentative populations (often because of their easy availability) to either obtain convergent evidence from other populations or provide explicit comparisons of their data with those obtained by other researchers.

Returning to the Prinz and Prinz (1979) study, these investigators reported that Anya used "baby signs" comparable to the "baby words" frequently produced by hearing infants. She also was observed doing something like manual babbling: "She exhibited a type of manual 'babbling' behavior in that she would wave her hands around in apparent imitation of signs produced by her parents. Interestingly, Anya's imitative signs were generally more accurate and visually distinct than those that she spontaneously produced. The spontaneously produced signs were often truncated in the formation of hand configuration, the place within signing space in which a sign is normally made, and/or sign action" (Prinz & Prinz, 1979, p. 286).

It is noteworthy that Prinz and Prinz referred to such productions as manual babbling rather than approximations to signs (cf. Schlesinger & Meadow, 1972b). In fact, their examples suggest that Anya's manual babbling was composed of distortions of signs rather than the repetitive and variegated components of future words observed in the oral babbling of hearing children. Together with the fact that Anya is a hearing child, these observations appear to leave open the question of the frequency and status of manual babbling in deaf infants.

Beyond the Prinz and Prinz (1979) study and occasional anecdotal references to apparent manual babbling, its possible role in the origins of sign language has been largely ignored. Instead, the focus has been on early gesture in deaf children (considered in a later section). If deaf children do exhibit the formational precursors of manual communication in something akin to babbling, however, it would add to the arguments in favor of the equipotentiality of sign and speech development. Such evidence might detract somewhat from the presumed linguistic origins of vocal babbling, but it would not seriously impair the notion of babbling drift so long as the latter is assumed to result from the filtering of input as well as a spontaneous vocalization device. Suppose, however, that deaf and hearing children are found to produce similar frequencies and varieties of simple cheremic (manual) components of language at early ages with gradual divergence as manual babbling emerges (cf. Stoel-Gammon & Otomo, 1986). We then could examine the refinement of early repertoires of manual behavior in the same ways as a variety of investigators have with vocal behavior.

A study relevant to this issue was reported by Petitto and Marentette (1991). They videotaped the progression of manual babbling by two deaf infants of deaf parents and three hearing infants of hearing parents over the ages of 10, 12, and 14 months. Using criteria parallel to that required for attribution of vocal babbling, Petitto and Marentette found that both deaf and hearing children produced manual activity that (1) consisted of a subset of the potential phonetic inventory of sign language, (2) demonstrated syllabic organization comparable to that in ASL, and (3) was apparently devoid of meaning or reference (p. 1494). Only the two deaf children's productions appeared to progress through the stages characteristic of vocal babbling, however, and their productions were more complex and varied than the ones of the hearing children.

Perhaps the most surprising finding in Petitto and Marentette's study was that by 14 months of age more than 60% of the two deaf infants' manual activity was classified as syllabic babbling (compared to 4 to 15% of that produced by the three hearing children). This rate contrasts with the level of 20% typically taken to represent the stage of vocal babbling in hearing infants. It also seems remarkably high for native signing children of deaf parents who one would have been expected to be well started on their way in vocabulary development at this age (see Bonvillian & Folven, 1993; Petitto & Charron, 1991; and following sections). In any event, Petitto and Marentette (1991, p. 1495) concluded that "babbling is an expression of an amodal brain-based language capacity capable of processing speech and sign." Insofar as manual and vocal babbling appear to consist of similar units, they argued that there must be an innate predisposition to discover the patterned input of language.

Petitto and Marentette's data do not rule out the possibility that babbling reflects learned behavior, its precise form in infants being based on input from parents sharing a common language modality. The ruling out of that alternative would require examination of babbling by infants without language models (e.g., deaf children whose hearing parents do not sign). Nevertheless, the observed differences between deaf and hearing infants and the similarity of the manual activity produced by Petitto and Marentette's deaf subjects and the cheremic sign components of ASL argue strongly that babbling is intimately tied to the acquisition of language.

Just as the earliest vocal repertoires of infants are defined by the extent of neuromotor maturation and configuration of the articulators, so it is with deaf infants. Battison (1974), for example, has described the earliest handshapes acquired by deaf children, finding a relatively small set of hand configurations that appear to be uniform across deaf infants learning sign language as a first language. These handshapes also comprise the primary stuff of later signs. Battison referred to these canonical handshapes as *unmarked* in the sense they are found across all documented sign languages and are both formationally and perceptually distinct such that they could generate *minimal contrasts* within the language. These handshapes include the six handshapes shown in Figure 5-1. Lane, Boyes-Braem, and Bellugi (1976) later found these six shapes to characterize more than 80% of the productions of a 2-year-old deaf child whose sign language development they were studying. Whether those handshapes might constitute a similarly large percentage of handshapes in young hearing children remains to be explored. The Lane et al. (1976) classification system for distinctive features of handshapes would provide a perfect tool for this investigation.

The relation of deaf children's chereme production and manual babbling has yet to be explicitly compared to the oral productions of hearing age-mates. Perhaps most interesting would be an examination of the manual babbling of deaf children whose hearing parents sign to them compared to a group with hearing parents who do not sign. This situation would allow a comparison of the effects of lacking *auditory* feedback from babbling (already available from other studies) versus lacking *any* linguistic feedback. Together with the comparison of the effects of manual feedback to deaf children of deaf parents and auditory feedback to hearing children of hearing parents, this information would provide a better understanding of the social-behavioral implications of parental input during the babbling stage in addition to its role in phonological and speech development.

Vocal Babbling by Deaf Infants

The emergence of vocal behavior in normally hearing children follows a fairly regular and well-defined course. The first 2 months generally see a *phonation stage* in which infants produce "quasivowels" with normal, speech-like intonation; combinations of vowels with consonants are rare. This phase is followed by a *cooing stage* (more accurately referred to as a *gooing stage*), from 2 to 3 months, in which quasivowels are linked to articulated sounds produced for the most part in the back of the oral cavity. These quasiconsonants are joined by trills, vibrants, true vowel

FIGURE 5-1. Relatively universal set of hand configurations that appear across deaf infants learning ASL as a first language. (Source: Battison, 1974. © 1988, Sugar Sign Press; reprinted by permission.)

sounds, and a variety of grunts, growls, and squeals during the *expansion stage*, from 4 to 6 months.

Although some children produce what is called "marginal babbling" during the expansion stage, production of the well-formed syllables needed for babbling does not fully emerge until the *canonical stage*, beginning at about 7 months for most infants and continuing until about 11 months (cf. Petitto & Marentette, 1991). It is during this period that sounds are reduplicated to form the first productions interpreted as words by overzealous parents: /mama/, /dada/, and /kaka/ (regarding the origins of conversation in preverbal interactions see Feyereisen & de Lannoy, 1991, Ch. 5). Oller and his colleagues (e.g., Oller, 1980; Oller & Eilers, 1988; Oller, Eilers, Bull, & Carney, 1985) saw this stage as particularly central to speech development because it is the stage at which infants produce syllables that can function as the phonetic building blocks of words. It also seems likely to be the stage at which the building blocks of interpersonal linguistic interaction emerge.

In contrast to the relative paucity of literature concerning manual babbling by deaf infants, there are many studies and nonempirical writings concerning their vocal babbling and other early vocalizations. This literature is fraught with apparent contradictions, although it appears that most of the controversy derives from the nonexperimental work. The empirical data, in contrast, appear relatively clear.

The controversy appears to have begun with the intuitively appealing suggestion of Whetnall and Fry (1964, p. 79) that, at the point when hearing children would begin to benefit from auditory feedback to their babbling, "babbling fades in the deaf child because he lacks the external auditory stimulus from an adult and also the auditory stimulus of his own babbling." This description was followed by a study by Lenneberg, Rebelsky, and Nichols (1965) in which they explored the vocalizations of one deaf infant and three hearing infants of deaf parents in comparison to a group of hearing infants of hearing parents. All of the infants in the Lenneberg et al. study were observed during the phonation and cooing stages, and data were presented based on six categories of vocalization: rhythmic and arrhythmic crying, fussing, vegetative sounds (e.g., coughing, grunting), cooing, and "neutral" sounds. Their data indicated that the infants of deaf and hearing parents did not differ on any of the six dimensions.

Lenneberg et al. (1965, p. 32) went on to describe characteristics of the "normal," *later* sequence of vocalization in which crying gives rise to cooing and thence to babbling, before variegated babbling yields to the first words. Unfortunately, that description has been interpreted by several investigators as a statement of empirical findings, even though the children examined in the Lenneberg study were not in the older age range described (e.g., deVilliers & deVilliers, 1978; Stoel-Gammon & Otomo, 1986; cf. Gilbert, 1982). This misinterpretation has been compounded by Lenneberg's (1967, pp. 139–140) later description of his observation of two deaf infants of deaf parents and 16 other deaf children observed "between their second and fifth year.[2] Lenneberg noted that "in certain respects" the development of vocalization in the deaf infants paralleled that observed in hearing children (although without words). He also mentioned observing relatively normal babbling in many of the older (2 to 5 years old) deaf children. Neither of these observations is unusual for deaf children (e.g., Stoel-Gammon & Otomo, 1986), but the latter statement was subsequently interpreted by many to refer to the two younger children who were observed during the canonical stage.

The Lenneberg studies thus frequently have been interpreted as indicating that deaf and hearing infants show similar patterns of vocalization and babbling, albeit with the deaf showing somewhat less variety in their babbling, up to the point of the first words in hearing children (e.g., Locke, 1983). In contrast to the real and alleged findings of Lenneberg (1967; Lenneberg et al., 1965), however, a variety of single-subject and small-sample studies have found vocalizations of deaf children to decline in both frequency and diversity over the first, "prelingual" months of life. Mavilya (1972) and Maskarinec, Cairns, Butterfield, and Weamer (1981), for example, observed decreases in the frequency of vocalization by deaf children over the first 6 months. Stark (1983) observed a smaller range in the vocalizations of hearing-impaired infants from 15 to 24 months compared to a group of 2- to 11-month old hearing infants. Oller and his colleagues (Oller et al., 1985) went even farther, reporting the complete absence of canonical babbling by severely to profoundly deaf infants during the first year.

These findings suggest that both degree of hearing loss and parental hearing status might have significant effects on the quality and quantity of deaf infants' early vocalizations. Deaf infants might well show effects of reacting to those portions of parental vocalizations that are received as well as kinesthetic feedback from their own productions (cf. Abrahamsen et al., 1985; Petitto & Marentette, 1991). This suggestion is supported by findings from Stoel-Gammon and Otomo's (1986) study involving 11 moderately to profoundly deaf infants (five of whom were deaf before 7 months) aged 4 to 28 months and a group of 11 hearing infants aged 4 to 18 months. They found a significant decline in the variety of consonantal sounds produced by the deaf infants over the period of observation, whereas that of the normally hearing sample increased. The divergence was most marked after 8 months of age, when only the hearing children showed age-appropriate canonical babbling. Stoel-Gammon and Otomo observed this difference between deaf and hearing children across the age ranges of their samples and reported that the differences were smaller in the two cases of moderate hearing impairment than in the severe and profound cases. Stoel-Gammon (1988) later reexamined the inventory of consonantal sounds produced by infants in the 1986 study plus three new deaf subjects and reached the same conclusions.

Oller and Eilers (1988) compared the early vocalizations of 21 normally hearing infants to those of 9 severely to profoundly deaf infants, all of whom had undergone early auditory amplification and speech stimulation. In particular, they examined the transition from precanonical, marginal babbling to true babbling. Oller and Eilers found that the hearing sample showed the typical onset of canonical babbling at about 7 months (range 6 to 10 months), whereas the deaf infants did not begin canonical babbling until 11 to 25 months, despite the early interventions. Although all of the deaf subjects babbled eventually, they showed a much lower proportion of babbling in their vocalizations (≤ 0.1 canonical syllables per utterance) than their hearing age-mates (0.5 to 1.5 canonical syllables per utterance). Oller and Eiler concluded that audition apparently does play a role in babbling (cf. Locke, 1983), although the differential effects of self-stimulation versus stimulation by others remains unclear (cf. Gottlieb, 1980).

In summary, there is now a variety of evidence to indicate that deaf and hearing infants do produce similar, prelinguistic vocalizations (Lenneberg et al., 1965; Oller et al., 1985; Stoel-Gammon, 1988). There is equally strong evidence, however, that deaf and hearing infants differ in their vocalizations *before they reach the one-word stage*. At the points where hearing babies are producing regular, canonical reduplication (/mamama/, /gaga/—at around 7 months) and variegation (/maka/, /paka-pakapaka/—at around 10 months), deaf babies are showing a reduced complexity in vocal production. This difference occurs despite early use of amplification and concerted efforts to provide speech stimulation. Residual hearing would be expected to ameliorate the lag of hearing-impaired infants, but at least in those with moderate losses (two infants studied by Stoel-Gammon & Otomo, 1986) the difference is still apparent.

At the age when parents should be beginning to respond rather specifically to their infants' vocalizations, when grunts and babbles are first "comprehended" by significant adults and older children, deaf babies thus may be disadvantaged socially and communicatively as well as auditorally and orally. It may be that deaf (or hearing) children of deaf parents are producing (Petitto & Marentette, 1991) and receiving (Rea et al., 1988) comparable stimulation via the manual system. This manual system might even be developing at a rate faster than the speech system (Holmes & Holmes, 1980; Orlansky & Bonvillian, 1985; Prinz & Prinz, 1979), although the reasons for such a difference are still at issue (Abrahamsen et al., 1985; Meier & Newport, 1990) (see Chapter 6). For most deaf children, however, this time is the point at which parents are beginning to suspect a problem with their child: Some children are being diagnosed as deaf, and those whose deafness has already been identified are (hopefully) beginning intervention.

The lack of vocal-auditory communication between hearing parents and their deaf children is thus a real and significant factor in development, with implications even at this early age for cognitive and social development as well as language development and day-to-day functioning (Hopkins, 1983). This conclusion is not meant to imply that there are no other modes of communication at play. Hearing mothers and their deaf infants presumably have developed some reciprocity and synchrony in their physical contact at this point, and they soon will begin to use manual gestures and "body language" to communicate, similar to dyads containing a deaf mother and a hearing infant (Spencer, 1991). We thus now turn to the gestural domain and a communication medium that has a relatively continuous pattern of development during the toddler and preschool years.

The Role of Gesture in Sign Language Acquisition

As noted earlier, the focus of most research concerning deaf children's early manual behavior has been on the emergence of meaningful gestures rather than the components of those gestures that might be formational precursors of signs (for surveys of both see Volterra & Erting, 1990). It was suggested at that point that parallel studies of the emergence of formational components of sign and speech are still lacking. With regard to gesture, more comparable studies of deaf and hearing children have been conducted, even if, as we shall see, some of them may have been "biased" in favor of deaf children (perhaps a fair deal given the apparent bias against them in the babbling literature). Once again, however, the emphasis should be on providing equal footing for the two groups if we expect identification of similarities between deaf and hearing children to reveal some of the still unsolved mysteries of the mechanisms of language development. In this context, the present discussion of the emergence of gesture in deaf children's behavioral repertoires represents only the tip of the iceberg. For a more complete consideration of the status of gesture as an accompaniment to spoken language see McNeill (1993); McNeill, Levy, and Pedelty (1990); and Feyereisen and de Lannoy (1991). The distinction between gesture and sign language is considered in more depth by Marschark (1993), McNeill (1993), and Petitto (1987, 1988).

Just as the gestures of hearing adults (McNeill, 1985) and hearing children (Church & Goldin-Meadow, 1986) appear to provide insights into the mental representations underlying speech production, deaf children's gestures and pantomime might yield new understanding of their perceptions and conceptions of the world (Marschark, 1992; Marschark & Clark, 1987). Distinction of those gestural characteristics common to children acquiring signed and vocal languages from those manual elements that are specific to sign also might be informative with regard to the structure and origins of deaf children's linguistic competencies.

This suggestion is supported by Klima and Bellugi's (1979) distinction between several means of elaborating regular lexical items in ASL and the "extrasystemic" or "nonconventionalized gestures" that frequently are interspersed with the signs made by deaf adults. Klima and Bellugi (1979, p. 15) noted that, "When hearing-speaking people communicate, they too use gestures in varying degrees, but the gestures are clearly distinguishable from words. In signing, the various kinds of gesturing are in the same channel of communication as the regular lexical items. Since nonconventionalized gesturing is extensive and varied in deaf communication, and since it occurs in the same linguistic context as signing, a central question for the analysis of ASL is how to distinguish in the signing stream those gestures that constitute the lexical signs of ASL."

Nevertheless, consideration of nonconventionalized gestures within sign language appears anathema to some sign language investigators. Perhaps it is because it is all too recently that manual communication emerged from a hazy status in which *gestures* had distinctly negative connotations, signaling that sign language could never "be considered comparable to a verbal symbol system" (Myklebust, 1960, p. 235) and was explicitly not a verbal language (p. 241; see also Evans, 1988). In fact, the pendulum has swung the other way, and many investigators now use *sign* and *gesture* interchangeably, e.g., the "symbolic signing" of hearing children (Acredolo & Goodwyn, 1985), or refer to all gestures produced by deaf children as "signs," regardless of whether those manual productions are lexicalized (Goldin-Meadow & Mylander, 1984).

Salient Gestures of Deaf Children

Marschark (1992) distinguished several classes of meaningful, manual behavior on the basis of the extent to which they are lexicalized (having linguistic, word-like status), conventional, or extrasystemic to children's sign language. The important two issues in that discussion were (1) the extent to which these classes might have similar psycholinguistic functions and (2) the degree to which they serve similar roles for deaf and hearing children who encounter or create them within the context of language acquisition. Although some of the descriptions used there go beyond the present purposes, it is worthwhile to consider three specific classes of gestures that are particularly frequent in deaf children's communication: (1) pointing, or deixis; (2) iconic gestures; and (3) character-viewpoint, or pantomimic, gestures (see also the discussion of sign language in Chapter 2). All three of these forms remain in their repertoires as children become more fluent in sign language, and each serves a variety of functions in communication (e.g., Marschark et al., 1987).

POINTING

Gestures such as finger- and hand-pointing comprise the class of gesture most clearly lexicalized in ASL and one that emerges relatively early. For these reasons, there is an inclination to suggest that *deixis* (pointing to a location in space) should not be considered a (nonlinguistic) gesture for competent deaf signers, even if it is for prelinguistic children. Instead, lexicalized pointing should be considered signing. Marschark and colleagues (1986, 1987), for example, classified pointing as gesture for hearing children but did not do so for deaf children unless it accompanied, rather than replaced, signed production and contributed iconically either manner, course, speed, or quantity. This contrast of supplementary versus replacement pointing may be an important one, distinguishing linguistic pointing within ASL from the gestural pointing common to both deaf and hearing children.

The pointing gestures produced by deaf as well as hearing children typically have a referential function. In their earliest incarnations (9 to 12 months), they are used for directing attention to objects, people, or locations, typically expressing wants. For older hearing children, pointing gestures frequently describe a location or motion of something into a location and set up some place in the gesture space to represent this locus. Almost always, however, the gesture is accompanied by a verbal description and generally is used only a single time or within a single context (Marschark et al., 1987). If repeated, the gesture is again accompanied by verbal description. Deaf children produce essentially identical gestures, but they are reusable, frequently referred to, and do not require verbal accompaniment once someone or something has been placed either by body movement, head movement, or a deictic gesture.

The supplementary uses of deictic pointing by deaf children frequently appear

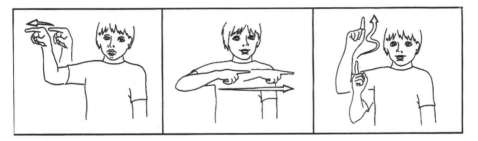

FIGURE 5-2. Three-gesture sequence (involving supplementary deixis and possibly a classifier) in which a boy describes seeing a bear, running to a tree, and quickly climbing upward through the branches. Based on descriptions in Marschark et al., 1986.

to be instances of classifier use (see Chapter 2) or combinations of deictics and classifiers. Figure 5-2, for example, shows a three-gesture sequence drawn from the corpus obtained by Marschark et al. (1986). The sequence was produced by a young deaf child after a signed description of a boy being chased by a bear. First, he is shown using a deictic to indicate the location of the boy when he sees the bear; then there is movement to another location (a tree); and finally he shows rapid movement through branches as the boy scampers up the tree. Had the finger position in the sec ond gesture been in the canonical upright form of the person classifier, the classification of that production (as a sign) would have been clear. The child's use of the horizontal position, however, clouds the issue of gesture versus classifier—of nonlinguistic versus linguistic. Perhaps the difference has no psychological reality to the child, even if it might to an adult psycholinguist. In any case, it would be interesting to examine the development of classifier use as distinct from deixis and supplementary (nondeictic) pointing in the same way that Petitto (1987) distinguished prelinguistic pointing from personal pronoun pointing (for evidence concerning classifier acquisition see Hoffmeister, 1982; Wilbur, 1987).

ICONIC GESTURES

Iconic gestures bear a close formal relation to the semantic content of ongoing language for both deaf and hearing children, and they can involve either symbolic actions or descriptive features (Marschark et al., 1987). The determination of what qualifies as an iconic gesture in deaf children requires identification of intended referents (McNeill et al., 1990). The supplementary quality of such a gesture follows from the fact that a signed or spoken description typically is needed to provide a context in which the receiver of the message can understand the iconic qualities. In this sense, iconic and other supplementary gestures provide the best examples of the complementary relation of language and gesture described by McNeill (1992).

  Together with pantomimic (*character-viewpoint*) gestures (see following section), which typically are not accompanied by literal descriptions, iconic (*object-viewpoint*) gestures, provide the insight into mental representation suggested by McNeill (1985). Because of the dissociation between gesture and speech in the case of true pantomime, however, the character-viewpoint and object-viewpoint gestures can fill different roles in communication and may derive from different sources (Cohen, Namir, & Schlesinger, 1977). In particular, pantomime and character-viewpoint gestures may be particularly useful and frequent when literal, verbal "terminology" is unknown or temporarily unavailable (Marschark & West, 1985). Iconic gestures, in contrast, by virtue of their typical accompaniment by sign or speech, apparently have a somewhat different origin. This difference suggests that pantomime might decrease with increasing vocabulary size whereas iconic gestures remain relatively stable. Interactions with the hearing status/language modality could indicate differences in the courses of language development in deaf and hearing children or in the functional status of gesture in the development of signing and oral children.

The above considerations apply to iconic modifications of existing signs as well as to iconic gestures that are interspersed within the sign stream. Wilbur (1987, pp. 168–169) emphasized that, "When iconicity does appear [in modification of ASL signs], it must obey the constraints on allowable signs . . . such that (1) the resultant sign cannot violate the phonological conditions on allowable signs, (2) it cannot destroy the syntactic or morphological content of the sentence, and (3) it cannot be semantically distinct from the original meaning in the sense of a minimal pair." Certainly, conditions (2) and (3) also hold for the use of iconic gestures within a signed sequence, or the complementarity of speech and gesture would be violated. The status of condition (1) has not been evaluated, however, and it is possible that the gestures of deaf children and perhaps deaf adults have some features that do not occur in sign. Identification of such characteristics would provide one "tracer" with which to map the transition from gesture to sign + gesture in deaf children and to distinguish gesture and sign in more mature signers.

Iconic gestures sometimes appear similar to pantomimic gestures (considered below), and they frequently have been treated as a single class. Petitto (1988), for example, described the emergence of iconic gestures in children between 16 and 20 months, using examples such as the "twisting motions of the wrist" that accompany and represent opening of jars. Importantly, Petitto found that such gestures did not emerge until after children had already acquired the related sign or word. That sequence may be different in the case of gestures that are object-viewpoint gestures and supplement descriptions rather than replacing them (as in Petitto's case). Consistent with this suggestion, Acredolo and Goodwyn (1988) observed pantomimic gestures of hearing children functionally serving the same roles as words, but their subjects tended to have *either* the word or the iconic gesture in their repertoires. In contrast, to the extent that nonpantomimic (object-viewpoint) iconic gestures function primarily in a supplemental manner, they might be expected to emerge later than the literal sign or word.

CHARACTER-VIEWPOINT GESTURES

Many of the gestures observed by investigators of hearing children's gestures (e.g., Acredolo & Goodwyn, 1988; Bates, 1979) consist of pantomimic actions rather than deictic or iconic gestures. In some cases the children are actually holding relevant objects, perhaps offering or showing toys (Acredolo & Goodwyn, 1985; Bates, Bretherton, Shore, and McNew, 1983). Perhaps more interesting is the comparison between object-independent gestures that do and do not mirror the actions they represent (or the objects used in those actions). Also relevant to this discussion is whether the gesture represents the desired/requested/demonstrated action or is metonymically related to the action.

These issues are best considered in terms of the following ordering of the gestures observed in deaf children's productions:

Object-viewpoint —→ metonymic —→ character-viewpoint —→ object-dependent

Object-viewpoint gestures, again, are those relatively pure cases in which shapes, locations, directions, or manners are depicted. In a sense, these are all *metonymic* or *synecdotal* insofar as they involve using a part, characteristic, or associate of a thing to stand for the whole; but the emphasis for the present purposes is on the absence of pantomimic quality. *Metonymic gestures*, in contrast, are those in which actions are explicitly used by children to represent related outcomes. For example, Petitto (1988, p. 209) noted that her observation of a jar opening gesture was "not literally the enactment of the designated activity (e.g., the child does not actually open a jar)," as in object-dependent gestures. However, she did not indicate whether the child actually wanted a particular jar opened, in which case it could be considered a character-viewpoint gesture of request, or if jar opening was a symbolic gesture representing the child's desire for a particular something that typically was found in a jar (e.g., as a socially agreed on signifier for peanut butter). The latter case seems a clear example of metonymy in the sense described in treatments of figurative language (e.g., Marschark et al., 1987).

Unfortunately, object-viewpoint and character-viewpoint gestures have not been distinguished to any great extent within the developmental literature. Everhart and Marschark (1988) distinguished the two in productions by deaf and hearing children; and Marschark, Everhart, and Dempsey (1991) did so in productions by adults. Marschark and West (1985) and Marschark et al. (1986) separated pantomime from gesture but did not distinguish among types of gesture. The results across those studies, however, are clear: During the oral narration of stories, hearing adults and hearing children consistently produced iconic, object-viewpoint gesture with greater frequency than pantomime or pantomimic gesture. Deaf adults and deaf children, in contrast, consistently produced pantomime with equal or higher frequency than gesture. This same pattern held for ASL-English bilinguals (hearing adults) when narrating orally and in sign, respectively (Marschark et al., 1991). Moreover, the between-group (deaf versus hearing) differences in frequency of pantomime (favoring deaf producers) were consistently greater than those in frequency of gesture. These findings thus uniformly suggest that pantomimic gestures may have a privileged status in sign language and that they are distinct from iconic gestures.

The theoretical importance of the above continuum and the distinction between pantomimic and nonpantomimic gestures in particular does not so much concern their functional uses (at least in the present state of knowledge) as the extent to which they indicate symbolic processes beyond simple imitation or the observation of perceptual similarity. With regard to deaf children acquiring sign language, this issue is related to questions concerning the extent to which iconic signs are acquired earlier than arbitrary signs. The fact that this priority does not appear to be the case with any regularity (e.g., Orlansky & Bonvillian, 1984; Page, 1985) (see Chapter 6) adds further weight to the suggestion that gesture and sign productions of deaf children can be distinguished, at least when both are exhibited by the same individual. However, just as these various gestural forms might have similar functional properties, they also might share similar origins. We therefore now turn to the origins of gestures in deaf and hearing children and possible differences in their symbolic and functional characteristics.

Where Do Gestures Come From?

If deaf children's gestures are to give us insight into their underlying mental representations, we must understand the relation between early gestures, early words or signs, and children's knowledge of the things to which they refer. The relation of first words and early gesture has been of interest for a long time with regard to hearing children (for discussion of the phylogeny of gestures see Feyereisen & de Lannoy, 1991, Ch. 2). Piaget (1962) and Werner and Kaplan (1963), for example, suggested that related words and gestures should emerge at about the same time in development because both are reflections of children's underlying conceptual representations. Such productions were seen to indicate a transition from sensorimotor to symbolic functioning.

If particular gestures depict object-related behaviors as primitive forms of symbolic representation, one would expect that growth in speech and sign repertoires would be linked to reduction in gestural similarity and frequency—as symbols and referents become *decontextualized* (Werner & Kaplan, 1963). In contrast, if gestures and words are serving similar functions, one would expect a positive relation between gestural and verbal production in terms of frequency and in the shift away from being contextually bound to particular referents (Acredolo & Goodwyn, 1988).

There is now considerable evidence that linguistic and nonlinguistic competencies do not uniformly emerge in parallel in the strong sense implied by Piaget and by Werner and Kaplan (for discussion see Bates, Thal, Whitesell, Fenson, & Oakes, 1989; Petitto, 1987). However, the precise linkage and potential comparability of gesture and speech/sign in children is not as clear. In their pioneering work on the relations of gesture and early language, Bates, Benigni, Bretherton, Camaioni, and Volterra (1977) described a developmental sequence of prespeech gestural production that predicted the emergence of the first words. Bates et al. found that *showing gestures* and *ritual requests* for attention or instrumental action are used by children at about 9 to 10 months of age, followed by the *giving* gestures at around 12 months and *communicative pointing* or deixis at around 13 months.

These gestural schemes were reliably correlated with each other and with the size of children's vocabularies within this age range. Taken together, as a *gestural complex*, they accounted for the largest proportion of variance observed among all of the gestural communication measures. Insofar as the components of the gestural complex appeared just as regularized in form and to carry the same referential and communicative intentions as later emerging speech, Bates and her colleagues suggested that their findings reflected decontextualization of gestures from their communicative referents, consistent with the Werner and Kaplan (1963) position.

The Emergence of Gestures in Deaf Children

One central component of Bates's findings is that preverbal gesture appears to be a precursor of the first words or signs, providing social and symbolic structure for them. This conclusion meshes well with the long-standing observation that the gestural systems of young deaf children as well as older ones with impoverished language input are systematic and consistent (Charrow, 1976; Goldin-Meadow & Feldman, 1975; Kretschmer & Kretschmer, 1978). Such similarities could reflect either a biological predisposition for ruled-governed language or the demands of social communication behavior. Obviously, the intertwining of these two loci early in development makes their empirical differentiation difficult if not impossible. Comparisons of the gestural systems of deaf children with those of hearing children, however, are likely to be informative in this regard, insofar as they would reveal the commonality of early manual behavior that is eventually replaced by more conventional signed or spoken systems. The nature of the link between gesture and sign thus is a central issue of interest, as is the nature of the cognitive *interlingua* underlying them.

The role of gesture as a precursor of sign language and the correlation of gesture use and sign vocabulary size are particularly interesting given the claims of several researchers that deaf and hearing children learning sign language typically produce first signs earlier than oral-only peers produce their first words. Furthermore, bilingual English-ASL children have been reported to produce signs before words (e.g., Holmes & Holmes, 1980; Orlansky & Bonvillian, 1985; Prinz & Prinz, 1979; cf. Abrahamsen et al., 1985). Issues concerning language acquisition in manual versus oral deaf children and the effects of parental hearing (and language) status are considered in the next chapter, together with consideration of whether there is truly a *sign advantage* in early language. It is worth noting here, however, that deaf children acquiring oral language appear not to use gesture with any greater frequency than do hearing children (Gregory & Mogford, 1981). Research with deaf children thus appears likely to elucidate broader issues concerning the linkage of gesture and language during language acquisition.

Pointing, for example, has been of central interest to investigators interested in deaf children's transition from gesture to sign. In one relevant study, Petitto (1987) evaluated the position that language emerges from earlier nonlinguistic structures. She examined the emergence of the ASL personal pronouns ME and YOU in two deaf children of deaf parents. Rather than being arbitrary symbols, such as the words "me" and "you," personal pronouns in ASL are produced by pointing at the intended referent and thus are comparable to the indexical pointing observed in hearing children as early as 9 months of age. Petitto was able to examine the transition from prelinguistic gesture to linguistic expression in a case where both occurred within the same modality.

Following two subjects from ages 6 and 8 months to 26 and 28 months, respectively, Petitto found regular use of gestural pointing comparable to that observed in hearing children. Consistent with the findings of Bates (1979) and Acredolo and Goodwyn (1988) that hearing children tended to have either a gesture or a word for particular objects but not both at the same time, Petitto found a discontinuity in the development of indexical pointing. Her subjects began to use pointing to refer to people, places, and things at 10 and 12 months. At about 12 and 15 months, respectively, personal pronoun-like use of pointing completely dropped out of use, whereas other pointing forms remained intact. When person-pointing returned to their repertoires (in pronomial form) beginning after 18 months, both children evidenced errors of reference similar to those produced by hearing children, until they gained pronomial proficiency at around 27 months (see also Hoffmeister, 1982).

Petitto interpreted her findings as providing strong support for the hypothesis that gestural and linguistic components of communication are distinct—that the latter does not merely emerge from the former, even when both occur in the same mode. Perhaps most importantly for the present purposes, Petitto's results indicate that despite the sharing of a surface form, pointing gestures and the lexicalized pronomial pointing of ASL are not the same, at least during language acquisition (cf. Goldin-Meadow & Mylander, 1984).

Petitto (1988) reconsidered the issue raised by Bates and her colleagues concerning whether children's gestures function as symbolic names (see also Bonvillian & Folven, 1992; Folven & Bonvillian, 1985). She argued that the suggestions of Bates et al. (1983) and Acredolo and Goodwyn (1988) in support of this position depend on a rather loose, if not circular, definition of "naming" (p. 196). While indicating the presence of symbolic memory in young children, Petitto's (1987) data clearly indicated a dissociation between gesture and communicative naming in a most conservative situation. Although Acredolo and Goodwyn (1988) obtained better evidence than the Bates group for children's use of gestures in interpersonal communication (in contrast to solitary play), most of those gestures were pantomimic or context-bound (e.g., tapping on the refrigerator for food). Clearly, gestures can function in a referential sense, but does this linkage make them *names*?

In her longitudinal study of three deaf children acquiring sign language and three hearing children acquiring spoken language, Petitto (1988) found that deaf children's indexical and nonindexical gestures were neither more advanced nor more elaborated than those of their hearing peers. In fact, she found that deaf and hearing children produced almost the same gestures across a variety of functional contexts. The fact that the deaf children's gestures did not take advantage of the elaborative devices (e.g., inflection) available to them in the sign languages that they were acquiring indicated that "the children's early gestural forms and the parent's responses to them . . . have radically different properties than words (or signs)" (Petitto, 1988, p. 210). Furthermore, the fact that neither deaf nor hearing children understood the gestures that they themselves produced (when re-produced to them) argues against the position that the gestures truly functioned as *names*.

Petitto (1988) suggested that the question of why children gesture at all is a more important issue than the role of gesture in language acquisition. It seems likely that these two issues are not really separable, and in fact Petitto's discussion implicitly recognized that fact. Importantly, however, Petitto's (1987, 1988) results are consistent with the suggestions of Klima and Bellugi (1979) and others that there are gestures produced in the context of communication, by deaf as well as hearing individuals, that are not linguistic signs even if they share a common modality and some formational parameters. Still unresolved, however, are the disentangling of the role of different gestural types in children's sign language productions and the question of why they are more prevalent than those used by hearing children. Petitto (1988) found that both the onset (at 6 to 8 months) and decline (at 20 to 22 months) of gesturing was the same for her deaf and hearing subjects. My students and I (e.g., Marschark et al., 1986), in contrast, consistently have found gestures to be more frequent in deaf than hearing children, aged 7 to 15 years, although not in adults. Thus once young children have developed sufficient linguistic competence to communicate in a truly symbolic manner, the function of gesture appears to change.

Gestures During Social Interaction

Before moving on to other topics, one more issue should be addressed that concerns gestures and deictic gestures in particular. Beyond the similarity of nonlinguistic (or prelinguistic) pointing and lexicalized pointing with sign language, deictic gestures are likely unique in another way: as they relate to social interaction (e.g., Lederberg et al., 1986). Gesture and language emerge during childhood largely in service of the need for social communication of both the instrumental and emotional varieties. Thus it should not be surprising that deaf children or any others who lack language models spontaneously develop regularized, alternative communication systems (Goldin-Meadow & Morford, 1985; Goldin-Meadow & Mylander, 1984; Kretschmer & Kretschmer, 1978).

With regard to gesture in normally language-acquiring deaf children, deictic pointing plays a special role during social interactions—communicating needs, wants, foci of interest, and as stimuli for parental elaboration ("That's a doggie, what sound does a doggie make?"). Given this importance of pointing gestures, they might be expected to have a preeminent position in hearing children's gestural repertoires just as they appear to in deaf children's repertoires. Evidence in favor of this suggestion would support the position that at least some of the gestures observed in deaf children may be functionally the same as those observed in hearing children, that is, nonlinguistic even after they cease to be prelinguistic.

This hypothesis has not been explicitly tested, but some relevant data have been provided by a study of hearing children by Dobrich and Scarborough (1984). They examined the deictic gestures produced by verbally advanced versus other 2-year-olds. When contrasting the functional versus formal symbolic roles of gesture, Dobrich and Scarborough suggested that if both gesture and language are tied to maturation of an underlying symbolic system, verbally advanced children should show greater competence (e.g., precision, appropriateness) in gestural production as well. In fact, they found that mothers of high- and low-verbal children used deictic gestures equally often and that the children similarly did not differ in the frequency or quality of their pointing use. [On the simultaneity of maternal pointing and vocalization in deaf and hearing dyads, respectively, see studies by Caselli & Volterra (1990) and Baldwin & Markman (1989).]

Dobrich and Scarborough concluded that gesture is not replaced by language but maintains a central role in children's social communication; a conclusion supported by Bates (1979, Ch. 3). Unfortunately, they did not sample gestures other than deictics. Comparison of their findings with previous evidence indicating a decreasing reliance on gestures during later childhood (e.g., Ellenberger & Stayaert, 1978; Newport, 1981), however, suggests that deictics may have a special status as a supplement to language, regardless of the modality of primary linguistic development. Wilbur (1987) also provided a description of the special status of pointing in ASL, together with consideration of indexical nouns (e.g., for body parts), indexical verbs, and pronomial reference. Remaining to be determined are the differential functions of pointing for deaf and hearing language learners and possible differences in the social and cognitive implications of its use.

Cognitive Constraints on Language Development in Deaf Children

Complete consideration of the relation of language and cognition or even just that of the relation of language development and cognitive development could easily fill a volume the size of this book, leaving many of its facets still untouched. For the present purposes, therefore, only a few of the most relevant and interesting issues are raised, particularly as they might represent systemic parameters that guide, limit, or facilitate language growth in deaf children (see also Chapter 12).

The Relation of Language and Cognition

Discussion of the relation of language and cognition could take one of two forms. The most interesting and extensive discussion would concern the direct question of whether language structures thought, thought structures language, or the extent to which the two *have to be* interconnected in the way they are by the biological and cognitive structures of language users and the situations in which language and cognition are involved. The third of these alternatives suggests an interaction of language and cognition in which both are analogously (because of similar contexts or constraints) or homologously (because of common origins) shaped by other factors. It also appears to be the alternative that in some sense *has to be* correct (cf. Bates, 1979; Bates, et al., 1977; Greenfield, 1991).

Another way of addressing the language-cognition issue was typified by Pylyshyn's (1977) posing of the question "What does it take to bootstrap a language?" His central point was that any account of language acquisition requires "that a primitive conceptual system is already available" (p. 37). An essential component of such an argument is the distinction between the external, "manifest system" of communication and the internal system it reflects. The conceptual system is that which structures or is structured by experience (most likely both) and which guides children's attention to aspects of the environment that later are communicated via language and gesture (see also Macnamara, 1972; Potter, 1979).

From this perspective, deaf and hearing children's early gestures should provide an important insight into the salient features underlying the meaning of children's first words or signs (McNeill, 1985), an issue considered earlier. Note, however, that Pylyshyn's (1977) "primitive conceptual system" underlying language acquisition does not appear to be specific to language, a position that contrasts with that of authors such as Chomsky (1986) and McNeill (1966) but is consistent with that of others (e.g., Bronowski & Bellugi, 1970; Brown, 1973; Marschark, 1983).

Comprehension Versus Production

Once the basic language-cognition discussion is completed, or at least when the discussants are too worn out to continue, it undoubtedly will be agreed that language and cognition likely structure each other, with one or the other taking the lead in different domains. In this view, similar to Piaget's (1952) notion of *equilibration*, children are constantly attempting to "solve the problem" of analyzing incoming information as they carve up the world into figure and ground, information and noise (Bronowski & Bellugi, 1970; Marschark, 1983). One type, as well as a source, of information, is that which we refer to as *language*—and it has its own problems to be solved (Nelson, 1973). This situation raises the issue, related in principle to the competence–performance issue, of the relation of comprehension and production; that is, which, if either, comes first. Like the competence and performance question, this one likely can be resolved only in terms of a domain-specific account. In particular, it appears that comprehension generally appears to precede production in naturalistic settings. At the same time, children may produce particular linguistic constructions with contextual support while failing to show evidence of comprehension of those same constructions when placed in artificial experimenter-defined settings (e.g., deVilliers & deVilliers, 1978; see also Meier & Newport, 1990).

The domain specificity of language comprehension and production may be even more pronounced for deaf children than for hearing children. Initially exposed only to speech, many deaf children may understand more of a spoken message (using various cues) than they can produce. At the same time, they use gestures in social communication but may fail to comprehend those gestures when produced by others, as do hearing children (Petitto, 1988). In school, deaf children are the focus of concerted efforts by educators to have them map sign and spoken/printed language onto each other (see Chapter 11). In that context, they may be able to produce in writing less than they can understand from text and are able to read and remember incorrect English that has sign-like structure (Charrow, 1976; Charrow & Fletcher, 1974).

Despite the recognized difficulties of deaf children with English comprehension and production, their "language abilities" (as well as a variety of other cognitive skills) traditionally have been assessed using English-based evaluations only. It is now clear, however, that English- and sign-based assessments of deaf children's abilities do not necessarily give the same answers (e.g., Charrow & Fletcher, 1974; Everhart & Marschark, 1988; Suty & Friel-Patti, 1982) (see also Chapters 7 and 10). Some researchers thus have begun to consider the intertwining of language development in the oral and manual modalities and their effects on other abilities as well as on each other. Anything else seems destined to produce either an underestimate or a distorted view of deaf children's true language capabilities. This incorrect understanding, in turn, would have profound implications for any attempts to use language ability as a predictor of deaf children's performance (or competence) in other domains or to understand their performance of tasks that are likely to involve linguistic mediation.

Cognitive-Experiential Underpinnings of Language Acquisition

While maintaining the position that language and cognition are essentially independent but interconnected systems, there can be little doubt that children's early experiences simultaneously structure both (a point considered at length in Chapter 12). It is this common underlying experience together with the parameters imposed by the biological system that frequently give the impression of language and thought being one and the same. Issues concerning the experiential deficiencies of deaf children thus have a bearing on language acquisition as well as cognitive and social development.

Chapter 2 included a general discussion of the effects of auditory deprivation on development (see also Liben, 1978), Chapters 3 and 4 considered the effects of deafness on social development and some likely linguistic consequences, and Chapter 7 covers the effects of deafness on cognitive development. In addition to those treatments, however, it is worthwhile to consider briefly the effects on language development of the restricted range of experiences available to deaf children.

Some of the limitations on young deaf children's activities, imposed by their well-meaning parents, have already been described. These frequently overprotective restrictions on outdoor play, experimentation, and the diversity of playmates continue into the early school years and are accented by attendance at residential schools that are placed beyond walking distance to shopping and activity centers. (Alternatively, leaving campus simply may be forbidden.) Nelson (1973) found that the diversity of children's playmates was generally a poor predictor of hearing children's language development. In fact, the amount of time spent with other children was inversely related to vocabulary development, although it was not quite as potent a predictor as time spent watching television ($r = -.39$ versus $r = -.45$). This relation of language and peer–peer interaction might be different for most deaf children, however, at least if the playmates are also deaf, because deaf children of hearing parents likely have more linguistic interactions with their peers than with their parents.

The strongest positive predictors of vocabulary development in Nelson's (1973) study were the number of outings on which children were taken ($r = .60$) and the number of different adult language models to which they were exposed ($r = .42$). Unfortunately, these variables are ones on which deaf children of hearing parents would be expected to be short-changed relative to hearing peers with hearing parents or deaf peers with deaf parents. Nelson also found that those children whose mothers were less intrusive and directive had faster rates of vocabulary growth, another factor that may work against deaf children with hearing parents. Although these limitations certainly are not the only reasons for the observed lags in language acquisition of deaf children relative to hearing children of hearing parents, the available data certainly are consistent with such relations.

Nelson's (1973) view—like that of Macnamara (1972), Pylyshyn (1977), and Neisser (1976)—was that children acquire much of their earliest vocabularies by putting environmentally supplied labels on their own concepts. She also assumed that the features of an object that elicit a particular label from a child might differ from those that are significant for an adult. In the case of deaf children, the differences in their experiences with things, together with the frequently impoverished language input from adults and other children might well make for differences in the structure of concept knowledge. Although such differences do not appear to be salient in older deaf children (Tweney, Hoemann, & Andrews, 1975), they should be more visible in younger children (for whom far less evidence is available) (cf. Koh, Vernon, & Bailey, 1971) (see Chapter 9). Older children, as better language problem-solvers, should be better able to "build concepts" to match the language of others. This ability, however, depends largely on children's assumptions and hypotheses about the function of language, based on pragmatic (Halliday, 1975) as well as linguistic (Slobin, 1973) grounds (see the "operating principles" described in Chapter 12).

The impoverishment of deaf children's bases for language development regrettably is not remedied by the beginning of formal schooling (Johnson et al., 1989). Schooling does improve the communication abilities of deaf children, although there is also some evidence suggesting that schools for the deaf inadvertently may be training children to be relatively rigid and concrete in their language and cognitive skills (Marschark, 1989; Ottem, 1980; Tervoort, 1975). Deaf educators and researchers often overlook the overwhelming preponderance of language "training" that derives not from formalized language instruction but from the other subjects and activities encountered in school. Even beyond the motivational effects of subjects more interesting than language class, a large proportion of worldly vocabularies comes from learning about history, literature, and social studies. To give these topics less attention than more "practical" and concrete subjects all but ensures that children not only will have smaller vocabularies (Griswold & Cummings, 1974), but that the vocabularies they do have will be relatively concrete and specific (Blackwell, Engen, Fischgrund, & Zarcadoolas, 1978).

With regard to language obtained outside the home and school, there appears to be no substitute for diversity. A variety of early studies demonstrated that institutionalized deaf and hearing children suffer cognitive, emotional, and linguistic consequences of restricted environments (e.g., Templin, 1950; see Liben, 1978). Nonetheless, the perceived and real necessities of caring for hearing-impaired children, especially in today's lawsuit-inclined society, continue to impose restrictions that have pronounced and long-term consequences for language and cognitive development in deaf children. Some such effects are directly observable in the differences among deaf children raised by deaf parents, hearing parents who can sign, and hearing parents who, for whatever reason, do not establish any effective channel of communication with their young child. These patterns of language development are the substance of the next chapter.

Summary

The goal of this chapter was to elucidate the contexts, capabilities, and earliest components of language development in deaf children. Most centrally, it has been argued that understanding deaf children's language abilities, like understanding their social and cognitive abilities, requires consideration of the contexts in which they develop and the interrelations among these domains.

When considering the emergence of the rudiments of language, the possibility of manual as well as vocal babbling of deaf children was considered. Although manual babbling has not been extensively investigated, it appears that early sign-like productions in deaf children function similarly to early word-like productions by hearing children in terms of both "exercising" the articulatory apparatus and the generation of personal and interpersonal feedback. A variety of studies have indicated that deaf infants, like hearing infants, produce prelinguistic vocalizations related to oral language. At the same time, it is also clear that the two groups evidence marked and important differences in these vocalizations even before the use of "real" words would normally begin. At least by 7 months of age, deaf babies show less complexity than hearing babies in their vocalizations, even when they are exposed to speech stimulation via hearing aids.

If hearing babies show evidence of more adaptive early vocalization, deaf babies might be expected to show evidence of more adaptive early gesturing. In fact, both deaf and hearing children use gestures for making their goals, wants, and desires known. In the case of hearing children, those gestures are obvious and distinct from the ongoing speech stream. In the case of the deaf children, the fact that gestures and sign language use of the same (manual) modality makes the two difficult to distinguish. Accordingly, there appears to be more disagreement about the status of gestures used by deaf children prior to and within sign language than about those used by hearing children. Gestures produced by both deaf and hearing children have remarkable similarity, however, and there appears no strong reason to differentially assign the status of "language" or "gesture" when comparable manual movements serve the same functions in the same contexts.

In young children, gestures primarily serve pragmatic functions, relating to instrumental and emotional needs. As vocabularies develop, however, gestures take on a supplementary role, highlighting or elaborating accompanying speech or sign, while occasionally standing in for words or signs that are either unknown or temporarily unavailable. Research concerning the relation of gesture and early language has yielded inconsistent findings. Some researchers have found that gesture and words emerge at about the same time in hearing children and can be dissociated by their frequency and contexts of use. Others have suggested that gestures generally precede both speech and sign, and set the stage for it. Relations between the emergence of particular gestures (e.g., showing, giving, communicative pointing) and the size of children's sign language vocabularies are consistent with the latter view (for reports on both sides of the issue see Volterra & Erting, 1990).

Examination of children's gestures provides us with alternate access to the verbal system underlying the emergence of their language and to their understanding of social and referential communication. In neither sense should deaf children be considered any different from hearing children. The two groups may well diverge, however, in the conceptual bases of early language. Differences due to the diversity of deaf and hearing children's experiences with other children, adults, and novel contexts may make for some real differences in the subjective structure of knowledge. Such differences not only have an impact on the quality and quantity of early language production but also affect social and cognitive development. The implications and effects of early language abilities comprise a constant theme throughout the remainder of this book.

Notes

1. Another frequent misinterpretation of Chomsky (1957, 1965) involves the distinction between surface structure and deep structure. The *surface structure* of a sentence is what we see or hear, derived from an underlying deep structure. Contrary to popular opinion, *deep structure* is not *meaning*. Rather, it is an underlying lexical-syntactic description that can be transformed into a surface string or interpreted by a semantic component to yield meaning. Deep structures of signed sequences thus may be analogous to those of spoken sequences, but it is because they have common linguistic origins not because they may have the same meanings.

2. Note that this period constitutes the age range from 1 to 4 years rather than from 2 to 5 years, as claimed in Gilbert's (1982) evaluation of Lenneberg's research.

6

Language Acquisition

Meadow (1980) suggested that the most serious problem imposed by deafness is not the lack of hearing per se but the fact that it impairs or eliminates acquisition of language via sound. There is room for argument on this point, as beyond the lack of aural-oral language the lack of hearing has significant implications for social and cognitive development as well as for the pragmatics of day-to-day living. Meadow's point nevertheless underscores the centrality of language acquisition both in the normal course of child development and in the literature concerning deaf children.

Sign language clearly can serve as an effective mode of communication for young deaf children and reveals typical stages of normal acquisition under some circumstances. What is not clear, however, is the extent to which the products and correlates of sign language acquisition are comparable to those of a spoken language. Although there is strong sentiment to assume a functional equivalence of signed and spoken languages (i.e., beyond linguistic equivalence), the question remains an empirical one, not a political-emotional one. This chapter therefore examines the course of language development in deaf children in some detail, including sign acquisition and speech acquisition. Acquisition of reading and writing abilities is taken up in Chapter 11.

Understanding Language Development

Theoretical Difficulties

Understanding the empirical findings with regard to language development in deaf children is confounded by several factors. Inherent in the contrasts between manual versus oral training and having deaf parents versus hearing parents are several issues related to those differences. One of these issues is that, contrary to the way we typically talk about them, neither of these contrasts is truly a dichotomy with respect to language development. Deaf children, by design or by accident, are almost always exposed to both manual and aural-oral modes of communication. What differs is which mode is primary, a circumstance determined largely by the hearing status of the parents. Even the designation *primary mode of communication* is not entirely clear. Particular parents or children might have some residual hearing and thus might benefit from aural-oral language while still using sign language in particular contexts. Similarly, even when deaf children are orally trained, systems of gestural communication may develop between parents and children (e.g., Greenberg et al., 1984). These systems, also, may play a greater or lesser role in communication depending on the context. In any case, such variability plays an important role in the language models available to and utilized by children.

A related issue, touched on in the preceding chapter, involves the number of adult language models to whom the child is exposed. Young deaf children of hearing parents frequently do not have *any* truly competent sign language models. In cases of profound, congenital deafness, where there is essentially no benefit from auditory stimuli, this situation means perhaps no language models at all. To the extent that language acquisition is positively related to the diversity of adult models available (Nelson, 1973) and social reinforcement (Whitehurst & Valdez-Menchaca, 1988), such deaf children are at a decided disadvantage for language development.

Another theoretically confounding variable is age of language acquisition (Mayberry & Eichen, 1991). Two important aspects of this issue are (1) whether the children of interest are congenitally deaf or all or partial hearing was lost after some time of auditory experience, and (2) whether (noncongenital) hearing loss is acute or progressive. These issues aside, however, most hearing parents of deaf children initiate language training, by omission or commission, via the oral modality. Early language experience for these deaf children thus is different from that of hearing children. At worst, it may be nonexistent.

Of course, there is also an interaction to be considered between the degree of hearing loss and the extent of manual communication. Many of those hearing parents who begin to sign to their young deaf children with the best of intentions nonetheless do not sign with any consistency. Typically, they have had little formal sign training (Harmon, 1992), are uncomfortable signing especially in public, and use their children's mode of communication only when speaking directly to the child. Parents are generally surprised (if only briefly) when it is pointed out how much of language is learned indirectly from overhearing conversations of others, television exposure, and similar sources. Why should it be any different for deaf children? In principle, it should not be. However, it is clear that deaf children have far fewer opportunities for such vicarious learning and that the information value of the messages they do receive frequently is lower than that received by most hearing children.

Methodological Difficulties

Any discussion of research concerning language acquisition by deaf children must acknowledge that this literature seems particularly fraught with methodological and statistical shortcomings, which may impair both reliability and validity. Included among the most frequent problems are the lack of statistical analyses (or the use of inappropriate ones) and the overgeneralization of descriptive results based on only one or two subjects. Out of necessity, studies of language development frequently involve small groups of children, and care must be taken when drawing broad conclusions from them. This concern is especially important and problematical with longitudinal studies because the time and expense involved frequently rule out extensive replications. For example, although there is now considerable convergent evidence to support its validity, it often seems that much of what we know about hearing children's grammatical development is based on Roger Brown's (1973) study of three children: Adam, Eve, and Sarah (cf. Moerk, 1983). The generalization problem is compounded in the case of deaf children, however, because deafness can be accompanied by other physical, neurological, or emotional difficulties (see Chapter 2). These contaminants make for considerable heterogeneity in deaf children's language abilities and heterogeneity in the data from studies in which those abilities are evaluated.

Perhaps the most obvious methodological caveat to language development research with deaf children is that the factors noted above are seldom controlled statistically or by subject selection. On one hand, this lack of control limits the generalizability from some studies and makes acceptance of null hypotheses (e.g., deaf and hearing children do not differ) more tenuous. On the other hand, when statistically significant differences are found despite high variability within small groups of deaf children, one can be fairly certain that there is some real basis for that observation.

Problems of interpretation also arise from attempts to compare the language abilities of deaf children who are manually trained with those of deaf children who are orally trained. Such comparisons represent one of the most popular and potentially informative areas in deafness research but also one of the most intractable. "Manual" here is actually a misnomer for describing methods of simultaneous oral and manual training or for Total Communication. The problems, however, run deeper. One difficulty is that oral and manual education programs tend to have different philosophies and curricula. Thus differences observed between any two groups might be the result of any of a number of related variables rather than, or in addition to, variance due to language training factors per se.

Kretschmer and Kretschmer (1978) pointed out several other problems involved in the comparison of language abilities of manually trained versus orally trained deaf children. For example, although many studies have found linguistic advantages for manually trained children, Kretschmer and Kretschmer noted that careful examination of the data usually reveals that both manual and oral groups have significantly worse language skills than hearing age-mates (see also Chapter 4). Furthermore, although several studies have found rather large performance differences between orally and manually trained children, they are not all in the same direction (cf. Battachi & Montanini-Manfredi, 1986; Brasel & Quigley, 1977; Geers, Moog, & Schick, 1984).

Related to the issue of experimental control raised above, Kretschmer and Kretschmer also noted that deaf children drawn from oral programs tend to be "oral" only while they are in the classroom, frequently using sign language in other contexts. This situation was exemplified in an extreme form during a visit I made to a private school for the deaf in Italy, accompanied by the superintendent of the Central North Carolina School for the Deaf. Italy, by law, maintains an oral orientation in deaf education, and this particular school includes more than 50% hearing children, who serve as language models for the remaining (deaf) children. The teachers in this school, as in many others, do not know Italian Sign Language, and most believe that it can be used only for the most concrete and iconic of purposes. In fact, we observed both deaf and hearing children signing to each other inside and outside of the classroom. Furthermore, the children were seen apparently cheating via sign language, with the teacher oblivious to the fact that any communication was going on.

In short, it is difficult enough to conduct research on language development with deaf children because of the basic problems of access and communication. In addition, however, deaf children appear far more heterogeneous as a group than hearing children, and it is difficult to control variables likely to affect language development while at the same time having sample sizes large enough to be able to draw reliable conclusions. Such difficulties having been acknowledged, the focus in the remainder of this chapter is on the substance of deaf children's language development and its relation to other domains. For more complete description of the psycholinguistic details of deaf children's language acquisition, see Bonvillian and Folven (1992), Kretschmer and Kretschmer (1978), and Wilbur (1987).

Emergence of Sign

Recall that according to Bates et al. (1977), gestures serve as precursors of the first words, providing social and symbolic structure for them. The claims of several researchers that children learning sign language typically produce first signs earlier than oral-only peers produce their first words and that bilingual English-ASL children produce signs before words (for reviews see Bonvillian & Folven, 1992; Goodwyn & Acredolo, 1991; Meier & Newport, 1990) raises the issue of whether gesture precedes, follows, or emerges at the same time as the first signs. Of additional theoretical interest is the possible relation of gesture use and sign vocabulary size (cf. Acredolo & Goodwyn, 1988).

The Relation of Gesture and Early Signs

As a first approximation to the linkage of gesture and sign in deaf children, consider the work of Bonvillian and his colleagues on their emergence in hearing children learning sign language (as a first language) from their deaf parents (Bonvillian, Orlansky, & Novack, 1983a; Folven & Bonvillian, 1985, 1987). Consistent with the positions of Macnamara (1972), Pylyshyn (1977), and others, Bonvillian argued that symbolic functioning may develop earlier than can be assumed on the basis of vocal productions. If deaf children do indeed begin to sign at an earlier age than hearing children begin to speak, we might have a sensitive indicator of the knowledge underlying prelinguistic gesture and vocalization.

Folven and Bonvillian (1985) examined the Request, Showing, Giving, Communicative Pointing, and Noncommunicative Pointing gestures described by Bates et al. (1977) in a group of 12 hearing children and one deaf child all learning ASL as their first language. Folven and Bonvillian hypothesized that the acceleration of early language development in native signers might result in the co-occurrence of gesture and linguistic production rather than their sequential emergence.

Consistent with the most clear-cut findings from the Bates et al. (1977) study, Folven and Bonvillian found that both Giving and Pointing were reliably correlated to sign language vocabulary size. The gestural types that did not yield reliable relations with vocabulary nonetheless were strongly related to it, $r = .49$ to $.61$, still an impressive finding given the small sample size. Most importantly for Folven and Bonvillian, the gestures that tend to precede the first words of oral (hearing) children were found to follow the first signs of their manual children (cf. Folven & Bonvillian, 1987). They acknowledged that first words may not be equivalent to first signs, the latter possibly relying heavily on contextual clues to convey their meanings. In this sense, first signs may be more similar to gestures than to first words, a situation that could have important implications for understanding subsequent cognitive and language development (see also Petitto, 1988).

Findings concerning the question of when early gestures and signs emerge often appear to depend on how "gesture" and "sign" are defined (Goodwyn & Acredolo, 1991). Certainly, this question appears relevant to Folven and Bonvillian's work. Folven and Bonvillian (1987), for example, described the development of referential signing in a group of eight hearing children and one deaf child, all of whom used sign language as the principal means of communication with their deaf parents. Consistent with other studies of hearing children (Holmes & Holmes, 1980; Prinz & Prinz, 1979), children in Folven and Bonvillian's sample typically produced their first recognizable signs at around 9 months of age. However, these signs were limited in their use to requests, imitations, and familiar interpersonal interactions. It was not until near the children's first birthdays (mean age 11.9 months), around the normal time for first words, that they first used signs specifically as names or labels.

Ackerman, Kyle, Woll, and Ezra (1990) reported similar "first sign" results from a longitudinal study of five deaf and eight hearing children learning British Sign Language (BSL). The interpretation of what would qualify as a sign was left to the mothers of children in that study, and we thus are unable to be sure exactly where those signs fit on the gesture–sign continuum. Nonetheless, Ackerman et al. found that the hearing children's "first reported signs" (excluding BYE BYE) occurred at 11.4 months and those of the deaf children at 11.0 months. Consistent with Folven and Bonvillian's (1987) results, the first "object gestures" (names) occurred at around age 11.4 months in both groups. The results of both of those studies thus contrast with Acredolo and Goodwyn's (1988) finding of object gestures emerging at around 15.6 months in oral-only hearing children. Whether this difference is a function of the fact that the Folven and Bonvillian (1987) and Ackerman et al. (1990) subjects were learning sign language (ASL and BSL, respectively) or a difference in the criteria for assigning linguistic status to object gestures, however, is unclear.

First Signs

Whatever the functional connection between gestures and the first signs, early gestures establish a channel of social communication between children and significant others around them. Both deaf and hearing children develop pragmatic means of communication early and gradually refine them with experimentation and feedback. Meaningful, if perhaps nonarbitrary, gestures are the primary communicative stuff of most young children by about 6 to 8 months, developing into a consistent, conventional gestural system by the end of the first year. By the time they are 1 year old, deaf and hearing children use pointing, in particular, to refer to things, people, and locations. As the first words come to be used by children, near the end of the first year, they do not replace gestures but tend to fill other roles in the repertoire, regardless of whether the children are hearing (e.g., Acredolo & Goodwyn, 1988; Bates, 1979) or deaf (e.g., Caselli & Volterra, 1990; Folven & Bonvillian, 1987; Petitto, 1988).

Deciding when the first words occur has never been an easy task, even with hearing children. Between 9 and 12 months of age, hearing children make some sounds that are similar to adult words, at least to some parents' ears. These vocalizations generally, but not always, are produced in the correct context. The fact that these "words" are also produced at times that are incorrect from the adult perspective indicates to some investigators that children do not understand the language they are producing (production before comprehension?—see Chapter 5). Alternatively, such vocalizations may be imitations of adult utterances or evidence of linguistic hypothesis testing, two possibilities with considerably different theoretical implications but that arc observationally equivalent.

For the present purposes, it does not seem critical that we decide which of these sounds are protowords and which are true words. The point at which a theory or theory maker bestows *word* status on an utterance (together with the biological, linguistic, and cognitive states that it is assumed to reflect) is largely a function of one's general orientation with regard to Language. What is important is that, whatever they are, these productions elicit particular responses from listeners and either come to be used with greater and more appropriate regularity or are dropped from the repertoire.

A parallel scenario develops for deaf children with regard to the first signs.[1] Several investigators have argued that the first signs of deaf and hearing infants who are native signers can be seen 1 to 3 months prior to the first words of hearing peers, or somewhere around 7 to 9 months (e.g., McIntire, 1977; Orlansky & Bonvillian, 1985; Prinz & Prinz, 1979; Sachs & Johnson, 1976; Wilbur & Jones, 1974; see also the empirical manipulation of Goodwyn & Acredolo, 1991), if not earlier (e.g., Maestas y Moores, 1980). Many such reports have remain unpublished, however, and their frequent citations provide little detail on the specifics of the studies or observations. Such details are often important, as in the case of the frequently cited Prinz and Prinz (1979) report of manual babbling described in Chapter 5.

Some investigators have reported simple signs in individual children as early as 5.5 months (Schlesinger & Meadow, 1972a), although others report the first signs emerging closer to 12 months, or at the same age as hearing infants' first words (for discussion see Meier & Newport, 1990; Petitto & Charron, 1991). In view of the fact that manual dexterity matures earlier than the musculature of the vocal apparatus, observations of relatively early signing do not seem surprising if we consider the linguistics of the situation alone. McIntire (1977) has even suggested that the sequence of neuromotor maturation of the hand and fingers is reflected in the emergence of signs involving the thumb, index finger, and whole hand prior to those involving other fingers.

When combined with the corollary assumptions concerning the underlying processes of language production, it is difficult to know whether many of these early, parent-reported manual productions should be considered signs.[2] Particularly troublesome here is the fact that, like the first *proto-words*, parent-reported first signs tend to be rather simple approximations that, at least initially, could be spontaneous and nonlinguistic (cf. Goodwyn & Acredolo, 1991). One frequent example in this regard is the sign MILK, made by the opening and closing of a 5 hand. Flexing of the unformed hand undoubtedly occurs frequently in infants, and it seems "only a matter of time" before it is produced in an appropriate context and interpreted as a sign. Two other early signs, MAMA and DADA, are depicted in Figure 6-1 in their adult citation forms. Infant approximations to those signs can be imagined and seem likely to occur on some chance basis. Interestingly, the DADA sign is made incorrectly far more often than the MAMA sign. Presumably because it is outside the infant's visual field, DADA is made in various places on the head and with various handshapes (S. Shroyer, personal communication, February 10, 1992). The fact that the "sign" nonetheless is interpreted as DADA is the important point.

Examples of this sort suggest some caution when attributing intentionality or meaningfulness to the signs of the infant. Nevertheless, the implications of those "signs" for social responding by others are exactly the same as those created by hearing children's first "words." Once again, then, it seems that precise determination of when early production should be given lexical status may be less important than identifying their functional role in social communication.

Goodwyn and Acredolo (1991) reported a unique study of the sign language

FIGURE 6-1. Just as in speech, the ASL signs MOTHER and FATHER are sometimes made in approximate forms (MAMA and DADA) that are interpreted and reinforced by parents.

mother   father

advantage in language learning. They had the parents of 22 hearing children include eight symbolic gestures in their interactions with their children, beginning between 8 and 11 months of age. Goodwyn and Acredolo promoted use of the gestures by sending relevant toys home with the parents and encouraging them to incorporate other gestures into their interactive repertoires as well. They then followed the emergence of the gestures and words via telephone interviews from age 11 months onward.

Although the small manual repertoire (including five object labels plus gestures for MORE, ALL GONE, and WHERE IS IT?) limits its generalizability to deaf children receiving a full range of signed input, Goodwyn and Acredolo found a small but consistent advantage in the appearance of manual over oral productions. The first gestures appeared at a mean age of 11.94 months compared to 12.64 months for the first words. The point of having a five-item repertoire was reached at 13.55 months for gestures and 14.28 months for words. Goodwyn and Acredolo concluded that although signs may have an edge in early language learning the small (and significant) differences observed should not be taken as conclusive evidence for a true sign advantage. Given the limited range of specific gestures used and the fact that most of their subjects did not begin to receive exposure to the several gestures until 11 months, Goodwyn and Acredolo's skepticism appears healthy.

In their 1990 review, Meier and Newport considered a variety of studies on both sides of the sign advantage issue (see also Abrahamsen et al., 1985; Bonvillian & Folven, 1993; Petitto, 1988; Volterra & Caselli, 1985). They reexamined both theoretical and methodological aspects of previous investigations and concluded that, overall, the available evidence favors a small sign language advantage at the "one-word" stage of vocabulary development. Importantly, Meier and Newport also found that the sign advantage disappears by the "two-word" stage, when syntactic and semantic factors come into play, suggesting that there are likely multiple interactive mechanisms underlying early language development.

In this context, it must be kept in mind that relative rates of neuromotor development are not the only differences between learning sign and learning speech. For example, the increased rates of touching and visual contact between mothers and their deaf infants (e.g., Koester & Trimm, 1991; Spencer, 1991) may have the effect of calling attention to their manual productions in a more direct manner than is normally the case for hearing dyads. Furthermore, Meier and Newport (1990), Goodwyn and Acredolo (1991), and others have emphasized the fact that the distinctive features of signs—their component parts on the articulators of language models—are completely visible to the language learner. This 100% availability contrasts with speech, in which only the labial components are immediately available. Schlesinger (1978), in fact, suggested that 40% or less of speech can be observed by a recipient. Given the lack of correlated cues from other features of articulation and the naive status of the deaf infant, even 40% appears an overestimate of the functional availability of oral language to the deaf infant.

Growing Vocabularies

Consistent with claims that sign language can be acquired earlier than spoken language, several investigators have found that young deaf and hearing children who are native signers have higher rates of vocabulary growth than peers learning spoken language. The three most common benchmarks for hearing children are vocabularies that contain 10 words, 50 words, and 10 two- and three-word phrases. Nelson (1973) found that the 18 children she studied reached the 10-word point at around 15.1 months, the 50-word point at around 19.6 months, and the 10-phrase point at around 19.8 months. McIntire (1974), in contrast, reported a 20-sign vocabulary in a 10-month-old child; and McIntire (1977) reported an 85-sign vocabulary in a 13-month-old, who expanded to 200 signs at 21 months.

Petitto and Charron (1991) examined the rate of vocabulary development up to the first 50 signs in three deaf infants learning La Langue des Signes Quebecoise (LSQ) from their deaf parents. The boys, two of whom were twins, were observed from 9 to 30 months of age. Petitto and Charron reported that the rates of development and the semantic categories of signs produced were comparable to those reported by Nelson (1973). The latter finding suggests that, regardless of the mode of language, deaf and hearing children likely have similar things "to talk about." Although the samples were small (especially given that two of the three subjects had identical learning environments), Petitto and Charron's findings support Meier and Newport's (1990) suggestion that any sign advantage in early language should dissipate rapidly.

In contrast to that position is a study of early vocabulary development in deaf children reported by Schlesinger and Meadow (1972a). They examined the sign comprehension and production of four deaf children, two of whom had deaf parents and two of whom had hearing parents. Three of the four children were older than 2.5 years at the beginning of the study, but Schlesinger and Meadow reported that the youngest child, then 8 months old, was already using vocalization and gestures to "convey emphasis and emotions" when first observed (p. 57). First signs were reported as early as 10 months for that child; at 15 months she had a vocabulary of 19 signs; and by 19 months she had used 117 signs. The 10-phrase point was reached at around 17 months; and at 19.5 months, when Nelson's (1973) subjects were just achieving 50-word vocabularies, Schlesinger and Meadow's young subject had 142 signs.

Orlansky and Bonvillian (1984) observed 13 hearing children of deaf parents who were acquiring ASL as their first language. On average, the 10-sign point was reached at 13 months in that group and the 50-sign point just beyond 18 months. Perhaps the most important contribution of this study, however, was Orlansky and Bonvillian's analysis of the extent to which the early vocabularies were composed of iconic signs. Conventional ASL signs, like gestures, fall on a continuum from *iconic* [looking like their referents (TENNIS, CAMERA)], to *transparent* or metonymic [looking like a part or associated aspect of their referents (BOY, DOG)], to *arbitrary* (HONOR, CHURCH). It would not be surprising to find that the earliest-acquired signs are those falling toward the iconic end of the continuum. This finding would simply suggest that, like gestures and metaphors (see Vosniadou, 1987), some signs are less indicative of conceptual, symbolic reference than others.

Orlansky and Bonvillian, however, found that the early sign repertoires of their subjects were evenly divided across iconic, metonymic, and arbitrary signs, and that those proportions were relatively constant over the first year. As Markowicz (1977) has argued, it seems likely that deaf children might not understand the iconic or metonymic bases of some signs but acquire them in the same arbitrary manner as other signs. Only later, with more linguistic sophistication, do they understand the origins of those signs. This phenomenon is not unusual in the acquisition of various words and phrases for hearing children (e.g., Gardner, Winner, Bechofer, & Wolf, 1973; Marschark & Nall, 1985); and even as adults we still have new experiences of "lexical awareness" (e.g., anti + septic; Descartes and Cartesian; and "mares eat oats and does eat oats. . . ."). Two conclusions thus can be drawn from Orlansky and Bonvillian's results: First, iconic signs and arbitrary signs are learned with equal facility by children acquiring sign as a first language (see also Pizzuto & Williams, 1979). Iconic signs might well be easier to learn when mapped onto some other first language, but such studies have not yet been done. Second and most centrally, early signs, unlike early gestures, are not necessarily tied to physical similarities in the world but represent true linguistic symbols at a stage of development prior to spoken words.

Regardless of the details concerning early sign productions of manual deaf children, there is little doubt of the contrast they provide with the productions of oral deaf children. In general, even the best pupils of the best oral programs have limited early vocabularies—rarely beyond 10 words at 2.5 years of age. Meadow-Orlans's (1987) summary of the outcomes of several oral training programs indicates that the language of orally trained deaf preschoolers remains at least 2 to 3 years behind age-appropriate norms, even after more than a year of training. Part of this difference may be related to a failure of the parents of those children to recognize the effects of hearing losses. Meadow et al. (1981), for example, reported that the hearing impairments of children who were orally trained had been diagnosed at an average age of 19 months, compared with an average of 15 months for children who were manually trained. Although both of these statistics pale in comparison to deaf parents' abilities to "know" that their children are deaf by 3 months of age, even a 4-month delay in intervention can make for large differences during this most sensitive period of language development.

From Pointing to Naming

In the discussion of gesture in Chapter 5, it was noted that the relation between simple pointing and indexical naming is not entirely clear. Several researchers have assumed that both preverbal deictic pointing and other preverbal gestures that iconically or metonymically identify a thing can be considered names. One alternative to this position is that a gesture might be considered a name rather than a signifier only when (1) it is truly decontextualized (i.e., capable of being removed from its referent) (Werner & Kaplan, 1963), and (2) when it is used in social communication across a variety of contexts. The goal here is to distinguish children's gestures that call attention to interesting sights or are used in imitative play from gestures that serve communicative, identifying functions in the absence of that to which they refer. Underlying this distinction is an attempt to ensure that anything called a "name" serves a symbolic, linguistic function capable of satisfying Hockett and

Altmann's (1968) *displacement* design feature. Although the reliable classification of these productions might be difficult in practice, the two carry different corollary assumptions of cognitive and linguistic competencies, and hence the theoretical discrimination is a worthwhile one.

Regardless of where one draws the line between gestures and names—across classes of exemplars or within the development of a particular child's communicative repertoire—there is likely to be some disagreement. Clearly, however, if distinguishing referential gestures from names is difficult in the case of hearing children, the problem is compounded in the case of deaf children. The oral "end state" for hearing children's naming can at least be distinguished from prior gestural forms (cf. McNeill, 1985). For deaf children using sign language, in contrast, the two always share a single modality and similar if not identical forms (cf. Petitto, 1987).

Of particular difficulty in distinguishing the transition from gestures to names is the fact that pointing serves a central role in the productions of young deaf children during the one- and two-word/sign stages. Petitto (1987) has shown that indexical gesturing and use of deictic and pronomial pointing in ASL are distinguishable during the second and third years (see Chapter 5). The problem is that pointing serves a variety of semantic functions beyond simple naming. Hoffmeister (1982), for example, reported the study of a single child who began to incorporate indexical gestures into utterances between the ages of 2;4 and 2;6. This age range for the merging of pointing and naming also has been identified by Newport and Ashbrook (1977), Petitto (1988), and others. Hoffmeister, however, found that more than 56% of all semantic relations were expressed as a POINT + noun or POINT + adjective during this period. This number decreased to 5% by age 4;4, when sign inflections came to be used with some regularity.

Consistent with Hoffmeister's findings, Newport and Ashbrook (1977) followed five deaf children (aged 1;4 to 3;6) of deaf parents and found pointing and naming to be well established in even the youngest child. Because Newport and Ashbrook were interested in locations, datives, instruments, and existence relations, pointing was particularly central to their investigation. As in hearing children, they found that pointing and naming were used to express existence relations at the earliest observations, followed by designations of action, states, locations, and datives. Instruments did not emerge until much later, toward the middle of the fourth year (for convergent evidence see Fischer, 1975; Prinz & Prinz, 1979). The functions of pointing and naming thus appear to emerge at about the same ages for deaf and hearing children. Moreover, for both groups, the utility of these designators appears to expand and contract, at least if we use hearing criteria for classifying the manual behaviors of deaf children as either pointing or naming (for a variety of unpublished references see Hoffmeister, 1982).

Co-occurrence of Sign and Speech

One of the longest-running debates in deaf education has been whether introducing young deaf children to sign language impairs their ability or motivation to acquire spoken language. In fact, there is essentially no evidence to support such a position (Jones & Quigley, 1979; Schlesinger, 1978; Schlesinger & Meadow, 1972a; Stoloff

& Dennis, 1978; for a review see Caccamise, Hatfield, & Brewer, 1978), although one study is frequently cited in this regard. Todd (1976) reported a normally hearing child born to "deaf-mute" parents and raised with ASL as his only language until he was 3 years old. What Todd reported was that ASL structure frequently intruded into the child's productions of English, a phenomenon not uncommon in deaf children who acquire sign as a first language (e.g., Charrow, 1976; Geers et al., 1984; Schiff & Ventry, 1976) (see Chapter 11). Similar errors, in fact, occur for most children and adults learning a second language. Most references to Todd (1976), however, imply that he found that sign language acts as some more dramatic impediment to spoken language. Such misinterpretations, together with anecdotal evidence concerning individual cases, have been sufficient to keep the manual-oral debate alive (e.g., Evans, 1988).

What seems to be neglected in most pro-oral arguments is the importance of early linguistic stimulation of children, in *any* mode. Regardless of whether language acquisition is seen to involve the sequential "setting of switches" (Chomsky, 1986), rule learning (Dale, 1976), or social-cognitive experience and hypothesis testing (Bronowski & Bellugi, 1970; Macnamara, 1972; Slobin, 1973), it requires regular input and feedback during the sensitive period of the first 2 to 3 years. Oral training for young deaf children has not had great success in the United States, and several other countries that previously had oral deaf education philosophies have now come around to a simultaneous communication point of view.

A variety of studies have documented the deficiencies in oral deaf children's use of English (e.g., Charrow, 1976; Geers et al., 1984; Kretschmer & Kretschmer, 1978; Sarachan-Deily & Love, 1974), and others have indicated that manually trained children surpass their orally trained peers on a variety of language-related and cognitively related measures (e.g., Battachi & Montanini-Manfredi, 1986; Bonvillian & Folven, 1993; Brasel & Quigley, 1977; Caccamise et al., 1978; Geers et al., 1984; Hoffmeister, 1982; Kricos & Aungst, 1984; Vernon, Westminster, & Koh, 1971). These findings should not be interpreted as indicating early manual training to be a linguistic panacea, however. The issue is complicated, and all of the relevant variables have not yet been disentangled (see Chapter 11).

Early Signs and Early Words

Bates (1979), Acredolo and Goodwyn (1988), and others have observed that as young hearing children become verbal there is considerable overlap between those concepts that had been communicated via gesture and those now communicated via words. This observation, however, tends to be made *between-subjects*. As noted earlier, consideration of individual children reveals that they tend to have *either* a gesture or a word for things, but not both. These observations support the contention that gestural indication may be less a mandatory precursor of symbolic naming than an early form of social interaction. Similar between- and within-subjects findings from deaf children also are consistent with this position and are even more definitive precisely because the gestures and "words" of those children are in the same modality.

With regard to commonality between first words and first signs, Prinz and Prinz

(1979) noted that Anya's early oral vocabulary complemented her sign language vocabulary with little overlap. During their 14-month observation period, less than 16% of her repertoire consisted of both manual and oral forms for the same referent, and one suspects that some of her manual productions may have been supplementary gestures rather than signs per se (Marschark, 1992). Beyond this tendency to have language tokens in only one communication modality at a time, there is a tendency during later childhood to use only one mode of communication at a time (Geers et al., 1984; Jensema & Trybus, 1978) and an adult pattern of preferring one modality over the other. Longitudinal, within-subject assessments of these dispositions in children have not yet been made. Nevertheless, it is obvious that some deaf individuals are more comfortably and competently bilingual than others. Bilingual balance depends in part on the age and degree of hearing loss (Mayberry & Eichin, 1991), but other variables—such as parental language fluencies and involvement in their children's training, quality of early education and speech training, and socioeconomic status—seem likely to be relevant.

With regard to language in children who are initially trained in oral environments, several studies have indicated that subsequent sign training does not decrease the frequency of vocalization (Schlesinger, 1978; Schlesinger & Meadow, 1972a; Stoloff & Dennis, 1978). Rather, speech and sign may become increasingly complementary both in production and in their contributions to language reception (Crittenden, Ritterman, & Wilcox, 1986; cf. Jensema & Trybus, 1978). Oral performance, however, typically remains well below manual performance (for example, in Manually Coded English, or MCE) when evaluated in terms of English grammatical structures (Brasel & Quigley, 1977; Geers et al., 1984).

Griswold and Commings (1974) examined the expressive vocabularies of 19 deaf preschoolers enrolled in a Total Communication (TC) program that emphasized parental involvement, including their learning of sign language. The children ranged in age from 1;9 to 4;6; more than half had deaf parents or siblings, and 16 of the children's families (including all those of the younger children) were rated as "good" or "fair" in their use of TC in the home. Parents kept cumulative logs of the emergence of signs and speech in their children for the duration of the program, which apparently ranged up to 21 months for several children. Although the data for signs and words were not reported separately, Griswold and Commings reported that, "Most of the words which made up the individual [vocabulary] lists were signs without indications of accompanying speech" (p. 18).

Griswold and Commings observed no reliable differences between children from families with and without other deaf individuals, although there was a reliable lag in the vocabulary sizes of the deaf children in their sample compared to earlier reports involving hearing children. Perhaps the most interesting aspect of the study, however, was the finding that the deaf children's vocabularies were relatively concrete compared to those of hearing peers (for evidence from older deaf children see Fusaro & Slike, 1979). The deaf children generally lacked verbs relating to existence (e.g., *be, have, could, will*), and words referring to time and number were rare. Finally, Griswold and Commings found that rather than vocabulary size being related to children's ages, the best predictor was length of time spent in the preschool program. Although the findings from this study are difficult to interpret in the absence of more extensive controls and statistical analyses, it appears that both the quality and quantity of vocabularies may differ between deaf and hearing preschoolers even when the deaf children have the benefits of TC both at school and at home. Most (TC) deaf children's early expressive language appears to occur in sign rather than in simultaneous communication (Johnson et al., 1989), just as productions of single vocabulary items tend to occur in only one of the two available modes (Acredolo & Goodwyn, 1988; Folven & Bonvillian, 1987). The preference for signed communication over oral communication in deaf preschoolers also is consistent with the finding that manual communication is the primary mode of receptive vocabulary competence for deaf children during the early and middle school years (Crittenden et al., 1986).

How Extensive Are the Effects of Early Manual Training?

In view of the evidence indicating early linguistic and cognitive advantages in deaf children who have either deaf parents or competently signing hearing parents, it is not unreasonable to expect that early manual experience might have some general positive effects on oral language development, regardless of hearing status (Battachi & Montanini-Manfredi, 1986). Some investigators, however, have gone farther and predicted specific facilitative effects of early signing on subsequent acquisition not just of speech skills but of the grammatical and morphological rules of the vernacular (Caccamise et al., 1978). Unfortunately, this scenario appears not to be the case.

Geers et al. (1984) examined the signed (MCE) and oral English grammar skills of 168 deaf children enrolled in aural-oral programs and 159 enrolled in TC programs. All of the children were between 5 and 9 years of age, had profound congenital or early-onset hearing losses, and had been involved in early intervention programs. Using the Grammatical Analysis of Elicited Language (GAEL) developed by Moog and Geers, Geers et al. compared the oral productions of the aural-oral children with the oral and the signed productions of the TC children.[3] Consistent with the expectation that early sign advantages should be short-lived, Geers et al. found no significant differences between the oral and TC groups when the latter children used sign only or when they used speech and sign together. At the same time, the TC group showed significantly poorer oral performance than signed performance.

Lest these results be taken as a counterexample to the alleged facilitative effects of early sign language training, consider Geers and Schick's (1988) reexamination of a subset of the children from their earlier study, in which they compared children with deaf parents and those having hearing parents. Among 5- and 6-year-olds, Geers and Schick found essentially no differences between the groups in terms of either oral or signed English ability. Among 7- and 8-year-olds, however, the children of deaf parents showed small but reliable advantages in both modalities. These results were taken as evidence of the benefits of early language stimulation, although parental acceptance of their children's handicaps also was acknowledged as possibly having some role.

Geers and Schick largely dismissed any other nonlinguistic factors in the superior performance of children of deaf parents because the scores of children with deaf parents closely resembled those of orally trained children with hearing parents. "It was only [deaf children with hearing parents] enrolled in total communication programs who exhibited significantly poorer English skills, and they did not do so until age 7" (p. 141). Omitted from this disclaimer was the fact that the orally trained children were drawn from private schools and thus likely had more individualized instruction and higher socioeconomic status than the children educated in the state-run TC programs (cf. Geers et al., 1984). Without consideration of possible interactions of language fluencies with various familial factors, rejection of alternative interpretations of the Geers and Schick results seems premature. Finally, it should also be noted that the performance of the deaf children in Geers and Schick's study was never compared to that of normally hearing children. One would suspect that the English skills of both the oral and the TC groups were significantly below the normal (hearing) average (Karchmer, 1985; Kretschmer & Kretschmer, 1978), and the lack of significant differences could reflect floor effects rather than any degree of competence.

A Note on Individual Differences

Before leaving the issue of manual versus oral training, it is essential that the apparent implications of findings presented in the preceding section be tempered somewhat. At least since Nelson's (1973) demonstration that hearing children differ considerably in the classes and exemplars of the words they acquire, child language researchers have been interested in individual differences in language development. Nelson found that whereas some children tended to acquire vocabularies that consisted largely of names (*referential* vocabularies), others acquired vocabularies that were largely socially oriented (*expressive* vocabularies). Interestingly, whether particular children were expressive or referential in their early language was not related to whether the mother used expressive or referential terms frequently when communicating with them. Nelson thus suggested that, rather than being the result of the content of early mother–child interactions, expressive and referential vocabularies reflected different learning strategies. She concluded that children's perceptions of the functions of language ("language is for communicating" versus "language is for naming") influence its content.

This imposition of a problem-solving perspective on children's language acquisition could well be informative with regard to deaf children's acquisition of both sign and English. For example, it may account for some of the considerable heterogeneity seen in the language abilities of deaf children with hearing parents, as they may have relatively ill-formed early conceptions of what language is all about. Consistent with this hypothesis, Meadow et al. (1981) found that deaf mother–deaf child dyads engage in far more self-referential and less object-referential language than hearing mother–deaf child dyads.

Among researchers interested in deafness, it is well recognized that even when deaf children have no other obvious handicaps, their within- and between-subject variability is far higher than that of the hearing peers to whom they are typically compared. Such heterogeneity is evidenced in studies of language acquisition per se (e.g., Orlansky & Bonvillian, 1984; Suty, 1986) but is also omnipresent in the domains of social development, cognition, and memory. In part, this variability may reflect neurological or cognitive differences correlated with deafness either etiologically or as a consequence of development without audition (e.g., Mateer, Rapport, & Kettrick, 1984; Neville, Kutas, & Schmidt, 1982; see Chapter 12). As a group, deaf children, and those with hearing parents in particular, also may have greater heterogeneity in their early environments and language experience, although such differences would be difficult to quantify. They also appear likely to have greater heterogeneity in the quality of their social interactions (see Chapters 3 and 4) and the breadth of their cognitively stimulating experiences (see Chapter 7). Most broadly, however, diversity in language abilities typically increases rather than decreases during the early school years, and heterogeneity in language abilities contributes to heterogeneity in virtually all other psychological dimensions of interest.

This argument leads to the general prediction that greater variability in educational and familial interactions should lead to greater variability in language and other abilities. More specific predictions are also possible, such as the expectation that within groups of deaf children with hearing parents test score variability should be smaller across domains for those children who have been enrolled in early intervention programs (thus partially standardizing their early environments) compared to those who have not. The extent to which performance variability can be attributed to neurological or other peripheral factors largely could be determined by examining variance of the data of deaf children of deaf parents compared to hearing children of hearing parents.

Clear evidence bearing on this argument is not easily available, most notably because of the small samples involved in the relevant research. Nevertheless, there are several findings consistent with it at least in spirit and, as yet, apparently none that contradict it. Examination of the normative data collected by Geers et al. (1984) for both prompted and imitated production of English, for example, reveals that there are no cases, across either ages or output modalities, where children trained exclusively in (private) oral programs showed greater variability than those trained in TC programs; and the variability in scores obtained by the TC children tends to be considerably greater than that obtained by the oral children. Unfortunately, comparisons cannot be made for children of deaf versus hearing parents (where variability should be greater for the latter group) in the Geers and Schick (1988) data, because only difference score variability is reported. Data reported by Vernon et al. (1971), however, indicated that deaf children of deaf parents have slightly greater variability in their language scores than deaf children of hearing parents. Those data, as well as those from the Geers at al. study, first would need to be standardized in order to be interpretable beyond the observed absolute differences in performance.

Semantic Development as Indicated Through Sign Language

The preceding sections have examined the development of both English and sign language abilities in young deaf children. We now move beyond single signs to the syntax and semantics of early sign language acquisition. In view of the possible interaction of sign and English acquisition in hearing children who are native signers (e.g., Orlansky & Bonvillian, 1985; Prinz & Prinz, 1979), the focus is on deaf children acquiring sign language as their primary mode of communication.

This section, however, has an existential problem. At an obvious level, deaf children's acquisition of a sign language such as ASL would be expected to differ from hearing children's acquisition of a spoken language such as English in ways that parallel the morphological and grammatical differences between the two languages. In addition, there may be related differences inherent in the alternative (manual versus oral) modalities of their production (Sharpe, 1985). What would it mean to find that deaf and hearing children differ in their sequences of *semantic* development? Beyond possible differences in the ages at which various concepts are expressed linguistically—reflecting overall differences in language training and experience—one would expect that the relative sequence of semantic development would be the same for deaf and hearing children. At least with regard to language *production*, any other finding would suggest one of three conclusions: (1) sign language and spoken language are differentially suitable to the communication of particular ideas; (2) deaf children communicate about different things than do hearing children; or (3) deaf children "think" differently than hearing children.

At first glance it might seem that we can quickly abandon conclusion (3) as being too outlandish, if not downright chauvinistic. Chapters 7 through 9, however, present evidence from a variety of studies suggesting that even if the basic cognitive processes of deaf children are the same as those of hearing children they may be organized and utilized in different ways (see also Chapter 12). Such differences might come about from one of two sources. One is that deaf and hearing children may have sufficient differences in their mode of language production (Sharpe, 1985), their linguistic and nonlinguistic experience (Furth, 1966; Liben, 1978), and their concept knowledge (Koh et al., 1971) that they "carve up" the world differently (Bronowski & Bellugi, 1970; Neisser, 1976). Alternatively, deaf children might indeed be different from hearing children in their basic cognitive processes or resources. Such differences might involve the capacity or structure of short-term memory (e.g., a reliance on visual over verbal coding) or the organization of long-term memory. Looking ahead, differences in short-term memory functioning between deaf and hearing children provide one possible explanation for differences observed in a variety of other domains, such as conservation, concept learning, classification skills, and reading, to be considered in following chapters.

Closely related to conclusion (3), above, conclusion (2) suggests that differences in deaf and hearing cultures can create differences in the content of communication and that such differences would be reflected in what is thought about (or vice versa). This assumption seems undoubtedly true as one basis of cultural diversity within countries and across the world. In the case of deaf children, those with deaf parents (relative to those with hearing parents) might be especially affected by such cultural differences. To find such differences in deaf children of hearing parents who have little or no contact with deaf culture, however, would suggest that more central factors are at play. In the context of attending schools for the deaf, for example, some deaf students are exposed for the first time to "deaf" attitudes and values. In large part, this shift is the consequence of interactions with other deaf children (those deaf children who have deaf parents in particular). Deaf children of hearing parents, however, also now encounter a variety of deaf adults who interact with them in a manner different from that of many of the hearing adults to whom they have become accustomed.

Finally, consider conclusion (1). From a developmental perspective, the suggestion that languages may differ in the way that particular ideas are expressed directly implies that cognitive differences can derive from language differences. That is, it may be that spoken English and the sign languages used in English-speaking countries are sufficiently different to create subtle differences in the thinking of those who use them (e.g., Sharpe, 1985). This situation need not require the adoption of a strong position of *linguistic determinism* (Whorf, 1956)—that language determines thought. Rather, it would reflect a *linguistic relativity* whereby aural-oral and visual-spatial language might direct attention to different aspects of things, e.g., visual-spatial properties (Swisher, 1993), and thus influence conceptions and "perceptions" of the world.[4] Note that such differences may also exist among spoken languages and among various signed languages.

At this point, an important caveat is in order: It might be suspected that the modality difference between sign and speech could increase the effects of linguistic relativity just as greater differences between any two spoken languages could produce larger collateral effects than when those languages are more similar. In the case of signed and spoken languages, however, the two co-occur in the same culture (broadly speaking). This similarity of context means that, whereas the possible reciprocal effects of language and culture might contribute to observed differences between two aural-oral cultures, any such effects are attenuated for a deaf subculture immersed within a hearing culture. Deaf culture thus appears to provide a paradigm case for examining the effects of cultural and linguistic relativity, but such an exercise has not yet been undertaken.[5]

Early Acquisition of Semantic Relations

Early research on language and cognitive development in deaf children frequently led to the conclusion that they were, from the outset, more concrete than in hearing children (e.g., Griswold & Commings, 1974; Myklebust, 1960; Templin, 1950). More recently, however, it has been concluded that deaf and hearing children show essentially the same pattern of early semantic development (e.g., Schlesinger & Meadow, 1972a). How can this contradiction be reconciled?

One convenient answer would be to suggest that the earlier studies relied on children's performance within spoken and written language. In fact, the use of "gesture" was routinely taken as an indicator of cognitive and linguistic concreteness precisely because it was assumed that manual communication could only refer to the concrete, to the here and now. As indicated earlier, this assumption still lingers in the United States (e.g., Evans, 1988) and is strongly held among some groups of deafness educators and researchers in other countries.

Although the English versus manual evaluation argument may be a valid one (e.g., Everhart & Marschark, 1988; Marschark & Clark, 1987), expression of semantic relations can be considered at yet another level, where there is still an apparent contradiction. Consider, for example, Griswold and Comming's (1974) findings that deaf preschoolers' vocabularies rarely included signs for existence, time, number, and referential placeholders. Newport and Ashbrook (1977), meanwhile, reported that the five deaf children they had observed revealed competent use of existence relations as early as 16 months of age. Newport and Ashbrook's subjects also showed competence in the use of semantic relations involving intention and transitory states, constructions that seem to reveal some abstract linguistic competence.

The source of the contradictory findings in these two studies appears to lie in two differences between the investigations that are relevant to a variety of other studies as well. The first of these differences is that in Griswold and Comming's study 15 of the 19 children had hearing parents. In contrast, all five of the children in Newport and Ashbrook's study had deaf parents who exposed them to signing from birth. Perhaps most importantly in this situation, the children with deaf parents would have had a relatively smooth transition from manual gestures to signs, a transition in which parents would have been involved in active, continuous teaching and recasting of lexicalized manual communication (cf. Furrow, Nelson, & Benedict, 1979).

The second important difference between these studies concerns the fact that in the Griswold and Commings study children's semantic competencies were based on vocabulary diaries kept by their (mostly hearing, beginning signer) parents—diaries that contained all signs and words produced. In the Newport and Ashbrook study, children were videotaped during naturalistic interactions, and the tapes were interpreted by a deaf native signer. In the work we have done with nonliteral or nonlexicalized sign language of deaf children (see Chapter 10), we have found that many certified ASL interpreters, and especially native signers, tend to interpret rather than translate our videotapes, as indeed one would desire in most situations. The relevant difference here is that such interpreting provides transcriptions that include all of a child's gestural (i.e., nonsign) and quasiinflectional content as well as specific signs. For example, Newport and Ashbrook noted that a production transcribed as "He put it on the table" might be signed simply with the verb PUT moving toward a table. In their study, such a production would have been appropriately scored as indicating location as well as action. In the Griswold and Commings study, however, only the sign PUT would have been recorded in a diary and subsequently scored as an action.

Given the use of what appears to be a more sensitive methodology, it is not surprising that the Newport and Ashbrook (1977) study was better able to tap the semantic competencies of deaf children than was the earlier study (cf. Marschark & Clark, 1987). Meier and Newport (1990) have argued that parental reports generally are a more sensitive measure of deaf children's language competence than are videotapes, especially when the videotapes are of children's performance in unrelated experimental tasks (cf. Everhart & Lederberg, 1991). The comparison of these two studies, however, suggests some limitations on that conclusion, particularly in light of Griswold and Commings' having hearing parents as informants.

In any event, Newport and Ashbrook's results indicated that the emergence of semantic relations within manual communication parallels that observed in spoken language, despite the differences in the syntactic devices required to produce them. They therefore concluded that syntactic differences have little effect on the early expression of the basic semantic relations (see also Poizner, Klima, & Bellugi, 1987; Prinz & Prinz, 1979). It should be emphasized, however, that deaf children's demonstrations of semantic relations depend on the same *method of rich interpretation* employed by investigators of hearing children's semantic competence. To the extent that gesture and sign language share components that might influence determinations of semantic or other competencies, there must be some caution exercised when interpreting such data from deaf children. Just as usefully, however, we might look to the gestural productions of hearing children to examine the nonlinguistic expression of semantic information that might or might not be accompanied by speech (e.g., Church & Goldin-Meadow, 1986; Marschark, 1992).

Finally, it should be noted that there is a considerable gap in our knowledge concerning early conceptual development in deaf children compared to what is known about hearing children. The "existential discussion" above leaves open the possibilities that semantic concepts underlying language might or might not vary between deaf and hearing children. Maestas y Moores (1980) reported that the child she studied evidenced semantic overgeneralization of nouns by 11 months, but apparently no other data are available in this regard for young children. Possible differences in the conceptual knowledge of older children are considered in Chapters 7 and 9, as they relate to performance on cognitive and memory tasks. Clearly, however, the possible interactions of differences in early experience, language modality, and the development of meaning are in need of exploration.

Later Development of Semantic Relations

The preceding interpretation of findings concerning early semantic development is consistent with Ellenberger and Stayacrt's (1978) study of the representation of action in the sign language productions of one deaf child. They found that over the course of observations made from age 3;7 to 5;11 there was a decline in the child's use of gestures and pantomime to indicate actions and a corresponding increase in his use of conventional signs and classifiers (see also Newport, 1981). Such changes typically are reflected in the emergence of sign inflections for expressing semantic relations during deaf children's fourth year (i.e., 3-year-olds). Deaf 2-year-olds generally do not use inflected verb signs, even when they give all appearances of understanding them when produced by others in appropriate contexts. Instead, they use multiple sign sequences to communicate the same information, e.g., when the three-sign sequence I GIVE YOU is produced rather than the single directional sign I-GIVE-YOU. Similarly, from about 2;6 onward, pointing and other gestures are used in accompaniment to signs in order to "avoid" the need for more complex forms. These uses of indexing instead of inflections are most notable from about 2;6 to 3;6, although they remain in the repertoires of most deaf children until they are nearly 5 years old.

In 3-year-olds, one sees the emergence of some verb inflections, such as those indicating direction, location, and states of being. By the second half of the fourth year, instrumental relations are expressed together with inflections indicating manner, intention, and cause. As with hearing children, there is also incorrect overgeneralization of some constructions, most notably in directional verbs. Where hearing children of this age are often seen to regularize irregular verbs that they previously used correctly (e.g., *fell* becomes *falled*), deaf children "regularize" nondirectional verbs, such as TOUCH or SIT, giving them understandable points of origin and conclusion.

As indexing of verbs starts to fade in 3-year-olds and comes to be used correctly for identifying locations, demonstrative and possessive pronouns also emerge. Both types of pronoun appear to occur somewhat later in deaf children than in hearing children, but the relevant studies have involved too few subjects for us to be confident of the results. For example, both demonstratives and possessives are used regularly by hearing children at age 2;6. Kantor's (1980) study of two deaf children, only one of whom was in this age range, however, found production of possessives to be rare. Hoffmeister's (1982) study of one deaf child indicated the possessive not to be fully developed until age 4.

Pizzuto and Williams (1979) explicitly examined comprehension rather than production of possessives, using four tasks of the form *Where is your X? Where is her Y?* Their study involved two deaf siblings with deaf parents; one child was 1;10 and the other 4;0. As expected, the 4-year-old showed better performance than the 1-year-old, revealing full comprehension of MY, YOUR, and HER. Although the sequences of learning the various possessive forms seemed to follow the same pattern as in hearing children, it appears that an early reliance on pointing might delay appropriate use of possessive pronouns (cf. Petitto, 1987).

In general, there appears to be remarkably little research on semantic development in sign language for deaf children between the ages of 3 and 6 years. There now seems ample evidence that the order, if not the rate, of such semantic development in deaf children correlates well with that of hearing children. Beyond that general finding, however, the data are too sparse to make many firm conclusions. Some further information about meaning is available from studies of organization in short- and long-term memory (see Chapters 8 and 9), but that research largely concerns knowledge about things and their characteristics rather than the semantic relations that are involved in interpersonal communication. Still to be explored are the ways in which the development of semantic relations and their expression within sign language might affect other aspects of development. The latter issue is considered in the next chapter. We now turn to the effects of parental input on deaf children's language acquisition.

Parental Input and Language Acquisition

Language Input to Deaf Children

For the present purposes, we must set aside all of the possible effects of deaf children having hearing parents except those directly relevant to language acquisition. This suggestion is not to say that the social, emotional, and cognitive consequences of being deaf in a hearing family do not impact on language acquisition, but those considerations are dealt with elsewhere. It is relevant here, however, that deaf parents are likely to be more sensitive to the communication needs of their deaf children than are hearing parents. This situation is not just a consequence of the fact that they have a better channel of communication via sign language; the same would be expected of deaf parents who do not sign (Schiff-Myers, 1982). It is also true that some hearing parents have been shown to be remarkably sensitive to communication-related feedback from their deaf children even at young ages (e.g., Blennerhassett, 1984; Erting et al., 1990). Hearing mothers, however, generally evidence a lack of competence and confidence in their manual communication abilities—attributes that make them relatively inflexible when adapting to their children's needs (Swisher, 1984). For their part, fathers are even worse, rarely having more than a passing knowledge of sign language (e.g., Harmon, 1992), and leaving the mother as even more of a primary caretaker than is the typical case with hearing children (Luterman, 1987).

Given the responsibility placed on hearing mothers of deaf children, it is appropriate that investigators refer to the signed as well as the spoken language directed to young children as *motherese*. Regardless of whether a child is hearing or deaf and regardless of whether signed or spoken language is used, adult language to children is generally adapted to the presumed linguistic capabilities of the listener (e.g., Furrow et al., 1979; Newport, 1977). In the case of sign language used by both deaf and hearing mothers, motherese tends to be slower, less complex, and have some simpler, reduced forms than the sign language used to older children and adults (e.g., Erting, 1989; Kantor, 1982; Maestas y Moores, 1980). Perhaps most importantly, experienced signers keep their signs within the infant's line of sight, extending the size and extent of the signing space when necessary.

One would expect that motherese in deaf mother–child dyads would begin just as early as in hearing mother–child dyads. Findings reported by Erting et al. (1990) are consistent with this suggestion. These investigators examined the language used by deaf mothers interacting with their deaf 3- to 6-month-old babies. Erting and her colleagues found that single-sign utterances were most common, about 30% of them being names for things. Signs generally were made within the infants' visual fields, primarily by mothers' moving their hands there and not by physically orienting the children. Erting et al. also found that the mothers' signing was accompanied by positive facial expression and oral movements, while being exaggerated in size and shape. Clearly, these characteristics together with mothers' tendencies to use slower and simpler signs in closer proximity to the children parallel similar aspects in motherese directed to hearing babies (Newport, 1977).

Such modification in parents' child-directed language plays an important role in both communication success and in children's language acquisition. It therefore would not be surprising if a lack of maternal sign language skill impairs communicative, social, and educational interactions with their deaf children. MacKay-Soroka et al. (1987, 1988), for example, demonstrated that mother–child dyads using Simultaneous Communication (SC) performed poorly in referential communication tasks, usually because of failures to clearly distinguish the unique characteristics of target items. Even in cases in which the productions of SC-oriented children contained more complete information than the productions of more oral peers (viz. children with lesser hearing losses), MacKay-Soroka et al. (1987) still found that SC did not lead to more successful communication than oral interaction.

The tendency toward oversimplification and informational inadequacy in hearing adults' signing directed to deaf children has been observed both in the formal interactions of (hearing) teachers of the deaf and their students (Marmor & Petitto, 1979; Newton, 1985) and the informal interactions of hearing mothers with their young deaf children (Swisher, 1984). Swisher's (1984) investigation involved six mothers with children between the ages of 4;6 and 6;0. She found sign omissions (based on simultaneous speech) in more than 50% of all utterances, despite the fact that the average mean length of utterance was less than four morphemes. Swisher estimated that approximately 18% of spoken information was missing from the sign code even when the content of communication was concrete and literal (Johnson et al., 1989). These deficiencies are not surprising in a sample that for the most part had only beginning competence in sign language as a second language; their implications for subsequent language and cognitive development, however, may be considerable.

This conclusion is consistent with findings reported by Meadow et al. (1981) in their study involving deaf 3- to 5-year-olds. As noted earlier, their study found that oral mothers tended to spend less time in interactions with their deaf children than manual mothers or mothers using SC. Only the homogeneous deaf and hearing dyads displayed normal, complex, extended interactions involving both language and gesture. The mixed, oral dyads produced the fewest child-initiated interactions and the highest proportion of unelaborated, or uncompleted communicative interactions. Deaf mother–child dyads and hearing mother–child dyads showed roughly equivalent levels of communicative competence, with the mixed SC dyads falling between them and the oral, mixed dyads. Finally, the communicative *bouts* (i.e., multiple turns) of the mixed, oral dyads were characterized by a paucity of questions and self-references as well as significantly more frequent object references and imitations by the children. Such findings corroborate results obtained by Day (1986) indicating delays in questioning and responding in young deaf children of hearing parents. They also are consistent with findings of Brasel and Quigley (1977) showing that manually trained children outperformed orally trained peers when evaluated on both (English) linguistic and cognitive dimensions during the later school years.

One additional, interesting finding from the Meadow et al. (1981) study was that about 40% of maternal behavioral requests and commands for attention were ignored by children in the mixed dyads. The fact that those mothers made considerably more behavioral requests and relatively few attention calls compared to manual and SC mothers is consistent with the earlier depiction of hearing mothers of deaf children as being overly intrusive. It may well be that the oral mothers in the Meadow et al. study made fewer attention calls simply because they were accustomed to such attempts failing (cf. Lederberg, 1993). In either case, the result may be an attempt to control their children's behavior in a way that reduces the need for linguistic interventions.

The implications of the quality of linguistic interactions evidenced by the Meadow et al. study are highlighted by findings of Wood, Wood, Griffiths, Howaith, and Howaith (1982). Their study, conducted in Great Britain, involved oral and written language performance of deaf 6- to 10-year-olds. In Britain, 16-year-old deaf school graduates tend to perform at the levels typical of 8- to 9-year-old hearing children (cf. Allen, 1986). When examining the oral classroom interactions of their sample, Wood et al. were searching for some bases for such poor performance. Perhaps their most salient finding was the marked relation of the teachers' language style with the performance of their pupils. Those teachers who were more controlling in the language directed at pupils "produced" children who were the least likely to initiate language interactions and were poorest at it when they did. For example, Wood et al. found that the rate of teacher questioning was highly related, *in a negative direction*, to pupils' frequencies of communicative initiatives ($r = -.86$), elaborations of specific answers ($r = -.64$), and questions ($r = -.55$). Unfortunately, teachers' rates of controlling language interactions were positively related to the degree of hearing loss. In other words, those children who had the most difficulty with linguistic interaction in the first place were those who were verbally "assaulted" more by their teachers and reacted most negatively to it.

The results of Wood et al. (1982) were replicated and extended by Power, Wood, and Wood (1990), who examined the language interactions of 8- to 10-year-old deaf children with teachers who used aural-oral communication, Sign English, or cued speech. Once again, it was found that teacher control over conversations was related to students' responses: As teacher control increased (e.g., via the use of linguistic *repairs*), student initiatives in conversation decreased in all three groups. These results are consistent with earlier studies showing that continual shaping of hearing children's language was not beneficial (as the behaviorists had declared) and in fact was harmful to language acquisition (Cazden, 1972). Educators of deaf children would do well to take note of such results in their integration of language training into school curricula in general.

Sign Language Input to Hearing Children

The language addressed to hearing children by their deaf parents has been considered at various points throughout this and the last chapter. Also mentioned at those points were several published studies that have involved two deaf parents versus one deaf parent and, in one case at least, two hearing parents (Holmes & Holmes, 1980). For the present purposes, a brief discussion of several of these studies suffices. Ideally, a discussion of this sort would elaborate on the extent of oral language input derived from sources other than the primary caretakers and the relation of that input to oral and sign acquisition. Insufficient data on this point, however, make such elaboration impossible, leaving only the avenue of speculation.

Two of the most frequently cited studies of hearing children acquiring sign language are those supplied by Prinz and Prinz (1979) and Holmes and Holmes (1980). Recall that Prinz and Prinz (a hearing father and a deaf mother who are both teachers and researchers in deafness) reported that their daughter used her first signs several months earlier than her first words (7 versus 12 months, respectively); her first words occurred at about the same time as those of other hearing children. Abrahamsen et al. (1985), Meier and Newport (1990), and others have taken this finding from a balanced oral-manual environment as a strong indicator that the early sign advantage is a robust one.

Prinz and Prinz, in fact, reported that "Anya's first sign MAMA was identified when she was 7 months, 6 days old. Interestingly, she reversed the sign's forearm rotation . . . Anya made the sign consistently with the little finger touching her chin" (p. 286) (see Figure 6-1). It is unclear from their report why this particular gesture

was classified as a sign whereas previous ones were not. The likely resultant reinforcement, in any case, excludes subsequent use of the "sign" as an indicator of its
status.

Let us accept for the moment that it was a true sign in its communicative function, if not Anya's own comprehension. What other early benefits accrued from her
exposure to manual communication? At 1 year, Anya had a repertoire containing
one word and five signs; at 15 months she had three signs and eight words, or a total
repertoire of 11. This rate of vocabulary development is consistent with the 18 children studied by Nelson (1973): They reached the 10-word point at around 15.1
months. Recall, however, that Nelson's children reached the 50-word point at
around 19.6 months, whereas Anya was lagging far behind; she did not reach a
vocabulary of 38 items (14 words and 24 signs) until she was 21 months. Thus it
appears that the availability of sign language did not facilitate Anya's vocabulary
growth in either modality, or overall, beyond reaching the earliest language milestones (cf. Meier & Newport, 1990). Rather, one could argue that her lexical acquisition was slowed by the experience, especially given such capable and language-
interested parents (cf. Todd, 1976).

Holmes and Holmes (1980), who are both hearing teachers and researchers of
deafness, exposed their son Davey to both spoken and signed language from the
time of his birth. Davey is reported to have used his first sign (DADDY) at 6.2
months and to have reached the 10-"word" stage by 12 months if signs (seven) and
words (four) are combined (one unit was both signed and spoken) and by 13 months
if either signs or words are considered alone. That is, Davey was reported to have
10 signs at 13 months and 10 words at 13 months, even though he had a total of
only 10 items in his expressive vocabulary at 12 months. Davey thus appears to
have acquired 10 new vocabulary items during his 13th month and then 30 more
during his 14th month to reach the 50-"word" point at age 14 months. Meanwhile,
he reached the 50-word point for speech at 16 months and for sign at 15.3 months.

Davey's rate of acquisition was considerably faster than the 10-words-per-
month rate observed by Nelson (1973), and the pace apparently was maintained
over the next few months. He thus appears to be rather more than a "normal" language learner, making it difficult to know how far one can generalize from the findings of his parents. This difficulty is compounded by examination of Holmes and
Holmes's summary of the sign models presented to Davey (p. 248), which suggests
that he was provided with a limited sign language vocabulary rather than a complete, naturalistic one (Abrahamsen et al., 1985).

In any event, we now have examined the two most frequently cited cases of the
early sign advantage, one of which appeared to have accelerated vocabulary growth
and one that did not. The more extensive, 18-month longitudinal study by Orlansky
and Bonvillian (1985) of 13 children, 11 of whom had one or two deaf parents, was
described earlier. That study provided support for Holmes and Holmes' position
that the availability of sign makes for early, more rapid development of vocabulary
in hearing children. Orlansky and Bonvillian found that in their sample the first
signs emerged, on average, at 8.6 months; and the 10-sign point was reached at 13.2
months. By statistically comparing their subjects to those of Nelson (1973), examined 12 years before, Orlansky and Bonvillian found that their sample achieved a
10-item vocabulary significantly earlier than did Nelson's sample. Unfortunately,

the comparison was not made with a more current control group (cf. Goodwyn & Acredolo, 1991). Nevertheless, Orlansky and Bonvillian included only signs in the children's vocabularies, not spoken words (which are not reported). This practice put those children in the range of acquisition as Davey Holmes—fast learners indeed.

Orlansky and Bonvillian concluded from their results that sign language availability accelerates vocabulary development in normal children and can be a useful tool for language training of other children with a variety of learning and language-specific impairments. It should be remembered, however, that the Orlansky and Bonvillian sample represented a special case—that of having both manual and oral language available and spoken fluently in the environment at the same time (although sign language was the predominant mode of parent–child communication). Such a situation is unlikely to be encountered by most children with language or cognitive impairments, and thus the results of their study should be generalized cautiously. One methodological note adds to that caution.

Orlansky and Bonvillian (1985) did not describe who scored their videotapes, the extent to which the vocabularies depended on videotapes versus parents' vocabulary notebooks, or the reliability of their scoring. As argued earlier, designation of young children's gestures as vocabulary items may well inflate such assessments of lexical acquisition in a way that would not have affected Nelson's (1973) study. Moreover, we have no information as to how sign acquisition might have affected oral development in the Orlansky and Bonvillian sample. For the time being, therefore, it appears that the effects of early sign language exposure in hearing children are not entirely clear.

Language Acquisition in the Context of Impoverished Language Models

Consistent with the orientation of this book, this chapter and the preceding one have focused primarily on children with hearing impairments of sufficient severity that their primary form of communication was manual. Hearing children of both hearing and deaf parents also have been of interest in various respects, as they bear on the theoretical issues related to language acquisition and deafness. However, there has been little discussion of children with other disabilities who might benefit from sign language training (Orlansky & Bonvillian, 1985) or several other groups, some with and some without hearing, who have links either to deafness or to sign language in relatively atypical ways.

Children of Oral Deaf Parents

One such group is composed of children (either deaf or hearing) with deaf parents who communicate primarily via oral language. There has been little research conducted with children in this group, in part because there are so few deaf adults who have sufficient oral skill that they bring up their children in oral environments. The situation is even more complex than it might appear because the nature of parent–child language interaction depends on the degree of the hearing loss on both sides. For example, oral communication might be effective for children with degenerative hearing losses inherited from their parents if they learn speech before losing their own hearing. Experimental control in studies of such rare individuals would be complex, however, and there appear to be no relevant studies in the literature.

A related and more available group consists of hearing children of oral deaf parents. Again, the necessary controls would be difficult, and for the most part consideration of such a group is beyond the scope of this book. Three relevant studies are worth noting, however, as they bear on the larger issues concerning deaf children. Schiff-Myers (1982), for example, examined the language development of five 18- to 30-month-olds who had deaf mothers; observations extended over periods ranging from 6 to 10 months. The mothers of the children had in common their use of ASL with other deaf adults, but all primarily used speech to their children, often without even realizing it.

Schiff-Myers found that, in addition to being hearing, the children shared the condition of acquiring speech rather than sign, despite the fact that the oral production of three of the mothers was impoverished. When they did use manual communication, the children's productions tended to be simple gestures or transparent signs lacking syntactic regularity. This finding is important because it suggests that language development depends more on the language directed *to the child* than language indirectly picked up from the environment via some innate or acquired language acquisition device.

Two other studies of interest involved deaf children of deaf parents in a context in which the parents used oral parent–child communication. Sachs and Johnson (1976) reported a study of an admittedly atypical case involving a boy aged 3;9. "Jim" apparently was exposed to the sign and speech of his deaf parents, but he showed no evidence of sign language acquisition and had impoverished oral English ability. In fact, Sachs and Johnson found that Jim's parents did not expect their children to acquire sign language and communicated with them only orally. In other words, Jim "overheard" sign but never had sign directed to him. Clearly, the limited speech and gesture directed toward him was insufficient for normal language development. Sachs and Johnson concluded that children cannot just "pick up" language from the environment; it must be directed at them with appropriate modification (cf. McNeill, 1966).

Sachs, Bard, and Johnson (1981) added to their study Jim's younger brother, who was 1;8 at the time of the initial investigation. "Glenn's" situation was rather different from that of Jim in that Glenn benefited from both the regular visits of the investigator/therapists and (eventually) having an older sibling (Jim) who directed oral language to him. In fact, Jim turned out to be an active language teacher for Glenn, frequently providing explicit language tutelage and "interpreting services." The fact that Glenn subsequently showed relatively normal language development added support to the Sachs et al. argument against an innate, automatic language acquisition device and for an emphasis on experience and active learning (although the two are not mutually exclusive in principle).

Language Acquisition Despite Language Deprivation?

On the other extreme from the Sachs studies are several by Goldin-Meadow and her colleagues involving deaf children who had received only oral, essentially ineffective input from their hearing parents. Feldman, Goldin-Meadow, and Gleitman (1978), for example, reported a study of six moderately to profoundly deaf children who showed only minimal progress in speech- and lip-reading abilities via their oral programs. The children, aged 1;5 to 4;1, all had parents who had been instructed not to sign to their children for fear of impeding their oral development. Although the parents actually did use some manual gestures with their children, Feldman et al. indicated that the children had no specific language models. Their examination of the children's "language-like gestures" was based on identification of "attempts to communicate" but did not include "direct motor acts *on* the listener" (e.g., pushing to indicate *go*). Segments designated *signs* were "analogous to morphemes or words" but were not lexicalized ASL signs.

Feldman et al. found that, despite their linguistic deprivation, all of the children developed manual communication systems using common gestures (e.g., pointing), invented gestures, and regular combinations of those units. "They were iconic, certainly, but also highly stylized—just enough to render an intent, rather than an attempt to imitate veridically some scene or object in the visual world" (p. 375).

Goldin-Meadow and Mylander (1984) extended these observations to a group of four other children in similar situations, with particular attention to the development of semantic relations. As noted earlier, identification of semantic relations in situations such as this one depends largely on the method of rich interpretation, just as it does with young hearing children. For example, within a particular context, Goldin-Meadow and Mylander identified the sign sequence DUCK–BOX as "she/mother put the duck on the box," a patient–recipient relation. Taken together, Goldin-Meadow and Mylander's analyses were interpreted as indicating that the gestural productions used by the children were examples of "true" language: They were productive, communicative, social systems of communication comparable to the language development of hearing children of hearing parents [For further elaboration of one child's productions see also Mylander & Goldin Meadow (1991).]

The bearing of Goldin-Meadow and Mylander's (1984) findings on interesting questions such as Is language innate? What is language? and Who (e.g., chimpanzees) has language? is considered at length in the commentary by deVilliers (1984) following the Goldin-Meadow and Mylander (1984) report. For the present purposes, it is sufficient to note that studies of deaf children who fail to benefit from oral training indicate that social communication proceeds, nonetheless, in whatever medium is available. The emergence of regular gestural forms and combinatorial structures reflecting underlying semantic understanding demonstrates the resilience of children for achieving their communicative needs. The extent to which such productions reflect a "biological predisposition to language" or the social-biological needs of young children coupled with the receptive flexibility of caring adults is open to considerable argument. It may well be significant, however, that in those few reported cases in which the receptive, caring adult component was missing—studies involving "closet children" or "wild children"—there has been little evidence of communicative competence approaching that observed in the above studies.

Summary

Research considered in this chapter focused on the early language development of deaf children: the transition from gesture to sign, the first signs and first words, and the semantic and social implications of language input and language output. Any understanding of this area is clouded by a variety of methodological and theoretical difficulties, many of them inherent in the population and questions at issue. Moreover, it is precisely those ambiguous findings and confounded naturalistic situations that make the study of deaf children's language so important and so interesting to investigators. Questions concerning the effects on language development of children's degrees of hearing loss, manual versus oral early environments, parental hearing status, and social-educational situations must be considered in the context of real-world heterogeneity in all of those domains.

It is frequently claimed that sign language tends to emerge earlier than spoken language within hearing, bilingual children and earlier in deaf children of deaf parents compared to the emergence of speech in hearing children of hearing parents. Although the evidence in that regard is based on small samples and is far from consistent, it appears that such an advantage occurs through the one-word stage but disappears soon thereafter. The claim that deaf children of deaf parents show earlier, more normal language development than deaf children of hearing parents is clearly supported by the available literature. The problem lies in identifying all of the sources and implications of such findings.

If deaf children's early exposure to sign language does not lead to any consistent, long-term facilitation of normal language development relative to hearing children, it also does not appear to lead to any consistent impediments to subsequent, oral language learning. In fact, oral and manual communication may become increasingly complementary with age in regard to both production and comprehension, even if deaf children, like deaf adults, tend to have preferred language orientations (largely linked to degree of hearing loss). Oral training, in any case, does not appear to provide the benefits once hoped for in the linguistic realm and may create difficulties for deaf children in cognitive and social realms (but see Chapter 11).

The sequence of emerging semantic relations in deaf children's language productions parallels that observed in hearing children, at least when manual deaf children are evaluated using sign language. Research concerning the possibility that linguistic, cultural, or other aspects of deaf children's early environments might affect conceptual development or the semantic underpinnings of language is still too sparse to draw any firm conclusions. Nevertheless, it appears that deaf mothers tend to be significantly better than hearing mothers in terms of their ability to communicate to their deaf children both specific and general information about objects and events in the environment. Hearing mothers appear to be sensitive to the need to adjust their communication for their deaf children, but there is no evidence that the social editing of their language results in any facilitation of information exchange.

Consideration of what little research is available involving children who lack adequate language models indicated subsequent, related impairment in language comprehension and production. At the same time, the linguistic resilience of such children is evidenced by the fact that many of them manage to develop some regular means of communication despite their deprivation. However, one suspects that children in contexts of linguistic deprivation are likely to be deprived in other ways as well, most notably in the quality of their social interactions. Children who do not have any consistent language experience early in development may represent extreme cases, but there are many other deaf children whose early linguistic environments approach such situations. More or less by virtue of their hearing losses, most deaf children initially are at some disadvantage relative to most hearing peers; and by virtue of their language deficiencies, they initially are at some disadvantage in the extent of their experiental diversity, the effectiveness of their schooling, and their flexibility in dealing with the world. Whether these initial disadvantages are reduced or enlarged over the school years and the extent to which they yield differences, if not deficiencies, in deaf children's cognitive development is the substance of the next chapter.

Notes

1. A similar discussion with regard to deaf children's first spoken words would be informative if the available information were consistent enough to draw any reliable conclusions. Given the several theoretical and methodological issues raised earlier and the murky status of the vocalizations produced by most deaf children, it seems better to defer such consideration until more data are available (see Abrahamsen et al., 1985, for discussion).

2. Language researchers, in contrast, have a variety of rules for determining what qualifies as a sign in deaf children's repertoires. Confident that these restrictions are somewhat more objective than parents' perceptions, they are described below

3. The terms "oral" and "spoken" in the Geers et al. (1984) report referred to the mouthing of words. There apparently was no requirement of vocalization, and it is unclear how a more stringent methodology or scoring might have affected their results.

4. Perception appears in quotes here so that it will be understood in the generic sense rather than the strict psychological sense. Thus it is not being claimed that as a cross-country skier my 10 or so color words referring to snow make my perceptual apparatus better able to discriminate the stuff, only that there are benefits in my learning to do so, in that the labels allow social communication about snow conditions. Similarly, even if sign language does not explicitly affect the sensitivity of visual-spatial perception (but see Swisher, 1993), it could influence the focus of attentional and learning strategies of deaf children sufficiently to affect their conception and organization of the world.

5. Ashbrook (1977) is frequently reported (e.g., in Hoffmeister, 1982) to have compared the expression of semantic relations in English and ASL, concluding that the availability of parallel forms of expression should make for equivalent semantic development in hearing and deaf children. That unpublished study is not easily available, however, and it is unclear whether the data bear out a linguistic relativity hypothesis in any strong sense.

7

Intelligence and Cognitive Development

This chapter surveys several sources of evidence concerning the cognitive or intellectual abilities of deaf children. A variety of studies have explored the issues surrounding intelligence testing with deaf children—issues such as the confounding of intelligence and language ability, the *culture-fairness* of intelligence tests, and the validity of nonverbal versus verbal measures of intelligence. Regrettably, asking these questions has not led to many answers, and all of the issues remain open to debate. Research conducted from both psychological and educational perspectives, however, has brought us a long way toward a better understanding of intellectual development in deaf children and its interaction with language and social development (Marschark, 1993).

In large measure, progress in this domain has derived not from studies of intelligence per se but from investigations into differences in cognitive abilities of deaf and hearing children. Most of the relevant studies, especially the early ones, were aimed at understanding cognitive development in the "absence" of language. Recent studies have dealt more directly with deaf children's cognitive skills, with and without concerns about the influences of language fluency, mode of language training, and degree of hearing loss. Foremost among these studies have been a variety of empirical investigations concerning the performance of deaf children in conservation tasks. *Conservation tasks* tap children's abilities to consider problems or situations from alternative perspectives. Taken together, these studies and those on intelligence per se have indicated the need to distinguish the effects of language abilities on cognitive functioning in deaf children. Still at issue are the effects on cognitive development of deaf children's atypical histories of social functioning and educational experience, inside and outside the classroom.

Intellectual Functioning of Deaf Children

The earliest meaning of the word "dumb" (circa 1000 AD) and the first one listed in the *Oxford English Dictionary* (*OED*) is "destitute of the faculty of speech." In this original usage, dumbness was attributed to animals, not in the sense of lacking intelligence but in the sense of their being bereft of speech. More than 700 years later, the word was used to refer to the lack of physical brightness and, perhaps via that figurative link ("dull" originally referred the lack of mental faculties rather than physical brightness), the use of "dumb" in the intellectual sense came about. If we now were to ascribe fully to the *OED* (and to commit a social and political *faux pas*), most deaf children are surely dumb but also far from stupid.

Unfortunately, there is a long history of explicit and implicit suggestions that deaf children are stupid as well as dumb. Early studies by Pintner and his colleagues consistently indicated that deaf children were about 2 years retarded mentally, on average, compared to hearing peers. Those findings were taken to account for 2 of the 5 years of educational retardation seen in deaf children, and language deficits were presumed to account for the other three. During the 1920s and 1930s, Pintner and others therefore developed nonverbal, or *performance*, tests of intellectual abilities expressly designed for the purpose of better evaluating the mental abilities of deaf children. Such changes notwithstanding, deaf individuals still generally fared less well than their hearing age-mates, even if the differences were often small. Many of those early tests were not appropriately standardized, however, and the investigators frequently used samples that were either biased or too small to be able to draw any strong conclusions. [See Myklebust (1960) for discussion of these early studies and Braden (1985a) for discussion of their bias and appropriateness.] As a result, the issues of intelligence and intelligence testing of deaf children remain with us today, although the area has taken on a somewhat different character.

Perhaps the central question of current educational interest with regard to intelligence testing concerns the relation of test scores, or intelligence quotients (IQs), and achievement. Even now, when samples of deaf and hearing children are shown to have equivalent IQs according to some particular (almost always nonverbal) test, the deaf children generally still lag behind hearing peers in school-related academic performance. Sometimes intelligence scores are reliably related to achievement, but those relations typically account for relatively small proportions of the observed variance (e.g., Hirshoren, Hurley, & Kavale, 1979). Findings of this sort suggest that there are significant factors other than intelligence per se affecting academic achievement in deaf children, not a surprising conclusion. In previous chapters we have seen aspects of social development, language experience, and educational methods that might well have considerable impact not only on what deaf children learn but how they learn and how they apply learned knowledge in particular situations.

Several investigators have gone so far as to suggest that neuropsychological as well as experiential differences between deaf and hearing children may result in qualitatively different styles of information processing (e.g., Furth, 1966; Myklebust, 1960; Tomlinson-Keasey & Kelly, 1978) (see Chapter 12). Frequently, such arguments are taken as suggestions that deaf children are doomed to intellectual deficiency, and the conclusions are thus dismissed out of hand. The issue is a complex one, however, and the possibility that deaf children might have a *different* constellation of intellectual abilities from hearing children requires serious consideration. If true, these abilities might well demand particular kinds of educational experience to achieve "normal development." The lack of such training might produce the observed achievement deficiencies of deaf children even when they obtain normal scores on standardized tests. In addition to being of central importance for understanding and facilitating development of deaf children, information relevant to this possibility would be informative with regard to the relations among language, experience, and cognitive development. It therefore is worthwhile considering intelligence, IQ, and deaf children's cognitive functioning in more detail.

Nonverbal Intelligence Testing of Deaf Children

Despite Pintner's early findings, the most frequently cited conclusion on the relative intelligence levels of deaf and hearing children is a more positive one based on a literature review by Vernon (1969). Vernon argued that on the basis of his review of "approximately 50 independently conducted investigations, it is clearly evident that the deaf and hard of hearing population has essentially the same distribution of intelligence as the general population" (p. 547). Deaf norms now have been established for a variety of popular intelligence tests (e.g., Anderson & Sisco, 1977), although it is far from clear that such norms are either necessary or informative (Braden, 1985b).

Almost all of the evidence on which Vernon based his 1969 conclusion involved *performance* tests, which are nonverbal tests that involve manipulation, matching, or completion of test stimuli in ways intended to reflect abstract as well as concrete reasoning abilities. At the outset, the use of performance scales only for assessing intelligence of deaf children creates an interesting situation. On one hand, the exclusive use of nonverbal tests seems eminently fair. English is essentially a second language for most deaf children (Charrow, 1976), and they would not be expected to fare any better on an English-based test of intelligence than I would on an Italian-based test (my Italian is only slightly better than my sign language skill). In fact, there are several good reasons to expect that they would be at an added disadvantage (see Chapter 11). If performance tests provide fair and accurate assessments of intelligence independent of language skills (Bolton, 1972; Vernon, 1967), however, why do we persist in using verbal tests for hearing individuals? If we want to accept the nonverbal IQ approach, we must be sure that we know exactly to what we are referring when we speak of *intelligence*.

Normally, IQ is defined in an apparently circular fashion as "the hypothetical construct which is measured by a properly standardized intelligence test;" and (from the same source) intelligence is defined, more helpfully, as "the individual's total repertory of those problem-solving and cognitive-discrimination responses that are usual and expected at a given age level and in the large population unit to which he belongs" (English & English, 1958, pp. 268–269). Ruling out verbal abilities from assessments of deaf children seems necessary given "the large [deaf] population unit" to which they belong, but it also requires acceptance of the fact that we are tapping only one part of intelligence as it is typically understood. In particular, a considerable portion of problem-solving and cognitive-discrimination responses that are usual and expected at a given age level in the "hearing world" may require aspects of language ability that at least some deaf children are lacking. It thus appears that we are applying a different definition of intelligence to deaf children than we are to hearing children.

This bias may not seem like such a poor idea at the level of verbal versus nonverbal functioning, but then how do we reconcile that position with the assumption that nonverbal intelligence has the same character in deaf and hearing children?

Two issues are of interest here. First, it is unclear whether the possibility that deaf children might have different constellations or configurations of intelligence from hearing children demands that these differences be responsible for observed deficits in deaf children's academic performance. Intellectual and academic abilities are obviously related, but it remains to be determined how much of deaf children's observed academic deficiencies can be ascribed to intellectual differences rather than to other factors, such as language fluency or achievement motivation. Research on this question would require longitudinal studies of cognitive development and academic performance that have not yet been conducted.

Second, as is discussed later in the chapter, deficits also appear in deaf children's performance on tests that purportedly assess cognitive functioning independent of linguistic ability. At least two possible sources of such differences should be obvious by this point. One of them concerns the typical role of language in children's cognitive development and in the acquisition of nonverbal as well as verbal concepts. Concept knowledge derives in part from explicit teaching. Language-delayed deaf (or hearing) children thus may be at a disadvantage in "educational" interactions with adults prior to the school years and in ongoing lessons in the classroom (Johnson et al., 1989). Deaf children are also likely to spend more school hours in remedial speech-language training, to the exclusion of other, conceptually stimulating work.

Just as important, however, is the wealth of conceptual knowledge that children normally obtain from indirect teaching, either by overhearing the (real or televised) conversations of others or via informal language interactions with adults and other children. Chapter 6 considered some of the consequences of deaf children's interactions with parents who are typically far from fluent in manual communication. Even in those cases in which parents know and use sign language, however, the physical necessities of manual communication mean that parents and others are often unable to explain ongoing or transitory events if their hands are otherwise occupied. The need to free the hands for tool use and other manual tasks, in fact, is frequently suggested as one of the driving phylogenetic forces that led to the development of aural-oral language, and its ontogenetic role should not be taken lightly (Feyereisen & de Lannoy, 1991; Kimura, 1975; Tzeng & Wang, 1984).

A second concomitant of childhood deafness that might play a role in the assessment of nonverbal intellectual abilities is neurological damage. Although it certainly is not the case that all or even most deaf children also have "brain damage," there are a variety of conditions that can cause hearing loss (or predispose a child to deafness) that also may cause some degree of neurological impairment. As indicated in Chapter 2, maternal rubella, high fever during infancy, and meningitis are but three examples that figure significantly in the epidemiology of deafness and have such possible other consequences. Deafness-linked neurological damage also may be a factor in some mental illnesses that are more frequent in deaf than hearing populations (Vernon & Andrews, 1990), an issue considered in Chapter 2. The point is that most normative studies of intellectual differences in deaf and hearing individuals, of the sort reviewed by Vernon (1969) and several to be discussed below, have some proportion of subjects who do have neurological impairments in addition to their deafness. The variability contributed by such impairments could well be partially responsible for apparent overall, quantitative differences between deaf and hearing samples or qualitative differences in the configuration of abilities within the deaf population (Ulissi, Brice, & Gibbins, 1990).

On the other side of the coin, it has been suggested that deafness, especially hereditary deafness, might confer some intellectual advantages. Kusché, Greenberg, and Garfield (1983), for example, examined nonverbal intelligence and verbal achievement in four groups of deaf high school students: one group in which students had at least one deaf parent and evidence of hereditary deafness, one in which students had hearing parents but either deaf siblings or deaf cousins and other indications of genetic deafness, and two groups with hearing parents and no evidence of genetic deafness. Each of the nongenetic groups with hearing parents was matched with one of the groups with genetic deafness on age, hearing loss, and Stanford Achievement Test (SAT) scores; and the pairs were equivalent on a variety of other factors.

As would be expected, Kusché et al. found that the group with deaf parents exhibited earlier acquisition of sign language than did the groups with hearing parents. Most importantly, the two groups with genetic deafness had higher mean IQ scores—112 according to the Wechsler Intelligence Scale for Children–Revised (WISC-R) or the Wechsler Adult Intelligence Scale (WAIS)—than their matched groups with nongenetic deafness (scores of 101 and 102, respectively). Because only one of the genetically deaf groups had hearing parents, Kusché et al. ruled out early language stimulation and quality of parental communication as possible loci of the IQ differences. Instead, they suggested that "it is possible that natural, cultural, and/or historical selection have resulted in superior nonverbal intelligence for deaf individuals when genetic etiologies are involved" (p. 464). This conclusion was consistent with earlier findings by Sisco and Anderson (1980) indicating higher nonverbal intelligence in deaf children of deaf parents compared to deaf children of hearing parents. Sisco and Anderson, however, had interpreted their findings as the result of deaf parents having higher expectations for their children with regard to the potential for educational and rehabilitation success.

Chovan, Waldron, and Rose (1988) found that deaf middle school and high school students showed faster responses in visual cognition tasks than their hearing peers, adding weight to the deafness advantage hypothesis (regardless of its locus). The Chovan et al. study did not reveal any reliable differences between those deaf students enrolled in an oral educational program and those in a Total Communication program, but the etiologies of deafness and family characteristics of students in the two groups was not reported.

In an effort to clarify the relation of familial deafness and intelligence, Zweibel (1987) examined the intellectual abilities of 243 children varying in the number of deaf family members. All of the children were educated in oral settings and were between the ages of 6 and 14 years of age. Eighty-five percent had severe to profound hearing losses and 94% had congenital (80%) or early-onset deafness. The students were rated by their teachers on lip-reading skill, signing ability, intellectual potential, and their parents' signing abilities; all were administered the Snijders-Oomen Nonverbal Intelligence Test (SON) and the Goodenough-Harris Human Figure Drawing Test.

Consistent with the Kusché et al. findings, Zweibel found that deaf children with deaf parents or siblings (suggesting genetic deafness) scored significantly higher in intelligence than deaf children with hearing parents and hearing siblings, according to scores on the SON and Figure Drawing tests as well as teachers' ratings. Although the subgroup with both deaf parents and deaf siblings did not differ from a hearing control group on the Figure Drawing Test, they fell significantly behind that group on the SON. Most importantly, Zweibel found that (1) deaf children with deaf parents obtained higher IQ scores than genetically deaf children with hearing parents but deaf siblings; and (2) the latter group did not differ from deaf children with all-hearing (nongenetic deafness) families. Zweibel concluded that genetic background makes no difference in intelligence, suggesting instead that his results were best interpreted in terms of manual communication use in the home increasing the ability of deaf children to absorb messages and stimuli, thus leading to subsequent gains in cognitive development.

It is noteworthy that Zweibel's (1987) results with regard to intelligence are consistent with a variety of findings in the realm of reading and writing achievement, indicating that a combination of oral and manual training leads to the best cognitive performance (see Chapter 11). At the same time, his failure to demonstrate a genetic deafness advantage in either intelligence or perceptual-spatial abilities contradicts the findings of Kusché et al. (1983). One tantalizing explanation for these differences lies in the fact that Zweibel's subjects were enrolled exclusively in oral programs, whereas those of Kusché et al. were enrolled in Total Communication programs (there is no other obvious difference in the nature of their samples). Without further evidence, however, we have to look to other quantitative and qualitative aspects of deaf children's intellectual abilities for clarification.

Factor Analytic Studies of Intelligence Measures

While maintaining some caution interpreting the results of early verbal and nonverbal tests of intelligence in deaf children, there are several more recent studies that have addressed the possibility that deaf and hearing children might differ qualitatively or quantitatively in their intellectual functioning according to standardized tests. Bolton (1978), for example, reexamined data collected in the standardization of the Hiskey-Nebraska Test of Learning Ability (HNTLA) for deaf and hearing children. The HNTLA is a popular, performance-based intelligence test originally developed for deaf children. Bolton used data from 8 of the 12 HNTLA subtests (those appropriate for 3- to 11-year-olds). He submitted the scores of 1079 deaf and 1074 hearing children to factor analysis in order to extract apparent relations among the various subtests. Although several studies have shown that deaf and hearing children have comparable intelligence according to the HNTLA (Vernon, 1969), Bolton found that the two groups showed somewhat different factor patterns, indicating different interrelations among the tests and presumably the abilities they tap (cf. Furth, 1964).

Braden (1984) conducted a study similar to that of Bolton but involving the performance scale data obtained from the standardization sample for the WISC-R. The WISC-R is the intelligence test most commonly given to hearing children, and its scores are highly correlated with nonverbal tests, such as the HNTLA. Braden compared the scores of 2200 hearing children to those of 1228 deaf children with congenital or early-onset deafness and severe to profound hearing losses. In contrast to Bolton's HNTLA findings, Braden found that there was a quantitative difference between the deaf and hearing samples on their WISC-R performance scores. The deaf sample was far more variable than the hearing sample (standard deviations averaging 5.12 and 0.24, respectively) and scored significantly ($p \leq .007$) lower on five of the seven subtests. In contrast to Bolton's (1978) findings, Braden (1984) concluded that for deaf and hearing children, "Intelligence has the same character or structure . . . Even though there may be *slight* differences in overall intellectual ability" (p. 406; italics added).

Braden (1984) interpreted his findings as being consistent with Vernon's (1967) assertion that there is no relation between concept formation and level of verbal language. Although this conclusion may be appealing, the finding of similar configurations of *performance* (i.e., nonverbal) abilities in deaf and hearing children appears to have little bearing on the possible relation of language skills to concept formation. Imagine, for example, that deaf children's performance IQ scores increased uniformly, across all subtests, one percentage point for each percentage point increase in their English skills.[1] There would then be a strong relation between language ability and intelligence, but the relations among the performance scores would still be the same.

Leaving the language issue aside for the moment, there is the problem of reconciling the differences between Braden's (1984) study and that of Bolton (1978). Recall that Braden but not Bolton found overall quantitative differences in deaf and hearing children's scores on their respective tests, whereas Bolton but not Braden found qualitative differences. Braden (1985a) argued that Bolton's failure to consider the high correlation between the two HNTLA factors obscured the largest source of variance in that study, the "general intelligence (g) factor," also known as *fluid intelligence*. In addition, Braden (1984) and Bolton (1978) had used different factor analytic rotation techniques (principal component and oblique, respectively), and their samples differed in the distribution of ages (6 to 16 years and 3 to 10 years, respectively). Braden (1985a) therefore performed identical analyses on data from earlier deaf and hearing samples administered either the WISC, WISC-R, or HNTLA.

With the WISC and WISC-R data as well as the HNTLA data from an 11- to 17-year-old sample, Braden obtained essentially identical factors for deaf and hearing children, as both groups revealed only a single factor (g + performance) with loadings on all of the subtests. Only HNTLA data from a sample of 3- to 10-year-olds revealed different structures for deaf and hearing subjects. Both of the latter groups revealed one (g + performance) factor in common, but there was also a second factor that distinguished the deaf and hearing children. Braden left that factor uninterpreted because of its inconsistent loadings on memory and reasoning subtests, but it is interesting to note that the four tests that showed the largest differences in factor scores between the two groups were the same four that showed the largest differences in Bolton's (1978) study.

Although he did not report quantitative differences between deaf and hearing samples, Braden's (1985a) results, together with the differences between the findings of Bolton (1978) and Braden (1984), suggest that there are *qualitative* performance IQ differences between young deaf and hearing children that disappear with age and schooling. Meanwhile, *quantitative* differences between the groups may emerge only as the gap between their academic and linguistic competencies increases, especially with regard to reading abilities.

This interpretation of WISC-R and HNTLA results is also consistent with findings reported by Zweibel and Mertens (1985), using the SON. They found that when SON scores from a group of 251 deaf children, aged 6 to 15, were analyzed only a single, *g* + performance factor emerged. When the sample was divided into three age groups—6 to 9 years, 10 to 12 years, and 13 to 15 years—however, different factor structures emerged for each group. In the youngest group, general comprehension was linked to perceptual thinking in one factor, whereas perceptual and concrete thinking were linked in a second. In the middle age group, general intelligence emerged as a separate factor from perceptual skills, whereas a link to abstract thinking was only weakly suggested. In the oldest group, abstract thinking emerged in a second factor, following the first (general intelligence) factor. Even at ages 13 to 15, however, the deaf children still revealed greater emphases on perception and memory in intellectual functioning compared to SON scores from a single group (*n* = 101) of 10- to 12-year-old hearing children (cf. Zweibel, 1987). The hearing group revealed two factors, one reflecting only general intelligence and the other reflecting abstract thinking.

Zweibel and Mertens ascribed their results to a trend in cognitive development toward increasing organization and abstract thinking and a greater reliance by deaf children on visual-perceptual thinking compared to hearing peers (see Chapter 8). Such findings appear consistent with the suggestion that deaf children rely more on concrete experience than other forms of knowledge, an orientation that could affect their performance in a variety of cognitive domains including conservation performance, short-term memory, and reading. In some cases their performance on particular intelligence tests or cognitive tasks may be comparable to that of hearing agemates, but more often than not they appear to differ in either quantitative or qualitative ways. Still to be determined is the extent to which any such differences might be related to genetic versus nongenetic etiologies of deafness or differences in social development, schooling (see Paquin & Braden, 1990), and especially language and reading skills. Until studies of this sort are conducted, it is difficult to interpret findings of comparable nonverbal intelligence in the face of overwhelming differences in academic performance by deaf and hearing children.

Is IQ Really Independent of Language?

This section does not rehash the long-standing argument concerning the general relation between language and thought. For relevant historical discussions, readers can see the writings of Whorf, Vygotsky, and Hayakawa. At issue here is only the possibly informative or possibly misleading case of deaf children, primarily those acquiring visual-manual language. The potentially misleading aspect of this issue is that, as we have seen, deaf and hearing children differ on several developmental dimensions aside from the presence or absence of oral language. It is true that more deaf than hearing children might be characterized as having "no effective language," but these children also differ from the norm for deaf children in ways that are likely to affect intellectual development. Unfortunately, there are not many cases that allow unambiguous separation of the effects of language and other environmental experience, although there are some that are instructive (e.g., Goldin-Meadow & Mylander, 1984).

For the evaluation of intelligence in more typical deaf children, there is a continuing trend toward assessing their abilities using purely nonverbal tools. This situation suggests a possible alternative to Bolton's (1972) and Vernon's (1967) conclusions that nonverbal cognitive abilities are unrelated to language skills. Simply stated, the performance scales of most intelligence tests are designed to tap those aspects of intelligence that are independent of verbal ability. It could well be that intelligence and verbal ability are not fully independent in deaf children. We just may be evaluating those components of intelligence that are independent of language, whereas other, language related components are excluded from consideration.

When extended to deaf children, nonverbal intelligence scales have been helpful for assessing the extent to which those children might have developed intellectual skills despite probable language deficits. However, it does not seem to be of any service to the deaf population to ignore the possible role of language skills, manual or oral, in the ability to deal effectively with problem-solving in the real world. Whether deaf children obtain intelligence scores equal to their hearing peers is not the issue (aside from a possible political one). The issue is the need to determine the relative strengths and weaknesses in deaf children's psychological repertoires and to develop means of using the former to improve or compensate for the latter.

Braden's (1984) results notwithstanding, there appears to be a good possibility that deaf and hearing children might have somewhat different cognitive abilities or cognitive configurations. Such a position does not deny that deaf children might be deficient in some particular domains (e.g, seriation, grammar) but also does not rule out the possibility that they might be superior to hearing peers in some other domains (e.g., spatial memory, visuomotor coordination) when confounding factors are controlled. Although the suggestion that individuals of any minority might be psychologically different from those of any particular majority is not a popular topic, in the case of a handicap with implications as pervasive as deafness such a case might be made without bias.

This argument, in fact, was raised by Tomlinson-Keasey and Kelly (1978) in their attempt to reconcile the general comparability of deaf and hearing children on nonverbal tests of intelligence with the consistent lag of deaf children on school-related achievement measures. They suggested that the lag in language acquisition experienced by most deaf children would impair the development of symbolic thought, in which arbitrary symbols come to represent real-world objects, actions, and events and allow consideration of them when they are not present.

As an example of one way in which this relation might be evidenced, consider a study with hearing children by Baldwin and Markman (1989). They demonstrated that combined pointing and verbal labeling by adults led infants as young as 10 months of age to look at an indicated object longer and to attend to it longer afterward in the absence of language. Pointing alone helped to direct attention during the testing session but did not carry over in its effects on visual exploration in a subsequent play session. From Tomlinson-Keasey and Kelly's perspective, the lack of a consistent relation between verbal and manual indexing would be likely to reduce deaf children's formation of label-object links and thus eliminate a normally powerful source of early symbol learning.

This line of argument leads to the prediction that deaf children of deaf parents should reveal cognitive competencies and cognitive organizations more comparable to those of hearing children than do deaf children of hearing parents (possible cultural influences aside), a finding consistent with the results offered by Kusché et al. (1983) and Zweibel (1987). Furthermore, within the group of deaf children with hearing parents there should be a positive correlation between language ability and intellectual functioning, a finding supported by Zweibel (1987). Studies to be reported later indicate that such predictions are supported in the cognitive development literature as well.

Broadly speaking, then, the research described thus far supports the general point raised by Tomlinson-Keasey and Kelly (1978). Differences between young deaf and hearing children with regard to sensory input, diversity of experience, symbolic development, and early interaction with others theoretically demands that there be correlated differences in intellectual functioning. This issue is one that comes up repeatedly in studies of cognitive development in deaf children, not just in terms of their possible deficiencies but also in terms of the kinds of qualitative differences observed in several domains. In the next two chapters, consideration of memory development yields further information relevant to this point. In the meantime, we turn to a consideration of tasks commonly used to assess the abilities of young deaf children to deal with concrete and abstract concepts, problem-solving, and the possible relations of such tasks to language abilities.

Cognitive Abilities of Deaf Children

Most prominent among the early studies of cognitive development of deaf children were those conducted by Hans Furth and reported in a variety of journals and books during the 1960s and 1970s (e.g., Furth, 1966). Furth's goal was to understand the relation of cognition and language—or, rather, the lack of it—in deaf children. That is, at the time these studies were being conducted, sign language was not formally taught in schools and was acquired by deaf children only via their association with other deaf children and adults. As a result, Furth saw his work as being conducted with children who *"do not acquire functional language competence*, even after undergoing many years of intensive training" (Furth, 1966, p. 13).

Simple Concept Learning

Consistent with the methodologies of human experimental psychology during the 1950s and early 1960s, Furth, Oléron, and others conducted a variety of studies that examined the acquisition of simple single- or multidimensional concepts. Many of these studies involved nonverbal stimuli and responses and employed transfer tasks in which concepts were "learned" (actually, "discovered") through the use of trial-and-error learning. The nonverbal tasks were intended to avoid any confounds due to deaf children's linguistic deficiencies, whereas the transfer tasks allowed investigators to ensure that a child understood a task before beginning the more complex test phase of the experiment.

Oléron (1953), for example, had deaf adolescents sort a set of 27 stimulus cards that differed in the color, number, and identities of the shapes represented. The goal was to have the subjects successively sort the cards on each of the three dimensions, but Oléron found that only 6 of his 24 deaf subjects could perform the task, even with feedback. In contrast, 15 of 24 matched hearing subjects did so. Oléron concluded that deaf children think concretely, in terms of objects and attributes, rather than in terms of classes and interitem similarities and differences (see also Furth & Milgram, 1965).

If this study appears to be an underestimate of the abilities of deaf 15-year-olds, consider another concept-learning task employed by Furth (1961a). Furth had deaf and matched hearing children, 7 to 12 years of age, learn the concepts of *sameness*, *symmetry* and *opposition*. In the sameness task, children saw sets of four circles, each circle containing two simple figures. The task required only choosing the circle in which the two figures were the same. On the symmetry task, children were shown pairs of geometric figures, one of which was symmetrical and one of which was not. The task was to choose the symmetrical one. Finally, in the opposition task, children were first shown a randomized subset of four wooden disks varying in diameter; if the experimenter pointed to the smallest, the child had to point to the largest, and vice versa. Once the child had acquired the opposition concept (if they did), there was a transfer task in which similar trials were given on the dimensions of volume, length, number, brightness, position on a circle, or sandpaper texture (from smoothest to roughest).

On the sameness and symmetry tasks, Furth found no reliable differences between the deaf and hearing groups. On both tasks the deaf outperformed the hearing at ages 7 to 10 years, whereas the hearing outperformed the deaf at ages 11 and 12. In contrast, the deaf children performed less well than the hearing at all ages on the opposition task. From Furth's (post hoc) perspective, the opposition problem differed from the other two in that "opposite" is most often encountered in verbal contexts, thus explaining hearing children's advantage in that task.

To all outward appearances, the opposition task certainly appears to be nonverbal. Borrowing from Oléron, however, it also differs from the other two tasks in being the only one that required a *relational* response, dependent on the initial behavior of the experimenter and not just the characteristics of the stimuli themselves. It thus may be that there is some difficulty in integrating and maintaining the larger concept over the particular stimuli involved (Ottem, 1980) (see Chapter 9).

One frequent explanation for results of the sort presented by both Oléron (1953) and Furth (1961a) is that deaf children are distracted by irrelevant stimulus dimensions (cf. Youniss & Furth, 1970). That is, the problem may not be that deaf children are unable to form concepts or categories but that the dimension on which they are to form them is not as obvious as it might be for hearing children. This misdirection could result either from of a lack of verbal mediation (i.e., similar objects get the same category name) (Liben, 1979) or from a lack of experiential diversity in which such concepts might be acquired (Furth, 1966). Looking ahead, a study by Ottem (1980) indicated that deaf children appear to perform comparably to hearing peers when a response based on a single dimension is required, but that performance drops off when multiple dimensions or attributes are involved. This suggestion brings to the fore deaf children's abilities to *decenter* from a single dimension and not to be governed by unidimensional appearances of things. As these abilities lie at the heart of *conservation*, a topic of considerable interest to researchers involved with deaf children, several key findings in this domain should be considered. Throughout this discussion, the underlying themes are the extent to which deaf children are constrained by the visible and concrete and the degree to which more general and abstract concepts might depend on linguistic mediation.

The Origins of Studies of Intelligence in Deaf Children

The focus on deaf and hearing children's conservation performance, beginning around the mid-1960s, derived from the developmental psychology of Jean Piaget. Within his framework for intellectual development, young children were described as passing through a sequence of developmental periods characterized by qualitative changes in cognition. Although particular aspects of the theory can be debated on several dimensions (e.g., Siegel & Brainerd, 1978), Piaget's writings on cognitive development had a profound impact on the study of children's thinking. Of particular interest here are three periods of cognitive growth that were seen to take children from immature, subjective modes of thought to the mature, *operational* thinking of an adult. The theoretical underpinnings and implications of these periods are not of issue here, although they are essential for any comprehensive understanding of cognitive development (for complete coverage see Ginsburg & Opper, 1979). What is important for the present purposes is an understanding of the sequence of qualitative changes in cognitive ability observed as children gain experience and the implications of findings indicating differences between deaf and hearing children on several relevant dimensions.

For Piaget, it was the progression of cognitive development that was important, not the precise age at which particular children reached particular levels of functioning. Following infancy, children from approximately age 2 to age 7 were seen to be *preoperational* in their thinking. At this stage they were described more in terms of what they could not do than what they could, a position clearly out of step with North American psychology of the "modern" era. [For some "old school" views on deaf children see Myklebust (1960) and Oléron (1953).] Most notably, preoperational children are characterized as being *egocentric*—unable to consider the world from alternative perspectives—and constrained by *perceived appearances*. Because children focus on states rather than changes during this period of development they are unable to mentally reverse transformations or to recognize that something remains the same despite a change in its appearance (hence preschoolers' frequent fear of Halloween masks on familiar people). Although the discussion here concerns cognitive development, it should be apparent that changes in thinking along the lines suggested by Piaget also bear directly on social interactions, as they determine children's abilities to understand the bases of interpersonal behavior (e.g., Cates & Shontz, 1990) (see Chapter 4).

At the outset, it should be recognized that deaf children might be expected to be at a particular disadvantage, relative to hearing peers, during the preoperational period of cognitive development. For one thing, as Chapter 3 indicated, young deaf children are more restrained in their early experiences by their frequently overcontrolling, hearing parents. More broadly, however, the lack of hearing could be an especially potent impediment to children's recognition of constancy during perceived changes. Returning to Halloween, for example, deaf children would not have the reassuring experience of hearing mother's voice from underneath her witch's mask and would not hear the giggles of other young children from underneath their ghost and Teenage Mutant Ninja Turtle costumes. In more explicitly cognitively related situations, they frequently would not have the benefit of parental descriptions accompanying perceptual change ("Let's put *that* juice in this other glass") or the verbal rationale underlying qualitative changes in the environment. The latter qualification is particularly important when it is recalled that most hearing parents who have some sign language skill are limited to relatively concrete, pragmatic vocabularies and are largely unequipped to deal with children's naive questions of epistemology and teleology.

During the period of *concrete operations*, roughly between ages 7 and 11, mental representations are no longer confined to "snapshots" of appearances, but children come to be able to internally manipulate, compensate, and recognize identities of things despite perceived changes. Taken together, these abilities allow concrete operational children to *conserve*, that is, to maintain stability by recognizing relations among things, states, and actions. It is out of this period that *formal operations* emerge, as children are able to go beyond mental operations on concrete objects and events and can generate hypotheses about relations and perform "mental experiments," also known as abstract reasoning. According to Piaget, most hearing children achieve formal operations between the ages of 11 and 15 years. Several investigators, however, including Furth (1973), have argued that deaf children are unlikely ever to reach that level of cognitive performance but remain limited to concrete functioning in social interaction as well as cognition. To understand this claim, we can consider a representative sample of the many relevant studies conducted with deaf children to determine their status within the Piagetian framework of development.

Conservation Performance of Deaf Children

The ability of children to succeed in a conservation task is perhaps the hallmark of cognition in Piaget's theory because it reveals the presence or absence of operational thinking. At a less theoretical level, conservation tasks indicate children's understanding of the concepts underlying what they see, in contrast to their acceptance of the physical world solely in terms of its perceived attributes. In a conservation of weight task, for example, children are shown two identical balls of clay and routinely judge them as equal in weight. Then, one of the balls in changed in full view of the child, perhaps by breaking it into pieces, flattening it into a disk, or rolling it into a "snake." The question of which clay is heavier is then posed. With the standard form of the task, children are asked simply whether the changed clay is heavier, lighter, or the same weight as the unchanged clay; and they are asked to justify their answers. This task thus requires an understanding of weight and the ability to ignore changes in shape that do not affect the amount of substance, but it also entails an understanding of the words (or signs) "heavier," "lighter," and "same." To the extent that deaf children are more reliant than hearing age-mates on perceptual observations (versus conceptual understanding), they would be expected to perform less well on tasks of this sort (Oléron, 1953).

In one of the earliest studies of deaf children's conservation skills, Furth (1964) tested 22 deaf 8-year-olds together with a hearing control group of 6- and 8-year-olds. In order to avoid language confounds, Furth developed a nonverbal version of the task in which children could move their hands horizontally for "same weight" or lower one hand or the other to indicate that one of two pieces of clay held by the experimenter was heavier. After training on this task, he introduced nine transformations to one of two balls of clay. Three of the transformations were the critical test trials: a ball versus a snake, a ball versus a ring, and a disk versus a ring. Overall, Furth found that the 8-year-old deaf children correctly said "same" (i.e., conserved) on 45.5% of the trials. In comparison, the hearing 6-year-olds did so on 41.4% of the trials, and the hearing 8-year-olds responded correctly on 90% of the trials.

Furth (1966) reported similar results in a study of liquid conservation. The standard task involves showing a child two equal beakers of liquid and then pouring the contents of one into a taller, thinner beaker or a shallow, wider one. Judgments of "sameness" are easily obtained with the identical beakers, but judgments that the posttransformation beaker with the higher liquid level has "more" indicates failure to decenter from the height dimension and failure to conserve liquid. In Furth's version of the task, children initially were trained to point to the one of two piles of beans that had "more" or to make the sign SAME if the piles had the same amount. Transferring to the beaker task, children were asked "Which glass has more water?" or "Which has more to drink?" a difference that is of some importance later.

It is noteworthy that Furth (1966) reported that the liquid conservation task was first conducted with 8- to 10-year-old deaf children, but that the experiment had to be abandoned when all but one of the subjects failed to master the bean-pile task. Eventually, he tested one group of deaf 12- to 14-year-olds and another group aged 16 years and older. The hearing control groups were aged 9 to 10 and 11 to 12 years. Examining conservation on two critical trials, Furth found that the success rate of the deaf 12- to 14-year-olds was 45%, and that of the age 16+ deaf group was 100%. In contrast, the 9- to 10-year-old and 11- to 12-year-old hearing groups performed at 70% and 95%, respectively.

Furth's findings in both of these experiments indicated that deaf children's conservation performance lagged behind hearing peers by 2 to 4 years. Because the nonverbal versions of the tasks ruled out any linguistic confounds, Furth (1966) concluded that deaf children's deficits in concrete operational thinking resulted from their lack of experiential diversity in the real world. However, Furth attributed much of deaf children's lack of experience to their language deficits because lack of language skills limits deaf children's opportunities for developmental interactions.

In contrast, the argument put forward by Oléron (1953), consistent with later discussions by Bronowski and Bellugi (1970) and Marschark (1988a), was that language has a more direct effect on cognitive growth because it differentially allows explicit and implicit acquisition of categories and other conceptual relations. The difference between these two positions is an important one, although it is possible that both, or neither, might be correct.

One study particularly relevant to this issue was reported by Rittenhouse and Spiro (1979). Their primary interest was the role of language in conservation, and they suggested that deaf children's difficulty with conservation tasks was a consequence of the linguistic demands of such tasks, although Furth (1964, 1966) had shown otherwise. Rittenhouse and Spiro administered conservation tasks to groups of 36 hearing 4- to 16-year-olds and 40 prelingually and profoundly deaf 7- to 19-year-olds; 24 of the deaf students attended day schools and 16 attended state residential schools.

In an attempt to examine the effects of linguistic differences between their two deaf groups, Rittenhouse and Spiro used both standard and *attribute-specific* instructions. The latter clearly specified the dimension of interest, as in Furth's (1966) question of "Which has more to drink?" Directions of this sort were employed in conservation tasks involving number, weight, liquid, and volume. With the standard instructions, Rittenhouse and Spiro found that 31% of the hearing children and 17% of the day school deaf children could conserve on all four tasks, whereas none of the residential school children could do so. Individual task performance was not reported, however, so it is unclear whether the groups differed on one, particularly difficult test, or across the board. As expected, Rittenhouse and Spiro's attribute-specific instructions significantly improved performance in all three of the groups: 61% of the hearing children succeeded in passing all four conservation tasks under those instructions, whereas 50% of the day-school children and 38% of the residential school students did so. In contrast to Furth's findings, the use of dimension-explicit instructions largely eliminated significant differences among the groups (the hearing group marginally outperformed the residential group, $p \leq .06$).

Rittenhouse and Spiro concluded from their findings that characteristics unique to day-school experiences contribute to conservation comprehension in ways not available to deaf children who attend residential schools (see also Rittenhouse & Kenyon, 1991). They suggested, in particular, that the gestural nature of "the substantial amount of non-oral behavior to which deaf students in state residential schools are exposed to [*sic*] because of the predominant use of sign language . . . [leads to] cognitive confusion in the deaf student" (p. 509). The locus of such confusion is unclear from their results, however, and its relation to tasks involving relatively iconic signs (e.g., MORE in conservation of number, LESS in conservation of liquid) versus noniconic signs was not discussed.[2] Given the wide age ranges involved in the study, it is unfortunate that Rittenhouse and Spiro did not report any age effects. In fact, a large number of subjects in both deaf and hearing groups should have been well into or beyond the period of concrete operations and should have had little trouble with the tasks.

There are two further aspects of Rittenhouse and Spiro's (1979) results that are particularly interesting in the present context. One of them is the difference in performance observed between the day-school and residential school children. The other is the difference between their results and those of earlier studies, which had indicated significant lags in conservation performance by deaf relative to hearing children. In fact, these two findings might be closely related. Considering the day school–residential school difference, it now seems unlikely that Rittenhouse and Spiro's results can be ascribed to a deficiency on the part of children in manual communication settings. Lister, Leach, and Wesencraft (1988) examined the conservation performance of two groups of deaf children: a residential group with moderate to profound hearing losses and a day-school group with severe to profound losses. The residential group, consisting of 24 children aged 7 to 14 years (mean 12;8), and the day-school group, consisting of 28 children aged 4;6 to 16;0 (mean 11;8), were compared to a group of younger, normally hearing children aged 4;6 to 11;2 (mean 8;10). The study was conducted in England, and all deaf children were enrolled in oral programs. Thus tasks on conservation of number, substance, length, weight, area, and volume were given in their standard, oral form. This fact is important to the Rittenhouse and Spiro (1979) findings because Lister et al. found that both groups of deaf children lagged behind the younger hearing children by 3 to 4 years. At the same time, the deaf and hearing groups showed the same ordering of conservation performance across tasks.

The Lister et al. (1988) results from exclusively oral deaf children suggest that manual communication is unlikely to be the locus of conservation failure in North American deaf children. Consistent with this conclusion, Rittenhouse and Kenyon (1991) found that conservation performance was unrelated to hearing loss and did not differ in groups of children enrolled in Cued Speech versus oral programs. Still unclear, however, is the extent to which language fluency, rather than language modality, might be linked to conservation performance as well as other cognitive skills. This issue must be considered at two levels. At a broad level, those deaf children with better language skills are frequently those with greater parental involvement in their education, more experiential diversity, and a greater likelihood of having received earlier or more intensive educational intervention. Children with such backgrounds also appear more frequently in recent studies than they did in studies conducted 25 years ago. At a more specific level, those children with better language skills also are likely to have more productive interactions with other individuals and with printed media (see Chapter 11). At both of these levels, language no doubt contributes to cognitive development in deaf children, but the two typically are too intertwined to be considered separately. There are, however, several studies that have addressed the question of the role of language fluency in deaf children's conservation performance as well as its broader impact on their cognitive development.

Language Fluency and Cognitive Performance

Watts (1979) examined developmental changes in conservation (of number, weight, length, substance, and area), "horizontality" (i.e., water-level problems), and social thinking, as well as in language development. The study involved 70 "partially hearing" children, 70 "deaf" children, and 70 hearing children, all between 10 and

16 years of age. Watts reported that, overall, his results were consistent with find-ings from earlier studies suggesting that there is no functional relation between "verbal" (viz., *oral and written*) language and other cognitive processes. Watts found that up to age 14 conservation performance increased from the deaf children to the partially hearing children to the hearing children; whereas after age 14 the ordering of performance indicated that the deaf children fell between the other two groups. Insofar as the improved performance of the deaf group was not accompa-nied by relative increases in reading comprehension or writing ability, Watts con-cluded that the observed deficits in cognitive performance could not be ascribed to "linguistic deficiency." This conclusion was supported by the finding that deaf and partially hearing children performed equally well on the social thinking task (which required placing pictures in a social sequence), despite the superior language abili-ties of the partially hearing group. (The water-level problem showed no differences among the groups.)

Because Watts's subjects apparently were all oral (tested in England), his accep-tance of reading and writing as indicators of "linguistic ability" may have some validity. Nevertheless, it may be premature to conclude, as he did, that language has no direct role in cognitive development. Watts opted for an experiential deficiency hypothesis to explain increases in cognitive performance in the absence of increases in language performance. No evidence is provided concerning how the experiential deficiencies of the deaf children were remedied relative to the partially hearing chil-dren, however, nor is it clear what *nonlinguistic* experiences the partially hearing children had that produced their initial cognitive advantage.

Beyond Watts's (1979) study, there are several other examinations of the rela-tionship of language and cognitive functioning in deaf children, although most are not without difficulties of interpretation. Parasnis and Long (1979), for example, examined "concrete reasoning" (using the Spatial Relations Test, which requires mental paper-folding), abstract reasoning (via the Abstract Reasoning Test), and language abilities in 144 profoundly deaf freshman at the National Technical Institute for the Deaf (NTID). The only reliable difference on the cognitive tests between the performance of deaf students and 12th grade hearing norms was that the deaf males performed below the hearing male norms on the test of abstract rea-soning. Although Parasnis and Long did not discuss the relations among their vari-ous measures in any detail, examination of their Table 4 (p. 884) reveals that hear-ing loss was related to reading, writing, and abstract reasoning in males. Furthermore, whereas manual reception ability was not related to performance on either cognitive task, Simultaneous Communication (SC) reception but not Manual Communication (MC) reception abilities was strongly related to both concrete and abstract reasoning for both males and females. This pattern of results suggests that better speech comprehension is related to better cognitive functioning even in col-lege students (who represent a select group of deaf individuals).

Additional support for this conclusion is evident in the results of a study by Arnold and Walter (1979), also involving NTID students. They compared a group of profoundly deaf students to a group of hearing students who were training to become sign language interpreters. The two groups did not differ reliably in their reception skills for either lip-reading or Manually Coded English (MCE). However, the deaf students performed significantly worse on several tasks drawn from the Differential Aptitude Test battery, including tests of abstract reasoning, verbal reasoning, mechanical reasoning, and clerical speed. Rather than attributing those differences to any "central" cognitive differences between the two groups, Arnold and Walter concluded that the poor performance of the deaf students "may be explained by the contribution of language to performance in these non-verbal tests, in part through the printed instructions" (p. 194; cf. Rittenhouse & Spiro, 1979). Still at issue is whether there is a more direct link in young deaf children between language abilities and performance on various cognitive tests (rather than performance IQs).

Dolman (1983) specifically investigated the relation between syntactic comprehension and cognitive development, as assessed by tests of conservation, classification, seriation, and numeration. He tested fifty-nine 7- to 15-year-olds with severe to profound hearing losses and found that those children who had achieved concrete operations—using the specific dimension instructions of Rittenhouse and Spiro (1979)—also had better syntactic skills. In a more specific evaluation of the language hypothesis, Dolman compared the performance of 7 deaf children who had consistent, early experience with American Sign Language (ASL) learned from their deaf parents; 17 who had strong MCE backgrounds (from hearing parents); and 20 others who had no consistent language (NCL) backgrounds.

No difference was observed in the receptive grammar abilities of the ASL and MCE groups, and only the ASL group scored significantly higher than the NCL group. Conservation was also superior in the ASL group relative to the NCL group, but there were no other differences between groups on conservation or any other test. Dolman was careful not to suggest any causal relation between language and concrete operations but noted that advances in cognitive development are either accompanied or predated by advances in language development (with regard to linguistic development during the sensorimotor period see also Bonvillian, Orlansky, Novak, & Folven, 1983b). It should be noted, however, that scores on the syntactic test were uniformly low across the three groups, as the ASL and MCE groups were correct on 19% of the trials and the NCL group on 17% of the trials (mean conservation scores in the three groups were not presented). Any suggestion that conservation is related to language as indexed by syntactic comprehension therefore would be highly suspect.

If the preceding studies *suggest* that there is some implicit bias in the literature to treat oral or written ability as *language* ability, a study by Sharpe (1985) makes the issue explicit. Citing Furth's earlier claims that deaf children are unlikely ever to reach the stage of formal operations, Sharpe raised the nagging issue of why fluency in manual communication does not lead to deaf children's full competence in academic achievement relative to their hearing peers. In particular, she argued that the mode of language, manual versus oral, may be more important for cognitive development than is language fluency. "This theoretical premise reflects the proposition that the oral-aural mode uniquely facilitates the development of cognition because it facilitates the perception of contrast more effectively than any other mode" (Sharpe, 1985, p. 40; cf. Furth, 1961a).

Sharpe examined the formal-operational ability to solve analogy problems

(A:B::C:?) in a group of 12 congenitally, profoundly deaf students and 12 hearing students, all aged 14 to 19 years. When 22 analogies were presented in word form (with vocabulary controlled) and 22 in picture form, the hearing students significantly outscored their deaf age-mates on both tasks. Sharpe claimed that these results are best accounted for in terms of visual-gestural language being inferior to oral-aural language for cognitive development. Lacking from her study, however, is the obvious control group of oral deaf students who would possess the oral-aural mode but generally have less language fluency than hearing peers. Moreover, evidence from studies with younger hearing children learning ASL as a first language is at odds with Sharpe's position (e.g., Bonvillian et al., 1983b). In any case, without an oral deaf comparison group, her conclusion seems premature at best.

One relevant study has been done, however, by Parasnis (1983a). She compared the concrete and abstract reasoning skills (as per Parasnis & Long, 1979) of (1) deaf students who learned ASL early from their deaf parents; (2) deaf students who had learned to sign only later, between the ages of 6 and 12, and had hearing parents; and (3) a group of hearing students with hearing parents. Overall, Parasnis found no differences among the groups nor any interactions with gender on either of the cognitive tests. As in the Parasnis and Long (1979) study, abstract reasoning was related to SC but not MC receptive skills. Abstract reasoning was strongly related to reading only in the ASL group ($r = .69$), whereas it was strongly related to writing only in the delayed language group ($r = .51$). Concrete, spatial reasoning was not related to either in any group. Overall, the finding that the ASL and delayed language groups did not differ in their concrete or abstract reasoning skills suggested to Parasnis that parental deafness and early exposure to manual communication do not have differential effects on the cognitive abilities of deaf children.

Parasnis's view of her results thus contrasts with the results and conclusions of Sharpe's (1985) study. The limiting factor in the comparison, of course, is the fact that Sharpe examined younger children, and Parasnis examined NTID college students. Assuming that Sharpe's sample was more representative of deaf children than was that of Parasnis, the differences in their results have two possible explanations: (1) The manual versus oral difference in cognitive ability exists at an early age but is eliminated by college age (cf. Meier & Newport, 1990); or (2) those deaf children with superior reading and writing skills (i.e., those who will attend college) tend to have better cognitive skills than non-college-bound deaf peers, and such abilities are roughly comparable to those of hearing peers. A less interesting, third alternative would be that the Sharpe and Parasnis tasks simply tapped different abilities.

Nonverbal Factors in Deaf Children's Cognitive Performance?

At present, there appears to be no strong reason to prefer any of the above explanations for the Sharpe–Parasnis discrepancy, although there is some tangential evidence concerning nonverbal factors that bears on the issue. As is shown in chapters to follow, there appear to be differences between deaf and hearing children in several domains in which visual and verbal short-term memories are involved. Consistent with the general direction of those findings are the findings of Chovan et al. (1988), cited earlier, demonstrating that deaf middle-school and high-school children were more likely than hearing children to use visual strategies for cognitive tasks and showed faster reaction times on visual tasks. There were no consistent differences between TC and oral deaf groups within their deaf sample.

Youniss and Robertson (1970) examined the concrete operational abilities of young deaf children to take alternative perspectives in a nonverbal task. They asked younger (8;9 to 9;11) and older (11;0 to 12;11) groups of severely to profoundly deaf children and hearing controls (matched on IQ) to judge how a display would look from seven perspectives other than the one that was directly visible. Youniss and Robertson found no differences between the deaf and hearing groups at either age level, although the use of a multiple-choice test likely made the task simpler than the more standard Piagetian-type task.

The above studies, together with the conservation studies involving explicit, dimension-specific instructions appear to indicate that even if the cognitive performance of deaf children does not depend on verbal fluency it may be enhanced by language skill (or its correlates) and certainly can be disrupted by failure to understand verbal stimuli or verbal instructions. At the same time, studies such as that of Furth (1964), showing lags in conservation abilities in nonverbal tasks, suggest that there are factors involved in deaf children's concrete and abstract reasoning abilities that have not yet been identified.

There is also another thread running through most of studies described in this chapter that bears not on language abilities but on short-term memory and attentional factors. Ottem (1980) reexamined 51 "nonverbal" studies, conducted with deaf children and adults from 1917 to 1975. They included evaluations of discrimination learning, associative learning, memory, rule learning, sorting, and Piagetian tasks. Consistently across these studies, Ottem found that performance of deaf and hearing subjects was essentially equivalent when tasks required subjects to show their understanding by referring to a single dimension of the stimuli (e.g., number). When the task required the resolution of two or more dimensions (e.g., length and number), deaf subjects performed more poorly than the controls, presumably, according to Ottem, because of a tendency to center on a single aspect of the task situation in communication.

This distinction among nonverbal cognitive tasks focuses on the content of responses required by deaf subjects, not the cognitive competencies assumed to underlie such responses. Thus in a liquid conservation task in which the single dimension of *how much* is emphasized by asking a child which of two amounts would be better if they were thirsty, deaf and hearing children perform equally well, just as hearing preschool children have been shown to perform well in this task despite their presumably being in a preoperational period of development. In contrast, when deaf children have to "balance" differences in liquid height and width when deciding on which has *more*, they routinely perform below hearing peers. Similarly, for short-term memory tasks in which deaf children have to refer to only a single datum, as with sequencing in the Knox Cube Test (see Chapter 8), performance is comparable to that of hearing children. However, when two or more dimensions must be maintained in memory, as when both the identity and sequence of digits must be retained in a digit span task, deaf children's performance is inferior to that of hearing children (cf. Perfetti & Goldman, 1976).

Another possible locus of Ottem's findings lies in the ability of deaf children to allocate their attention during a cognitive (or social or academic) task. A tendency toward socialized impulsivity coupled with possible neurological concomitants of deafness (see Chapters 2 and 12) in many deaf children would contribute to difficulties of attention allocation and give some ideas about avenues for overcoming such problems. Alternatively, Ottem's observation of deaf children's disadvantages in responding to tasks that require retention or manipulation of multiple stimulus dimensions may indicate a limited capacity in deaf children's short-term memories or the use of alternative coding strategies that might not be adaptive for particular tasks. Both of these alternatives could implicate the range and diversity of deaf children's cognitive experience, and both could have profound impacts on academic achievement. In the next two chapters, therefore, attention is turned to consideration of deaf children's cognitive functioning in the context of memory tasks. Short-term memory is considered first so as to address the issues raised above. Long-term memory is then considered so as to evaluate the role of deaf children's knowledge of the world in cognitive functioning and to set the stage for consideration of reading and writing abilities (see Chapter 11) within the school setting.

Summary

Early investigations of deaf children's intellectual functioning routinely found it to lag behind that of hearing peers by several years. Many of the standardized tests involved, however, required comprehension of English, and most were conducted during a period when language and academic performance of most deaf children was far below current levels. More recently, a variety of intelligence tests and other tests of cognitive ability have been developed that depend only on nonverbal, performance measures.

Within the field of intelligence testing, there are a variety of studies indicating that even on the nonverbal, performance scales of standardized tests, such as the WISC-R, deaf children score consistently (and sometimes significantly) below hearing age-mates, but they show qualitatively the same "constellation" of cognitive abilities. Other studies, typically using tests designed specifically with deaf children in mind (e.g., the HNTLA), have shown deaf children to score comparably to hearing children in terms of their total scores but to evidence qualitative differences in the interrelations among their abilities. These differences are particularly evident in young deaf children, who are likely to be less competent in their language abilities as well as in their cognitive flexibility.

The question of whether language is, in fact, independent of intelligence or IQ scores is made more confusing rather than clearer by evaluating of deaf children. The problem is that those deaf children who are most severely lacking in language abilities are also likely to be different from other deaf (and hearing) children in other ways as well, including the diversity of their early experiences, parent–child and child–peer relationships, and ability to benefit from schooling (e.g., via reading).

Research that has focused on specific aspects of cognitive development, such as conservation, classification, and concept learning, similarly has yielded contradictory and confusing results. Explicit, nonverbal paradigms sometimes have eliminated differences between deaf and hearing children on these tasks, but in other cases significant differences have remained. Delays in these cognitive domains have been demonstrated in children who have been trained in oral settings, as well as those who have been trained in more manual settings.

One would expect that deaf children of deaf parents should perform "normally" on most cognitive tasks, but these expectations do not materialize. Such findings suggest that there are factors beyond the normal communication difficulties observed in hearing parent–deaf child dyads that contribute to delays in deaf children's cognitive development and thus appear to rule out any strong link between language and cognitive abilities in deaf children. However, it may be that the ranges of language skill examined have been too narrow to evaluate the issue fairly. Yet to be determined is the extent to which other differences between deaf children with deaf parents and deaf children with hearing parents may affect cognitive development. Of primary interest in this regard would be the quality and quantity of interactions that (implicitly or explicitly) foster various components of cognitive growth, such as concept learning, classification, conservation, and metacognitive abilities (e.g., Krinsky, 1990).

As the following chapters indicate, there are indeed marked differences in the processing strategies employed by deaf and hearing children that might provide both advantages and disadvantages for deaf children in various domains. One emerging possibility pertaining to cognitive development and language development is that deaf children and hearing children might differ either in the attentional strategies devoted to cognitive processing or in the functional characteristics of their short-term memories. Differences in the abilities of deaf and hearing children to retain or integrate verbal and nonverbal information over short periods, coupled with less experience in considering alternative solutions to problems, may have implications for social functioning as well as cognitive and linguistic functioning. Regardless of whether such divergence represents differences or deficiencies relative to hearing peers, alternative information processing styles are likely to effect differences in performance in academic settings, with implications for achievement and success across a variety of domains.

Notes

1. The assumption here is that Vernon intended to restrict this conclusion only to aural-oral language rather than to all languages. Times and terminology have changed, however, and sign language is now well established as a verbal, if nonvocal, language. It is doubtful that a case could be made for a complete independence of language and conceptual ability in any serious sense.

2. Schwam (1980) attempted to examine the relation of sign iconicity and liquid conservation in deaf children and found a reversal of the usual finding with hearing children that "more" is easier than "less." However, Schwam used "the non-iconic sign 'MORE,'" which sometimes has only an nominal meaning (e.g., I WANT MORE) rather than the comparative MORE (as in THIS HAS MORE THAN THAT). The relatively poor performance of MORE relative to the iconic LESS thus could be artifactual.

8

Short-Term Memory: Development of Memory Coding

Studies of human cognition have revealed a distinction between *short-term memory* (*working memory*) and *long-term memory*. Most generally, short-term memory refers to the dynamic system that "contains" new information for several seconds after input and from which that information either is "transferred" to some more permanent memory store or is forgotten. Short-term memory is also the "work space" into which information is retrieved from "storage" and manipulated in contexts that require the use of existing knowledge. Long-term memory, in contrast, refers to that "permanent memory store," the "residence" of existing knowledge to which new information may pass after its brief stay in short-term memory. Descriptions of this sort, of course, represent oversimplifications of rather complex mechanisms and issues. Nevertheless, these definitions suit the present purposes until they are filled in with more detail in this chapter and the following one.

One well-documented difference between short- and long-term memory, however, is essential for understanding the possible qualitative divergence in cognitive functioning of deaf and hearing children suggested in Chapter 7. That difference is best described in terms of the types of information involved in short- and long-term memory processing. In particular, short-term memory generally is seen as operating at a relatively superficial level, involving primarily physical characteristics of to-be-remembered information. Short-term memory thus tends not to be affected by the meanings of incoming information, except insofar as more meaningful information tends to be more familiar and thus more readily interfaced with long-term memory (for discussion see Paivio & Begg, 1981). Instead, short-term memory is most obviously characterized in terms of its susceptibility to interference from stimuli that look the same, sound the same, or are motorically made the same. In particular, for hearing individuals, short-term memory for verbal materials, whether presented in print or orally, usually involves a sequential articulatory or phonological code (Baddeley, 1986).

Meaning, on the other hand, is what long-term memory is all about. A variety of studies have shown that, for the most part, the superficial characteristics of to-be-learned information are forgotten rather quickly, whereas meaning, gist, or concepts are retained. This distinction between the types of information most central to short-versus long-term memory highlights another distinction relevant to memory research and especially to research involving deaf children: the difference between *memory codes* or *mental representations* and the *processes* and *strategies* that operate on them. In particular, the present chapter focuses on questions concerning the memory codes that deaf children apply in short-term memory contexts. The next chapter, focusing on long-term memory, considers the memory strategies deaf children use to maximize their performance. [For a general overview of research in memory development, see Kail (1990).]

Why do we need a separate chapter for short-term memory? As becomes evident below, short-term memory functioning seems to have attracted more attention in deaf children than in hearing children. For the most part, this interest derives from questions about the development of short-term memory codes in the absence of aural-oral language. The assumption that deaf children do not have available the acoustic, articulatory, or phonological codes that underlie short-term memory in hearing individuals raises the question of whether there are alternative codes that can support retention over brief intervals equally well. Examination of the relevant literature provides insights into several broader issues concerning the psychological development of deaf children.

On Memory Development

Before evaluating the research on short- and long-term memory performance of deaf children, two important issues should be outlined for later consideration. One issue concerns the nature of the materials involved in testing memory of deaf children. Most memory studies with older children and adults (both deaf and hearing) involve to-be-learned materials printed (or spoken) in English. The fact that deaf children frequently recall less than hearing peers on such tests perhaps should not be surprising insofar as oral language can be considered a second language for most of them (Belmont & Karchmer, 1978; Charrow & Fletcher, 1974). Although researchers interested in the memories of normal, hearing adults are rarely so foolish as to use materials that are unfamiliar to their subjects (unless that is the focus of their investigation), it has not been at all clear how the findings from such research with deaf children should be interpreted. The sword cuts both ways; however. If it is unclear what we should conclude when deaf children appear inferior to hearing peers in tests of memory for English, it is also unclear what we should conclude when their nonverbal memories are comparable. The deafness literature is rife with examples of explicit and implicit rejections of apparent performance differences that go against deaf children while accepting those in their favor. With the possible exception of literature concerning IQ scores (see Chapter 7), the memory literature is clearly the worst offender in this regard.

One other problem when interpreting this literature is that many studies have compared deaf children's memory performance with that of younger hearing children. Such methodological deviance arises in part from the desire to equate deaf and hearing children on linguistic abilities, but explicit evaluations of language skill are rarely made. At the same time, young deaf children often lack sufficient language or attention spans to perform adequately in the artificial situations demanded by most short-term memory tests (and tests of *implicit memory* have not yet been used with deaf children). Some of the problems created by these methodological confounds are solved by the use of nonverbal stimuli. Studies with deaf children uniformly have used visual stimuli in such tasks. Tactile, olfactory, and other memory stimuli also are available but thus far apparently have not been used.

Visual Short-Term Memory in Deaf Children

A variety of studies concerning short-term memory in deaf children have focused on their retention of simple nonverbal materials, such as colors, shapes, pictures, and digits. Using nonlinguistic stimuli, in fact, may not always prevent linguistic coding (Glucksberg & Krauss, 1967; Prytulak, 1971). Nevertheless, the goal of most of the studies reported in this section has been to examine deaf children's short-term memory codes and capacities in situations that seem unbiased with respect to possible differences in education, mode of communication, or language skills. In most cases, the related manipulations involve the retention of visual features rather than *meaning*. Insofar as visual processing has long been thought to be the "strong suit" of deaf children, this domain seems to be the appropriate place to start.

By far the most frequently cited investigation in this area, is Blair's (1957) comprehensive study of visual memory in deaf children. Because of the importance attributed to this study within the field, it is worthy of detailed consideration. His results are summarized in Table 8-1.

Blair's investigation involved 53 profoundly deaf children, aged 7;6 to 12;6, matched with a group of hearing children for age, gender, and nonverbal IQ. His visual memory battery included the Knox Cube Test, the Memory for Designs Test, and four memory span tests: digits forward, digits backward, a picture span task, and a dot pattern span (using dominos). Blair's primary hypothesis was that he would find evidence of *sensory compensation* in the deaf children. That is, because they lack hearing deaf children were expected to have augmented visuospatial abilities, leading to better visual short-term memory performance than their hearing agemates, a finding earlier reported by Mott (1899). In fact, Blair reported that deaf children's performance significantly surpassed that of their hearing peers only on the Knox Cube Test and the Memory for Designs Test.

In the Knox Cube Test, the experimenter taps a sequence on a set of four small

TABLE 8-1. Summary of Results from Blair's Study of Deaf and Hearing Children

	Mean Scores	
Test	Deaf Children ($n = 53$)	Hearing Children ($n = 53$)
Knox Cube	7.83	7.30
Memory for Designs	33.31	28.18
Forward Digit Span	2.92	4.75
Backward Digit Span	3.15	4.00
Picture Span	3.47	4.30
Domino Span	3.28	3.94

Source: Blair (1957).

cubes, and the child attempts to reproduce the sequence. Blair reported a "clear difference" in favor of the deaf students on that test (Table 8-1). The absolute difference is not a large one, however, and Blair did not report how many items were administered. The Memory for Designs Test involves a series of 13 individual geometric figures, each one viewed for 2 seconds before the subject is asked to draw it. The standardized scoring procedure and norms are based on an all-or-none decision about whether the design has been reproduced. Blair (1957), however, devised a new scoring system, allowing for partial credit. Unfortunately, he did not explain the scoring system, whether the designs were scored by an independent judge, the reliability of the system, or how a total score of 50 (p. 257) was possible with a 13-item test.

Although the results obtained by Blair on these two tests do not seem remarkable, they are important because he interpreted them as providing strong support for his sensory compensation hypothesis, and many subsequent investigators have accepted his interpretation. This conclusion seems especially surprising, however, in view of Blair's findings that on all four of the memory span tasks the hearing controls scored significantly higher than the deaf students (Table 8-1). In fact, Blair argued that *visual memory* per se does not differ in deaf (compared to hearing) children, but that deaf children are inferior on "abstract" or "conceptual" tasks. This interpretation was based on his assumption that memory span "involves the mental integration of a series of discrete yet related units into a meaningful sequence . . . in order that the sequence could be accurately reproduced . . . a relatively abstract type of mental process" (p. 260), whereas the other tasks involved "visual perceptual acts."

Beyond their apparent lack of face validity, Blair's conclusions are called into question by another aspect of his findings, not mentioned in the 1957 article but reported later by Myklebust (1960). Myklebust more fully described Blair's data, including the deaf and hearing children's performance on the 10 subscales of the Chicago Nonverbal Battery used to match them on IQ. In that context, Myklebust (pp. 67–71) expressed his concern about the fact that the hearing children significantly surpassed the deaf children on five of the ten Chicago scales, whereas the deaf children, as a group, never surpassed their hearing peers. In particular, he noted that the deaf children performed significantly worse than the hearing children on both of the subtests that involved geometric figures (Test 4: synthesizing geometric forms; and Test 5: noting details of geometric forms), as well as others that involved visual processing of meaningless stimuli. These results seem directly contrary to the sensory compensation account of Blair's (1957) performance data.

Another finding inconsistent with the sensory compensation position was provided by Goetzinger and Huber (1964). They asked deaf and hearing 14- to 18-year-olds to reproduce geometric designs from the Benton Visual Retention Test either immediately after viewing or after a 15-second delay. Although the two groups performed equally well on the immediate test (thus ruling out any visual deficits), the deaf students scored significantly below their hearing age-mates in reproducing the designs after the delay (see also Dodd, Hobson, Brasher, & Campbell, 1983; McDaniel, 1980; McGurk & Saqi, 1986). Goetzinger and Huber thus concluded that visual memory abilities of deaf children are inferior to those of hearing age-mates.

One alternative to the sensory compensation explanation for Blair's (1957) findings is the linguistic coding hypothesis, or the *inner speech hypothesis*, (Conrad, 1979). Because of the central role that verbal-linguistic coding appears to play in many short-term memory tasks involving hearing individuals (see Baddeley, 1986), a variety of authors have suggested that short-term retention of sequential information might be particularly difficult for deaf children or others who are less fluent in their language skills (e.g., Conrad, 1979; O'Connor & Hermelin, 1973b). The linguistic coding hypothesis would fit well with Blair's (1957) finding that memory span scores were the only ones that were consistently related to reading scores. It also would be consistent with his finding that, in contrast to the hearing children tested (and the usual pattern of results), the deaf children in his study showed greater backward digit spans than forward digit spans (see also O'Connor & Hermelin, 1976, described in the next section).

Generally, backward digit spans are presumed to be remembered via the use of a visual image code, whereas forward spans are remembered via a verbal code (see following section). Reduced dependence on verbal coding thus could be partially responsible for Blair's digit span results, although it is unclear why a visual image code could not have been used for forward as well as backward spans. Note, however, that the linguistic coding hypothesis rests on the assumption that deaf children lack linguistic coding abilities simply because they lack oral language (e.g., O'Connor & Hermelin, 1973b, p. 441; cf. Waters & Doehring, 1990). This assumption may be appropriate for deaf children who lack *any* language training (but see Chapter 6 for evidence that even they do not lack symbolic coding systems), but it certainly does not apply to most deaf children.

Blair's (1957) finding of longer memory spans in hearing children than in deaf children was unsurprising at the time, largely because it was consistent with earlier digit span results obtained in studies by Pintner and Patterson (1917) and others (see also Belmont & Karchmer, 1978; Waters & Doehring, 1990). Pintner and Patterson, for example, assessed digit spans in 482 deaf people, 7 to 26 years of age. Their results are well summarized by the finding that not a single one of their deaf subjects reached a digit span equal to that of hearing 7-year-olds, according to available norms.

The Pintner and Patterson (1917) study is now more than seven decades old, but their findings are still replicable. In a study of reading abilities of orally trained deaf children, for example, Waters and Doehring (1990) examined the memory spans of severely and profoundly deaf children (see Chapter 11 for discussion of the reading results). Their 54 subjects, ranging in age from 7 to 20 years, were administered printed and oral versions of memory span tasks for digits, words, and sentences. In all cases, those deaf children scored well behind hearing peers according to available norms (see also Belmont & Karchmer, 1978). Such findings, together with those reported by Blair (1957) and others, suggest that deaf children are at a disadvantage regarding cognitive or academic skills that depend on sequential (temporal) short-term memory. At the same time, deaf children may make use of other short-term memory codes that facilitate their performance in particular tasks. Visual-spatial coding seems one likely alternative in this context, and the issue has undergone extensive investigation.

Temporal and Spatial Bases of Sequential Coding in Short-Term Memory

A basic assumption underlying much of the research on short-term memory in deaf children has been that deaf and hearing individuals might have qualitatively different ways of organizing their experience. Hearing people, by virtue of their dependence on oral-aural language, are assumed to use verbal-sequential coding to remember short lists of simple stimuli. This code is variously seen as phonological, articulatory, or acoustic in nature (for discussion see Baddeley, 1986). Deaf people, in contrast, by virtue of lacking oral-aural experience and using a visual-manual language, have been assumed to rely more heavily on visual-spatial short-term memory codes (cf. Whorf, 1956).

Central to this area of research, at least as it concerns memory for simple visual stimuli, is a series of studies by O'Connor and Hermelin (1972, 1973a, 1973b, 1976; Hermelin & O'Connor, 1973, 1975). They drew on the work of Paivio (1971) and others in attempting to determine whether deaf children are more influenced by spatial organization, as evidenced when multiple visual stimuli are presented simultaneously, or by temporal organization, as evidenced when visual stimuli are presented in a rapid serial manner. In order to evaluate these alternatives, O'Connor and Hermelin developed a paradigm in which individual stimuli were presented through a series of small windows in a display box. Children were tested in tasks that varied in regard to whether stimulus presentations followed a *spatial*, left-to-right order (windows 1, 2, and then 3) or some other *temporal* order (e.g., windows 3, 1, and then 2).

O'Connor and Hermelin (1972) conducted one such study involving deaf, hearing, and blind children aged 13 to 14 years. The deaf children and one group of age-matched sighted/hearing children were visually presented with three digits using the display apparatus. The blind children and another group of age-matched sighted/hearing children were auditorally presented with digit stimuli similarly varying in spatial and temporal ordering of presentation via loudspeakers. All subjects were first presented with a series of *congruent* trials in which the second-presented digit was in the central position and the children were asked to identify the "middle" digit. They then underwent another series of trials in which spatial and temporal positions were not congruent and again were asked to identify the location of the "middle" digit.

O'Connor and Hermelin found that there were no overall quantitative differences in levels of performance among the groups. Qualitatively, however, they observed marked differences among the groups. In general, the blind children and matched sighted controls tended to code the auditorally presented sequences in a temporal fashion; that is, the digit reported as the "middle" one was the one heard second, regardless of whether it had been presented in the central position. The deaf children and their hearing controls, in contrast, tended to code the visually presented sequences in a spatial fashion, indicated by the fact that the digit reported as the "middle" one was the one seen in the central position, regardless of whether it had been presented second. These results indicated that temporal and spatial coding can lead to equivalent short-term memory performance with auditory and visual materials, respectively.

O'Connor and Hermelin's (1972) results were later extended in a study where they (1973a) presented children with stimulus arrays in which the spatial and temporal orders were different and asked the same children to recall the digits or to recognize the presented sequences in a set of two alternatives. The results indicated that hearing 8-year-olds usually recalled the digits in a temporal order and always correctly recognized presented, temporal orders. Deaf 8- to 11-year-olds, in contrast, frequently (incorrectly) chose the spatial, left-to-right order in the recognition task and recalled the digits in order of their spatial display rather than their temporal sequence. These results suggested that deaf children are likely to depend on spatial coding in short-term memory, whereas hearing children depend on temporal, sequential coding.

Hermelin and O'Connor (1973) then conducted a similar study, presenting sets of three digits to hearing children (aged 8;3 to 9;2 and 10;6 to 11;6) and deaf children (aged 9;9 to 11;5 and 12;10 to 13;2). The investigators hypothesized that temporal ordering at input would occur only for children who "implicitly verbalized," and they assumed that deaf children would be unlikely to do so. Consistent with that expectation, they found that more than half of the deaf children failed to recognize correct temporal sequencing. Instead, they falsely recognized spatial, left-to-right sequencing independently of whether temporal-spatial incongruence occurred in the input string or in the recognition items. This finding was consistent with other results in suggesting that deaf children are more likely than hearing children to depend on a visual-spatial short-term memory code. Most importantly, perhaps, Hermelin and O'Connor found that correct recognition was unrelated to either articulation ability (as rated by the children's teachers) or implicit verbalization (as indicated by the use of rhyme on a picture paired-associates test), findings contrary to their initial, linguistic coding hypothesis.

O'Connor and Hermelin (1973b) explicitly investigated the role of verbalization in short-term memory of deaf and hearing children, aged 12 to 13 and 11 to 12 years, respectively. They used pictures of faces and nonsense syllables as stimuli in a task similar to that used by Hermelin and O'Connor (1973), except that each trial involved presentation of five stimuli. O'Connor and Hermelin hypothesized that if verbal coding were crucial for the retention of sequential information, hearing children would retain the order of the nonsense syllables better than that of the photographs, a difference that was not expected in deaf children "because of their language impairment" (p. 438). That prediction was supported, as the hearing children recalled 68% of the syllables and 60% of the photographs following a five-window presentation procedure. The deaf children, in contrast, remembered 60% of the syllables and 65% of the photographs.

Insofar as memory for temporal order appeared independent of both the linguistic character of to-be-remembered material and the presence of "an intact auditory-vocal channel," O'Connor and Hermelin concluded that deaf individuals retain order information just as efficiently as hearing individuals but frequently "elect" to use a visual strategy rather than a temporal strategy for short-term memory tasks (with regard to the hearing, cf. Paivio, 1971). Consistent with that conclusion, O'Connor and Hermelin (1976) later found that deaf children showed equal facility in backward and forward memory span tasks involving digits and letters presented in their display apparatus. Such findings provide strong support not only for the primacy of visual-spatial coding in deaf children's short-term memories but also for comparability of that code to the verbal-sequential short-term memory codes typically employed by hearing children.

The research presented thus far indicates that alternative, visual and verbal-sequential short-term memory codes may be equally effective in tasks that involve visual presentation of three- to five-digit or letter stimuli. At the same time, the bulk of the literature indicates that deaf children generally have shorter memory spans than hearing age-mates (for a review see Conrad, 1979, Ch. 5), and are more likely to depend on visual than verbal-sequential coding in short-term memory. Taken together, these findings suggest that there may be basic information processing differences between deaf and hearing children, even if different approaches to memory can sometimes lead to quantitatively similar performance. Several words of caution are in order, however.

First, note that both the Hermelin and O'Connor presentation apparatus and their use of forced-choice recognition tasks (usually with only two alternatives) provide a different context than most other short-term memory studies. The extent to which those results would generalize to the larger memory literature and real world situations is unclear (see also McDaniel, 1980). Second, in their reports, Hermelin and O'Connor only rarely referred to the language abilities of their deaf subjects, occasionally indicating that one group had some degree of oral ability or lip-reading skill. In fact, all of Hermelin and O'Connor's research was conducted in England, and it likely involved children with little or no signing skill and considerable variability in oral skills (e.g., O'Connor & Hermelin, 1973b). Thus although spatial coding for short-term memory might well be adaptive for children with lesser verbal abilities, it is unclear whether such a strategy is used by those deaf individuals who either are competent in oral ability or use sign language as a primary or supplementary mode of communication.

Third, but not unrelated, is Furth's (1966) suggestion that the typically shorter digit spans evidenced by deaf children relative to their hearing peers may result from their having relatively less familiarity with digits and number concepts. This explanation may be relevant to Hermelin and O'Connor's studies insofar as most of their tasks involved numerical stimuli. Consistent with this suggestion, Olsson and Furth (1966) found that both hearing and deaf adolescents showed longer memory spans for nonsense shapes that were high in association value (i.e., easily labeled by another group of subjects) compared to shapes low in association value. There was no effect of hearing status in that task, even though the hearing students had significantly longer digit memory spans than the deaf students. Also consistent with Furth's proposal is the fact that neither O'Connor and Hermelin's (1973b) study with nonsense syllables and photographs as stimuli nor their 1976 study with letters as stimuli revealed main effects of hearing status.

Concern about inconsistencies in the O'Connor and Hermelin experiments, coupled with the subsequent unquestioning acceptance of those findings by several investigators, led Beck, Beck, and Gironella (1977) to replicate the basic O'Connor and Hermelin study using an essentially identical procedure. Their study involved Canadian deaf children aged 7 to 12 years and hearing children aged 7 to 9 years. Not only did Beck et al. fail to find a memory difference between the deaf and hearing children, they failed to observe the usual temporal coding preference in hearing children, as slightly more of their hearing subjects revealed use of a spatial rather than a temporal strategy. Among the deaf children, approximately equal numbers preferred temporal and spatial coding strategies. Strategy preference was unrelated to age, digit span memory, gender, or reading levels; and subjects receiving purely oral training were no different from those receiving combined oral and manual training (cf. Wallace & Corballis, 1973).

Beck et al. (1977) unfortunately did not discuss the possible sources of difference in their results versus those of O'Connor and Hermelin, and there are two limitations of their study for the purposes of that comparison. First, their use of subjects with an average age of 8 years contrasts with Hermelin and O'Connor's consistent use of 12-year-olds. Beck et al. cited previous research with 8-year-old hearing children that indicated a preference for temporal coding, but that finding was not replicated in their 1977 study. There was also a wider age range among the hearing than among the deaf students, but no age analyses for the hearing sample were reported. Second, the deaf subjects tested by Beck et al. (1977) had hearing losses ranging from a moderate 45 dB to a profound 110 dB. No information is given on the relation of hearing loss to coding strategy preference or to recall, although one might expect from Hermelin and O'Connor's findings that the more oral children (with respect to training and hearing loss) might be more likely to adopt temporal strategies.

Belmont, Karchmer, and Bourg (1983) suggested that the inconsistencies in both the Beck et al. (1977) and the O'Connor and Hermelin findings might lie in the obvious individual differences observed in strategy preferences. In particular, they were interested in the extent to which deaf children's spatial or temporal short-term memory coding strategies might affect their information-processing strategies in general. Belmont et al. used a computerized version of the O'Connor and Hermelin (1972) procedure with groups of deaf and hearing 11-year-olds. Unlike Beck et al. (1977), Belmont et al. found that all 16 of their hearing subjects adopted temporal coding strategies. Like some of the earlier findings (e.g., Beck et al., 1977; Hermelin & O'Connor, 1973), however, the 16 deaf children were approximately equally split between spatial coding ($n = 9$) and temporal coding ($n = 7$).

Perhaps the most interesting part of the Belmont et al. study was that after determining children's coding preferences in one set of trials the investigators required them to switch to the alternate (spatial or temporal) strategy. In all groups, this switch led to a decline in performance. The hearing groups, however, showed a clear recovery of performance within several trials, whereas the deaf groups did not. Furthermore, the pattern of error data and response times indicated that for the deaf subjects the spatial coding scheme was the more efficient strategy. These results thus clearly indicate that preferences among deaf children for visual versus verbal coding represent rather durable and consistent strategies. Although Belmont et al. did not report whether the deaf children were orally or manually trained and did not evaluate the relation between oral skill and coding strategy, all of their deaf subjects were profoundly deaf, and thus the possible range of oral skill was likely smaller than in the Beck et al. (1977) study. The Belmont et al. (1983) study also does not speak to the failure of Beck et al. to obtain a temporal ordering preference among their subjects, insofar as Belmont and his colleagues tested 11-year-olds rather than 8-year-olds. The results of Belmont et al. do emphasize, however, the importance of considering individual differences in coding strategies among deaf children, not only for short-term memory tasks but as they might affect performance in other cognitive domains that contain an explicit or implicit memory component.

Clearly, there are some relatively basic information-processing differences among deaf children, as well as between deaf and hearing children, even if the loci of those differences are not yet determined. Before considering such differences further, it is worthwhile examining several studies that concern deaf children's use of alternative short-term memory coding strategies in studies using letters, hand-shapes, and lip-read stimuli—all components of larger linguistic units.

Short-Term Memory for Linguistic Component Stimuli

Evidence from Studies Using Printed Letter Stimuli

The "classic" study in this area is that of Conrad and Rush (1965) on the effects of visual and acoustic similarity in short-term memory for consonants. Forty-one American deaf children, aged 13 to 20 years, were compared to 53 hearing seventh-graders (presumably 12 to 13 years old) in their ability to remember visually pre-sented five-consonant strings. The strings were exposed for 3.5 seconds each, after which the students attempted to reproduce them by writing five letters from a nine-letter set that remained visually available throughout the session. Of central interest was the pattern of confusion errors for acoustically and visually similar letters.

Insofar as previous findings had indicated the importance of acoustic coding in short-term memory of hearing adults, Conrad and Rush were not surprised to find a pattern of errors in their hearing subjects indicating acoustic coding of the letter strings (i.e., intrusion of acoustically similar alternatives: B for V). The deaf sub-jects, however, showed no evidence of acoustic coding. Shape-related intrusions (e.g., Y for V) were produced with more than chance frequency by those deaf stu-dents who showed the poorest recall performance but generally were not produced by those students who showed the best performance.

Conrad (1970) presented oral British deaf students (aged 12 to 17 years) with consonant strings or words that explicitly varied in visual and acoustic similarity. Their performance was compared to that of a group of age-matched hearing con-trols. Conrad found frequent acoustic confusions among the hearing subjects indi-cating phonological/articulatory short-term memory coding. Among the deaf stu-dents, he found phonological/articulatory confusions in some and visual confusions in others (cf. Belmont et al., 1983). Conrad (1972) later replicated those results with deaf and hearing children aged 11 to 16 and 10 to 11 years, respectively, and sug-gested that the use of phonological/articulatory coding versus visual coding depended on the articulatory abilities of the deaf children. Those with better oral skills were believed to use "inner speech" when coding the strings, whereas those with lesser oral skills used visual memory codes. Conrad even suggested that an *articulatory index* of the proportion of total errors that was phonologically/articulatorally based might be used as a measure of internal, verbal sequential coding.

Although Conrad's subjects typically were drawn from oral schools, they were all aware of the British Sign Language (BSL) manual alphabet and no doubt used it outside the classroom. Hopefully, readers familiar with deafness or sign language have already asked themselves the question "What about similarity of the hand-shapes used to make the letters?" Conrad (1970, 1972; Conrad & Rush, 1965) did not evaluate that alternative, but it was evaluated by Locke and Locke (1971). Their frequently cited study involved both oral and nonoral British deaf students, aged 14 to 20 years. The oral versus nonoral classifications were made on the basis of speech intelligibility. A hearing control group was comprised of public school students, aged 10 to 14 years.

Locke and Locke's stimuli were letter pairs designed to be either phonetically similar, visually similar, or dactylically (literally, "of the fingers") similar in BSL. Although the details are unclear, it appears that three pairs were presented at a rate of 5 seconds per pair, followed by a 15-second "rehearsal" period, and then a 10-second (written) response period. In total, 54 three-pair lists were presented. A trained lip-reader and fingerspeller observed the children for evidence of lip movements and finger movements that might be involved in rehearsal (although this monitoring was likely difficult in the group testings of 26 to 28 subjects).

Locke and Locke reported that "the groups recalled with differing levels of accuracy," the oral deaf performing best and the hearing controls performing the worst (p. 144). In fact, however, an examination of their data (Locke & Locke, 1971, Table 2) reveals essentially no overall differences among the groups, as the mean accuracy of the hearing group was reported as 0.335, the nonoral deaf group 0.333, and the oral deaf group 0.333. The oral deaf group, in fact, was never significantly more accurate than any other group, whereas the hearing group reliably surpassed both deaf groups in their memories for both phonetically similar and visually similar stimuli. The nonoral group, meanwhile, recalled the dactylically similar stimuli more accurately than the hearing controls. Consistent with their accuracy data, Locke and Locke concluded that the hearing subjects were "more aware" of phonetic and visual features (cf. Blair, 1957) of the stimuli, whereas the nonoral deaf subjects were "more aware" of the dactylic features. The confusion data, however, only partially support that position. Those errors indicated that the hearing subjects made more phonetic confusions than the oral deaf subjects, who in turn made more than the nonoral deaf subjects. At the same time, the nonoral group made more visual confusions than the hearing controls and more dactylic confusions than either the oral deaf or the hearing groups.

One interesting observation from the Locke and Locke study was that most of the deaf subjects were reported to have engaged in obvious dactylic rehearsal prior to the response period. The two deaf groups were observed to use both phonetic rehearsal and simultaneous phonetic and dactylic rehearsal at approximately equal rates, whereas the nonoral group showed more dactylic encoding and the oral group more "noncoding." Unfortunately, the rates of rehearsal were not given for any of the groups, and so we are unable to draw any firm conclusions. It is clear, however, that these oral and nonoral students used some kind of *verbal* coding in short-term memory with considerable frequency.

Wallace and Corballis (1973) explicitly examined possible differences in short-term memory coding between manual (aged 14 to 27 years) and oral (aged 11 to 14 years) Canadian deaf children and a hearing control group (aged 11 to 14 years). The deaf children were enrolled in a program employing the Rochester method, in which Simultaneous Communication is augmented by the frequent use of finger-spelling. The visually presented stimuli were four- and five-letter strings of upper- and lower-case letters, similar to those used by Conrad (1970).

Both accuracy and confusion measures in the Wallace and Corballis study indicated that with shorter strings oral and manual deaf subjects relied primarily on visual coding, whereas hearing subjects relied on phonological/articulatory coding. With longer strings the oral deaf children evidenced phonological/articulatory coding as well as visual coding. Part of the evidence for the observed coding difference derived from observations of the children made during a 10-second interval between presentation and recall. During that time all of the students in the oral group were seen to use articulatory rehearsal (i.e., they moved their lips), whereas those in the manual group frequently were seen using dactylic rehearsal (i.e., they moved their fingers). Dactylic confusions, however, were not evident in the error data. Finally, Wallace and Corballis observed two spontaneous rehearsal strategies in their deaf subjects, one cumulative and the other involving "chunking" (or group-ing). Consistent with memory research with normal children (Kail, 1990), the cumulative rehearsal strategy was clearly the more effective.

Wallace and Corballis's (1973) finding of a greater reliance on visual coding in the manual deaf students than the oral deaf students is intuitively appealing. Most simply, it suggests that training in a visual-spatial language environment can create a bias for visual encoding in short-term memory, at least as far as we can generalize from studies using letter stimuli. It is also interesting to note that Wallace and Corballis's manual students were older than the oral ones, suggesting that the cod-ing effect was not due to a confounding of age and English proficiency.

Age-related differences in short-term memory coding strategies do occur, of course, and related findings obtained by MacDougall (1979) indicate the impor-tance of controlling language fluency in such tasks. MacDougall's deaf and hearing subjects comprised a younger group, aged 10 to 12 years, and an older group, aged 15 to 18 years. All deaf students had been trained in an oral program, although MacDougall reported that they were acquainted with fingerspelling and sign lan-guage. He presented the children with five-letter strings, using several typefaces, each string presented for either 2.2 or 8.0 seconds (for older and younger groups, respectively), followed by an 8-second recall period. The pattern of accurate recalls and (typeface) confusion errors clearly indicated that the younger hearing children used primarily acoustic/articulatory coding, whereas the older ones supplemented that coding with visual coding. The deaf children, in contrast, heavily relied on visual coding at both ages, although the older ones appeared to supplement their visual coding with acoustic/articulatory coding. These differences notwithstanding, MacDougall suggested that older hearing children may be more efficient in visual coding than their deaf peers because they made fewer errors than deaf subjects with the visually presented stimuli (see also Conrad, 1970; Wallace & Corballis, 1973). Unfortunately, a similar comparison cannot be made with auditorally presented material, so it is unclear to what extent MacDougall's results may have been due to deaf children having a general memory span deficit versus (the presumed) visual coding deficit.

Evidence from Studies Using Lipshapes and Handshapes

The findings of MacDougall (1979), Conrad (1970), and Wallace and Corballis (1973) have been clarified by a series of studies concerning memory for digits and letters presented via lip-reading, sign, and print. Dodd et al. (1983), for example, conducted three experiments aimed at elucidating short-term memory for graphic (numeric) and orally produced (but silent) digits in orally trained schoolchildren. They found comparable performance, overall, between deaf 13- to 16-year-olds and hearing 14- to 15-year-olds and between deaf students who were either good articulators or poor articulators (aged 11 to 18 years). Dodd et al. (1983) concluded that coding of lip-read stimuli involves an internal speech code (Conrad, 1972) that is similar for deaf and hearing students and based on phonological rather than articulatory information (cf. McGurk & Saqi, 1986).

Harris and Arnold (1984) examined short-term memory for letters presented via lipshapes, handshapes, and print. Groups of six profoundly deaf students, six moderately to severely deaf students, and six hearing controls were tested; all three groups had mean ages of 15 years. Harris and Arnold presented sets of six stimuli per trial, either sequentially or simultaneously. Overall, they found no (written) recall differences *within* any of the three groups in memory for the three stimulus types when they were presented sequentially. When the stimuli were presented simultaneously (for 18 seconds), however, letters were remembered better than handshapes, which were remembered better than lipshapes for all three groups.

Surprisingly, Harris and Arnold (1984) did not report analyses of any *between-group* differences in recall. Examination of their Table 1 (p. 67) shows that, in terms of memory for both letters and lipshapes, the hearing students exceeded the moderately hearing-impaired students, who exceeded the profoundly deaf students. In terms of memory for handshapes, the hearing group exceeded the profoundly deaf group, which in turn exceeded the moderately hearing-impaired group. This pattern of results indicates that oral ability improves memory for orally relevant stimuli among oral deaf children, whereas those who likely have less oral ability (i.e., the profoundly deaf) are more proficient in their memories for manually related signs. Consistent with this hypothesis, Harris and Arnold found that the moderately hearing-impaired students and the hearing students did not differ significantly on a speech-reading test. Regrettably, no comparison with the profoundly deaf students is possible, insofar as they "lacked the confidence or the ability to even attempt" the speech-reading test (Harris & Arnold, 1984, p. 67), and it was not administered to them. Most importantly, note that the hearing subjects outperformed the profoundly deaf subjects with all materials—even the sign handshapes.

Taken together, the findings in this section lead to several conclusions. One, perhaps unsurprising finding is that, at least in the case of orally trained students who are competent in speech-reading, memory for lip-read stimuli is equal to or approaches that of hearing peers. Articulatory ability does not appear to be a good predictor of memory for orally produced stimuli (Dodd et al., 1983), even if it does appear to distinguish students who use an acoustic- or phonological-like coding strategy from those who use a visual strategy for short-term memory for letters (Conrad, 1970). Importantly, it should be remembered that the children in these two studies were British and probably were all orally trained. The possibility remains that to the extent that their speech-reading skills are superior to those of manually trained deaf children, any differences in memory ability as a function of articulation skill might have been attenuated in these studies (i.e., due to the restricted range). Comparable studies with manual deaf children, however, apparently have not yet been published.

The studies by O'Connor and Hermelin have led to the popular conclusion that there are qualitative differences in short-term memory coding for deaf and hearing children even when overall (quantitative) performance does not differ. Once again, however, it should be noted that their studies exclusively involved orally trained deaf children, and there have been relatively few comparable studies with manually trained children. On the basis of the Wallace and Corballis (1973) study, it appears that there are, in fact, differences in short-term memory coding by manual and (hearing or deaf) oral children, although further study is clearly needed to disentangle all of the relevant variables.

Conclusions concerning overall levels of short-term memory performance for oral, manual, and hearing children are not easily drawn. The above studies, largely with oral deaf children, have split fairly evenly on this issue. These investigations, however, involved deaf children in their teenage years, usually between 12 and 15. At this age, language development is consolidating in deaf children, but it is also a time of large individual differences and hence experimental variability. True, it may be difficult to keep the attention of young deaf children and to obtain materials that are meaningful and yet amenable to short-term memory testing. Kernohan (1986) attempted to resolve those difficulties, presenting familiar (object and action) shapes to deaf children as young as 5 years in a short-term memory paradigm. Regrettably, neither his methodology nor his results are presented in sufficient detail to permit drawing firm conclusions with any comfort. Some other studies, however, have had better success.

Short-Term Memory for Familiar, Meaningful Stimuli

Hoemann, Andrews, and DeRosa (1974) attempted to resolve some of the issues concerning stimulus familiarity in deaf children's short-term memory coding through a study involving memory for pictures of familiar objects. Their study included deaf and hearing children 8 to 12 years of age, with the deaf children demonstrating at least minimal manual communication abilities. The question motivating the study was somewhat different from those underlying the above studies, as Hoemann et al. were interested in whether deaf children were as likely as hearing peers to engage in *categorical encoding* in short-term memory. That is, they wondered if young deaf children would spontaneously and automatically activate taxonomic information pertaining to presented items. This question was assessed by examining whether a change in the categorical composition of a list resulted in a *release from proactive inhibition.*

Proactive inhibition (PI) refers to the fact that as successively presented stimuli are drawn from the same category or semantic class short-term memory declines, presumably from the build-up of interference from earlier, similar items. When a semantic change in the stimuli is made (e.g., DOG MOUSE DEER TIGER STOVE), recall increases, reflecting a "release" from the build-up of interference. Hoemann et al. (1974) used release from PI as an indicator of whether children were using categorical encoding in their short-term memory task. Although they used only a single categorical shift, from the familiar category of animals to other "common objects" (e.g., tree, airplane, house), Hoemann et al. found clear evidence of release from PI in both deaf and hearing children as young as 8 years; and there were no effects of age in either group. Furthermore, the deaf and hearing students showed essentially equivalent memory performance overall, leading Hoemann et al. to conclude that "deaf children's memory on this task is functionally similar to that of hearing children and adults" (p. 430). In addition to the use of only one categorical shift and small sample sizes (five to seven in each of the deaf age groups), however, Hoemann et al.'s study is limited by the fact that age and hearing status were never included in the same analysis, and the data were not broken down by age. It thus remains unclear whether categorical encoding in short-term memory is the norm for young deaf children and if it can be obtained for stimuli other than the single, highly overlearned category of animals.

Similar concerns about the possible influences of stimulus characteristics and differences in information-processing strategies in deaf and hearing children led Liben and Drury (1977) to study deaf children's short-term memories for pictures (either animals or meaningless forms) and letters (either in print or using the manual alphabet). One of the most notable aspects of this study is that it involved relatively young children (6 and 8 years), compared to most of the previous research. All of the children were hearing-impaired to the extent that they were enrolled in a Total Communication school program and had "a severe enough hearing loss to inhibit normal development of oral-aural language" (p. 62).

Liben and Drury used a serial probe task for examining short-term memory. In that task, the experimenter first showed the children a set of six stimulus cards, one at a time, and placed them face down on a table. The children then were presented with a probe card identical to one they had seen and were asked to locate the matching (face-down) card. In this task, deaf children showed better performance on animals than meaningless shapes, with no effect of age; but they showed no difference in their memory for printed versus signed letters.

Analyses of picture versus letter memory were not presented, but inspection of Liben and Drury's data suggests that the pictures were remembered better. Differences between the deaf children and the hearing 4- and 5-year-old children also were not reported; and given the differences in age, they may not be useful. Nevertheless, it is worth noting that, in contrast to some of the findings from the previously described literature in which the performance of young hearing children sometimes surpassed that of older deaf children, Liben and Drury's results appear to indicate better memory in the deaf 6-year-olds than the hearing 5-year-olds, at least in terms of their memory for animals, printed letters, and handshapes.

The Liben and Drury (1977) and Hoemann et al. (1973) studies augur well for manually trained deaf children (this time there are no comparable studies with oral deaf children). Both of those investigations indicated that there are some functional similarities between the short-term memory processes of deaf and hearing children that could have significant consequences for performance in other domains (Belmont et al., 1983; Waters & Doehring, 1990). Further understanding of the role of visual versus verbal-semantic processes in both manually and orally trained children can be obtained by considering their performance on slightly more complex tests of long-term memory, to which we turn in the next chapter.

Summary

Studies examining short-term memory in deaf children have involved a variety of verbal and nonverbal materials. In many cases, the intention has been to use stimuli unlikely to elicit verbal coding so as to control for language differences. In fact, a variety of studies with hearing children as well as adults have indicated that nonsense stimuli, be they linguistic or pictorial, are rarely dealt with as such but are "transformed" into some more meaningful form that is easier to remember. To the extent that these transformations involve verbal labeling, the purportedly nonverbal studies with deaf children might well involve a language-related component after all. Regrettably, nonverbal materials typically are used *in place of* controlling or matching for language ability, so the possible effects of language coding on memory for nonverbal materials are difficult to discern at this time.

It is now fairly clear that the extent of hearing loss is inversely related to short-term memory performance for a variety of materials, whereas oral ability, for orally trained children at least, is directly related to short-term memory performance (Conrad, 1979). These findings suggest the possibility that vocabulary and communication fluency would be positively related to memory in more manually oriented deaf children if they were evaluated in sign language rather than by English-based assessment. At issue here is not only the extent to which the to-be-remembered stimuli are familiar, although that clearly makes a difference; in addition, children with better communication skills are more likely to have metalinguistic and metamemory interactions with others from whom memory strategies and memory-relevant content knowledge can be learned, either explicitly or implicitly. They also are more likely to have interactions with diverse individuals with whom remembering things might be important (see Chapter 4).

It is not surprising to find that deaf children might have a greater reliance on visual-spatial short-term memory coding than temporal-sequential coding, at least in comparison to hearing children. The fact that this difference also is observed between young and older deaf children again suggests the importance of language fluency and memory experience to cognitive development and memory performance. One important comparison that would clarify this issue is the extent to which deaf children of deaf parents might differ from hearing children of deaf parents in terms of their short-term memory coding.

The evidence reviewed here has indicated that deaf children generally have shorter memory spans than hearing children. Most early demonstrations in this regard, however, used digit stimuli, with which deaf children might have less familiarity (e.g., Furth, 1966). In general, sequential-linguistic coding has been found to be beneficial for short-term memory, even if it remains uncertain that it is *necessary*. A variety of studies with hearing adults and children have shown that verbal-linguistic coding is superior to a visual-imaginal coding in memory for sequential information, and Blair (1957) found that memory span was the only measure consistently related to reading ability in his deaf sample. Although most child-related studies have considered only English-based verbal coding, there is considerable evidence that sign language coding is used in memory tasks by deaf adults (e.g., Bellugi, Klima, & Siple, 1975; Hanson, 1982; Krakow & Hanson, 1985). As yet, however, there have been no assessments of whether sign language coding in short-term memory is available to young deaf children, regardless of whether they know when and how to use it effectively.

9

Long-Term Memory: Codes, Organization, and Strategies

The previous chapter reviewed a variety of apparent consistencies and inconsistencies in the short-term memory performance of deaf children and hearing children. Aside from the general finding of shorter memory spans in deaf children, the most consistent finding was that for tasks requiring the short-term retention of simple nonverbal stimuli such as digits deaf children are more likely than hearing children to use spatial memory codes rather than temporal or sequential verbal codes. This difference notwithstanding, deaf and hearing children most frequently showed similar levels of (subspan) recall overall, suggesting that their alternative information-processing strategies were in some sense equally effective.

In contrast to studies involving memory for nonverbal stimuli, studies involving memory for meaningful verbal material yielded less consistent results. This difference derives in part from the fact that memory for meaningful stimuli is more likely to depend on linguistic coding than is memory for nonmeaningful stimuli. The verbal fluency differences between deaf and hearing children (especially when to-be-remembered materials comprise linguistic stimuli such as words) favor hearing children and those deaf children with better language skills over deaf children with poorer language skills. At the same time, the language skills of deaf children, as a group, are clearly more variable than those of hearing children.

Intimately tied to memory for meaningful material, especially verbal material, is the knowledge that children bring to the memory situation, in terms of the breadth of their conceptual knowledge and the strategic knowledge about their own memory functioning. In these domains, also, differences between deaf and hearing children might not be unexpected. We therefore now turn to consideration of deaf children's long-term memory processes and the roles of concept knowledge and alternative memory codes in long-term memory performance.

"Early Classics"

As might be expected from the discussion in Chapter 7, one of the pioneers in early studies of long-term memory in deaf children was Hans Furth. Consistent with his investigations of conservation and cognitive development, Furth and his colleagues designed memory experiments that held the need for linguistic mediation to a minimum. Furth (1961b), for example, tested groups of deaf children (hearing losses $\geq$ 50 dB) and hearing children, aged 7 to 12 years, in a paired-associate learning paradigm in which they had to remember which of two toys went with each of four colors. When the colors were later presented alone, children had to match each with the correct toy and achieve 10 consecutive correct matches (out of 40 trials) to be considered "successful." Furth found no differences in performance at ages 7 to 10 years, but the deaf 11- and 12-year-olds performed significantly worse than their hearing age-mates. Those results led Furth to conclude that the basic visual memory capacity of deaf children is equivalent to that of hearing peers (see also Hartman & Elliot, 1965; Putnam, Iscoe, & Young, 1962). Furth suggested that the results from the 11- and 12-year-olds were likely due either to motivational differences between the deaf and hearing children or to the cognitive development of deaf children falling behind that of hearing children, as the latter group achieved *formal operations* (see also Furth, 1973) (see Chapter 7). He gave no basis for why such motivational or cognitive differences affecting memory should occur only at formal operations, however, citing only variation in "experience and training."

Furth and Youniss (1964) compared deaf and hearing 6- to 7-year-olds and 10- to 11-year-olds on another nonverbal task in which toys were paired congruently, incongruently, or neutrally with their real-world colors. For example, a red rectangle with a fire engine was a congruent pairing, a white rectangle with a fire engine was an incongruent pairing because one toy in the set was a normally white refrigerator; and an orange rectangle with a fire engine was a neutral pairing because there were no normally orange toys in the set (cf. the Stroop effect described in Chapter 11). Furth and Youniss reasoned that, if deaf children are more "perceptually bound" and rigid than their hearing age-mates (cf. Blair, 1957), over a series of trials the deaf children would show greater interference than the hearing children on the incongruent pairings. In fact, there were no differences in cued recall of the incongruent and neutral pairings for the deaf subjects at either age, but there were significant interference effects for the hearing children at both ages. Furth and Youniss offered two interpretations for these findings, one verbally based and one nonverbally based.

The nonverbal explanation was that deaf children might have less experience with things such as trees, locomotives, and refrigerators and hence be less prone to interference from color-object mismatches. The verbal explanation was that the greater interference in the hearing children was a consequence of their verbal superiority, in that they might have been implicitly responding to the real-world colors of the toys' referents. That is, Furth and Youniss suggested that hearing children might have been coding the materials verbally, whereas the deaf children were coding them nonverbally (e.g., visually). Regrettably, Furth and Youniss had no independent measure of language ability within their samples, and hearing losses were not reported; thus it is impossible to determine the viability of their alternative explanations. Their results are important, however, because they raise the issue of the nature of long-term memory codes in deaf children and how they might correspond to the representations involved in short-term memory. We now consider in some detail the possibilities for long-term memory coding in deaf children.

Alternative Codes of Long-Term Memory in Deaf Children

One of the most frequently cited explanations for deaf children's allegedly inferior long-term memories relative to hearing peers is what was referred to in Chapter 8 as the *linguistic coding hypothesis*. Most generally, this hypothesis is that some tasks either require or are facilitated by sequential, linguistic coding (i.e., internal or external speech), so the lack of such coding results in performance deficiencies. The most obvious result of linguistic coding in memory is that meaningful words and pictures are better remembered than nonsense syllables and random shapes (under most conditions), and even nonsense syllables are better remembered as they become more word-like (Prytulak, 1971). However, as indicated by the Furth and Youniss (1964) study, linguistic coding sometimes can be invoked to account for relatively good memory performance (i.e., retention of a linguistic code) as well as relatively poor memory performance (i.e., linguistic or phonological interference created by that code).

With regard to deaf children, Hermelin and O'Connor's extensive work on spatial versus temporal coding in short-term memory provides support for a weak form of the linguistic coding hypothesis, insofar as the use of visual-spatial processing and sequential-linguistic coding resulted in different patterns of memory performance. When considering long-term memory of deaf children, however, Koh et al. (1971) went farther. They invoked a strong form of the linguistic coding hypothesis, arguing that because "a person's capacity to derive associative and linguistic relations among the input materials and to organize the items into higher-order subjective and conceptual units is crucial for an efficient recall performance.   We expect . . . that the prelingual deaf Ss should have a special difficulty in this recall task due to their extremely impoverished acoustic and linguistic systems" (p. 542). The fact that deaf individuals, by definition, have "extremely impoverished acoustic systems," however, does not imply that they have "extremely impoverished linguistic systems."

So why do even well-informed investigators and teachers of the deaf regularly assign deaf children inferior capabilities on the basis of the linguistic coding hypothesis? History likely plays a role here, as those who are unable to communicate in the vernacular traditionally have been assumed to be mentally deficient. Indeed, the lack of both internal symbolic ability and social communication certainly would lead to mental deficiency by all of the standards of civilization, but there is no basis for ascribing such status to deaf children. Deaf children raised in the absence of parental language interaction have been shown to develop their own communication systems (e.g., Goldin-Meadow & Morford, 1985; Goldin-Meadow & Mylander, 1984) (see Chapter 5), and even the few documented cases of solitary "wild children" (e.g., Fromkin, Krashen, Curtiss, Rigler, & Rigler, 1974; Itard, 1962) reveal some context-appropriate cognitive processing in the absence of language ability. It thus seems that the issue is really one of the extent to which deaf children's long-term memory coding might involve nonlinguistic instead of linguistic symbolic systems (Rodda, Cumming, & Fewer, 1993). Alternatively, deaf children may rely on linguistic coding for long-term memory, but the language abilities that serve as the bases for such processes may be more idiosyncratic than that observed in hearing children. Let us therefore examine differences in deaf children's recall performance due to the presence or absence of several hypothesized coding media, including phonological/articulatory, visual, semantic, and orthographic codes.

"Phonological" Effects on Long-Term Memory

Blanton, Nunally, and Odom (1967) tested four groups of deaf and hearing students, matched either on the basis of reading achievement or IQ scores, in a task in which they learned pairs of semantically related, graphemically similar, and rhyming words (cf. Bellugi et al., 1975). Interestingly, in the deaf and hearing groups that were matched on reading ability, the hearing students were both younger than the deaf students (14.4 versus 17.0 years, respectively) and had considerably lower IQ scores (84.7 versus 104.4). In the two groups matched on IQ, the hearing students were also younger than the deaf students (15.0 years versus 17.7 years, respectively) but had much higher reading achievement scores than their deaf peers (grade levels 8.0 and 4.7, respectively). On the cued recall task, Blanton, et al. found that the oldest (IQ-matched) group of deaf students showed significantly better performance than any of the other groups, and the younger deaf group surpassed their (even younger) reading score-matched hearing peers (see also Putnam et al., 1962). This pattern of results held for all three stimulus types. In short, the deaf students showed better memory performance than hearing peers, regardless of how they were matched.

Potentially the most interesting aspect of Blanton et al.'s study was that the deaf students in the older group attended a school that "primarily uses manual language," whereas the younger (by 1 year) deaf group attended an oral school. What makes this point important is that the IQ-matched deaf group showed superior performance even for the rhyming words. This finding means that the manual deaf students surpassed their hearing and oral deaf peers even in recall of visually dissimilar, rhyming words. Blanton et al.'s (1967) explanation of these results was similar to those offered by Furth and Youniss (1964) and Putnam et al. (1962) for results obtained with nonverbal stimuli: They suggested that because the deaf must rely "more on visual memory" their retention was less likely to be disrupted by "competing auditory-vocal processes during input and/or retrieval" (p. 231). This explanation leaves unclear, however, whether the deaf subjects actually did rely on visual coding in this task (cf. Belmont et al., 1983; Krakow & Hanson, 1985) and how visual coding could account for the observed superior retention of semantically associated pairs relative to visually or phonologically similar ones. In fact, both deaf and hearing students showed poorer memory for the rhyming words than the other two types, so a linguistic explanation for these results seems unlikely to be the whole explanation for these results.

Relevant to Blanton et al.'s (1967) concern about visual versus phonological long-term memory codes is a study by MacDougall and Rabinovitch (1971), who investigated the roles of overt vocal and sign verbalizations during learning. They had oral deaf (8 to 15 years old), manual deaf (9 to 18 years old), and hearing (8 to

13 years old) students learn lists consisting of six pairs of nonsense syllables, words, or pictures. The students were then tested in a forced-choice recognition task for the response members of each pair, given the stimulus members as cues. During one of two trials with each stimulus type, the two oral groups were instructed to name vocally the stimuli as they were presented; the manual deaf group was instructed to sign the words and picture labels; and, presumably, they fingerspelled the nonsense syllables. On the other trial, there were no verbalizations.

Unfortunately, possible effects of age were not analyzed, despite the large age ranges in each group; and mean first-trial scores were not reported. Using the number of trials to criterion as a dependent variable, however, MacDougall and Rabinovitch (1971) found no differences among the three groups in their recognition performance and no differences between the verbalization and no-verbalization conditions. They interpreted their failure to find an expected deficiency on the part of the deaf children as likely due to their use of a rather simple recognition paradigm rather than a recall paradigm. Consistent with the traditional thinking described in Chapter 8, MacDougall and Rabinovitch suggested that recognition memory for their stimuli might have been "primarily *visual* in nature" or translated from visual to kinesthetic codes, whereas a recall task would have prompted rehearsal "in the auditory modality" (p. 348).

Consistent with MacDougall and Rabinovitch's (1971) interpretation of their findings, D. V. Allen (1970) predicted that because deaf children do not use acoustic coding during paired-associate learning their recall would not be impaired by interference from acoustically similar words. Her subjects comprised three groups of 10- to 13-year-old children with reading levels between grades 3.5 and 6.0 and varying in hearing loss: 0 to 25 dB, 26 to 65 dB, and 66+ dB, respectively. Allen's stimulus pool consisted of eight pairs of visually dissimilar but phonologically similar words (e.g., DOOR–MORE and SIGH–LIE). In her "consistent" test list, words from rhyme pairs were combined with responses from other rhyme pairs (e.g., DOOR–SIGH, MORE–LIE). In her "inconsistent" list, the pairs did not follow that rule (i.e., DOOR–SIGH, MORE–WHILE) (D. V. Allen, 1970, p. 231).

Allen found no effect of hearing loss on the mean number of cued-recall trials to criterion, but the most severely impaired deaf group remembered significantly more of the consistent pairs (i.e., paired according to a phonological rule) than inconsistent pairs (63% versus 44%, respectively). In addition, she found that the least-impaired group performed significantly *worse* on the consistent pairs (36%) than the most-impaired group (63%). In line with the short-term memory research described in Chapter 8, Allen concluded that the better performance of the children with greater hearing losses lay in their use of visual coding as the "primary dimension of encoding," thus allowing them to "circumvent the [acoustic] source of interference" (p. 233). At the same time, however, she accounted for the better memory for consistent than inconsistent pairs in the severely deaf group by suggesting that "they were able to use the rhyming quality [of phonologically governed pairings] as a cue to aid learning" (p. 233). Can she have it both ways?

Allen's assumption that a primary visual code reduced rhyming interference for her subjects and a "secondary" phonological code allowed them to take advantage of that dimension seems inconsistent. This interpretation would be bolstered, however, by evidence that both visual and phonological codes are used simultaneously in long-term coding by deaf children. Let us therefore consider alternatives to phonological or acoustic memory codes in deaf children's long-term memories, just as we did for short-term memory.

Effects of Imageability and Signability on Long-Term Memory

Whether it makes sense to think of profoundly deaf children employing a truly *phonological* coding strategy for short- or long-term memory (see Chapter 11), the possibility of a kinesthetic, sign language-based code seems plausible. There are two issues involved here. The first issue is if deaf children are able to make use of a sign-based memory code and if they typically do so. The second issue concerns the form that such a code could take. That is, a memory code based on manual communication could be either (1) akin to the visual codes evidenced by research described in Chapter 8 (e.g., Hermelin & O'Connor, 1975); (2) like the *motor imagery* available to hearing adults (Engelkamp, 1990); (3) similar to the articulatory/phonological codes of hearing individuals; or (4) something else altogether.

Perhaps the first investigation of the role of sign-based codes in long-term memory was performed by Odom, Blanton, and McIntyre (1970). They asked 40 deaf students (mean age 16 years) and 40 hearing students (mean age 10.4 years—"as a control for reading achievement grade equivalent," p. 55) to learn a set of printed English words, half of which had sign-language equivalents and half of which did not. The words were matched for word length and printed frequency (which may or may not be relevant for deaf students); and signability was a between-subjects variable (i.e., each student received only signable or unsignable words). During eight study-test trials, Odom et al. found significantly better recall by deaf than hearing students and better recall of signable than unsignable words. Not surprisingly, the effect of signability was larger for the deaf than the hearing subjects.

Odom et al. concluded that deaf children "access the visual image of the word in memory more readily with one motor-encoding (a sign) response than with a series of fingerspelling responses" (p. 57), although no evidence was presented that any of the subjects used fingerspelling in the task. As for their unusual finding of memory superiority by deaf subjects, Odom et al.'s preferred hypotheses were that either (1) the (presumed) larger vocabularies of hearing children would make for more "inter-response interference" (Furth & Youniss, 1964); (2) motor-based codes are particularly powerful for memory; or (3) matching the deaf and hearing subjects on reading ability rather than age might have left them unequal in mnemonic ability. Although the second alternative is certainly true (Engelkamp, 1990), the large age difference between the deaf and hearing children was also a likely factor in this case.

Conlin and Paivio (1975) also obtained evidence of the power of the signability variable in their examination of the effects of visual and sign-based memory coding in a paired-associate learning task. They assumed that because visual experience is central to both deaf and hearing individuals both groups would show better memory for high- than low-imagery words (Paivio, 1971). Signability, in contrast, was assumed to be a relevant dimension only for deaf individuals, and thus only the deaf were expected to show better memory for high- than low-signability words. Finally, on the basis of the previous research described above, Conlin and Paivio expected an overall superiority of their hearing subjects over their deaf subjects, all of whom were about 15 to 17 years old.

In two important control studies, Conlin and Paivio had word imageability rated by a group of 90 deaf subjects and word signability rated by a group of teachers at a school for the deaf. After the fact, the wisdom and importance of these controls was revealed by the fact that the correlation between the hearing and deaf imagery ratings [using the Paivio, Yuille, & Madigan, (1968) imagery norms from hearing college students] was only .58. Although a statistically significant relation, this value is relatively low compared to, for example, the correlation between imagery ratings for the same words in different vocal languages (e.g., Cornoldi, 1974) and suggests that visual imagery may represent somewhat different things to deaf and hearing individuals.

Conlin and Paivio's (1975) cued recall findings (with written recall) supported all three of their predictions: Hearing students recalled more than same-age deaf students, high-imagery words were recalled better than low-imagery words, and high-signability words were recalled better than low-signability words by the deaf students but not by the hearing students. Conlin and Paivio also reported that deaf and hearing groups were equivalent in their reported (infrequent) use of verbal mediation, whereas the deaf students reported greater use of sign-based mediation.

Bonvillian (1983) replicated the Conlin and Paivio (1975) study with four important differences: (1) half of the severely to profoundly deaf 15- to 19-year-olds had deaf parents and half had hearing parents; (2) free recall rather than cued recall was used; (3) signability and imageability were manipulated within subjects; and (4) the control group consisted of undergraduates, averaging 2 to 3 years older than the deaf students. Bonvillian also chose stimuli from the Paivio et al. (1968) norms and had them rated on imageability by a group of 10 deaf students, yielding a correlation of .76. High- and low-signability was determined using the Stokoe et al. (1965) dictionary of signs and classifications by two independent raters. Both presentation and recall were via written English, although here both immediate and delayed recall were evaluated.

Bonvillian's results were consistent with those of Conlin and Paivio (1975) in that he found significant advantages in memory for high- over low-imagery words and for high- over low-signability words in both short- and long-term memory (cf. Cornoldi & Sanavio, 1980). As expected, signability was an important factor for deaf but not hearing subjects, whereas imagery value was more important for the hearing students. Bonvillian also found that in both recall conditions the hearing students performed better than the two groups of deaf students, who did not differ. He suggested that this finding might have resulted from the age difference between the hearing and deaf groups as well as the hearing group's possible advantages in education, facility in English, and verbal intelligence (although the latter variables were not examined).

Bonvillian's (1983) demonstration that imagery apparently played a lesser role for deaf subjects in his task than in the paired-associate learning task of Conlin and

Paivio is consistent with other results indicating rated imagery to be a far better pre-dictor of memory in cued recall than in free recall tasks (Marschark & Surian, 1989). His results are also consistent with previous findings that deaf students might have more difficulty than hearing students in terms of memory integration in the absence of effective organizers or mediators (Koh et al., 1971). Finally, Bonvillian's findings support the more general conclusion that deaf children may make use of different coding strategies than hearing children for long-term as well as short-term memory. Although reported strategies of his hearing subjects were not given, Bonvillian noted that the deaf subjects reported frequent use of fingerspelling, sign-ing, and imagery in memory rehearsal. The use of a sign-based rehearsal was largely limited to the deaf children of deaf parents, further supporting the need to examine individual differences in memory strategies of deaf children (Belmont et al., 1983).

The Conlin and Paivio (1975) and Bonvillian (1983) studies with deaf adoles-cents are complemented by a study with manually trained deaf children, aged 6 to 15 years, reported by Frumkin and Anisfeld (1977). Using a simpler, continuous recognition paradigm, they had children examine a list of words in which the recog-nition foils were related either semantically or in surface form (i.e., similar in orthography or in sign formation) to the target words. In one experiment involving memory for printed words and two others involving memory for signs, Frumkin and Anisfeld found that both older and younger deaf children tended to falsely recog-nize all three types of foil. These results thus lend support to the suggestion that both visual (letter shape) and sign-based (visual or kinesthetic) coding play a part in the long-term memory functioning of deaf children.

Frumkin and Anisfeld's (1977) findings are also consistent with those obtained by Moulton and Beasley (1975). Moulton and Beasley tested 16-year-old deaf stu-dents enrolled in a Total Communication program. Students learned lists of paired associates that were presented either as signs or words and were physically either similar or dissimilar. Like Frumkin and Anisfeld (1977), Moulton and Beasley found their subjects to utilize coding on both semantic and formational (*cheremic*) dimensions, but semantic coding appeared to be the more efficient insofar as it led to more accurate recall [see also the similar findings of Liben, Nowell, and Posnansky (1978) with deaf college students].

Although consistent with each other, the results from both the Moulton and Beasley (1975) and the Frumkin and Anisfeld (1977) studies are inconsistent with results obtained by Cavedon, Cornoldi, and DeBeni (1984) using a paradigm simi-lar to that of Frumkin and Anisfeld (1977). The Cavedon et al. continuous recogni-tion task was administered to groups of deaf and hearing 11- to 15-year-olds. The printed target words were intermixed with foils having "structural" similarities (either orthographic or phonetic) or semantic similarities (either synonyms or strong associates). Cavedon et al. found that the hearing students made more semantic (approximately 12%) than structural (9%) confusions, whereas grade-matched deaf students made more structural (17%) than semantic (6%) confusions, indicating that the deaf children were more likely to depend on structural than semantic coding. Alternatively, however, deaf students may be less accurate in terms of recognizing structural differences due to their lesser fluency with printed stimuli. This hypothe-sis is supported in part by results of the second experiment in the Cavedon et al.

study in which the hearing–deaf difference in the frequencies of phonetic confusions was eliminated when students were matched for grade or school achievement rather than age. The differences in orthographic and semantic confusions remained.

Assessment of possible sign language coding was not possible in the Cavedon et al. study because of the infrequency of sign language instruction in Italian schools. Given the lack of information on relative differences between deaf and hearing students in Italy, it is difficult to resolve the differences between the Cavedon et al. and the Frumkin and Anisfeld (1977) studies. Methodological differences also may have played a role in their results, as the Italian deaf students' error rates were far lower than those of the American students. It is important to note, however, that, despite apparent differences in the strategies adopted in long-term memory by deaf and hearing students in the Cavedon et al. study, overall recall was essentially equivalent for the two groups. Similar results were obtained by Marschark (1989) in a memory study involving *modality-specific interference* during learning of printed and signed sentences by oral deaf adults, American Sign Language (ASL)-oriented deaf adults, and hearing interpreters. Although the details are beyond the scope of this book given the age of the subjects, such results serve to reemphasize the point that *differences* in cognitive processes need not imply *deficiencies*. Rather, it appears that there may be different but equally effective learning strategies for both deaf and hearing children within the same language (Cavedon et al., 1984) and across signed and spoken languages (Marschark, 1989). The situation is not straightforward, however, as there may be interactions among cognitive and language abilities that go beyond simple learning studies.

One surprising aspect of Frumkin and Anisfeld's (1977) findings, for example, was the relatively high frequency of semantically related false recognitions in the deaf students (28 to 50%) compared to their hearing subjects (19%) and the subjects in the Cavedon et al. study (approximately 11%). Typically, young hearing children do not show strong semantic effects in this task, and yet young deaf children consistently did so in the 1977 study. Frumkin and Anisfeld suggested that those results reflected the early emergence of semantic coding in deaf children, which likely results from the absence of the competing speech code that predominates in verbal memory of hearing children. One implication of this conclusion is that deaf children may be in advance of hearing age-mates with respect to semantic (meaning-based) memory organization. At the same time, however, these findings suggest that "the formational properties of signs do not have for deaf children the coding prowess that speech has for hearing children" (Frumkin & Anisfeld, 1977, pp. 491–492). That is, speech may have evolved as a fundamental component of human information processing and may have no equivalent substitutes.

Organization and Memory

Before drawing any strong conclusions from the above studies about the effects of deafness and sign language on children's long-term memory, it is essential to distinguish possible effects on recall due to differences in memory organization or memory strategies from differences due to linguistic coding per se. One would expect, for example, that gross differences in stimulus familiarity would affect memory, and such differences may well be a factor when deaf and hearing children are tested on tasks that require memory for printed stimuli. Furthermore, the experiential differences of deaf compared to hearing children might well make for differences in motivation and cognitive styles (see Chapters 2 and 4), semantic memory organization, or their approaches to learning situations (aside from their responses to university researchers asking them to perform difficult, often boring laboratory tasks).

In view of the findings linking deaf children's experiential deficiencies to various aspects of cognitive functioning (Furth & Youniss, 1964; Liben, 1978; Ottem, 1980; Watts, 1979), it is surprising that there has been so little research examining possible relations between deaf children's memory proficiencies and the breadth and organization of their conceptual knowledge. This omission, in part, derives from the fact that it is only recently that developmental researchers have come to realize the importance and power of jointly considering the qualities and organization of children's knowledge and other aspects of cognitive growth (e.g., Bjorklund, 1985; Chi & Ceci, 1987). The problem has been particularly salient with regard to deaf children for more than a quarter-century, however, and it is discomfiting that investigators interested in deaf children did not recognize the importance of such research much earlier.

There are some indirectly related findings that have been taken to suggest that deaf children generally are more concrete and rigid than hearing age-mates with regard to specific concepts and in terms of their flexibility in problem solving situations (Stafford, 1962; Youniss & Furth, 1970). If true, it would not be surprising if these characteristics had an impact on memory performance. Such findings, in fact, have been interpreted as indicating both a lesser degree of conceptual organization in deaf children and a lesser ability to utilize what information is available, either within the task situation or from memory (Blair, 1957; Furth, 1973; Liben, 1978; Ottem, 1980). However, the generality of some of these results are called into question by demonstrations that deaf children's linguistic and cognitive flexibility appears comparable to that of hearing peers when the two groups are evaluated in terms of signed and oral production rather than tasks requiring the comprehension of printed English (e.g., Marschark et al., 1986; Suty & Friel-Patti, 1982) (see Chapter 10).

Relevant findings within the memory literature also are inconsistent. Several studies, for example, have indicated that young (5 to 15 years old) deaf children are less likely than hearing peers to adopt a strategic approach to long-term memory (e.g., Bebko, 1984; Koh et al., 1971), suggesting differences in the ability or likelihood of utilizing information that might be available. Other studies, however, have indicated that young deaf children use spontaneous memory strategies just as frequently as hearing peers, even if they do not equally facilitate performance (e.g., Liben, 1979). Insofar as deaf children's spontaneous rehearsal and application of categorical organization have also been demonstrated in short-term memory (Beck et al., 1977; Hoemann et al., 1974; Liben & Drury, 1977), it is tempting to conclude from these results that deaf children do not have any consistent memory organization deficits relative to hearing peers. However, both short- and long-term memory studies favoring this conclusion have used simple materials, and none has evaluated the role of deaf children's knowledge in terms of their use of organization during learning and memory. Interpreting findings of differences and similarities in memory performance between the two groups therefore remains problematical, and it is thus worthwhile to consider the long-term memory results in some detail.

The Role of Category Knowledge in Memory

Consider first a study by Tweney et al. (1975). They explicitly examined the semantic organization of deaf versus hearing adolescents, 16 to 18 years old. They asked students to sort sets of common nouns, pictures, and onomatopoetic words, and then submitted the sortings to hierarchical clustering scheme analyses (HCS). HCS is a statistical method that provides a description of organization or meaningful associations among stimuli based on the results of such a sorting procedure. Tweney et al. (1975), for example, reported that in the sortings of pictures and nouns the deaf and hearing differed only in "minor ways." With the unfamiliar sound words, in contrast, the two groups showed different organizations, as the deaf and hearing students sorted the words into qualitatively different piles. These results were taken to indicate that, at least by late adolescence, deaf and hearing children have similar semantic organizations for familiar concepts. It would not be surprising, however, if one were to find evidence of similar memory organization in older deaf and hearing children and in adults owing to the relative familiarity of the linguistic materials, while still observing differences between young deaf and hearing children.

Although the effects of semantic organization on memory performance were not evaluated in the Tweney et al. (1975) study, Koh et al. (1971) examined the free recall of categorized and unrelated word lists with groups of 13- to 14-year-old and 18- to 20-year-old deaf and hearing students. Their categorized list was composed of words from four categories: foods, animals, actions, and a "nature" category consisting of MOON, GRASS, LEAF, and RAIN. Each of these words has a simple sign equivalent, but the words were presented in print. With unrelated lists, Koh et al. found greater recall by the hearing than the deaf students at both age levels and more semantic clustering in recall by the older hearing students than by the other groups. Deaf students, in fact, showed no differences in the extent of their clustering as a function of age. With categorized lists, there were no hearing or age differences in recall (likely due to ceiling effects), but the hearing students showed greater clustering than the deaf students at both age levels.

The HCS analyses of the recall protocols revealed considerable variability in the clustering of the deaf students, and Koh et al. suggested this "noisy" organization as the major factor in their lower recall. Alternatively, the relative superiority of hearing students' recall performance might have been due to the use of printed English stimuli (Olsson & Furth, 1966). In either case, it is important that the observed differences in semantic organization at recall did not produce differences in the amount remembered. Once again, we have evidence that deaf and hearing individuals can have different memory processes that lead to similar overall outcomes (Marschark, 1989).

In contrast to the printed stimuli of the Koh et al. (1971) study, Liben (1979) examined free recall of taxonomically related line drawings by groups of deaf and hearing children aged 9, 11, and 13 years. Half of the children at each age level were trained in semantic clustering after the first memory trial, and all were told the category labels and sizes after the second trial. Liben found that training increased memory performance at all ages (Bebko, 1984; Beck et al., 1977) and that providing category labels increased memory independent of training. Most surprisingly, deaf children showed just as much semantic clustering in recall as hearing children, even before training. Nonetheless, their recall remained lower than that of hearing children. Liben concluded that, although deaf children can recognize and attempt to use the categorical nature of a list to improve memory, they might lack either flexibility in task-appropriate classification of individual items or sufficient knowledge of category membership and structure.

Although Liben did not address the differences between her study and that of Koh et al. (1971), the contradictory results might reflect their use of pictorial and printed English stimuli, respectively. That is, the attempted use of organizational strategies for recall (as well as recall per se) may be more likely or more successful with more familiar material. Alternatively, deaf and hearing children may have similar conceptual organizations for familiar stimuli but different organizations for unfamiliar stimuli (see Tweney et al., 1975). Parallel findings also might emerge as a function of age: With increasing age there may be convergence in the utilization or success of applying conceptual knowledge to memory tasks both within and between the populations of deaf and hearing children.

In an effort to evaluate the validity of the above alternatives, consider the Liben and Drury (1977) study described in Chapter 8 and two others reported by Bebko (1984; Bebko & McKinnon, 1990). Recall that Liben and Drury examined memory for pictures, nonsense shapes, fingerspelling, and printed words in 6- and 8-year-old deaf children. Given their hypothesis that deaf children might not use memory rehearsal because they lack oral labels for stimuli, Liben and Drury were surprised to find evidence of oral and manual labeling and of spontaneous rehearsal but no reliable relation between overt rehearsal and memory. Bebko (1984) explicitly examined the extent of spontaneous rehearsal and the success of rehearsal training in profoundly deaf children. The subjects ranged in age from 5 to 15 years and were enrolled in oral or Total Communication programs; they were compared to hearing children from an earlier study. The stimuli were pieces of colored paper presented in random sequences and rearranged for the "recall" task. This study thus did not involve verbal stimuli but allowed examination of recall strategies in the absence of confounds due to stimulus familiarity or language fluency.

During the first phase of the study, Bebko observed children's learning and recorded any evidence of rehearsal. He found that (overt) spontaneous rehearsal emerged later in both deaf groups relative to his hearing controls (tested 6 years previously), appearing at 7 to 8 years for the hearing, 10 to 11 years for the oral deaf, and 12 to 13 years for the TC sample. Overall, the hearing rehearsers recalled more than the deaf rehearsers, but this effect likely resulted from the fact that there were three times as many "borderline" (i.e., inconsistent) rehearsers among the deaf as among the hearing subjects. In fact, after training in overt cumulative rehearsal, the deaf subjects were as good or better than their hearing peers.

Bebko's results indicate that when the complexity of the materials is held constant and is not an impediment to learning, deaf children may still perform more poorly than hearing peers across a wide age range because they fail to employ the appropriate strategies, or if they employ them covertly they are unsuccessful. Clearly, however, when instructed to use strategies consistently and overtly (or when rehearsal is prevented), recall can be the same for the two groups. This finding indicates only that when given simple materials and explicit training deaf children can immediately perform as well as hearing peers.

Why do they not use such strategies as frequently and effectively as hearing children? Why do those strategies not transfer? What are the implications of success only with drastically simplified materials?

If the above findings are considered in terms of an approach to memory development emphasizing relations of knowledge organization and memory, three competing hypotheses emerge to account for the frequently observed differences in long-term memory performance between deaf and hearing children. First, the two groups may have different long-term memory organizations (e.g., Koh et al., 1971). These organizational differences might mistakenly be interpreted as indicating differences in memory ability (i.e., the use or effectiveness of strategies) if the materials are not carefully controlled. Second, the two groups might have similar long-term memory organizations, but deaf children may not utilize that organization in memory tasks (e.g., Bebko, 1984). Thus even when material is familiar and has the potential for meaningful processing, deaf children may not know how or may not try to use the "tools" at their disposal. Third, although deaf children may use organizational strategies for remembering, their attempts may be ineffective (e.g., Liben, 1979). More realistically, one would expect some interaction among these alternatives.

Consistent with this expectation are results from a study by Bebko and McKinnon (1990). They considered the relation between strategic memory rehearsal and serial recall performance in 41 deaf children (aged 5 to 15 years) and 45 hearing children (aged 5 to 8 years). All of the deaf children had profound hearing losses and were enrolled in a TC program. Bebko and McKinnon presented the children with sequences of three, four, and five colored squares (two trials with each). After each sequence there was a 15-second unfilled delay before the children attempted to order a series of colored blocks in the same order they had seen at the presentation. During stimulus presentation and the pretest interval, children were observed for evidence of cumulative rehearsal either orally or manually (or through repeated head or body movements). They were classified as *producers* if they showed evidence of cumulative rehearsal on two or more trials or if they reported cumulative rehearsal; otherwise, they were classified as *nonproducers*.

Bebko and McKinnon found that the deaf children lagged behind the hearing children in their spontaneous use of rehearsal, as 58% of the hearing children and 22% of the deaf children were classified as producers.[1] More importantly, perhaps, they found that children's language experience was the best predictor of rehearsal use. Using the number of years of training in children's preferred language modality as a measure of language experience, Bebko and McKinnon found that in both deaf and hearing samples language experience fully accounted for the age differences observed in the emergence of rehearsal. These results thus provide strong evidence for deaf children being less likely than hearing peers to employ memory strategies even for simple, nonverbal stimuli (cf. Liben, 1979). Still to be determined is the role of language experience and concept knowledge in the retention of more complex materials.

Item-Specific and Relational Information Processing

One additional explanation for the pattern of memory findings described here seems to cut across the alternatives described above. A variety of studies have demonstrated that memory for items in any particular verbal or nonverbal context (e.g., words or pictures in a list) depends on information unique to each of the items (*distinctive information*) and on relations among the items (*relational information*) (e.g., Marschark & Surian, 1989).

Beyond the obvious example of remembering words presented in categorized versus unrelated lists, one excellent example of the joint functioning of relational and distinctive information is the processing that goes on during text processing. That is, as the meaning of individual words are accessed in memory, an integrative semantic processing is also in progress, based on the grammatical and conceptual structure of the text. Similar processes are engaged simultaneously at several levels, but the gist of the argument should be clear: Lack of attention to these structural characteristics of the material results in only a fragmented understanding of what has transpired, hindering both comprehension and memory.

This framework appears consistent with the evidence concerning deaf children's reading and writing abilities, reviewed in Chapter 11 (e.g., Banks, Gray, & Fyfe, 1990) and the memory data considered in this chapter. To the extent that deaf children are lacking in either vocabulary knowledge or the grammatical abilities needed to relate the meanings of words, phrases, and sentences, their comprehension and memory for text suffer. Similarly, lack of either conceptual knowledge, including associative links with other concepts, or relational processing strategies for learning impairs memory performance.

Results of one preliminary study lend support to this relational-distinctive account as it relates to deaf children's memory for text. Marschark, DeBeni, Polazzo, and Cornoldi (1992) presented simple paragraphs to groups of hearing and deaf Italian students. The 37 severely to profoundly deaf students were between the ages of 15 and 22. They were matched with two groups of hearing children, one on the basis of age (forty-seven 16- to 18-year-olds) and the other on the basis of reading ability (twenty-six 8- to 9-year-olds). The students all read one of two passages constructed with the help of teachers to be appropriate for even the youngest deaf group. After each passage the students were tested for free recall, which was subsequently scored for the recall of relational information (i.e., ordered events) and item-specific information (i.e., individual propositions). As can be seen in Figure 9-1, the deaf children recalled significantly less, overall, than their hearing agemates but more than the younger, reading-matched children. Most importantly, the deaf students remembered less relational than item-specific information, whereas the reverse was true for both groups of their hearing peers. The fact that this finding occurred with both age- and reading-matched hearing peers means that the effect cannot be ascribed to reading deficiencies per se. Rather, deaf children may attend to and remember different things.

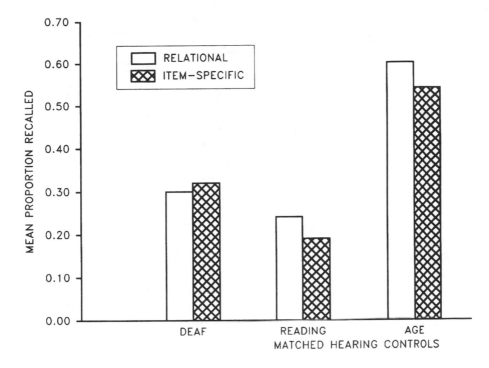

FIGURE 9-1. Proportions of relational and item-specific idea units recalled by deaf adolescents and hearing controls matched according to age or reading level. Based on descriptions in Marschark et al., 1992.

The suggestion that deaf children might attend less to relational information than their hearing peers could account for what appear to be differences in both verbal and nonverbal classification abilities when more than a single dimension is involved (Ottem, 1980) (see Chapter 7). Such a difference is also consistent with findings indicating that deaf children perform more poorly than hearing children in studies of long-term memory for verbal materials. At the same time, the failure of Tweney et al. (1975) to find memory differences between deaf and hearing students after a card sorting task and Hoemann et al.'s (1974) finding of release from proactive inhibition in response to a semantic category shift suggest that deaf children may spontaneously categorize stimuli when they comprise clearly defined categories. The extent of such categorization across memory tasks, language abilities, and age has not been determined.

Summary

Whereas studies of short-term memory in deaf and hearing children focus primarily on the temporal versus spatial bases of memory coding, studies of long-term memory focus on the semantic bases of concept knowledge, encoding strategies, and retrieval. Many studies of long-term memory in deaf children thus have made use of nonverbal materials, which are assumed to allow examination of semantic processing while controlling for language-related differences within samples of deaf children and between them and their hearing peers. Two factors appear to qualify such an assumption, however. First, it is well established that when attempting to learn even apparently meaningless materials children and adults tend to label them. One can safely assume that learning meaningful materials for a later memory test, labeling is the rule rather than the exception. Language fluency, whether in sign or speech (via articulatory or phonological processes), thus may play a role in long-term memory of deaf children regardless of the task. If it does not, linguistic coding certainly plays a role in observed differences in memory performance between deaf and hearing children. Second, several investigators have suggested that deaf children may have less, or at least different, experience with the stimuli used in nonverbal memory tests, and thus they may evidence patterns of memory performance different from those of hearing peers (e.g., Furth, 1961b).

The latter alternative does not eliminate memory factors per se as a major determinant of memory performance. Even if the likelihood of applying memory strategies is not directly affected by conceptual differences in the knowledge base, the resulting organization at both encoding and retrieval would be affected by differences in the breadth and depth of concept knowledge. At a simple level, knowledge concerning the possible taxonomic classifications of an object determines the extent to which to-be-learned stimuli can be hierarchically organized at encoding and clustered at retrieval. Evidence concerning possible differences in semantic organization between deaf and hearing children has been mixed, however, and studies examining the conceptual organization and use of semantically based memory strategies have not been done with young deaf children. It therefore is difficult to know whether semantic memory organization of deaf and hearing children becomes more similar with age or the two groups become better in terms of using what organization they each possess. In either case, it appears that the likelihood of verbal labeling and the use of semantic organization in learning-for-memory are affected by the child's familiarity with the concepts at issue and their fluency (i.e., speed or spontaneity) in verbal labeling.

In general, the *linguistic coding hypothesis* has been invoked to account for a variety of memory findings from studies with deaf children. When deaf children evidence memory performance superior to that of hearing children, it is frequently suggested that linguistic coding on the part on hearing children might have impaired their performance—regardless of whether the stimuli were constructed in a way that would be likely to cause or reflect linguistic interference (alternatively, the task might not have been as "verbal" as originally intended). On the other hand, when deaf children evidence memory performance inferior to that of hearing children, the linguistic coding hypothesis is often invoked to account for that difference as well, by assuming that deaf children are less likely to encode supplementary verbal codes that might facilitate memory. Frequently, however, the assumption that deaf children do not use "linguistic coding" is based on their presumed facility in the oral vernacular only. In fact, a variety of studies have shown that deaf children do show evidence of sign language coding in memory tasks, revealing patterns of both cheremic similarity interference and memory benefits from the use of signable compared to unsignable stimuli. Unfortunately, evaluations of individual differences in memory performance as a function of sign language and receptive speech abilities generally have not been reported, although such studies are underway at this time.

It seems likely that deaf and hearing children do have somewhat different organizations in long-term memory as a function of differences in both verbal and nonverbal experience as well as differences in language fluency. Although these differences may be partially responsible for observed differences in the quality or quantity of memory, there is some evidence to indicate that the two groups might also differ in terms of the extent of their available memory strategies, their experience with these strategies, and their knowledge about the *what*, *where*, and *how* of effective strategy use. If the possible interaction of these factors in memory performance remains unclear, their implications for more complex tasks involving memory are even more obscure. Memory clearly plays a central role in a variety of situations within the laboratory and without, and is a fundamental tool of thinking and problem solving.

Notes

1. Of the 26 hearing producers, 25 reported using cumulative rehearsal when asked how they remembered the colors. In contrast, only 5 of the 9 deaf producers did so.

10

Creativity and Flexibility:
The Myth(?) of Concreteness

Perhaps the most general and frequently invoked characterization of deaf children is that they are literal and concrete in both their language and cognitive functioning (Blackwell et al., 1978; Conrad, 1979; Furth, 1966, 1973; Heider & Heider, 1941; Liben, 1978; Myklebust, 1953; Oléron, 1953; Quigley & Paul, 1984; Watts, 1979). Historically, this conclusion has derived from numerous observations indicating that deaf children tend to be relatively limited in their abilities to grasp complex, abstract, or nonliteral concepts, even when those concepts involve nonverbal domains. Most frequently, however, both teaching and assessments of deaf children's abilities were (and still are) conducted using printed materials. It therefore is unclear to what extent observed deficits in such abilities reflect language-specific deficits rather than more pervasive intellectual limitations—with or without linguistic origins or correlates.

Most deaf children, as noted in Chapter 6, receive far less direct and indirect linguistic tuition than their hearing peers prior to the school years. The resulting unavailability of effective communication reduces the diversity of deaf children's linguistic and nonlinguistic experience (Furth, 1973; Liben, 1978; Watts, 1979). These limitations, in turn, affect their abilities to function in educational, experimental, and even day-to-day settings that might normally tap or require flexibility and creativity. Furthermore, the language training most deaf children receive later involves heavy emphasis on English. This training is frequently literal and concrete in both syntax and vocabulary (Furth, 1973; King & Quigley, 1985) with a variety of implications for reading and writing, to be considered in the next chapter. For the present purposes, it is important that, within deaf education, deaf children generally are not expected to exhibit much diversity or creativity in the linguistic realm (Johnson et al., 1989). Moreover, they rarely are exposed to these characteristics outside of school unless they have deaf parents.

The possibility remains, however, that deaf children may have some linguistic and cognitive abilities just as creative and flexible as those of hearing peers but not easily tapped by assessments involving the reading or writing of English. Evaluation of this possibility constitutes the primary focus of this chapter.[1] The issue is considered here in terms of the literature concerning the linguistic and nonlinguistic creativity of deaf children. The goal is to provide an overview of empirical results concerning the relative rigidity or flexibility of deaf children's cognitive skills, apart from traditional cognitive tests that have been considered in other chapters and by other authors (see also Dolman, 1983; Liben, 1978; Myklebust, 1953; Rittenhouse & Spiro, 1979).

Defining Creativity for Deaf (or Hearing) Children

As is evident from the methodological diversity in the studies reviewed here, there seems to be little consensus on exactly what is meant by "creativity" in deaf children. Most of the available studies have employed the Torrance Tests of Creative Thinking (Torrance, 1966, 1974) and have implicitly accepted Torrance's definition of creativity, described below. Other studies have employed more creative evaluation methods, operationally defining creativity as that quality measured by their procedures (see the discussion of IQ in Chapter 7). Few of these studies, however, have discussed possible definitions of creativity. It thus often remains unclear with what deaf children are being credited when they excel on one of these tasks and what they are presumed to be lacking when they appear less capable than their hearing peers.

Even within the creativity literature there is debate over the definition of its central concept. Whether creativity is seen as an ability, an achievement, a disposition, a response, or a strategy differs depending on the theoretical orientation of the investigator (for a review see Barron & Harrington, 1981). Torrance (1974) provided a general definition of creativity, one that goes beyond simple test performance and focuses on problem solving rather than production of some novel product. For him, creativity was "the process of becoming sensitive to problems, deficiencies, gaps in knowledge . . . searching for solutions, making guesses, or formulating hypotheses about the deficiencies, testing and retesting these hypotheses . . . and finally communicating the results" (p. 8). Accordingly, Torrance's test battery was intended to tap a "constellation of abilities" rather than a particular capacity.

Foremost in this constellation, on both verbal and nonverbal tests, was the ability to restructure one's perception or experience with a stimulus in terms of the needs of a given situation. That is, Torrance saw creativity as going beyond what is given and inventing new "structures" (see also Amabile, 1983). This view of creativity bears a striking resemblance to Piaget's (1952) view of cognitive development, and there are at least some domains of creativity, such as artistic ability and metaphor comprehension, in which competence has been reported to be highly related to children's levels of development according to Piagetian stages (e.g., Billow, 1975; Silver, 1977). Before considering such possible connections further, we should examine the available research concerning verbal and nonverbal creativity of deaf children.

Nonlinguistic Creativity of Deaf Children

When one encounters descriptions of the academic deficiencies of deaf schoolchildren, they are quickly followed by disclaimers suggesting that on many nonverbal tests deaf children are comparable to hearing age-mates (see Chapter 7). In the domain of creativity, as in cognitive and intelligence testing, nonlinguistic measures do tend to indicate that deaf children are more competent than is suggested by linguistic measures (Tomlinson-Keasey & Kelly, 1978). Even within this limited literature, though, there is considerable disagreement. Insofar as the same handful of such published papers are continually cited as bearing on this issue, careful consideration of them is worthwhile.

One would expect that the frequent emphases on nonverbal tests of intelligence and cognitive ability for deaf children would be accompanied by nonverbal tests of creativity. Yet there have been surprisingly few recent assessments of deaf children in this domain. "Recent" is an important word here, because of the advances in deaf education and in the early use of manual communication, in particular, that are giving deaf children greater access to more diverse experiences. Developmental investigators also have become more adept in recent years at tapping children's abilities with a minimum of confounding created by the testing materials or by skills and competencies other than those of particular interest. At present, however, the area of nonlinguistic creativity in deaf children, including play, art, and cognitive flexibility, remains sorely in need of investigation.

In keeping with traditional terminologies, nonlinguistic creativity is considered here in terms of previous evaluations involving the Torrance tests and several other measures purported to tap the divergent thinking abilities of deaf children, independent of language fluency.[2] The nonverbal (or Figural) Torrance tests, which have been the most popular tools for studying creativity of deaf children, include Picture Construction, Incomplete Figures, and Repeated Figures subtests, which examine the ability to construct and elaborate on likeness of people, objects, and scenes (Torrance, 1966). Productions are scored on dimensions of *originality*—the ability to break away from the ordinary or conventional and think in a novel or unique manner; *elaboration*—the addition of greater complexity to a normally simple idea; *flexibility*—the ability to generate a variety of ideas and to shift categories; and *fluency*—the ability to generate a relatively large quantity of ideas. Consistent with both Amabile's (1983) and Torrance's (1966, 1974) definitions of creativity, the primary issue of interest here is whether a particular behavior or mode of behavior reveals a shift from one approach to another, from the commonplace to the novel and apt.

Creativity and Imagination Evidenced in Play and Art

Heider and Heider (1941) reported that at a general level the linguistic deficiencies of young deaf children limit them to the present and immediate past, thus restricting the quantity and diversity of their imaginary play (see also, Cornelius & Hornett 1990; Singer & Lenahan, 1976). Furth (1973), in contrast, described the play of young deaf children as essentially identical to that of hearing peers. This discrepancy clearly needs resolution because such deficiencies in the play of hearing children have been taken to indicate a more pervasive lack of symbolic maturity (McCune-Nicolich, 1981), which in turn negatively affects linguistic development (cf. Lederberg, 1993; Spencer & Deyo, 1993) (see Chapter 3).

One study related to this issue was that reported by Schlesinger and Meadow

(1972a). They examined the behavior of 40 severely to profoundly deaf preschoolers and 20 age-matched hearing peers. Children were observed in videotaped interactions with their mothers, 10 minutes of which involved free play with toys and 10 minutes intentionally interactive activities such as sharing refreshments and looking at pictures. Examining those videotapes, Schlesinger and Meadow selected for analysis behaviors that appeared to differentiate the two hearing status groups of mothers and children. They reported that the hearing children were significantly more "creative and imaginative" than the deaf children, as 70% of the hearing but only 38% of the deaf children were above the median. When the deaf children were equally divided into groups with good and poor communicative skills, however, 60% of the good communicators were above the median, whereas only 15% of the poor communicators were in the more creative/imaginative half of the sample.

These findings are tantalizing because they suggest that good mother–child communication is positively related to children's cognitive flexibility (Cornelius & Hornett, 1990). Nonetheless, two limitations indicate the need for caution when interpreting those results. First, Schlesinger and Meadow gave no indication of the behaviors that were considered "creative" or "imaginative" or how they might have differed during free play or more structured settings (cf. Everhart & Lederberg, 1991). We do not even know whether both linguistic and nonlinguistic creativity were assessed, although the nature of the settings suggests the primacy of nonverbal behaviors. Second, Schlesinger and Meadow analyzed their data (using the chi-square statistic), in terms of the number of children in each group above or below the median. However, there were twice as many deaf as hearing children. Insofar as the hearing children were rated as significantly more creative than their deaf peers, the median would most likely have been lowered relative to a situation in which there were equal numbers in the two groups. As a result, when the deaf children were grouped on the basis of communication skill and then compared to the original median, the criterion would have been more lenient than otherwise would have been the case. In other words, we cannot be entirely sure that deaf preschoolers who are good communicators are really just as creative as hearing age-mates. For that conclusion, we would need a better understanding of what "creativity" meant in this context and groups with equal numbers of subjects.

Singer and Lenahan (1976) attempted to tap the imaginative abilities of deaf children by examining their daydreams, play, and fantasy reports. They obtained reports from 20 profoundly deaf students using structured interviews and an elicited story production. All of Singer and Lenahan's results were descriptive in nature, and no hearing subjects were included for comparison purposes. Nevertheless, they reported several findings purported to indicate that the deaf children were lower in creativity and imagination than hearing age-mates. For example, Singer and Lenahan found that their subjects did not report playing such games as "cowboys and Indians or pirates or cops and robbers" (p. 47) but preferred such activities as playing cards, playing ball, and watching television. This finding does not seem surprising given that those students were 12 to 13 years of age. Not many hearing children of that age play cops and robbers either.

More generally, Singer and Lenahan reported that their deaf informants tended to use past and present time frames (see also Vernon, 1967), and that, "for the most part, the fantasies were very ordinary . . . these children usually related experiences that they had actually encountered rather than some they wished to encounter" (p. 47). Singer and Lenahan therefore concluded that "the play activity, elicited fantasy, and dreaming of these deaf, bright and average IQ, children are of concrete, ordinary, day-to-day events with only a minimal amount of fantasy of imaginative content" (p. 47). Superficially, these results appear consistent with those of Heider and Heider (1941) in suggesting that deaf children are inferior to hearing children in terms of their flexibility of imagination. Their report, however, did not describe the communication modality of the interviews with the children or their language backgrounds. Furthermore, the lack of hearing comparison groups and naturalistic observations in these studies make generalizations from their results tenuous at best.

Silver (1977) accepted Singer and Lenahan's (1976) conclusion that deaf children lag behind hearing children in terms of abstract thinking, imaginary play, and originality, at least within the verbal domain. He argued, however, that "deaf children do *not* in fact lag behind when we bypass verbal expression and use nonverbal instruments to assess these capacities" (p. 349). Citing three unpublished studies, Silver provided several types of evidence for his claim. In one study, the originality of 54 deaf and hard-of-hearing children and adults was assessed using the Torrance figural tests and three measures of performance in art classes. Hearing losses were not described, nor were any other differences between the "deaf" and "hard-of-hearing" subjects. Silver reported administering the Torrance test to 12 of the 54 hearing-impaired subjects, although the basis for their selection was not described. Those 12 scored, on average, in the 88th percentile on flexibility, the 97th percentile on *fluency*, and the 99th percentiles on *originality* and *elaboration*. The three art-related measures involved having "university professors of art," "art educators," and "teacher-observers" compare the artwork of deaf and hearing students. In all three cases, the deaf students' work was judged equal to or slightly above the work of hearing students.

In a second study, 25 deaf students selected by school administrators were enrolled in experimental art classes. Their drawings and paintings again were evaluated by a panel of "education specialists," who were asked either if they found "evidence that art afforded opportunities for various kinds of cognition" or "evidence of story-telling as well as ten other categories of art qualities" (p. 352). More than 93% of the responses were affirmative.

In a third study, Silver evaluated the "cognitive skills" of 18 students attending experimental art classes at a school for the hearing-impaired, but again no information was given on their hearing losses or other abilities. Those students were found to exceed "control groups" (about which no information was provided) on Piagetian-like measures of conservation, seriation, categorization, and prediction of spatial relations. In addition, when drawings of the 8- to 15-year-old subjects were examined for evidence of artistic improvement over the term of the course, 11 of the 18 subjects showed significant gains.

It is difficult to interpret findings from the studies reported by Silver (1977) without knowing more about the deaf subjects involved. That is, individuals who enroll in art classes, whether deaf or hearing, may well be more original, creative, and perhaps even more intelligent in the first place. Another problem for interpretation is that judgments of children's artwork were made by "blind" judges on only one measure in one of the three studies, a situation not conducive to methodological confidence. Drawing any firm conclusions from Silver's null results is thus difficult. If one accepts his data and their interpretation, however, Silver's data suggest that deaf children's artwork evidences a creativity not found in other domains of their symbolic expression.

Nonverbal Creativity and Flexibility as Evidenced by Standardized Tests

Like Silver (1977), Pang and Horrocks (1968) used artistic ability (the Barron-Welsh Art Scale) as one indicator of creativity and employed the standardized Torrance tests in their study of 11 "deaf" children, aged 11 to 12 years. Pang and Horrocks accepted previous assumptions of concrete thinking in deaf children and thus chose evaluation scales that "eliminated language fluency and conceptual thinking" (p. 845). Contrary to Silver's conclusions, Pang and Horrocks reported deaf subjects to be inferior to (hearing) norms on the Torrance (1974) scales of *originality* and *fluency*, even while they were superior on scales of *elaboration* and *flexibility*. All of the reported differences were small, however, and no statistical analyses were reported. The mean *originality* scores, for example, were 31.3 and 31.6 for deaf and hearing groups, respectively, showing essentially equivalent performance. For the Barron-Welsh Art Scale, not even normative comparisons are reported. Pang and Horrocks simply provided a mean score for the group and noted that it was lower than reported for "other *S*'s" in a 1957 study. They concluded from the latter finding that "it appears that [the 11- to 12-year-old deaf subjects] were not interested in the abstract figures but more oriented toward the concrete" (p. 845).

Johnson (1977) also used the Torrance tests to measure *originality, fluency, flexibility*, and *elaboration* in deaf children. Johnson, however, employed a larger sample (*n* = 131) of deaf students, from a broader age range (11 to 19 years), and included a comparable hearing control group. Most of his hearing–impaired subjects were congenitally deaf and were classified as severely to profoundly deaf. In Johnson's subgroup of 15 deaf and 15 hearing 11- to 12-year-olds (comparable to those in the 1968 Pang and Horrocks study), the deaf subjects surpassed the hearing subjects in *fluency* and *flexibility*, but the hearing subjects surpassed the deaf subjects in *originality* and *elaboration*. The *fluency* and *elaboration* results thus contradict Pang and Horrocks's findings. Like the earlier study, however, Johnson found that the mean *originality* scores were essentially the same for the two groups (22.50 and 23.33 for deaf and hearing groups, respectively). Finally, Johnson (1977) found that over the entire age range of his subjects the deaf students scored significantly higher than hearing subjects on the tests of *fluency, flexibility*, and *elaboration*, findings "contrary to the widely held view [including that of Pang and Horrocks, (1968)] that intellectual development is retarded in the absence of language" (pp. 54–55).

Kaltsounis (1971) similarly used the nonverbal subtests of the Torrance battery in an examination of creativity in 172 "deaf" and 605 hearing children in grades 1 to 6. Overall, as well as in the separate 11- to 12-year-old (grade 6) sample (comparable to the Pang and Horrocks and Johnson samples described above), deaf subjects surpassed hearing subjects considerably on measures of *fluency, flexibility*, *elaboration*, and *originality*. The finding of superior *elaboration* scores in the deaf 11- to 12-year-olds was consistent with the finding of Pang and Horrocks but contrary to that of Johnson. Kaltsounis's finding that deaf children obtained greater *originality* scores than their hearing peers contrasts with null findings on that dimension by both Pang and Horrocks and Johnson.

In summary, on the basis of findings drawn from studies employing the nonverbal forms of Torrance's tests of creative thinking, deaf children, at least in the 11- to 12-year-old range, generally appear to be more flexible in their thinking than hearing age-mates (cf. Furth, 1961). Methodologically, the studies of both Johnson (1977) and Kaltsounis (1971) appear sound, suggesting that the advantage they observed for deaf over hearing subjects in *fluency* (the ability to generate a large number of ideas) is reliable. The *fluency* difference obtained by Pang and Horrocks in the opposite direction was so small (22.4 versus 23.4 for deaf subjects and Torrance's norms, respectively) that it likely would not be reliable. Finally, with regard to nonverbal tests of *elaboration* and *originality*, findings from studies employing the Torrance tests are inconsistent. Certainly, deaf children can be trained to be creative in nonverbal test situations (Kaltsounis, 1970; Lubin & Sherrill, 1980). However, the extent to which they naturally exceed hearing peers in relevant domains remains unclear.

Linguistic Creativity of Deaf Children

Because of the importance laid to the language–cognition relation in deaf children, somewhat more research has been conducted concerning linguistic than nonlinguistic creativity. Nonetheless, it is still surprising how little attention has been given to deaf schoolchildren's abilities in this domain, even in books devoted to their cognitive and language abilities (e.g., Quigley & Paul, 1984; Rodda & Grove, 1987). This omission is likely due to the common assumption that there is little to evaluate (e.g., Furth, 1973). In their discussion about using abstract and nonliteral language in the classroom, for example, Blackwell et al. (1978, p. 138) noted that, "A constant frustration of the secondary school teacher is the literalness with which hearing-impaired students approach new information. Either something is literal or it is absurd and thus usually regarded as insignificant."

This and other conclusions about deaf children's lack of linguistic creativity, however, largely have been based on observations of educators concerning flexibility within English. Although the need for English fluency is a laudable goal for the deaf educational system, determination of cognitive and linguistic competence on the basis of second language performance might be expected to lead to underestimation of those abilities (see Chapter 7). Assessment of deaf children's linguistic creativity thus should be seen as a somewhat different enterprise from assessment of their capabilities within any particular language. The more general evaluation requires consideration of their comprehension and production capabilities in sign language as well as English (Klima & Bellugi, 1979; Marschark & West, 1985; Marschark et al., 1986; Suty & Friel-Patti, 1982). All of these possibilities have been evaluated in one study or another and are considered here, together with several direct comparisons across domains.

Linguistic Creativity Based on English Evaluations

Laughton (1979) examined the English grammatical complexity of deaf children's picture descriptions in an attempt to determine the extent to which their linguistic creativity might correspond to their nonlinguistic creativity as assessed by the non-verbal Torrance tests. Her suggestion that the "creative" component of Chomsky's (1957) transformational generative grammar might correspond to creativity in the aesthetic sense, however, was based on the common but erroneous assumption that Chomsky's *deep structure*, from which his creativity arises, is based on semantic or underlying meaning representations (see Chapter 5). In fact, Chomsky used *creativity* to refer to the openness or productivity (Hockett & Altmann, 1968) of human language systems. That creativity, he asserted, was driven by a deep structure that was most decidedly syntactic and thus unlikely to be related to any nonverbal form of creativity.

Laughton tested 77 hearing-impaired students between 8 and 12 years of age who had severe to profound hearing losses. About half ($n = 30$) were drawn from programs using the orally oriented, auditory/visual/oral (AVO) method, and the remainder were drawn from a Total Communication program. Using the Torrance figural test battery, Laughton found that *flexibility*, *elaboration*, and especially *originality* scores were reliably correlated with the frequencies of producing various linguistic units during their picture descriptions. She thus concluded that a relation exists "between cognitive/semantic/syntactic systems" (p. 416). Laughton also found that the AVO students performed better (i.e., were more "creative") than the TC students on both nonverbal and verbal measures. The verbal finding is not unexpected given her English-based measures, but the finding of greater nonverbal creativity in the AVO students was contrary to "the frequent speculation of superiority in cognitive, language, emotional and other abilities of children using sign language" (p. 417).

Using a verbal subtest of the Torrance battery, Thinking Creatively with Words, Kaltsounis (1970) compared verbal and creative thinking abilities of deaf ($n = 67$) and hearing ($n = 351$) children. "The deaf group included boys and girls from Grades 4, 5, and 6 [in a residential school], whose age, mental, and hearing abilities were not controlled" (p. 727). Like the nonverbal Torrance tests, the verbal form of the Torrance battery includes several activities that require the subject to fill in, extrapolate, or elaborate on tester-supplied partial information. Over the seven tasks involved, Kaltsounis found deaf subjects to surpass their hearing age-mates on measures of verbal *fluency* and *originality*, whereas the hearing subjects were superior in verbal *flexibility*. The advantages of the deaf subjects were especially large in the fourth and fifth grade samples relative to the sixth grade sample. Interestingly, Kaltsounis did not draw any conclusions from the overall superiority of deaf subjects in his study, other than noting their consistency with Silver's (1967) earlier findings involving measures of nonverbal creativity.

In contrast to Kaltsounis's (1970) findings, Johnson and Khatena (1975) found that deaf children ($n = 181$) scored significantly lower than hearing peers ($n = 236$) on a different test of verbal creativity developed by Torrance and his colleagues, the Onomatopoeia and Images test (Torrance, Khatena, & Cunningham, 1973). Johnson and Khatena ensured that instructions for this task were understood by their deaf subjects through the use of both sign and speech in extensive explanation sessions. They then played audio recordings of onomatopoetic words ("ouch," "groan," "jingle," "zoom," and "fizzy") to their subjects, asking them for imaginative and original associations. However, as in Johnson's (1977) nonlinguistic study, "Most of the deaf *S*'s were deaf since birth and 98% were classified as severely to profoundly deaf, i.e., they did not benefit from hearing aids" (p. 632).[3] There is no mention of the stimulus words being either fingerspelled or written for the subjects, although even if they were the deaf subjects would be unlikely to be familiar with them and would lack appropriate associations. Thus it is not surprising, that Johnson and Khatena found that "the hearing *S*'s scored much higher than the deaf *S*'s" (p. 633). What would be surprising is anything other than random responding by the deaf subjects.

Lacking further information from standardized tests of verbal creativity, Kaltsounis's (1970) findings seem to have more face validity than those of Johnson and Khatena (1975). Kaltsounis, however, did not report whether his subjects responded in sign or in writing; and the possible reasons why deaf subjects should surpass hearing peers in English verbal creativity are not at all clear.

One other study of deaf children's linguistic creativity, as assessed in terms of English production, was reported by Kramer and Buck (1976). They examined the poetic creativity of a group of deaf schoolchildren aged 11 to 16 years old but whose hearing and other abilities were not specified. Kramer and Buck conducted intensive, one-on-one training sessions in poetry with the children and then obtained written productions from them. The selections on which their analyses were based were chosen and evaluated by the authors, but the bases for either selection or evaluation were not provided. Kramer and Buck reported only that the deaf subjects involved represented "as wide a range of strength in poetry" as did the authors' usual (presumably university-aged) students.

Methodological problems aside, there still is some question as to what conclusions can be drawn from consideration of Kramer and Buck's findings. To this admittedly untrained observer, at least, most of their examples seem just as likely (if not more so) to be cited as indicating poetic disfluency as the "fresh and right" creativity described by Kramer and Buck. The following examples (Kramer & Buck, 1976, p. 33), like most others, do not appear at first glance to indicate "the merging of openness of fantasy with the enhancement of technical dexterity" that Kramer and Buck claim to see in their deaf students' productions; nor does the first one seem "particularly moving."

> Remember when I was a little boy,
>   that you gave me bubble gum all the time.
> Now, I don't have any more gum.
> I like chewing gum because I always
>   think about when you gave me the gum.

> I remember, when I was
>   a little boy, I always
>   played outside, because
>   I felt so wonderful.

Although this evaluation is admittedly from the viewpoint of a psychologist rather than a poet, it seems doubtful that the average teacher of deaf children would be as exuberant with such productions as were Kramer and Buck (1976)—which is not to argue that deaf children in general might not have aptitudes for poetic expression within written language (cf. Everhart & Marschark, 1988; Klima & Bellugi, 1979). Without some comparison or control relevant to the presence or absence of spoken English as a native language, however, the relation of Kramer and Buck's training program to the other indices of deaf children's creativity and the poetic sign language creativity of deaf adults (Klima & Bellugi, 1976) is indeterminate.

Figurative Language Abilities of Deaf Children

One alternative means of evaluating deaf children's linguistic creativity involves examination of their comprehension and production of various nonliteral language devices. Most generally, figurative language evidences both linguistic flexibility and a more global cognitive ability to consider the world from alternative perspectives (Gardner et al., 1978; Petrie, 1979), precisely the kind of divergent thinking that investigators have sought to examine in deaf children using the verbal and nonverbal forms of the Torrance tests. More specifically, nonliteral language abilities have been shown to depend on classification skills and especially the ability to cross-classify, that is, to see abstract relations across domains as superseding superficial similarities (Billow, 1975; Marschark & Nall, 1985).

If deaf children are as concrete and literal as some investigators have reported, (e.g., Conrad, 1979; Furth, 1973; Liben, 1978; Myklebust, 1960), they would not be expected to either comprehend or produce nonliteral language. Because of its *compactness*, however, figurative language provides an efficient and vivid form of communication that could well be especially important for deaf children. Furthermore, because metaphors and other figurative constructions holistically predicate information from one concept to another, they reduce the need for a speaker to provide all details of an intended message and allow communication of ideas that otherwise might be inexpressible (Ortony, 1975). Such constructions therefore should reduce both the processing load and the time required for linguistic production and comprehension relative to exact, literal transmission; and they should be of particular utility to deaf children, who typically have smaller vocabularies than hearing agemates (Griswold & Commings, 1974). Several researchers (e.g., Gardner et al., 1978; Petrie, 1979), in fact, have emphasized the importance of this aspect of figurative language for young hearing children who, like deaf children across a wider age range, have much to say but meager linguistic resources at their command.

Figurative Comprehension by Deaf Children

A variety of studies have now examined the nonliteral language abilities of hearing children; relatively few, however, have involved deaf children, and almost all of those have investigated the comprehension of nonliteral English. Insofar as deaf children generally lack both experiential diversity (Liben, 1978) and English syntactic and semantic skills (Quigley & Paul, 1984), it would not be surprising to find that they have little skill in understanding the many nonliteral aspects of English (Boatner & Gates, 1969).

Conley (1976) was apparently the first to directly evaluate these assumptions. She tested samples of 643 hearing students aged 7 to 19 years and 137 deaf students aged 13 to 20 on a test of English idiom comprehension. Subjects in the deaf and hearing samples were described as having comparable reading abilities, ranging from 2.0 to 11.4 for the deaf and 1.5 to 12.9 for the hearing. Conley employed a multiple-choice, sentence completion task involving 100 idioms, such as "knowing something by heart." Despite the fact that the vocabulary of test sentences were selected from lower reading levels, Conley found that her deaf subjects were significantly poorer in their (English) idiom comprehension than their hearing peers, at least at the middle range of reading levels. However, Conley also found that deaf and hearing children at lower reading levels did not differ significantly in their performance (cf. Furth, 1961).

Iran-Nejad, Ortony, and Rittenhouse (1981) argued that the lack of linguistic creativity suggested by Conley's (1976) findings was the result of factors other than the nonliteral nature of idioms per se. They suggested that deaf children might well be able to comprehend English figurative language if they possessed the relevant knowledge of syntax, vocabulary, and the world. As stimuli, they therefore used a set of short stories in which these variables were controlled at a level appropriate for their deaf, 9- to 17-year-old subjects. All of the children had profound congenital or early-onset hearing losses.

Subjects read the stories, accompanied by a simple picture depicting the main point of the story. They then were required to select from a set of four literal sentences, similes, or metaphors the sentence that best completed each story. No hearing control groups were involved, but Iran-Nejad et al. found that even their youngest deaf subjects could select nonliteral sentences as best completions for the stories. Rittenhouse, Morreau, and Iran-Nejad (1981) replicated the Iran-Nejad et al. (1981) results and further showed that metaphor comprehension and performance on Piagetian conservation tasks were significantly related, a finding later replicated by Rittenhouse and Kenyon (1991) with children from oral and Cued Speech programs. Rittenhouse et al. (1981) concluded that metaphor comprehension and conservation "stem from the same or similar underlying cognitive processes" (p. 453), depending largely on children's real-world experience and problem solving (see also Billow, 1975).

In a reevaluation of Conley's (1976) finding that deaf children were inferior to hearing peers in their comprehension of English idioms, Fruchter, Wilbur, and Fraser (1984) employed a methodology similar to that of the Iran-Nejad et al. (1981) and Rittenhouse et al. (1981) studies. Fruchter et al. demonstrated that when idioms were accompanied by pictures depicting their interpretations as one of four response choices, hearing-impaired students across a wide range of reading abilities chose the correct picture during more than 90% of the trials.

Taken together, the findings from the above studies appear to support the claim that deaf children's poor performance on previous tests of figurative English comprehension may not have been the result of any nonliteral language-specific deficiency but, rather, underestimates of their abilities due to the use of inappropriate stimulus materials (Iran-Nejad et al., 1981). Billow (1975) has obtained evidence from hearing children consistent with this possibility. Marschark and Nall (1985), however, argued that the use of multiple-choice tests and accompanying interpretation-depicting pictures in all three of these studies may have created a liberal criterion for figurative comprehension, thereby overestimating figurative comprehension. Moreover, neither the "unassisted" comprehension paradigm of Conley (1976) nor the "assisted" paradigms of Fruchter et al. (1984), Iran-Nejad et al. (1981), Rittenhouse et al. (1981), and Rittenhouse and Kenyon (1991) provided naturalistic assessments of linguistic creativity, and the latter four lacked hearing control groups.

Figurative Production by Deaf Children

Although the results of studies of deaf children's figurative comprehension indicate these subjects to have more linguistic flexibility than previously was assumed, the extent of their linguistic creativity also requires consideration of their production abilities beyond highly structured, cue-laden comprehension tasks. Several such studies have demonstrated that, when evaluated in sign, deaf children display linguistic competencies not evident from their use of and evaluation in English. Suty and Friel-Patti (1982), for example, asked two deaf 6-year-olds to produce signed stories about cartoon-like picture sequences. They then compared those samples to samples obtained from a hearing child and to the deaf children's own responses on an English competence test. Observed modifications of the deaf children's manual signs indicated "linguistic maturity" comparable to that of the hearing child tested and independent of the deaf children's skills in written English.

In an attempt to examine deaf children's linguistic creativity more directly than had previous researchers, Marschark and West (1985) examined creative story productions signed and spoken by four severely to profoundly deaf and four hearing 12- to 15-year-olds, respectively. They videotaped the children, individually, telling stories on two experimenter-supplied, fantasy themes. The production samples then were examined for any use of nonliteral language constructions. The most important general finding was that there were several creative language constructions that were used consistently across deaf as well as hearing subjects. In contrast to Conley's (1976) study of deaf children's comprehension of English idioms, Marschark and West (1985) found that their deaf subjects produced novel and *frozen* figurative constructions just as often as their age-matched hearing peers. The deaf children also reliably surpassed their hearing age-mates in their frequency of using gesture, pantomime, nonliteral linguistic modifications, and linguistic inventions (Klima & Bellugi, 1976, 1979).

In general, Marschark and West's (1985) results suggested that deaf school-children are not necessarily tied to concrete, literal language when using sign language, even if they may be when using English (Conley, 1976; Conrad, 1979; Furth, 1973). Furthermore, to the extent that nonliteral language reflects both abstractive mapping of attributes between conceptual domains and vivid ways of expressing information that otherwise might be inexpressible, our sample of deaf children was at least as creative as their hearing counterparts. Marschark et al. (1986) obtained further support for those conclusions in an investigation of possible developmental changes in nonliteral language production by deaf and hearing children (for discussion see Gardner et al., 1978; Marschark & Nall, 1985; Pollio & Pollio, 1974). Our subjects were 20 deaf and 20 hearing children aged 7 to 15 years; 17 of the deaf students had severe to profound hearing losses, and the remaining 3 had moderate losses. Each of the children told two stories each on experimenter-supplied themes (one fantasy-based, one more mundane). In general, all of our earlier findings were replicated, indicating deaf children's considerable linguistic creativity when evaluated in sign language rather than English. The most interesting finding, however, was an apparent "literal period" in deaf children's language productions. Previous investigations of hearing children's language production have revealed a point at around 8 to 9 years of age when figurative language is at a minimum. This hiatus has variously been described as a consequence of perceived academic demands (Pollio & Pollio, 1974), the emergence of an analytical attitude in concrete operations (Gardner et al., 1978), and the point at which linguistic and cognitive skills have matured enough that children stop producing apparently figurative category violations that stem from conceptual error; that is, they are intended literally because children do not recognize the metaphoric *tension* (Marschark & Nall, 1985). According to the latter interpretation, it is only after the literal period that true figurative language use begins.

The literal period in deaf children's language production observed by Marschark et al. (1986) represented its first demonstration within sign language. Perhaps the most interesting aspect of that finding, however, was that the literal period of the deaf sample was observed at around age 12 or 13 years, 3 to 4 years later than it was observed in the hearing sample, and corresponding to the approximate lag in language development observed in deaf relative to hearing children (Furth, 1973; Quigley & Paul, 1984). This result is consistent with the suggestion of Iran-Nejad et al. (1981) that deaf children's lack of linguistic experience should be reflected in various aspects of their language use. More generally, it indicates that the development of linguistic creativity in deaf children follows a similar, if slightly delayed, course relative to that in hearing children.

Signed and Oral Production Compared to Written Production

The above results indicated that deaf children are not as rigid in language as has generally been assumed. Everhart and Marschark (1988), however, pointed out that deaf children's use of nonliteral sign language could reflect a language deficiency. Petrie (1979), Ortony (1975), and others have argued that figurative language frequently serves the function of allowing expression of ideas when literal vocabulary is either unknown or is temporarily unavailable. Marschark and Nall (1985) further argued that much of the apparent nonliteral language produced by preschool children might be intended literally owing to the lack of correct (i.e., adult-centered) conceptual and linguistic knowledge. Greater use of nonliteral constructions by deaf than by hearing children thus may be a product of their relatively impoverished vocabularies (Griswold & Commings, 1972; Meadow, 1980; Sallop, 1980).

To examine this possibility and to obtain a direct test of deaf children's figurative abilities within sign language and written English, Everhart and Marschark

(1988) contrasted the frequencies of nonliteral language use in signed and oral story productions by deaf and hearing children, respectively, with their use of nonliteral language in written English productions. If one accepts the conclusion that previous assessments of deaf children's linguistic creativity were biased by testing in English, it would be expected that deaf children would produce more nonliteral language in their signed than in their written productions, even when the nonliteral constructions considered are limited to those appropriate for both written and signed forms. Alternatively, if figurative language in children reflects primarily vocabulary deficits, manual deaf children would be expected to produce even more nonliteral constructions in written than in sign language because their fluency in English generally lags behind their fluency in sign language.

In two experiments, Everhart and Marschark (1988) asked deaf and hearing children to produce stories using the Marschark and West (1985) paradigm. Overall, we found that the hearing students produced more nonliteral constructions in their written than in their oral stories, whereas the deaf students produced marginally more nonliteral constructions in their signed than in their written productions. More importantly, the deaf students used significantly more nonliteral constructions in their signed productions than did their age-matched hearing peers in oral production, whereas the hearing students used significantly more nonliteral constructions in their written productions than did their deaf peers. Those findings supported the arguments of several investigators who have tried to differentiate the usefulness of English-based assessments of deaf children's academic competencies from more general issues concerning their intellectual competencies (e.g., Furth, 1973; Marschark & Clark, 1987; Suty & Friel-Patti, 1982). Written and signed/oral assessment of deaf as well as hearing children's psycholinguistic competencies simply do not offer the same conclusions. It is now clear that overemphasis on English in teaching and evaluating deaf children can lead to inaccurate understanding of their abilities and may even retard their linguistic and cognitive development (Furth, 1973; Griswold & Commings, 1974; Liben, 1978; Watts, 1979).

Creativity "Directed" at Deaf Children

Schlesinger and Meadow's (1972a) assessment of deaf and hearing preschoolers' creativity and imagination was described earlier in this chapter, as it involved their behaviors in free and semistructured play situations. In addition, Schlesinger and Meadow evaluated the behaviors of the hearing mothers who accompanied those children. As noted in Chapter 4, mothers of deaf children tend to be more directive than mothers of hearing children. Schlesinger and Meadow's (1972a) results supported that stereotype, as the mothers of deaf children were more intrusive and didactic and less flexible, permissive, and encouraging. In addition, those mothers also were described as being significantly less "creative and imaginative" in dealing with their deaf children. Interestingly, when the comparisons were considered within educational levels (i.e., with or without any college), creativity was the only difference that was no longer significant. This result suggests that mothers of deaf children who have more education are more likely to interact with their children in creative ways that, in turn, have positive effects on their children's creativity. Unfortunately, this possibility has not been directly evaluated. Anecdotal evidence and one empirical study concerning teachers in schools for the deaf (Newton, 1985), however, suggest that the creativity link also applies to teachers and their pupils.

In recent years the nature of linguistic interactions between deaf and hearing adults and deaf children have been of considerable interest to linguists, psycholinguists, and developmental psychologists (e.g., MacKay-Soroka et al. 1987, 1988; Meadow et al., 1981; Newton, 1985; Schlesinger & Meadow, 1972a) (see Chapters 3 and 5). To date, however, little attention has been given to the extent to which adults might use nonliteral sign language for communicating with deaf children (cf. Marschark et al., 1991; Newton, 1985; see also the informal observations of Maestas y Moore, 1980). Generally, adult language to children is adapted to the presumed linguistic capabilities of the listener (e.g., Furrow et al., 1979; Newport, 1977), and thus one might predict that adults would use less nonliteral language to deaf children than they would to hearing children. This expectation was supported by Swisher's (1984) finding that use of colloquial language was "notably absent" in the productions of the six bimodal mothers of deaf children she observed. Such literalness is not surprising, given that Swisher's sample consisted of mothers who for the most part had only beginning competence in sign language as a second language. More generally, use of literal and concrete language in the home as well as in school likely contributes significantly to deaf children's concreteness and apparent cognitive inflexibility in a variety of tasks (e.g., Liben & Drury, 1977; Marschark, 1988a; Ottem, 1980).

Newton (1985) made observations similar to those of Swisher in her study of nonliteral language by teachers of deaf children. She examined the use of indirect requests (e.g., "You could bring me the scissors") and English idioms in the classroom language of teachers of deaf children who used either oral language only or Total Communication (TC) for teaching. These two groups were compared to a group of teachers of hearing children. Although the frequency of nonliteral language was about the same for teachers of oral deaf and hearing students, Swisher found that its use was markedly reduced, in both speech and sign, by teachers using TC. This finding suggests that teachers of manual deaf children may not be good nonliteral language models for their students (Johnson et al., 1989). It also provides a partial explanation for the marked lack of nonliteral English by those children in academic settings (Blackwell et al., 1978; Everhart & Marschark, 1988).

When considered in this context, Newton's (1985) study has three important limitations. First, she reported only the use of English idiomatic language in sign or speech. Although using fewer English idioms, teachers using TC nonetheless may have used nonliteral sign language devices just as frequently as teachers of hearing children used idiomatic speech. This possibility may be somewhat reduced by the fact that the TC teachers were rated only as good or above average signers (p. 339), rather than being fluent—an unfortunate but not uncommon situation in schools for the deaf. Second, Newton's (1985) criteria for idiomatic language apparently included only *frozen* figures of speech—those that have become part of the language because of their frequent use. These constructions included nonprimary uses of language (e.g., It *got* stuck; That's *kind* of funny; He *made up* the answer), that are likely to be learned as "natural" lexical units. Other constructions were nonliteral phrases (e.g., *sink or swim, flew the coop, How are you?*) of varying degrees of figurativeness (Newton, 1985, p. 344). Third, Newton compared the language directed at deaf school-aged children (aged 5;11 to 9;3) with that directed at hearing preschoolers (aged 2;4 to 3;0), leaving open the possibility that the apparent TC versus speech difference observed was an artifact of the different age groups involved (cf. Marschark et al., 1991).

Newton's (1985) study thus leaves largely unresolved the question of whether the language directed at deaf children by their teachers contains the diversity of novel nonliteral constructions typically observed in the language of deaf and hearing children (Marschark et al., 1986; Vosniadou, 1987). Nonetheless, the study is particularly interesting in light of the demonstrations that, when evaluated in terms of their nonliteral sign language production, deaf children of both deaf and hearing parents have a far greater nonliteral competence than is revealed by tests of nonliteral English comprehension. Newton's study also brings up the question of whether deaf adults would use nonliteral sign when addressing deaf children, as they apparently do in adult-to-adult interactions (Klima & Bellugi, 1979).

Marschark et al. (1991) explored the use of nonliteral constructions in child-directed language productions of deaf and hearing mothers, using the same methodology as in our earlier studies. In addition, we included a group of "bilingual" mothers, women who were hearing but had deaf parents and had acquired American Sign Language (ASL) as their first language. Beyond the direct issue of whether deaf adults use nonliteral sign to deaf children in the same ways that hearing adults use nonliteral speech to hearing children, inclusion of this group allowed us to address another question left unresolved by the previous studies: Is the relatively high frequency of nonliteral sign language observed in deaf children (relative to both their own written productions and their hearing peers' oral productions) really an indicator of deaf children's creativity, or is it simply the result of sign language being "open"? That is, one possible explanation of our previous results was that sign language provides more opportunity for nonliteral production than does spoken English, regardless of the language user [but see Ortony's (1975) discussion of the central role of nonliteral devices in spoken language]. If this explanation were true, the bilingual women would be expected to produce more nonliteral constructions in their signed stories than in their oral stories, just as the stories of the deaf women would contain more nonliteral constructions than those of the nonsigning, hearing women. In addition, we had two other predictions: (1) If the previous work with children generalized to adults, the deaf women should produce more nonliteral language in sign than their hearing counterparts would produce orally; and (2) if Newton's (1985) results generalized to nonliteral productions other than English idioms, the bilingual women (corresponding to her TC teachers), should produce fewer nonliteral constructions in sign than the hearing, monolingual women would produce in speech.

In this study, 11 deaf women told two stories in sign, 11 hearing women told two in spoken English, and 11 bilingual women told two stories in each mode. They were initially informed that we were conducting a study of children's story comprehension for which we needed videotaped stories for 4- and 10-year-olds. Overall, we found that the bilingual mothers' oral stories were significantly shorter than those produced by hearing mothers. This result is noteworthy because it indicates that the large difference in mean story length observed between deaf and hearing mothers was not one of hearing status per se. Whether the difference between the hearing mothers and the other two groups in this regard is merely a product of the high variability typically seen in the lengths of such productions (e.g., Marschark et al., 1986) or is somehow related to differences in their early linguistic environments remains unclear.

In any case, when story length was controlled, deaf mothers were found to produce significantly more nonliteral constructions than hearing mothers, replicating the previous findings with deaf and hearing children. Considering the bilingual mothers, their total frequencies of using nonliteral constructions did not differ with production mode. Contrary to Newton's (1985) findings concerning the production of English idioms, they also did not differ from hearing mothers in their frequencies of orally producing nonliteral constructions. However, bilingual mothers did produce significantly fewer signed nonliteral constructions than deaf mothers. This result suggests that the findings of greater total, nonliteral language use by deaf than hearing individuals, both here and in the previous studies, were not solely the consequence of a greater likelihood of nonliteral production in sign language relative to spoken language. Rather, they represent either a real difference in the language content of deaf and hearing individuals or an interaction of hearing status and style of sign language use.

Either way, the results clearly indicate not only that deaf mothers use a variety of nonliteral language constructions in their language to children, but that they do so even with children as young as 4 years. In short, nonliteral language is a central component of linguistic competence (Ortony, 1975) that appears in both young language learners and mature adult users of signed as well as spoken languages.

Where Does Nonliteral Language Come From?

Taken together, the research considered in this section has indicated that nonliteral sign language is as much a natural and integral part of sign language as nonliteral speech is of spoken language (Boatner & Gates, 1969; Petrie, 1979). Deaf children of deaf parents appear most likely to learn about this flexibility in language at home from their parents and other members of the deaf community (either explicitly or implicitly). Most deaf children of hearing parents, in contrast, are unlikely to learn the ways of figurative language at home; and at least as indicated by teachers' infrequent use of signed English figures of speech (Newton, 1985), they are also unlikely to learn it in the classroom. One possible alternative is that the deaf children observed using nonliteral constructions in our studies have acquired both specific exemplars (especially likely for frozen devices) and a more general nonliteral competence from more adept signing peers in the school setting. This possibility would be easily tested by examining the frequencies of nonliteral use by students in residential schools compared to those in mainstream or oral programs (although a variety of possible confounds still would have to be resolved).

A second alternative is that nonliteral sign, and nonliteral speech for that matter, may not have to be learned from models but might emerge naturally from children's early categorization and labeling errors (Macnamara, 1972; Marschark & Nall, 1985). Evaluation of this possibility would be a bit more complex than the previous one, requiring either extensive examination of the productions of children who lack language models (e.g., Goldin-Meadow & Mylander, 1984) or a detailed analysis of the frequencies and types of naming errors produced and the subsequent use of those erroneous labels in other contexts. Both studies would be interesting, however, and seem worthwhile for other reasons as well.

Finally, it should be noted that the acquisition of figurative language from other language users has implications far beyond the study of nonliteral production per se. As important tools in both education (Petrie, 1979) and social communication (e.g., McNeill et al., 1990; Vosniadou, 1987), metaphor, novel gesture, and other creative devices have significant impact on several aspects of cognitive and social development in addition to their important roles in language acquisition in general.

Summary

This chapter has reviewed a variety of evidence concerning nonlinguistic and linguistic creative abilities of deaf children. Throughout, an attempt has been made to set aside the strong desire to declare deaf children just as creative as hearing children, or even more so, on the basis of results regularly cited in this regard but never critically examined. Evaluation of those findings indicates the need for some qualification of previous conclusions concerning deaf children's creativity and considerably more well-controlled research.

With regard to measures of nonlinguistic creativity, numerous investigators have cited deaf children's traditionally poor performance on various nonverbal tests of cognitive abilities as evidence of their conceptual concreteness and rigidity. Direct tests of nonverbal creativity per se have been relatively rare, however, and those that are available generally lack appropriate statistical controls and convergent validity. Somewhat more literature is available concerning deaf children's linguistic creativity. Research in this area, too, however, has been plagued by a lack of appropriate methodological control. Most of the relevant studies have examined deaf children's abilities in comprehending English idioms and metaphors. In general, the evidence suggests that deaf children can understand figurative English only when the relevant tasks are simplified and carefully structured. In contrast, evaluations of deaf children's sign language production have indicated that these children are just as creative in their use of novel, nonliteral constructions as their hearing peers. These findings support the hypothesis that deaf children might be cognitively and linguistically creative, but not necessarily in ways that are easily tapped by testing English comprehension.

Until more evidence is available, generalizations concerning the linguistic and nonlinguistic creativity of deaf children remain tenuous. What evidence is available nonetheless strongly suggests that they are not as literal in their language and cognition as early observations suggested. Although the charge of being more concrete than hearing peers may be warranted for some deaf children in some domains, cognitive differences should not be taken for cognitive deficiencies.

Notes

1. Portions of this chapter are based on the paper "Linguistic and nonlinguistic creativity of deaf children," originally published with M. Diane Clark in *Developmental Review*, 7, 22–38, 1987.

2. A variety of other simple tests of verbal and nonverbal creativity are available, but they have not yet attracted the attention of deafness researchers.

3. Although the descriptions of the subjects appear virtually identical, it is unclear if the two studies involved the same children and what effect, if any, that may have had on the results.

11

Learning to Read and Write

Perhaps more than any other area relating to deafness, the reading and writing abilities of deaf children have been the focus of attention from deaf educators, educational psychologists, and language researchers for decades. Although the empirical studies on reading and writing may number no more than those on short- and long-term memory, they have been accompanied by numerous surveys and evaluations of standardized test scores for schoolchildren and young adults in high schools or college. Taken together, these investigations present an enlightening, if disappointing, picture of deaf children who typically begin school with a language disadvantage and then consistently lose ground from there on in terms of their reading and writing abilities.

It is important to keep in mind here that "reading and writing" refer to performance in *English*, a second language for many deaf children (Charrow & Fletcher, 1974). Comparisons of deaf schoolchildren's literacy skills with those of native English speaking, hearing children thus may create some difficulties for theoretical interpretation (if not for applied considerations). At the same time, however, English is the vernacular in which those deaf children will have to function if they are to receive adequate educations and achieve their potentials in the work force and intellectual life of society (cf. Johnson et al., 1989). It therefore is necessary to consider both the several levels of cognitive and psycholinguistic functioning that are involved in the literacy (or illiteracy) of deaf children and the cognitive, academic, and social consequences of their typical reading and writing deficiencies.

Like the data available from several domains considered in earlier chapters, the literature on deaf children's literacy skills is not always consistent, and several variables must be taken into account when interpreting relevant findings. First, a large portion of the research on the component skills of deaf children's reading has been conducted in England, and research based on U.S. populations largely has involved children in oral programs or deaf college students. As a result, much of the relevant data on deaf children's use of phonological versus visual codes underlying spelling and similar "basic" processes is derived from studies with subjects who may not be representative of most North American deaf children. Rather more research has been done in the United States on the syntactic component of reading and writing. Primarily involving children in Total Communication (TC) and Simultaneous Communication (SC) programs, these data complement findings from oral and adult deaf populations and allow us to arrive at some fairly secure conclusions about reading, writing, and deafness.

Second, as in other domains of psychological development, we must take into consideration the backgrounds of the children from whom we wish to generalize. The finding that deaf children of deaf parents, on average, outperform their deaf peers with hearing parents surfaces in the reading domain, as it has elsewhere. As is seen below, however, the correlation of reading ability with parental hearing status does not entail any simple causation, as the effects of parental hearing on deaf children's reading are rather complex and indirect. Similarly, although reading is linked to several other aspects of cognitive development, it is not always the case that better functioning in domains such as short-term memory, attention allocation, and vocabulary knowledge operates in a unidirectional manner from cognition to reading. There are several instances, in fact, where reading also appears to improve other processes (e.g., short-term memory), which then feed back into reading achievement in what has been referred to as *reciprocal causation* (e.g., Lichtenstein, 1985; Stanovich, 1986). It is therefore worthwhile to keep the "whole-functioning child" in mind while evaluating the reading literature. As with the other domains considered earlier, examination of this one area in isolation could lead to some misdirection.

Can J-O-H-N-N-Y Read?

Evidence indicating that deaf children lag behind hearing peers in reading ability has been available for more than 70 years, although studies that predate the use of manual communication and amplification are of relatively little interest here. Regrettably, there is still sufficient evidence to conclude that the reading abilities of deaf children, as a group, are poor and not getting much better (Allen, 1986).

In one of the largest surveys yet conducted, DiFrancesca (1972) found that in a sample of 17,000 deaf children, 6 to 21 years of age, reading scores increased only 0.2 grade levels per year of schooling. This figure contrasts with the full year improvement in reading with each year of schooling defined by hearing children's performance. Vernon (1972) painted an even more dismal picture of deaf students 10 to 16 years of age, during which time, he reported, they gain little more than .1 grade levels per year in reading achievement. In fact, Allen (1986) found that the lags of deaf children relative to their hearing peers in reading comprehension (as well as mathematics) actually increase through the school years (see Chapter 4), despite the concerted efforts of teachers and deaf education researchers to reverse that trend. In other words, deaf students leaving school are at a relatively greater disadvantage than when they matriculated.

Traditionally, *functional literacy* has been designated as corresponding to a fourth to fifth grade level of reading and writing, although some educators now argue that the demands of the "information age" make an eleventh to twelfth grade criterion more appropriate (Waters & Doehring, 1990). Allen's (1986) data, however, indicated that as a group the 18-year-old deaf sample involved in the 1983 norming of the Stanford Achievement Test (SAT) did not reach even the third grade level of reading comprehension (scoring slightly below deaf 14- to 17-year-olds). Accordingly, it appears that more than 30% of deaf students now leave school functionally illiterate, compared to fewer than 1% of their hearing peers.

Importantly, deaf children's reading deficits do not appear to be the result of any particular educational orientation, such as manual or oral training, but occur across various curricula (Johnson et al., 1989). Children trained in oral programs do appear to show enhanced performance in those reading skills that depend heavily on articulatory-phonological coding (Conrad, 1979; but see Waters & Doehring, 1990). Overall, however, the inclusion of a manual component in language training appears to result in somewhat higher reading scores than does its exclusion (Brasel & Quigley, 1977; see also Rittenhouse & Spiro, 1979).

Are Deaf Children of Deaf Parents Better Readers?

Discussions in several previous chapters have emphasized that there are more differences between deaf children with deaf parents and those with hearing parents than just their early exposure to manual communication. Nevertheless, several investigators have attributed deaf children's reading deficiencies almost exclusively to their relative language deprivation at home (e.g., Brasel & Quigley, 1977; Meadow, 1968). This conclusion appears to derive from the observation that deaf children of deaf parents generally read at about two grade levels above their peers with hearing parents. Deaf and hearing parents, however, also have different expectations for the rehabilitation and education of their deaf children (Sisco & Anderson, 1980) and those children might have different academic and personal goals. Although it is tempting to interpret reading differences between these two groups of children as implicating early linguistic (and especially manual) interaction, it is not at all clear that the relationship is so direct.

Schlesinger and Meadow (1972a), for example, reported a study that included well-matched residential school samples of deaf children of deaf parents and deaf children of hearing parents as well as a group of day-school deaf students who had hearing parents. All children were between 11,5 and 17,0 years of age. Schlesinger and Meadow found that residential students with hearing parents were, on average, one grade level behind those with deaf parents in SAT reading abilities (grade levels 3.8 versus 4.8). The day students scored midway between them (4.4). These differences did not approach statistical significance, however, indicating that there was no reliable advantage for the group with deaf parents.[1] More interesting for the present purposes was Schlesinger and Meadow's discovery that the younger (11 to 13 years old) day students had come from two different programs, one of which employed an oral curriculum and the other a TC program. When these samples were considered separately, the TC day students (who had hearing parents) significantly surpassed the other groups, including the group with deaf parents (see also Quigley, 1977; Charrow & Fletcher, 1974).

Schlesinger and Meadow's (1972a) results suggest that the use of manual communication in a day-school classroom had a larger effect on reading ability than did parental hearing status per se, a conclusion later supported by findings of Brasel and Quigley (1977). Of course the day school groups possibly differed from the residential school groups in ways other than the hearing status of their parents (e.g., socioeconomic status and a variety of "parental involvement" measures) (see Chapters 2 and 4). There is no evidence, however, that the type of curriculum employed by the day-school programs differentially attracted particular parents, and thus some combination of day-school "attitude" and manual communication seems to have been at play. This suggestion is not meant to imply that involvement of the day-school parents was greater than that of the residential school parents, or that such involvement was the "active ingredient" in the Schlesinger and Meadow results. Vernon and Koh (1970), in fact, found that in two residential school samples children of deaf parents obtained higher SAT reading scores than children of hearing parents even though the hearing parents were better educated and gave their children more preschool experience.

Beyond the findings of Schlesinger and Meadow (1972a), there is further evidence suggesting that it is not just early exposure to manual communication (i.e., the length of time a child has been signing) that makes the difference in reports of superior reading abilities of deaf children with deaf parents. Jensema and Trybus (1978), for example, argued that an observed reading advantage by deaf children with deaf parents could not be attributed to parental use of manual communication. This conclusion was based on their study of families of deaf children that varied in whether one, both, or neither parent was deaf. Jensema and Trybus found that in the families with one deaf and one hearing parent speech was the primary form of home communication, whereas in the families with two deaf parents sign language was used more frequently. Nonetheless, deaf children with one deaf parent were still superior readers relative to those with two hearing parents.

Kampfe (1989) examined the relation between reading comprehension and maternal communication methods in a sample of 201 deaf residential school students who had hearing parents. She compared groups of children who came from backgrounds in which they began signing before age 5, after age 5, or had never learned to sign. No significant relation was found between reading comprehension and age of sign acquisition. However, within those dyads in which the mothers had used sign, the children had higher IQs, the mothers had more education, and mothers' signing skills were positively related to reading comprehension (see also Griffith, Ripich, & Dastoli, 1990). Unfortunately, interactions observed among those variables make it difficult to identify the locus of the children's improved reading abilities.

Consistent with Kampfe's findings, Charrow and Fletcher (1974) failed to find a difference in the reading comprehension scores of groups of 17- to 18-year-olds with either deaf or hearing parents. Charrow and Fletcher, however, did observe marked advantages for the native-signing group on several other dimensions of English reading and writing ability, including measures of vocabulary, paragraph meaning, and English structure. The pattern of results in both SAT and TOEFL (Test of English as a Foreign Language) scores indicated to Charrow and Fletcher that the deaf children of deaf parents performed like hearing children learning a second language (see also Johnson et al., 1989).

Kusché et al. (1983) also failed to find a relation between deaf children's reading abilities and the age at which they had started signing, provided they had hearing parents (as in the 1989 Kampfe study). Those children who had deaf parents, in contrast, showed a strong relation ($r = -.54$) between the ages of sign acquisition and reading comprehension. The Kusché et al. study involved three primary groups of deaf high school students, almost all of whom had severe to profound hearing losses and who had been deaf since before age 2. One group was composed of children who had deaf parents, a second of children who had hearing parents and hearing siblings, and a third of children who had hearing parents and deaf siblings. All were given grade-level appropriate versions of the SAT, including vocabulary and reading achievement subtests. Overall, the deaf children with deaf parents were superior in terms of vocabulary and reading achievement compared to the groups with hearing parents. Their advantage in reading comprehension over the group with deaf siblings and hearing parents, however, was not significant, indicating that the presence of deaf siblings in the home facilitated reading development. This advantage likely was related at least in part to the greater pressure on hearing parents to use sign language when they have more than one deaf child (Luterman, 1987). In addition, having deaf siblings suggests hereditary causes of deafness, making concomitant social and neurological problems less likely.

Reynolds (1986) provided yet another study indicating that reading ability is not strongly linked to the age at which children begin signing. He tested 100 freshman entering Gallaudet College (now Gallandet University) and found that reading ability was not related to speech-reading ability or even to degree of hearing loss. Consistent with findings reported by Conrad (1970) for oral children, the best predictor of reading comprehension in Reynolds' study was students' articulation abilities, leading Reynolds to conclude that some knowledge of the phonological form underlying the language was essential to reading skills in deaf children. This issue is considered at length in the next section.

Reynolds' finding that reading ability was unrelated to hearing loss contrasts with the finding by Parasnis and Long (1979) indicating a significant relation between those two variables in college-age males but not females. His findings, however, were consistent with results obtained by Parasnis (1983a). Parasnis found that deaf college students with hearing parents were better at speech-reading (without sound) and had better speech intelligibility than classmates with deaf parents, although the two did not differ in their reading abilities according to the California Reading Comprehension Test (CRCT). Unfortunately, Parasnis used the junior high school version of the CRCT, and thus it is unclear whether the two groups were fully comparable in terms of their reading abilities. Nevertheless, her results are consistent with those derived from the Vernon and Koh (1970) study that showed deaf children of deaf parents to be better readers and writers than peers with hearing parents, despite their not differing on hearing loss, speech-reading ability, or speech intelligibility.

In summary, it appears that the reported differences between reading abilities of deaf children with deaf parents and those with hearing parents are at best inconsistent. To the extent that such differences do occur, it is clear that early exposure to manual communication and even the extent of children's signing experience are insufficient explanations for such findings (Conrad, 1970; Conrad & Weiskrantz, 1981). Although it is tempting to assume that early exposure to language would provide a linguistically based advantage in reading development for deaf children with deaf parents, this advantage may be offset by the fact that the American Sign Language (ASL) vocabulary and syntax do not parallel those of printed English. This discrepancy suggests that early training with a manual form of English could be particularly beneficial for the reading abilities of such children, giving them the advantages of early exposure to language and English-relevant linguistic experience. In fact, a now classic study by Brasel and Quigley (1977), to be considered later, provides strong support for that prediction (see also Schlesinger & Meadow, 1972a).

Insofar as early exposure to manual communication is insufficient in itself to account for reading differences observed between deaf children with deaf parents and those with hearing parents, it becomes necessary to consider more broadly based variables, such as motivation, cognitive ability, general language fluency, and exposure to reading (Sisco & Anderson, 1980; Webster, 1986). The effects of early exposure to reading via parents and early school environments seems a particularly fruitful avenue for such study, given the findings indicating that children who read more become better readers, rather than the other way around (Stanovich, 1986).

In this context, several investigators have considered deaf children's reading problems in terms of their general academic difficulties relative to hearing peers. Johnson et al. (1989), for example, focused on the language used in deaf children's classrooms. They argued that even those children whose teachers use Sign English competently and consistently (a minority in their view) never gain genuine competence in English. At the same time, Woodward and Allen (1987) reported that although 7% of teachers reported using ASL regularly in the classroom only 0.3% of them actually did so. Johnson et al. thus attributed many scholastic difficulties of deaf students to their inability to understand the English-based materials used in school owing to the impoverished language used in the classroom and their lags in language ability already present at school entrance. In addition, Johnson et al. cited low standards and expectations for achievement both by and for teachers of the deaf. Moores (1990) provided an strong reply to Johnson et al. and to their suggestion that the use of English-based sign systems such as Sign English be "suppressed" [*sic*] in academic settings. Although copies of the exchange may be difficult to find, it provides an interesting insight into the issues and politics of deafness and deaf education viewed from "within the system." Unfortunately, the debate is beyond the scope of the present discussion.

Taking a narrower rather than a broader approach to reading, it is important to consider the various aspects of reading within which deaf and hearing children differ and within which deaf children of deaf parents might differ from deaf children of hearing parents. Accordingly, three primary components of reading are considered below: phonology and spelling, vocabulary, and syntax.

Components of the Reading Abilities of Deaf Children

Basic Processes: Phonological Knowledge and Spelling

At its most essential level, competent reading requires recognition of the words on a printed page. Such recognition can be achieved by either of two basic processes (with the possibility of a third, hybrid, alternative). One of these routes is *direct orthographic recognition* (or *whole word visual recognition*), to be considered more in the next section. The other, perhaps more fundamental method of word decoding is that used when words initially appear unfamiliar or are indeed new. This *indirect phonological assembly* depends on the ability to make grapheme-to-sound or spelling-to-articulation transformations and results in the "sounding out" of a word (which then may or may not be recognized). More proficient readers can rapidly access many word meanings on the basis of visual information but also make regular use of the orthographic and phonological structures of words when necessary.

The central issue in this area seems to be how deaf children, especially those who are severely to profoundly deaf, can make use of phonological coding in the absence of hearing. Looking ahead, there is now considerable evidence suggesting that deaf children's apparent phonological proficiencies are not solely derived from articulation patterns (cf. Conrad, 1970). Rather, the representations underlying their word decoding processes are derived through a combination of lip-reading, finger-spelling, articulation, and exposure to writing, no one of which is sufficient in itself (Leybaert, Content, & Alegria, 1987).

Although one would expect that the decoding of spelling patterns would be a primary obstacle to deaf children's reading competence, several studies have indicated that their abilities for using some kind of phonological code are surprisingly good, emerging by around the second grade. Moreover, variability in phonological coding does not seem to be directly tied to degree of hearing loss, at least among children with more severe losses. Evidence in this regard largely comes from spelling studies of the sort provided by Dodd (1980). In one experiment, Dodd presented British 14-year-olds (either hearing or profoundly and prelingually deaf) with a list of 18 words varying in the regularity of their grapheme-to-sound correspondence (e.g., *problem* versus *scissors*). The children lip-read the stimuli and then had to write them. Dodd then matched the deaf and hearing children on the total number errors in this task so there was no overall difference between the groups. However, she found an interaction of spelling regularity and hearing status such that the hearing children made fewer errors when they spelled phonetically regular (12.2%) than phonetically nonregular (37.7%) words, whereas the deaf children performed equally well on both types (28.8% and 27.2%, respectively). Of potential importance later, the most common error of the deaf students was omission, as they refused to respond on those items of which they apparently were not sure.

The pattern of spelling errors Dodd observed in this and two other experiments (involving memory for ambiguously and unambiguously pronounceable nonsense words) indicated that hearing children relied primarily on direct sound-to-grapheme correspondence (producing errors such as *sizzers*). Deaf children appeared somewhat less likely to employ phonological coding, but still showed better memory for regular than irregular nonsense words. Dodd concluded that deaf children can make use of a phonological code when unequivocal graphemic information is not available.

In contrast to Dodd's (1980) finding a greater reliance on phonological codes by hearing children than by deaf children, Hanson, Shankweiler, and Fischer (1983) found no interaction of hearing status and phonological regularity, as both deaf and hearing groups were found to perform better with phonetically regular than phonetically irregular words. They used a modified cloze ("fill in the blank") paradigm in which students had to complete partial words omitted from sentences. A group of profoundly deaf college students with congenital or early-onset hearing losses did not differ reliably from hearing college students on that task, at least when Hanson et al. excluded from analysis those subjects who omitted at least 15 responses. This criterion, however, eliminated 11 of 27 deaf subjects but none of the 37 hearing subjects (cf. Dodd, 1980). Subsequent analyses of the deaf subjects showed that those deaf students who were excluded were the poorest readers by a highly significant margin, although their observed spelling impairment was not reliable.[2]

When analyzing the relation of spelling and reading, Hanson et al. included all 64 subjects and found that the hearing subjects were more proficient readers and spellers, according to the Gates-MacGintie Reading Test. However, there was no relation between spelling and reading among the deaf students, $r = .28$; and there was only a marginal effect among the hearing students, $r = .36$. Furthermore, Hanson et al. reported that there was no reliable relation between speech intelligibility and either reading achievement or spelling proficiency in a subgroup of 25 deaf subjects for whom speech intelligibility scores were available (cf. Parasnis, 1983a; Reynolds, 1986).

The fact that the subjects in the Hanson et al. study were college students makes it difficult to draw any firm conclusions about reading development or to make any strong comparisons with Dodd's (1980) results. It is interesting to note, however, that the pattern of spelling errors exhibited by Hanson's deaf subjects indicated that they relied more often than the hearing subjects on a visual or orthographic coding. That finding is consistent with earlier results obtained by Chen (1976), Locke (1978), and others and bears on the short-term memory findings presented in Chapter 8.

Chen (1976), for example, used a silent reading task in which students had to cross out occurrences of the letter *e* in a passage. The typical finding among hearing subjects is that more letters are missed when they are phonologically silent than when they are voiced, indicating an acoustic/articulatory component to reading. Chen compared the performance on this task of four groups of college students: (1) congenitally, profoundly deaf students; (2) adventitiously, profoundly deaf students; (3) students with less than profound impairments (losses ≤ 80 dB); and (4) a normally hearing group. She found that only the less than profoundly impaired group and the hearing group missed more silent than pronounced *e*s, suggesting that the two profoundly deaf groups were more likely to rely on visual coding than acoustic/articulatory coding during reading. Gibbs (1989), however, noted that studies employing the *e*-canceling paradigm, like that of Chen (1976), did not actually relate performance on that task to reading performance. In fact, Gibbs found that *e*-canceling performance was unrelated ($r = .02$) to reading scores on the Gates-MacGintie Reading Test in a group of profoundly deaf 16- to 19-year-olds, even though they missed more silent (7.11%) than sounded (3.28%) *e*s.

The Hanson et al. (1983) findings that speech intelligibility was unrelated to reading appears to contrast with conclusions from the Reynolds (1986) study, described earlier, in which reading ability was strongly related to college students' speech skills. Hanson (1986) further examined that relation by contrasting sensitivity to orthographic regularity with sensitivity to summed, single-letter positional frequency in a perceptual identification task. In that task, students judged whether a target letter appeared in a briefly presented letter string. Hanson found that deaf and hearing college students used positional frequency information at about the same rate, whereas the use of orthographic regularity depended on speech production ability. Hearing subjects showed greater benefits from orthographic regularity than deaf subjects, overall, but post hoc tests indicated that the difference was entirely restricted to those deaf subjects who had relatively poor speech skills (cf. Waters & Doehring, 1990). Those deaf students with better speech skills were also those who made frequent use of orthographic regularity in their reading. This result appears consistent with the results of a variety of studies by Conrad (1970, 1973, 1979) indicating that greater hearing losses are associated with less frequent use of phonological codes in orally trained children.

Hanson, Goodell, and Perfetti (1991) used a semantic acceptability judgment task in another examination of phonological processes in deaf college students who were all native users of ASL and had reading levels of 3.3 to 12.9+. Their reasoning was that use of phonological codes for reading would be disrupted by the presence of tongue-twisters, resulting in more errors and slower responses in acceptability judgments. When deaf and hearing students' judgments on sentences with and without tongue-twisters were compared, the deaf students produced significantly faster but less accurate performance. Both groups showed reliable tongue-twister (interference) effects in their accuracy scores, and the effects were influenced specifically by the phonetic content of the sentences. The deaf students yielded much smaller tongue-twister effects than the hearing students, but this difference apparently was not significant. Hanson et al. therefore concluded that their deaf subjects must have made use of a phonological code during reading. They acknowledged, however, that such codes might be visually derived from the way words look on the lips of speakers.

Phonological coding by deaf readers also was examined by Waters and Doehring (1990) in a study of the reading, writing, and memory performance of 56 severely to profoundly deaf children. All of them were aged 7 to 20 years and enrolled in oral programs. In contrast to findings obtained by Hanson and Fowler (1987) with deaf college students, Waters and Doehring found no phonological effects in children's lexical decisions (word versus nonword judgments) about letter strings with regular or irregular grapheme-to-phoneme correspondences or words that varied in their visual and phonological similarity. In view of their finding that short-term memory for phonological information was unrelated to reading ability (Gibbs, 1989), this result led Waters and Doehring to suggest that phonological processes in deaf readers might involve *whole-word* codes rather than the phonological assembly implied by the findings of Hanson and her colleagues.

The conclusions of both Hanson et al. (1991) and Waters and Doehring (1990) are consistent with findings reported by Beech and Harris (1992), who also used a lexical decision task as a means to explore the phonological processes of deaf and hearing readers matched on reading age. Again, in contrast to findings obtained with deaf college students, lexical decisions by their severely to profoundly deaf 6- to 12-year-olds were significantly less likely to be disrupted by the effects of regularity and homophony. The deaf children were also less likely to be adversely affected by the visual disruption of to-be-judged irregular words (by zigzagging their component letters above and below center). Taken together, these results were interpreted as indicating that deaf children make use of *logographic*, whole-word processes in word identification, processes similar to those suggested by the findings of Waters and Doehring (1990).

Findings reported by Treiman and Hirsh-Pasek (1983) indicated that native signing deaf adults may make use of a sign-based recoding during reading rather than one based on articulation or fingerspelling. Similar data have been reported by Ewoldt (1981) from four prelingually deaf children. Together these studies suggest that in the absence of or in addition to automatic, "lower-level" processes, some deaf readers rely on sign-based, semantic processing (see also Fischler, 1985). Treiman and Hirsh-Pasek's finding that manual coding did not appear to occur in their better readers suggests that, like logographic reading, such a strategy is more useful with familiar than unfamiliar material and may be more of a fall-back strategy than a reliable one that is particularly suited to deaf readers. The relation of manual coding to reading abilities in children, however, has yet to be determined.

Apparently, proficient reading, even by deaf children, depends on some underlying knowledge of phonology. That knowledge, in turn, is linked to oral ability in children trained in SC settings as well as those trained in more oral programs. Phonological coding also may be related to proficient syntactic processing, as such codes would be more efficient for working memory during reading than would visual codes (Lichtenstein, 1985), a possibility to be considered later (see also Chapter 8). For the present, it appears safe to conclude that deaf children rely on both phonological and visual codes during reading. When sufficient orthographic regularity is available, phonological coding appears most beneficial. Those students with better oral abilities seem better able to take advantage of such coding or to have a "higher threshold" for irregularity. Deaf students are more likely than hearing students, however, to depend on visual spelling regularities and thus are more likely to omit letters (e.g., writing OR___GE for "orange") and to make transposition errors (writing SORPT for "sport") (e.g., Dodd, 1980). Whole-word codes appear especially useful for deaf readers, allowing them to draw on both phonological and visual word information.

The linkage of reading development to increasing phonological proficiency also is evidenced by the production of more phonologically accurate misspellings by older than by younger deaf students (Leybaert et al., 1987) and by good articulators than by poor articulators (Hanson, 1986; Reynolds, 1986). Generally, then, deaf children display sound-to-spelling correspondences, although their use of such information may be less frequent, proficient, or rapid than that of hearing age-mates (e.g., Hung, Tzeng, & Warren, 1981). Such findings are not limited to orally trained children, as they are also obtained in studies involving manual deaf students, at least by college age (Hanson, 1986; Hanson et al., 1983). It thus appears that at least some portion of deaf children's observed reading deficiencies derive from sources other than the most obvious one—their inability to hear the sounds of words.

Vocabulary Knowledge and Knowledge of the World

Although it has been well documented that vocabulary is a primary component for reading, consideration of deaf children presents the issue in a somewhat different light. We already have seen that most deaf children come from environments that are relatively restricted in experiential diversity as well as in linguistic stimulation.

One therefore might expect that there would be some interaction of such factors as having less knowledge about things in the world, knowledge about fewer things, and less linguistic experience related to such knowledge. Young deaf children of hearing parents have been shown to have fewer verbal labels for things around them than hearing children of hearing parents (Griswold & Commings, 1974), and deaf children of both deaf and hearing parents are less likely to gain such verbal knowledge from reading (Trybus & Karchmer, 1977). In this context, the finding of reciprocal causation in reading—that more reading produces better readers as well as the other way around—suggests that it is imperative we expand the breadth of vocabulary to which deaf children are exposed, away from the concrete and familiar. Otherwise, they may be caught up in a cycle of having smaller expressive vocabularies, smaller receptive vocabularies, and fewer opportunities to expand either (Marschark, 1988a).

A variety of early studies involving word-association and word-sorting tasks demonstrated that young deaf children evidence less extensive and less associatively organized vocabulary knowledge than hearing age-mates, as well as a lesser ability to organize words into semantic categories (Griswold & Commings, 1974; Myklebust, 1960; for a review see Kretschmer & Kretschmer, 1978; cf. Tweney et al., 1975). More recently, those vocabulary deficits have been attributed to the linguistic and experiential shortages encountered by young deaf children and, in turn, held to be largely responsible for low reading scores (Johnson et al., 1989; Quigley & Paul, 1984). Contrary to any simple version of this deprivation hypothesis, however, Brasel and Quigley (1977) found that Word Meaning and Paragraph Meaning SAT scores of deaf children whose deaf parents used manual English were significantly better than those of a group whose deaf parents used ASL (cf. Dolman, 1983). Both groups received early language experience in the home, but the group that had experience with English as well as sign language clearly showed superior performance on meaning-related reading tests (cf. Schlesinger & Meadow's, 1972a, TC group; see also Rittenhouse & Spiro, 1979).

Aside from deaf children's having relatively less breadth in vocabulary knowledge as a function of exposure, it is unclear whether even familiar vocabulary is recognized as quickly by deaf children as by hearing students. Deaf children typically perform poorly on evaluations of vocabulary knowledge, even when reading comprehension abilities are equated (for a comparison with hearing children see Moores, 1967; for a comparison of deaf children with hearing versus deaf parents see Charrow & Fletcher, 1974). Lack of reading experience, among other consequences, may well reduce the automaticity of word finding even when words are relatively familiar (Fischler, 1985). Alternatively, deaf children simply may perform meaningful processing more slowly in both nonverbal and verbal contexts. These alternatives can be considered in two domains: (1) meaning derived from individual words; and (2) meaning derived from syntactic structuring of those words. Recognition of vocabulary is considered first, holding syntactic processing for consideration in a separate section later.

EVALUATING WORD RECOGNITION VIA THE STROOP PARADIGM

One of the most popular paradigms for examining the automaticity of word recognition is the Stroop task. In the original and most common form of the paradigm, color words ("blue," "red," "yellow") are presented in colored inks that are congruent or incongruent with respect to the words (e.g., "blue" printed in either blue or red ink, respectively). Although reading the colored words typically is not affected by the irrelevant ink colors, naming of ink colors is disrupted by their presentation in the form of incongruent color words, compared to being presented as simple color patches or strings of colored Xs. This slowing of response times is typically taken to indicate that the meanings of the (irrelevant) words are automatically activated, and that as competent readers most Stroop subjects cannot "turn off" their word recognition abilities. Consistent with this interpretation, Stroop studies involving bilinguals have indicated that when stimuli are presented in the same language as that in which responses are made, there is more interference than when different stimulus and response languages are used. Furthermore, in between-language tasks the magnitude of the Stroop effect decreases as the orthographic similarity of translation equivalents decreases in stimulus and response languages (for discussion see Marschark, 1988b).

In the context of deaf children, the Stroop paradigm could be particularly informative, because the lack of automatic, low-level reading skills such as word recognition requires greater demands on cognitive capacity, leaving fewer resources available for high-level components such as syntactic and semantic processing. D. V. Allen (1971), for example, used the Stroop task for evaluating the word recognition abilities of severely to profoundly deaf students, aged 10 to 15 years. All were enrolled in an oral deaf education program and were reading at grade levels from 3.5 to 6.0 (above average for deaf students of that age). They were compared to a group of hearing students, aged 9 to 12, matched with the deaf children on reading ability (placing them below average for hearing students). Allen reported that the deaf students exhibited significantly smaller Stroop effects (i.e., less interference) than did the hearing students. Nevertheless, the deaf students still showed a large, no doubt reliable Stroop effect of almost 10 seconds. This finding is inconsistent with Allen's conclusion that the "deaf seem able to view verbal material without attending to its 'verbalness' " (p. 296) and her preference for an explanation in terms of deaf children having a slower "personal tempo."

The latter conclusion was based in part on Allen's finding that her deaf subjects were slower in (baseline) word reading than the hearing subjects, despite their being matched on reading ability. As noted earlier, however, it is not at all uncommon to find that deaf and hearing children who are matched on general reading ability (i.e., in terms of comprehension) nonetheless reveal differences in subcomponents of reading. The finding of such a large Stroop effect for the deaf students in Allen's study clearly indicates the operation of an automatic word recognition system, even if it does not function as quickly or consistently as that of hearing students.

Leybaert, Alegria, and Morais (1982) further examined Stroop interference in deaf children, comparing the performance of an orally trained group of early-onset or congenitally deaf students aged 12 to 25 years and a control group of hearing students aged 11 to 26 years. To remove the demand of having the children respond verbally, Leybaert et al. (1982) modified the Stroop task by having them sort the stimulus cards rather than name each one. In this manual task, both deaf and hearing subjects revealed interference effects, with the deaf showing a slightly larger overall effect. Leybaert et al. concluded that their findings indicated that D. V. Allen's (1971) finding of smaller Stroop effects in deaf than hearing children was the result of response suppression at output (not involved in the manual task) and not a problem of word recognition (meaning access) per se.

That conclusion was supported by another study conducted by Leybaert, Alegria, and Fonck (1983) in which they compared a different manual (button-pushing) version of the Stroop task with the traditional, naming version. Their deaf subjects comprised a group of profoundly deaf children with congenital or early-onset hearing losses. They all were aged 10 to 18 years and were enrolled in an oral education program. The deaf students were matched according to reading ability with a group of hearing students who ranged in age from 9 to 14 years. Leybaert et al. (1983) found that with the manual version of the task the deaf and hearing subjects experienced equivalent interference from incongruent color-word pairings. With the naming version, however, deaf and hearing performance was equivalent only for the subgroup of deaf students who had been rated by their teachers as having relatively good speech intelligibility. Poorer deaf speakers showed smaller Stroop effects relative to both the good deaf speakers and their hearing peers. This finding indicates that deaf children who are poorer speakers also are less likely to make use of a phonological code during reading, a result similar to that obtained in the studies of Conrad (1979) and Hanson (1986).

In contrast to the D. V. Allen and Leybaert studies, all of which involved children enrolled in oral education programs, Marschark (1988b) conducted a Stroop study involving deaf students enrolled in a TC program and deaf adults who use ASL as their primary mode of communication. As in the standard Stroop paradigm, subjects saw printed words and colors, but all responded in sign rather than orally. In addition, we developed a sign language version of the Stroop task in which subjects named the color of a signer's hand that was either painted the color named by the sign or painted a color different from the sign (e. g., BLUE made with a red hand). Note that the use of sign language as a response modality means that signed stimuli provided a within-language Stroop task, whereas printed stimuli provided a between-language Stroop task. On the basis of previous studies involving hearing bilinguals, larger interference effects were expected with signed (within-language) stimuli than with printed (between-language) stimuli.

The first experiment involved a group of nine deaf students, eight of whom had congenital or early-onset deafness, eight of whom had severe to profound hearing losses, and all of whom began to learn sign language before 5 years of age. A second experiment included a group of 12 prelingually deaf adults who had been exposed to sign language from an early age. Regardless of the age of the subjects, the results of both of these color experiments were consistent: Stroop effects were obtained with both printed stimuli and signed stimuli, and interference effects were actually larger when the colors were presented as printed words (between-language) than as signs (within-language). Children showed an average interference effect with printed word stimuli that was more than twice as large as that obtained with sign stimuli. The adults showed an interference for words that was more than 35% larger than for signs.

Taken at face value, these results suggest, somewhat counterintuitively, that the deaf adults and children we tested had more automatic processing of printed than signed stimuli. In fact, all of the adults in that sample were either teachers of deaf students or teachers' aides and thus might be more print-oriented than the average deaf adult. Furthermore, the children in our sample were drawn from North Carolina schools for the deaf where vigorous reading programs and parental intervention programs have led to considerable gains in reading achievement (R. Wilson, personal communication, April 14, 1992; see Marschark, 1988a).

We therefore conducted another study to examine the relation between language fluency, hearing status, and response mode in a Stroop task with deaf and hearing adults (Marschark & Shroyer, 1992). Three groups responded in sign (i.e., within-language for signed stimuli): one composed of manually oriented deaf adults, one of oral deaf adults, and one of hearing, nationally certified interpreters. Three other groups, in which all subjects had normal hearing, responded orally (i.e., within-language for printed stimuli): a group of beginning (first-semester) sign language students, a group of intermediate (second semester) sign language students, and another group of nationally certified interpreters. Thus three groups had approximately equal sign language skill with varying skill in English, whereas the other three had approximately equal English skill with varying skill in signing. This study thus provided a means of determining the effects of sign skill and English skill on the automaticity of sign and word naming.

The results revealed that manual responding took longer, overall, and led to more Stroop interference than responding orally, regardless of hearing status. All of the hearing subjects (regardless of response mode), however, showed more interference for printed stimuli than for signed stimuli, whereas the deaf subjects showed more interference for signed than printed stimuli. Only the interpreters responding in sign showed greater between-language than within-language Stroop effects. Perhaps most interesting was the finding that variation in language fluency, at least within the ranges tested here, did not produce variation in the magnitude of the interference effects. Apparently, once the meanings of words and signs are acquired, the Stroop task is relatively insensitive to variability in overall language fluency and thus should not be taken as an indicator of language skill. This conclusion is consistent with other studies showing the separability of vocabulary and reading skills, even though the former is intimately involved in the latter (Quigley & Paul, 1984).

THE RELATION OF VOCABULARY KNOWLEDGE TO READING

Studies by Moores (1967), Kyle (1980), and Quigley and Paul (1984) have indicated that deaf children typically show their largest reading-related deficits in the area of vocabulary knowledge. Moores (1967), for example, found that deaf children obtained significantly lower scores than hearing children on a vocabulary test involving the cloze technique despite the fact that the two groups had been matched on SAT reading scores. Charrow and Fletcher (1974) similarly found that deaf 17- and 18-year-olds who had hearing parents showed their worst performance on the TOEFL Vocabulary subtest, relative to peers with deaf parents, despite the fact that the nonsignificant trend in TOEFL Reading Comprehension scores favored the students with hearing parents.

It should no longer be surprising that deaf children score lower than hearing peers on vocabulary tests that involve comprehension of words in isolation. The Word Meaning subtest of the SAT is a particularly good example in this regard, as it generally yields the lowest scores obtained by deaf children and adolescents on the SAT battery. Deaf children also reveal deficits in their expressive vocabularies, in signed and oral productions as well as in writing (Everhart & Marschark, 1988; Griswold & Commings, 1974; Myklebust, 1960), indicating that vocabulary deficits go beyond difficulties with English and entail general linguistic and experiential factors as well (Furth, 1973). Not only do deaf children have smaller vocabularies than hearing peers, but the classes of words they do know are often different. Deaf children generally are more likely to understand and use concrete nouns and familiar action verbs rather than more abstract or general words with which they may have less experience, especially if they have hearing parents (King & Quigley, 1985).

Compared to their performance on vocabulary tests involving words taken out of context, deaf children typically perform somewhat better on meaning-related tests that include context, such as the Paragraph Meaning subtest of the SAT. They still lag behind hearing peers (Gaines, Mandler, & Bryant, 1981; Kretschmer & Kretschmer, 1978; Marshall, 1970), however, and Trybus and Karchmer (1977) found that their vocabulary abilities tended to lag a year behind their own reading abilities (a situation likely to create difficulties in both domains). Deaf children also perform better on vocabulary items that have only a single meaning. When words can have multiple meanings, and especially when those meanings may not all be literal, deaf children perform poorly even when context is supplied (Blackwell et al., 1978).

Fischler (1985), for example, examined deaf students' abilities to make lexical decisions for a task in which words were preceded by either (1) the "most likely" sentence context, (2) an incongruent sentence context, (3) an unlikely but congruent sentence context, or (4) no context. The task was administered to 40 hearing college students and 39 deaf Gallaudet College students, most of whom had severe to profound, congenital or early-onset hearing losses. Fischler found that both groups made faster decisions when words followed likely contexts and slower decisions when they followed incongruent contexts, relative to following unlikely but congruent contexts. The effects of sentence context were larger for the deaf than the hearing students, indicating that deaf students used context to help offset their lesser automaticity in word recognition skills. Findings such as those of Moores (1967), using the cloze technique, however, indicate that such higher-level syntactic and semantic processes cannot compensate fully for the lack of vocabulary skill. Demonstrating that deaf children can understand simple, well-controlled materials in semantically restricted contexts tells us relatively little about their reading potential or the reading strategies employed in more naturalistic contexts.

Vocabulary deficits in either deaf or hearing children are likely to impede higher-level reading processes by giving them only impoverished "bottom-up" information and by tying up available cognitive processing capacity (Hung et al.,

1981). One immediate impact of these limitations is the disruption of syntactic processing, as working memory becomes overloaded and inefficient (e.g., Spencer & Delk, 1989). It thus would not be surprising to find that deaf children also exhibit difficulties of syntactic parsing during reading. The question is whether those difficulties are primarily due to grammatical deficiencies per se or an inability to attend to grammatical markers because of insufficient short-term memory capacity (Jarvella, 1971; Perfetti & Goldman, 1976). In either case, the result would be impaired comprehension and a tendency to remember disconnected portions of texts without higher-level conceptual schemes, particularly when the material is unfamiliar. Precisely such findings have been demonstrated by Gaines et al. (1981), Banks et al. (1990), and Griffith et al. (1990).

Understanding Syntactic Structures

During the 1960s, the focus of many language researchers turned to the role of grammatical structures in psycholinguistic processing. Although *prescriptive* grammar had long been involved in teaching and evaluating reading abilities, a movement to *descriptive* grammars (i.e., models) of language structure, initiated by Noam Chomsky (1957, 1965), brought linguistics into the classroom—and into the deaf classroom in particular. In retrospect, this introduction was sometimes inappropriate, as investigators tried to map Chomsky's (transformational generative) model of linguistic structure (or linguistic competence) onto the individual as a psychological model of language ability (see Chapter 5). Although Chomsky's theory was not intended as a model for linguistic performance, many deaf children participated in reading programs designed to "teach" them transformational generative grammar as a means of increasing syntactic knowledge and reading ability. On the positive side, however, the many studies of deaf children's understanding of syntactic structures provided more thorough analyses of their grammatical knowledge than previously had been undertaken.

The center of the syntactic movement in deaf education was the University of Illinois at Urbana-Champaign. The expertise and interactions of a number of investigators in the departments of Communication Disorders and Psychology, as well as the Center for the Study of Reading and two developmental institutes, led to a variety of studies of deaf children's grammatical knowledge as indicated by reading and writing abilities. Most visible among them was a series of studies by Quigley and his associates, which detailed the syntactic performance of a national sample of deaf students 10 to 19 years of age (e.g., Quigley, Power, & Steinkamp, 1977; Quigley, Wilbur, Power, Montanelli, & Steinkamp, 1976). That project examined the comprehension and written production of eight classes of syntactic structures tapped by the SAT and the Illinois Test of Syntactic Ability (TSA). The results of that project, documenting the grammatical deficiencies of deaf children compared to hearing peers, have been presented in several contexts and are summarized by Quigley and Paul (1984; reprinted in King & Quigley, 1985).

Quigley and his colleagues found that whereas hearing children's performance varied from 78% to 98% correct on the 21 specific structures examined (collapsed across ages), their deaf sample's performance ranged from 36% to 79%. On the basis of these data, Quigley et al. concluded that the syntactic abilities of the average deaf

18-year-old were at a level below that of the average hearing 8-year-old. The biggest gaps between deaf and hearing scores occurred in question formation, complementation, pronomialization, and disjunction and alternation, whereas the most similar performance was observed in the relatively simple constructions of negation and conjunction. These results, together with the results of Perfetti and Goldman's (1976) comparison of good and poor hearing readers, suggest that the most difficult syntactic constructions for deaf children may be those that involve short-term retention of verbal information while awaiting subsequent (semantic or syntactic) resolution (see also unpublished studies reported by Quigley and his colleagues).

This conclusion also can be seen as consistent with evidence presented earlier concerning the impulsivity and lack of concentration that characterize many deaf children (see Chapter 4), as well as evidence indicating their verbal short-term memory deficits (Lichtenstein, 1985) (see Chapter 8). In addition, this suggestion would help to explain findings indicating that deaf children are consistently less able or less likely to draw inferences from contextual information, regardless of whether that context is verbal or nonverbal (e.g., Odom et al., 1973; Wilson, 1979) (see Chapter 7). Once again, it appears that nonlinguistic, experiential and cognitive factors affect reading at levels beyond those of phonological coding and vocabulary.

Consideration of the roles of global cognitive factors, such as concept knowledge, cognitive style, and memory in deaf children's reading, bears on the issue raised earlier of whether deaf children of deaf parents are better readers than deaf children of hearing parents. For example, Brasel and Quigley's (1977) study (initially described in the context of language development) explicitly examined the development of syntactic abilities in groups of 10- to 18-year-olds as a function of parental hearing status and early linguistic experience. All of the children in that study were deaf by age 2, and all were profoundly deaf. One group included children whose deaf parents had good English skills and communicated with them via manual English; a second included deaf children of deaf parents who were less competent in English and used primarily ASL in the home; a third included children who received exclusively oral training at home and at school and whose hearing parents had received training in using oral methodologies; and a fourth included children who also received oral training at school but whose hearing parents did not have any relevant training and did not attempt to initiate oral education prior to enrolling them in school. There were 24 children in each group, matched for age.

Using both the SAT and the TSA, Brasel and Quigley found that, overall, the manual English group showed the best syntactic competence, and that the two manual groups surpassed the two oral groups. In fact, although children in the manual English group performed significantly better than those in the two oral groups on most of the syntactic structures tested by the TSA, they performed better than the ASL group only on the most difficult structure, relativization. The Brasel and Quigley (1977) study is frequently cited as indicating that deaf children of deaf parents are better readers than those with hearing parents, but such an assertion misses an important component of their results. That is, Brasel and Quigley's *ASL group did not significantly exceed the intensive oral group on any of the component tests.* Consistent with the Schlesinger and Meadow (1972a) study described earlier, the Brasel and Quigley results most clearly indicate that a combination of sign language and English training is the most beneficial language environment for deaf children learning to read, at least with regard to the acquisition of syntactic abilities and gist comprehension (cf. Ewoldt, 1981; Treiman & Hirsh-Pasek, 1983).

Viewed another way, although it is true in Brasel and Quigley's study that the two groups of children who had deaf parents collectively performed better than the two groups with hearing parents, those children who received oral training at both home and school showed syntactic skills comparable to their peers who had deaf parents and were exposed to ASL from birth. This finding appears to cast doubt on the argument that deaf children with deaf parents are better readers than peers with hearing parents simply because of their exposure to language from birth. Evidently, there are other factors involved here, including the attitudes of parents toward their children's deafness and their involvement in teaching their children to read (see Janos & Robinson, 1985). Perhaps most importantly, it seems likely that the benefits accruing to syntactic abilities in the context of early language training likely result not only from exposure to syntax but also from exposure to and acquisition of an expanded vocabulary.

It is unfortunate that the Brasel and Quigley (1977) study did not include a control group of hearing children with hearing parents and perhaps a group of deaf children whose hearing parents used sign language intensively during their children's early years. Most generally, it would be helpful to know how the manual English group compared to a group of normal hearing children. As an estimate of such a condition, however, Brasel and Quigley's (1977) TSA data can be compared to the Quigley et al. (1976) data from hearing children also tested with the TSA. In that comparison, the manual English group is within 1% of the hearing group on negation, pronomialization, and relativization; within 8% on question formation and conjunction; and surpasses hearing age-mates by 3% on verb use.

With regard to deaf children of signing, hearing parents, one might expect that they would resemble ASL and intensive oral groups, at least if the parents were competent enough and consistent in their signing skill. That prediction is supported by the findings reported for hearing children learning ASL as a first language from their deaf parents (e.g., Jones & Quigley, 1979; Meier & Newport, 1990). Moreover, Jones and Quigley's (1979) study of question formation indicated no apparent interference in English acquisition caused by the fact that the syntax of ASL differs from that of English, even when parental language use is biased against speech (cf. Schiff & Ventry, 1976; Todd, 1976).

In summary, the findings reported in this section indicate that deaf children, *on average*, show marked deficits in syntactic abilities compared to hearing peers. These deficiencies can be reduced or eliminated when such children receive early language training either manually from their deaf parents or orally from hearing parents who seek out early intervention programs and regularly use oral training methods in the home. As was the case in early vocabulary development, however, it appears that the best situation for deaf children learning to read is to be exposed to both sign and English, regardless of whether their parents are deaf or hearing (Moores, 1990).

Such findings clearly contradict the strong proposals of Johnson et al. (1989) concerning the undesirability of Sign English in deaf education. One question left unresolved by the existing data, however, is the extent to which deaf and hearing children acquire comprehension of (written) syntactic structures in approximately the same or different orders. Wilbur et al. (1983) presented some evidence concerning the sequence of comprehending nine syntactic structures by deaf children, using a picture-based, multiple-choice test. However, the confounding of syntactic and semantic factors in their alternatives makes any generalization to naturalistic reading somewhat tenuous. We therefore now turn to an examination of deaf children's writing abilities as another perspective from which to view their literacy skills.

Writing by Deaf Children

In the domain of writing, as in reading, there have been numerous demonstrations of deaf children's relatively meager vocabularies and their poor grasp of English syntax (for a review, see Quigley & Paul, 1984). Evidence from several studies, however, indicates that the writing abilities of deaf children fall far short of their manual production skills (Everhart & Marschark, 1988; Suty & Friel-Patti, 1982) and may be independent of their cognitive abilities and general language flexibility (e.g., Parasnis, 1983a; Yoshinaga-Itano & Snyder, 1985). Such findings suggest that literacy should be within the grasp of deaf children. Nevertheless, the intimate relation of reading and writing is such that it does not come as a surprise to discover that deaf children's performance in the "input" domain is mirrored in the "output" domain."

Perhaps the most obvious characteristic of deaf children's writing, relative to that of hearing age-mates, is their use of shorter, less structurally variable, and frequently incomplete sentences (Heider & Heider, 1941; Myklebust, 1960; Powers & Wilgus, 1983; Webster, 1986; Wilbur, 1977). In addition to its lesser syntactic complexity, the writing of deaf children also tends to be less well-interconnected (Cohen, 1967; Yoshinaga-Itano & Snyder, 1985), and these children consistently score below hearing age-mates in grammatical correctness even in simplified situations (e.g., employing the cloze technique; King & Quigley, 1985). Given that deaf children also tend to have smaller and more concrete vocabularies than hearing peers, it should not be surprising that their writing is more literal (Blackwell et al., 1978; Everhart & Marschark, 1988).

Findings of this sort have been replicated in a variety of contexts and across the school years, leading to the general conclusion (similar to that in the reading literature) that the average deaf 18-year-old writes on a level comparable to that of a hearing 8-year-old (Kretschmer & Kretschmer, 1978). As an example of such performance, consider the following passage from Kramer and Buck (1976):

Wednesday is joyous
It is arrival of friends
Our friends assist us with poetry.
They communicate with me.
We discuss many things
So, we may comprehend.
There's a professor I admire.
He makes me chuckle.

This passage was written by a deaf adolescent who had had extensive practice with poetry as part of a long-term project conducted by college English faculty and students (as described in the passage). Although a final draft of the work, the passage exhibits many of the shortcomings noted earlier: short, repetitive sentences and simple syntactic and conceptual structures. Interestingly, although Kramer and Buck (1976) admitted that there "is not a line of poetry in this poem," they declare, "this piece was an exciting demonstration of how ready she was, more ready than we had hoped, to leap ahead in vocabulary richness . . . [her] verbal progress strengthens our belief that it has been a mistake to characterize her as 'literal-minded' " (p. 34).

Lest one conclude that the structural rigidity of the passage (aside from the short lines) was the result of its being an attempt at poetry, consider the following three short stories. All were written by deaf adolescents in the context of Everhart and Marschark's (1988) study of nonliteral language in deaf children (see Chapter 10) and were chosen at random from our corpus. The instructions asked only that the students write a story about being picked up by a UFO "as part of a project to teach other deaf children about stories."

> When I get in ufo They look funny. They have long pointed ears and have round face They speak different from our. They brought strange foods and Purple beverage. When I taste it I spill and begin to cought [cough][3] I taste like dog food. But It was very pretty inside with many feather and clothes were very pretty. But one thing people in ufo stare at me because they never see large musclar [muscular] and can pick up Heavy thing like weight, people or table. They feel it and said wow and start to teach me how to talk but they speak Russian language. I hate to learn Russian language. So I stay in ufo for 5 hours so they stop to place where they take me and drop their and they sent me a dog with long sharp teeth and was very tame I egan [began] to cry and miss them.

> One day I walk to Dark. Then UFO come to Dark. Then UFO take Me. I go with UFO. UFO Look at goBot. I Friend with UFO. I play with Baby goBot. The [Then] I go Back to my home. UFO go Far away from my home. (The Eend)

> I walk outside. That is come form [from] ufo. I hear it ufo come here. I grab in ufo. I saw little that is ufo people. Now I have to happend [happened] with ufo. I will become ufo. I live in ufo. That is a people live ufo. The ufo live in night sky. That I can see ufo in night sky that is an ufo. The ufo is an pretty in night sky. I want to became ufo. It is many ufo in night sky. That is good story. I make an ufo. I like an ufo in night ufo.

Among the other typical characteristics of deaf children's writing, the most noticeable in these passages is the frequent omission of words. A variety of studies and surveys have documented the fact that deaf children use fewer adverbs, conjunctions, and auxiliary verbs than hearing age-mates, whereas the frequencies of nouns and verbs is about the same (note again the similarity to reading performance) (Quigley & Paul, 1984). In part, this difference may stem from a concrete orientation to school writing and to school instruction in general (Marschark, 1988a; Tervoort, 1975). Consistent with this view, Wilbur (1977) argued that word omission, as well as many of the other errors evident in deaf children's writing, results from their failure to adopt a "discourse orientation." She suggested that for many deaf individuals writing is often seen as a laborious, sentence-by-sentence task, rather than an attempt at verbal communication. With such a view of writing, it should not be surprising that deaf children fail to use pronouns correctly, to use definite and indefinite articles, or to be concerned with intersentence issues of verb tense and agreement.[4]

Webster (1986) suggested that one reason why deaf children fail to make use of discourse structure in their writing is that they lack the rules of conversation normally acquired from monitoring ongoing verbal interactions. Webster reported a study in which deaf and hearing children each wrote two stories. One story was written with a pen and other was written with a stylus and carbon paper so that the children were unable to see what they were writing (thus inhibiting content rehearsal and review). Deaf children's performance was unaffected by this manipulation, but hearing children's errors increased sharply in the "no-see" condition and approached the error rate of the deaf students. This finding was interpreted as indicating that deaf children generally do not use make use of contextual discourse rules in their writing.

If Webster's (1986) premise and conclusion are valid, one would expect that deaf children with deaf parents (who have a fluent mode of parent-child communication) would show writing skills superior to those of deaf children with hearing parents. This prediction is consistent with the frequent finding that deaf children of deaf parents are better readers, overall, than deaf children with hearing parents. At the same time, however, there is another aspect of the Everhart and Marschark (1988) passages that lead to the prediction that deaf children of hearing parents might show writing skills superior to those of deaf children of deaf parents: Experienced signers will note that the syntax and morphology of those passages appear to parallel sign language structure, and the omitted words frequently correspond to aspects of the message that would not be explicitly signed. P. A. Jones (1979) argued that writing produced by deaf children parallels the structural and content characteristics of ASL, omitting words that would not be produced if the passage were being communicated using a pidgin signed English. Although the Jones paper is frequently cited in this regard [for example, see Quigley & Paul's (1984) extensive discussion], it is important to note that neither Jones nor any other investigator has offered empirical evidence to support such a position. In Jones's case, the argument was based solely on his impressions of writing produced by deaf college students. Hence there appears to be no strong basis on which to prefer the manual coding account of deaf children's writing deficiencies over the discourse deficiency and related short-term memory deficiency hypotheses.

The evidence necessary for making such a decision, of course, would have to include a comparison of the writing produced by oral versus manual deaf children. All other things being equal (which is rarely the case), the manually oriented children should show poorer writing skills (more omissions in particular) relative to children with oral orientation. On the basis of evidence provided earlier in the context of reading skills, one could even predict that deaf children with deaf parents who use manual English at home would exhibit better writing skills than those whose parents use ASL.

In one of the few studies relevant to this issue, Yoshinaga-Itano and Snyder (1985) compared the written productions of 27 deaf children enrolled in an oral school program and 22 others enrolled in a TC program to the productions of 49 hearing children. Frequencies of word omission were not considered in that study, but syntactic complexity and semantic cohesion were evaluated. Yoshinaga-Itano and Snyder found that the deaf and hearing children were comparable in both domains at age 10, but that hearing children showed a more rapid increase in syntactic and semantic discourse fluencies with increasing age. The hearing children increased approximately 50% to 150% between ages 10 and 14 on various measures, whereas the deaf children increased only 8% to 17% over the same age range. As for reading abilities, there was no apparent relation between hearing loss or speech intelligibility and either writing index. Furthermore, when age-matched subgroups of deaf and hearing children were matched according to reading ability, there were no differences in their writing scores on either semantic or syntactic measures. Although Yoshinaga-Itano and Snyder did not provide any analyses comparing their oral and TC subgroups, Snyder (personal communication, January 30, 1991) reported that there were no reliable differences between the two. It is to be hoped that future research will elaborate on the results of this study, including consideration of the hearing statuses of the parents of children in the two subgroups and the early linguistic environments they provided.

In general, the above results provide evidence for the expected parallels between deaf children's reading and writing performances. Although there are few data from which to draw conclusions about differences between deaf children of deaf versus hearing parents, it appears likely that the writing abilities of those groups would follow the same patterns as their reading abilities. Charrow and Fletcher's (1974) study of college students, for example, indicated that deaf children of deaf parents showed significantly better performance on the TOEFL writing test than deaf children of hearing parents. Similar findings were obtained by Parasnis (1983a), who found that deaf college students who had learned ASL early from their deaf parents performed significantly better on the NTID Writing Test than those who had learned to sign later in life. On the basis of these findings and the reading results described above, one would also expect that the writing abilities of deaf children whose hearing parents provide both early sign language stimulation and bimodal education should surpass those children who lack either early exposure to language or subsequent, intensive English training.

Before leaving the topic of reading and writing by deaf children, it is worth re-emphasizing the importance of social-emotional factors as well as linguistic variables to the development of literacy and to academic success in general (see Chapter 4). Studies involving hearing children have shown that parents spending time with their children, facilitating their academic and extracurricular interests, and answering their questions in supportive environments foster academic excellence as well as psychosocial maturity (Janos & Robinson, 1985). Unfortunately, such behaviors are not typical of interactions between deaf children and their hearing parents, although we have seen that there is considerable variability on this dimension.

Just as factors such as vocabulary and grammatical knowledge operate in a bidirectional manner in literacy development, one would expect variables such as locus of control and achievement motivation would operate in this manner for deaf children as they apparently do for hearing children. One essential aspect of achievement and mastery motivation, for example, is that children have to notice that the outcomes of achievement-related behaviors are self-produced, a characteristic directly related to locus of control (Janos & Robinson, 1985). This relation is consistent with the finding that intellectually achieving hearing children tend to be internal and independent—dimensions on which deaf children tend to vary more widely and lag behind hearing age-mates (Greenberg & Kusché, 1989).

The relative lack of achievement by deaf children in literacy-related domains also may be related to their tendency toward impulsivity (R. I. Harris, 1978) or their relatively concrete orientations toward academic subjects (Blackwell et al., 1978). Knowledge about language is quite abstract, and from the relatively literal and impulsive modes of thinking characteristic of many deaf children reading and writing may be viewed differently (Furth, 1973) than from the perspective of hearing children. Deaf children thus may be less invested in achieving literacy due to either their own attitudes and values or those of their parents. For the 90% of deaf children with hearing parents, there is the added difficulty of (typically) inefficient, concrete, and superficial parent-child communication. Hearing parents of deaf children generally have lower educational expectations for their children than do deaf parents (Sisco & Anderson, 1980), and deaf children of hearing parents likely receive less information concerning parental values toward literacy and achievement. As important as these issues are, research in this area is just beginning.

Summary

One of the most frequently cited and well-documented difficulties of deaf children (and adults) is their impoverished reading abilities. Although at first one might expect that the most disrupted component of reading would be the ability to decode the spelling patterns of words, many deaf children show surprisingly competent performance in this regard. True, their reliance on orthographic and phonological information is greater for words with regular grapheme-to-sound correspondence and more familiar spelling patterns, compared to irregular words, but there is considerable evidence that deaf children develop some form of phonological decoding that assists them in reading from at least the second grade on. At the same time, deaf children are more likely than hearing children to use visual and whole-word decoding strategies during reading, and the same pattern appears in comparisons of deaf children with lesser, compared to more extensive, oral abilities.

The most pronounced difficulties of deaf children compared to those of hearing children with regard to reading skills concern vocabulary knowledge and syntactic abilities. Relative deficiencies in the breadth and depth of deaf children's vocabularies indicate contributions (or the lack thereof) of early nonlinguistic as well as linguistic experience. Less automatic word recognition skills also affect the ability to make use of syntactic information, however, as a working memory tied up with word decoding has less capacity available for the integration of semantic information relevant to specific grammatical units and to their interrelations (see also Chapters 8 and 9).

The failure to use syntactic information effectively both reflects and contributes to possible limitations in short-term memory functioning during reading. Findings described in Chapter 8 indicated that deaf children tend to rely more on visual than verbal-sequential coding for short-term memory tasks. During the course of reading, adoption of such strategies would be relatively inefficient for both speed and comprehension (Lichtenstein, 1985). The demonstration that reading ability is intimately linked to the span of linguistic short-term memory in hearing children (Perfetti & Goldman, 1976) points to short-term memory as a potential bottleneck for both vocabulary and syntactic processing in deaf children, but there have not yet been any explicit evaluations of this possibility.

Exactly which variables are the most important for predicting reading success in deaf children is yet to be determined. Deaf children with deaf parents are frequently reported to be better readers than deaf children with hearing parents, but the locus of such findings is unclear. At this time, it does not appear that simple early exposure to sign language is sufficient to account for the observed difference. The best deaf readers, in fact, appear to be those who have received exposure to both early (usually manual) communication and the vernacular in which they eventually learn to read. A host of other variables are intertwined here, however, as deaf parents have greater expectations for their deaf children than do hearing parents; they also seem likely to spend more time in educationally relevant interactions with their deaf children than do hearing parents, and their children develop in more "natural" social contexts than do the deaf children of hearing parents. In addition, deaf children of deaf parents appear to show more normal patterns of cognitive development than deaf children of hearing parents (see Chapter 7), although there is too little evidence available to make any strong claims with respect to the impact on reading.

Finally, the literature reviewed in this chapter indicates that the sources of difficulty apparent in deaf children's reading performance are also readily apparent in their writing. Relative deficits in vocabulary, syntax, and relational discourse processing result in deaf children's written productions appearing concrete, repetitive, and structurally simplistic relative to both the written productions of hearing peers and to their own signed productions (see Chapter 10). The implications of deficiencies in writing ability, together with the limitations imposed by lack of reading ability, are centrally involved in deaf children's generally poor academic performance. At the same time, reading and writing form an essential link to the worlds of social and cognitive interaction, and the consequences of illiteracy have increasing impact on all realms of functioning as deaf children grow up.

Notes

1. The increasing reading lags as deaf children get older are evidenced by the difference between this report and Meadow's (1968) earlier report of her data (see also Allen, 1986). Her research originally involved two groups of thirty-two 11- to 17-year-olds each: one group of children with hearing parents and the other with deaf parents. In that study, she found a reliable difference of 2.1 grade levels in SAT reading ability in favor of the group with deaf parents. When Schlesinger and Meadow (1972a) dropped the oldest six students in each group (in order to match them with the day-school students), the difference dropped to the nonsignificant 1.0 grade level difference noted here.

2. The analysis of spelling ability differences between the excluded and included deaf subjects yielded $t(25) = 1.82, p > .05$, by a two-tailed test. However, that difference would be reliable according to a one-tailed test. The latter test seems well justified by the finding that

the excluded subjects were the poorer readers, and that analysis supports the suggestion of an important bias in the Hanson et al. sample.

3. Square brackets contain some editorial clarification; all other spelling is as originally produced.

4. Note also that these characteristics are consistent with a relatively limited capacity for linguisitic, short-term memory in deaf children relative to hearing children.

12

Development of Deaf Children: Toward an Integrated View

This final chapter is intended as an overview of the preceding eleven. Rather than being a complete summary of what has gone before, however, it provides only a partial recapitulation of the central themes and theoretical perspectives of earlier chapters. A chapter of this sort provides both writer and reader an opportunity to look back, to sort out the various conclusions that have seemed of greater or lesser importance, and to notice emergent issues that might have been lost in the context of any particular discussion. As noted in Chapter 1, my primary goal in this volume has been to provide an integration and critical examination of data pertaining to the psychological development of deaf children. In going about this business, several coherent threads have emerged that I had not even imagined at the outset. Although some of them have now been woven into the text, there are others that just now are becoming obvious.

It is helpful at this juncture to reacknowledge three aspects of my own approach to deafness and development that have shaped the way in which I have thought about and presented this material. Unlike most puzzles, this one likely has several ways in which it can be put together, yielding a different picture each time. Recognizing those alternative perspectives, I still believe that the one offered here is, in its essentials, the correct one.

Generally, the material considered has been viewed from the perspective of an experimental psychologist—not a deaf educator, not a sociologist, not a clinician of any sort. This perspective means that the literature has been reviewed with an empirical eye and perhaps more attention to methodological and statistical details than might have been expected. Through several of the chapters, however, it became clear that some of the common assumptions about deaf children have been based on methods, conclusions, or interpretations whose validity has been less than certain. For example, early conclusions about the "absence of language" in deaf children were biased by the assumption that manual communication was not a true language (e.g., Myklebust, 1960); the purported lack of linguistic creativity of deaf children was biased by the use of tests involving English comprehension (e.g., Conley, 1976); and it remains unclear whether the finding of similar distributions of deaf and hearing children's scores on nonverbal IQ tests really indicates that the two populations have comparable intelligence or is a consequence of using a restricted set of tests and subscales.

The perspective here on deaf children's development is also one of someone with a cognitive orientation. This viewpoint means that various aspects of social, cognitive, and linguistic development have been explained in terms of the mental processes (e.g., memory, problem solving, knowledge organization) that underlie behavior rather than simply trying to describe it in more superficial, if practical, terms. Admittedly, this particular cognitive psychologist has a rather eclectic view of learning, especially in infants. Thus the initial bootstrapping of social, cognitive, and linguistic processes has been viewed here from a perspective that had healthy doses of environmental and biological control. As the basic processes and structures fall into place, however, cognitive control also comes into play, so that qualitative as well as quantitative changes occur and make infants active participants in shaping the course of their own development.

Finally, as a researcher originally trained in psycholinguistics, I did not "grow up" academically with deafness as my primary field of investigation. Deaf children's language and cognitive development, however, have been my major area of interest for almost 10 years—although not the only area. My research focus has always been on the relation of language and thought, broadly defined. It was my original interest in verbal and nonverbal components of cognition that led me to interests in development, deafness, and the interaction of language acquisition with other domains of development. My thinking about deaf children, and its expression here, therefore has been molded in large part by my understanding of the roles of communication and language throughout the course of development. Communication is the tie that binds children to parents and to society, and provides for social, cognitive, and academic education. Communication also breeds communication; and language development facilitates language development as well as all other areas of psychological functioning.

With these perspectives in mind, the remainder of this chapter focuses on gaining some closure on what appear to be the central issues facing investigators and educators of deaf children. For the most part, no new research is be introduced. One section, however, considers the literature pertaining to the possibility of neuropsychological constraints on deaf children's development. The remainder of the chapter provides the conclusions and aspirations that drive research on the psychological development of deaf children.

On Causes, Constraints, and Correlates

As any graduate student in psychology knows (or should know), *correlation does not imply causation*. There are certainly a variety of cases in which causation is discernible, through statistical or rational methods, and many others for which we can make some pretty good guesses about its directness and direction. For example, it is unlikely that the negative correlation between deaf children's behavioral problems in school and their hearing parents' sign language ability (Harmon, 1992) indicates that children's disruptive behaviors cause parents to have lesser sign fluencies. It is of course possible that poor communication between parents and children contributes to social skills that either are generally maladaptive or are sufficiently idiosyncratic that they do not generalize well outside the family setting (see Chapters 3 and 4). Even in this case, however, it is unlikely that inefficient communication *causes* those social difficulties in any simple or strong sense. There are a variety of factors involved in determining the course of social development in deaf children, their precise "mix" varying to a greater or lesser extent on the (1) etiology and degree of hearing loss; (2) quality, quantity, and mode of early communication; (3) diversity of social, cognitive, and linguistic experience; and (4) myriad other variables that affect hearing children as well.

In several previous chapters (especially Chapters 2, 5, and 7), various "constraints" on deaf children's development have been considered. For the most part, these discussions have focused on the conditions that are most conducive to normal development, although the remarkable plasticity of children has been acknowledged. Unlike the distinction between correlation and causation, the line between correlation and constraint is rather more difficult to draw. Taken individually, the observed correlations between deaf children's academic performance and such factors as parental hearing status and early parent–child communication may not indicate limitations on the potential for development. There is a level, however, at which such factors do appear to affect the rate of skill acquisition if not their upper limit (cf. T. E. Allen, 1986; Furth, 1973; Marschark et al., 1986).

Beyond the general and somewhat intractable constraints on development directly imposed by deafness, there is the possibility of *secondary constraints*, linked to the secondary effects of deafness considered in early chapters. As a means of conceptualizing such constraints, consider a set of operating principles for cognitive development, based on Slobin's (1973) operating principles for language (and especially grammatical) development.[1] *Operating principles*, both here and for Slobin, refer to a set of heuristics that children bring to bear—or should bring to bear—on the task of organizing and storing their experience. Ultimately, observance of such principles should help lead to "normal" functioning within any particular domain. In this sense, such principles can be thought of as having real causal roles in development: *If* these heuristics are followed, *then* the child benefits from experience. The precise nature of the input may vary, of course, but the same general processes should come into play. At the very least, the ability to use such heuristics seems likely to be correlated with adaptive psychological functioning. The inability to use them similarly seems likely to impose considerable limitations on psychological development.

1. OPERATING PRINCIPLE A: *Pay attention to the outcomes of events.* For most practical purposes, the meaning or purpose of a (successful) event is defined by its end-state. This statement is not meant to imply that transitions are not important. In his many writings, Piaget made it clear that the ability to "see" and understand transitions from state to state represents an important developmental accomplishment (e.g., Piaget, 1952). At the same time, if a deaf or hearing child wants to understand why some physical, social, or linguistic event is occurring, looking at the outcome should be helpful more often than not. Especially in those cases in which parents or others are unable to explain the bases or purposes of particular actions (e.g., deaf children with hearing parents), children's comparison of beginning- and end-states would provide a particularly powerful heuristic for knowledge acquisition.

2. OPERATING PRINCIPLE B: *The superficial form of behaviors can be systematically modified (yielding the same result).* Linked to Operating Principle A, this principle makes explicit the fact that behaviors directed at a particular goal are not always identical; they vary from person to person, from situation to situation, and

perhaps even day to day. Among the characteristics most frequently attributed to deaf children is their rigidity or concreteness when approaching new situations, as they repetitively use the same models or forms (Furth, 1973; Myklebust, 1960). Some investigators have ascribed this lack of flexibility to explicit and implicit educational methods used with deaf students, particularly those within residential schools (e.g., Johnson et al., 1989; Tervoort, 1975; Watts, 1979). In social and cognitive domains, as well as in language acquisition, it is essential that deaf children have the flexibility with which to approach, and hopefully solve, novel problems. Such flexibility is less likely when children are taught at home or school in repetitive, unchanging terms.

3. OPERATING PRINCIPLE C: *Pay attention to the order of events and actions within events.* Flexibility of psychological functioning requires understanding of the fact that there are various means possible to achieve the same ends (Operating Principle B), and that similar discrete actions in a different order may achieve different ends. This principle has been made explicit at various linguistic levels by both Slobin (1973) and Hockett and Altmann (1968). Viewed more generally with regard to children's psychological functioning, it is useful for them to attend to the orders in which discrete behavioral units are combined. Eventually, those units and apparent combinatorial rules that are epiphenomenal drop out of the repertoire. In the meantime, it is important that children notice how things can be combined to yield different results. As a goal for parents and teachers of deaf children, the fostering of this operating principle requires the time and patience to work through alternatives during play as well as work. For children with almost any handicap, there are some contexts in which this principle is problematical (as in linguistic interactions with deaf children). Most likely, those areas are also the contexts in which it is most important.

4. OPERATING PRINCIPLE D: *Avoid interruption of ongoing events.* In the case of deaf children, this principle has two important senses. The most basic one, perhaps equally important for hearing children, pertains to the need to complete actions, events, and goals in order to be able to measure their success and their viability for use in other situations. In addition, there is a complementary need to see such connections in the behavior of others (e.g., in threatened consequences for particular actions). As one attempt to examine deaf children's understanding of such relations, our laboratory is just completing a study in which we have explored the temporal and causal relations of goals, actions, and outcomes in the stories told and written by deaf and hearing children of various ages (Marschark, Mouradian & Halas 1992). In addition to comparing the production of complete and coherent event descriptions in different modes (signing or speaking versus writing), our primary interest is the ways in which deaf and hearing children of different ages "package" their descriptions of events. Several studies have indicated that deaf children are less likely than hearing children to remember stories as coherent sequences of events, regardless of whether they are written (Banks et al., 1990) or signed (Griffith et al., 1990). Possible explanations for such findings include (1) a lack of initial language comprehension, (2) lack of initial organization due to inadequate knowledge of discourse structures or relevant experience, and (3) limitations on the functioning of working memory, especially for linguistic materials (see Chapter 8). The latter alternative, in fact, is the second sense in which this operating principle is

intended: To the extent that deaf children do encounter difficulty maintaining attention and encoding temporal sequences in memory, disruptions of ongoing events should be more likely to be detrimental to performance and learning.

5. OPERATING PRINCIPLE E: *Underlying meanings and intentions should be marked overtly and clearly.* Slobin's (1973) emphasis in his parallel principle (concerning semantic relations) was that those linguistic units that are most transparent in their meanings are the earliest acquired and the easiest to understand. In the present sense, this principle indicates that if deaf children are to understand and remember those things and events to which they are exposed, the more complete and obvious are their implications (or meanings) the more likely it is that children will succeed. Deaf children, for example, have been shown to have considerable difficulty linking examples of social situations with corresponding emotional states (see Chapter 4). If parents are unable to explain the reasons for their actions and emotions to their deaf children, an important source of early social and cognitive learning is absent (Calderon & Greenberg, 1993; Greenberg & Kusché, 1987). If teachers are unable to fully explain the bases of their lessons in terms their pupils can understand, classroom learning cannot succeed (Blackwell et al., 1978; Johnson et al., 1989; Webster, 1986). At the same time, deaf children also must acquire the necessary strategies for extracting meaning from events. If their early environments and interactions do not bootstrap such problem solving, later learning will be at a marked disadvantage.

6. OPERATING PRINCIPLE F: *Avoid exceptions.* One of the most widely noted aspects of language production in both hearing and deaf children is *overgeneralization.* Hearing children produce verbs such as "goed" and "falled," whereas deaf children make directional verbs out of the nondirectional TOUCH and TELL. Similarly, young children who have only rudimentary notions of taxonomic organization may call a horse "doggie" and a skunk CAT. Although such productions are errors from the adult perspective, they indicate that children are using underlying rules to generate exemplars in particular linguistic or conceptual classes (Marschark & Nall, 1985). In the long run, the formation of such rules is beneficial and necessary; and incorrect as well as correct categorizations can be educational. A hearing child of hearing parents or deaf a child of deaf parents who spies a horse and says "doggie" may be corrected with, "No, that's a different animal; that's a horse." A deaf child of hearing parents more often than not misses such instructional opportunities, although similar ones may be created by parents who have the time and motivation to do so.

It is from this domain, one suspects, that some of the relations between maternal education and deaf children's linguistic and cognitive abilities derive. Kampfe (1989) thus found that the level of hearing mothers' education was positively related to their own signing skills and to their deaf children's IQs and reading abilities, even while the age at which the children began to sign (before or after age 5) was not a reliable predictor. In short, the formation of rules and categories, carving up the world and avoiding exceptions (Bronowski & Bellugi, 1970), is perhaps the most basic of cognitive processes. Handicaps that impair this ability either directly (e.g., neurological damage) or indirectly (e.g., deafness) have diffuse consequences for comprehension and production in linguistic, cognitive, and social domains.

The above six heuristics provide some general rules for children's going about the world—for organizing experience and learning from it. They include both correlates and constraints on psychological development and point the way to causal relations between deaf children's experience (or lack thereof) and subsequent demonstrations of competence in several areas. There is one basic assumption underlying these principles, however, that needs to be explicit. In its simplest form, this premise is that deaf and hearing children come to the learning situation with essentially the same or comparable "hardware" and "software" (except for that directly related to hearing). Chapter 2, in contrast, suggested that the possible co-occurrence of deafness and other physical or neurological dysfunction put deaf children at some higher risk than hearing children for central and peripheral deficits that might affect basic psychological processes.

Beyond such differences in the *initial states* of deaf and hearing children, previous chapters have suggested several domains in which the nature of their early experience appears to create subtle or not so subtle differences in the ways in which they go about "data gathering" in the world. In some sense, differences of this sort are causal or constraining by definition because they determine the quality if not the quantity of what is acquired. Until now, however, such information-processing differences have been considered solely in terms of relations between acquired behaviors and interactions with the world. Such relations are informative with regard to both theoretical issues relating to development and the practical aspects of deafness and deaf education. Still unresolved is whether the differences from which they derive are purely psychological in nature or reflect physiological differences in the brains of deaf and hearing children. We therefore turn to one final area of research and consider the possibility of neuropsychological correlates of deafness.

Do Deaf and Hearing Children Have Different Brain Organization?

Aside from any neurological idiosyncrasies linked to the etiology of deafness, it is possible that deaf and hearing children's brains develop different patterns of organization as a function of their early experience. It is well known that children's brains are remarkably malleable in that they are able to accommodate and adjust to various brain traumas. Although such flexibility decreases with age, there appears to be significant reorganization and recovery of function possible at least up until adolescence (Kolb & Wishaw, 1990; Lenneberg, 1967). Lying somewhere between the self-adjustment of brains following injury or surgical intervention and the subtle (and still largely unknown) differences as a function of normal experience are the variations in cortical organization that one might expect when one of the major senses is absent. In the terms often voiced by students of the area: If deaf children do not use auditory cortex for hearing, do its resources become mobilized for vision or other functions? If language is normally localized in the left hemisphere and visual-spatial abilities in the right hemisphere (at least for right-handers), what happens when language is visual-spatial as for sign language?[2] It is precisely these sorts of questions that led Blair (1957) and others to hypothesize a *sensory compensation* in deaf children. [See Parasnis (1983b) for discussion of visual perception of verbal information in deaf individuals and work by Samar and his colleagues on perception and cerebral asymmetries in deaf adults.]

There are at least four ways in which investigators might go about searching for differences in brain organization between deaf and hearing individuals: (1) examining the effects on language and visual-spatial abilities of damage to one or the other hemispheres; (2) comparing the abilities of left (LVF) and right (RVF) visual fields, and thus the right (RH) and left (LH) cerebral hemispheres, respectively, to recognize verbal and nonverbal stimuli; (3) measuring the electrical or metabolic activity at various brain locations during verbal and nonverbal tasks; and (4) determining the extent of brain lateralization by examining the frequency and degree of right- and left-handedness in deaf and hearing populations. All of these methods have been used in studies of deaf adults, although for practical reasons, studies with children have been restricted primarily to methods (2) and (3).

Poizner et al. (1987) examined the verbal and nonverbal abilities of a group of deaf adults who had suffered LH or RH lesions. Their findings clearly indicated that even with a visual-spatial language it is the left hemisphere that is dominant for language, as the patients with LH damage showed significant sign language deficits while retaining the capacity for nonlinguistic visual-spatial processing. Conversely, deaf patients with RH damage exhibited normal sign language abilities but impaired visual-spatial processing. Perhaps most important, Poizner et al. found that despite the fact that grammatical information in ASL is expressed spatially, RH damage disrupts spatial relations but not syntax, and the reverse is true following LH damage. Moreover, their findings indicated that it is language per se that is disrupted by LH damage, not the motor control necessary to produce manual signs. Deaf patients with LH damage apparently retain the ability to make nonlinguistic manual gestures even when they are unable to make linguistic ones (cf. Kimura, 1981).

In contrast to the findings of Poizner and his colleagues, Neville and coworkers (1982; Neville & Lawson, 1987) have reported finding differences between deaf and hearing individuals in the amplitude and location of event-related potentials (ERPs), or brain electrical activity following a stimulus presentation. Neville et al. (1982) reported that congenitally, profoundly deaf adults (without known neurological damage) were just as accurate as hearing adults in a word identification task but failed to show the usual RVF advantage. In addition, hearing subjects showed normal patterns of occipital and parietal ERP activity, whereas deaf subjects exhibited more heterogeneous activity. Neville and Lawson (1987) further found that whereas hearing adults showed the normal pattern of contralateral parietal activation to peripheral visual presentations, deaf adults also showed bilateral occipital activity.

Neville and Lawson concluded that auditory deprivation from birth in deaf individuals has a major effect on the development of the peripheral visual system. Because deaf individuals normally must devote more attention than hearing individuals to the peripheral visual environment in order to receive orienting signals and simultaneously process language and object information (see Chapter 3), it would not be surprising if they have relatively more cortex devoted to peripheral vision (Neville et al., 1982; Swisher, 1993). Neville and Lawson (1987), in fact, found both behavioral and ERP evidence indicating that their deaf subjects showed greater RH involvement in peripheral visual attention than did their hearing subjects. Although these findings do not explicitly contradict those of Poizner et al. (1987), they suggest that there may be more heterogeneity in the cerebral organization of deaf than hearing adults. The differences in their findings also might be partially attributable to the fact that Neville's subjects all had been raised by deaf parents, whereas most of Poizner et al.'s subjects were born to hearing parents (parental hearing status for two of them is unclear).

The possible relation between early language experience and cerebral organization is not clear but seems likely to be important for understanding neurological differences between deaf and hearing individuals. Bonvillian, Orlansky, and Garland (1982), for example, surveyed the strength and prevalence of left- and right-handedness in samples of 226 deaf and 210 hearing high school and college students. They found a significantly higher incidence of left-handedness (indicating lesser LH dominance) in the deaf students than would normally be expected, and more than one-third of them reported that they used their left hands for finger-spelling as often or more so than their right hands. Importantly, the deaf left-handers were distinguished by the fact that, on average, they learned to sign later in life, suggesting to Bonvillian et al. that handedness (and hemispheric dominance) may be related to age of language acquisition rather than auditory deprivation. Consistent with this view, Gottlieb, Doran, and Whitley (1964) had found that strong LH dominance was linked to better speech production abilities in a group of 82 deaf children, most of whom had congenital and profound hearing losses.

Investigations of cerebral organization in deaf children are relatively rare, but what studies have been conducted generally support the findings obtained with neurologically intact adults indicating greater heterogeneity and less lateralization in deaf than hearing individuals (cf. Poizner et al., 1987). Kelly and Tomlinson-Keasey (1977), for example, examined hemispheric laterality in 39 mostly profoundly deaf children in grades 3 to 5. They used a visual matching task involving both word and picture stimuli; the fact that the instructions were given in Sign English suggests that the children were enrolled in some kind of manual education program. Contrary to their expectations, Kelly and Tomlinson-Keasey did not find a significant RH advantage in their subjects, although there was a trend in that direction. In fact, they failed to find any significant hemispheric lateralization and observed considerable variability across subjects.

Vargha-Khadam (1983) examined visual field asymmetries in a group of congenitally deaf children aged 12 to 17 years who had had 3 to 10 years' signing experience. Deaf and hearing children were shown words, faces, or ASL signs that were either static or moving. As is typically the case with hearing adults, the hearing children showed an RVF (LH) superiority for moving sign sequences and words and an LVF (RH) superiority for static signs and faces. The deaf children, in contrast, showed an RVF advantage for faces but no significant LVF or RVF advantage for words or signs. Consistent with the conclusions of Kelly and Tomlinson-Kelly (1977), Vargha-Khadam concluded that "in the absence of auditory experience, there is a greater chance that an anomalous pattern of cerebral activity may develop" (p. 385). Converging with the findings of Bonvillian et al. (1982) and Gottlieb et al. (1964), Vargha-Khadam also observed that those deaf children who showed evidence of RH language localization had poor speech abilities and relied exclusively on signing. Those children with LH language representation had good speech skills and used vocalization while signing.

The findings of Vargha-Khadam (1983) and Kelly and Tomlinson-Kelly (1977) point to the relative absence of normal hemispheric specialization in congenitally deaf children who had early sign language experience. This conclusion is consistent with the findings of Bonvillian et al. (1982) and Neville et al. (1982; Neville & Lawson, 1987) regarding neurologically intact deaf adults. In contrast to the results obtained by Poizner et al. (1987) with deaf adults who had suffered strokes, it appears that deafness and early manual language experience are related to neurological development in ways amenable to experimental detection.

It is worth noting here that in their more extensive review of the literature (including many earlier studies), Rodda and Grove (1987) described a variety of findings for, against, and indeterminate with regard to hemispheric lateralization in deaf individuals. Rodda and Grove suggested that the pattern of results they described was complex, "[p]robably because all of the studies reviewed have serious defects" (p. 286). Based primarily on the clinical literature of the sort described by Poizner et al. (1987), Rodda and Grove concluded that the case for "dramatic" hemispheric differences between deaf and hearing individuals had not yet been made. Considering newer results with apparently better controls and methodologies, it now appears deaf children and adults do have a far greater heterogeneity of brain localization than do hearing peers, and it seems safe to conclude that differences in early auditory and language experience are linked to some (not necessarily "dramatic") differences in brain organization. Indeed, it would be strange if anything else were the case.

Interestingly, the direction of the causal relation between the observed differences in hemispheric specialization of deaf individuals and their early experience is not at issue. That is, it clearly is not the case that differences in brain organization result in auditory deprivation or an advantage for early manual communication. Any observed neurological differences between deaf and hearing children must go in the opposite direction. The goals for future research in this area include better specification of the correlates of such differences and their potential effects on psychological functioning in deaf children. We already know, for example, that greater LH specialization for language is linked to better speech abilities in deaf children (Gottlieb et al., 1964) and better language skills, in general, for hearing children (Tomlinson-Keasey & Kelly, 1978). Whether there are other academic implications of deaf children's having relatively less hemispheric dominance and, if so, whether behavioral interventions can compensate for those differences remains to be determined.

Are Deaf Children Taught to Be Deficient?

In keeping with the perspective maintained throughout this volume, it is essential to stress here that the findings of possible neurological differences between deaf and hearing children do not imply neurological deficiencies. At our present state of knowledge, it seems just as likely that such differences might serve to enhance as to diminish cognitive proficiencies in various domains. The findings of apparent neurological and other differences between deaf and hearing children, however, do imply that the two populations are not strictly comparable in many respects, which means that expectations, interactions, and educational methods (broadly defined) appropriate for hearing children may not generalize to deaf children.

Earlier chapters have presented evidence indicating that deaf children, on average, are relatively more restricted in their range of experience; they tend to have more concrete and informationally deficient linguistic interchanges with others and do not have as many available sources of content and social knowledge as hearing age-mates. In a real sense, then, many of the interactions observed between deaf children and their early environments appeared to orient them toward the concrete, the superficial, and the immediate. Such patterns held primarily for deaf children of hearing parents, especially the children of parents who for whatever reason had minimal or only later communication with their children. Deaf parents, on average, are found to have greater expectations for and involvement in their children's educations, in addition to having more consistent child-rearing practices. It is therefore difficult to separate child-related from parent-related factors in deaf children's successes and failures. We can be sure only that the two interact in a variety of ways, and then we can try to identify the dimensions that appear most salient in determining the course of psychological development in deaf children.

Three such factors now appear to stand out as having central implications for deaf children's competence in dealing with the world. One such factor is *early language experience*. Regardless of its mode, all evidence from deaf and hearing children alike points to the need for effective early communication between children and those around them. Obvious in some sense, the need for symbolic, linguistic interaction goes beyond day-to-day practicalities and academic instruction. The deaf children who appear most likely to be the most competent in all domains of childhood endeavor are those who actively participate in linguistic interactions with their parents from an early age. From those interactions, they not only gain facts, they gain cognitive and social strategies, knowledge of self and others, and a sense of being part of the world. In social as well as academic domains, lack of the ability to communicate about the abstract and the absent prevents children from reaching their potential (Johnson et al., 1989).

A second essential factor for normal development is *diversity of experience*. It is through active exploration of the environment and through experience with people, things, and language that children acquire knowledge, including learning to learn. The operating principles for development outlined earlier in this chapter are unlikely to be innate. They derive from the application of basic perceptual, learning, and memory processes (which are more likely to have innate components) *as a result of experience*. With sufficient resources, learning becomes a self-motivating and self-sustaining pursuit. In the absence of diversity, there are no problems to solve and so no need for flexibility. When attempting to ensure that deaf children have the necessities for academic and practical pursuits, we sometimes forget that the basic elements must fit the larger puzzle if they are to make sense, be retained, and be appropriately implemented (Tervoort, 1975; Watts, 1979).

A third prerequisite for child development is *social interaction*. Social development was considered in detail in Chapters 3 and 4, where the interactions of social, linguistic, and cognitive development were emphasized. Deaf children's relationships with others frequently have been characterized as impulsive, remote, and superficial. Deaf children with deaf parents and those whose hearing parents are involved in early intervention programs, however, show relatively normal patterns of social development (Calderon & Greenberg, 1993; Lederberg, 1993). Beyond the biological and cognitive functions of social interaction, children use such relationships to develop secure bases for exploration and to identify with others who are like them; moreover, they use others for instrumental and emotional support. Social relationships make children part of peer and cultural groups; and they lead to self-esteem, achievement motivation, and moral development. Children who are denied such opportunities early in life because of child-related, familial, or societal factors cannot fully benefit from other aspects of experience.

Future Directions

Education of Deaf Children

While recognizing the motivations of many hearing parents and educators of deaf children, the concerns raised in the preceding section reflect a belief in the need to make deaf education and the experiences of deaf children as normal as possible. This conclusion is not a call for mainstreaming deaf children into regular classrooms. Concerns about the appropriateness of a "segregated, sheltered environment" for deaf education have been with us for more than a century (Schildroth, 1986, p. 83) and likely will be with us for some time to come. Public Law 94-142 (Education for All Handicapped Children Act) mandates that deaf and other handicapped children should be educated with nonhandicapped children "to the greatest appropriate degree." It also recognizes, however, that regular classrooms may be inappropriate. In practice, the mainstreaming of deaf students frequently consists in integration in nonacademic or vocational domains but not in academics (Moores & Kluwin, 1986). Being in a normal school or normal classroom does not necessarily provide deaf children with the same education as hearing peers. Quite the contrary: In the absence of comparable early environments, many deaf children are ill-equipped to deal with either the content or the context of the hearing public school classroom. Such a setting would be neither "normal" nor facilitative.

Moores and Kluwin (1986) pointed out that neither the fears of isolation nor the great expectations engendered by PL 94-142 have come to pass. If that law and the Americans with Disabilities Act of 1990 are to be fruitful for deaf children and the deaf community, the focus of attention must be placed, prior to the classroom, on early diagnosis and intervention and on parent counseling and training in manual communication (Greenberg & Kusché, 1987). The problems facing deaf education go far beyond children's inability to hear, speak, and read. Most of those problems did not develop during the school years, and it is unlikely that they can be resolved there.

Where Does Deafness Research Go From Here?

In a very real sense, the background work that has gone into this book has convinced me that deafness research is going in exactly the right direction—or, rather, directions. Investigations of early social development, the pragmatics and content of early communication, and the course of cognitive development of deaf children must continue, with increasing attention devoted to understanding the interactions among these domains (Marschark, 1993). At the same time, we need more empirical research on educational methods and on neuropsychological correlates of deafness in children. These latter two areas may appear to fall at opposite extremes on a dimension of practical versus scientific import, but ultimately the two are essential to each other. To the extent that there are, in fact, neuropsychological differences between deaf and hearing children, those differences are a reflection of differences in early experience and may help to guide deaf education toward greater facilitation of academic and intellectual pursuits for deaf children. Looking at the creativity, culture, and sense of identity that exist in the deaf community, we can see the potential of deaf children; the issues that divide us concern only the best way to facilitate their achieving that potential.

As an academic psychologist and researcher of language and cognition, I came into this project primarily with empirical questions. Many of these questions have been answered and many more raised. Like other researchers, I frequently have been frustrated by the lack of rigor in many studies involving deaf children and the "passing down" of findings that did not always have their bases in established facts. Adopting a broader perspective, however, has allowed detection of some unexpected and exciting patterns of results in several domains. The remarkable flexibility and creativity of deaf children in their sign language productions as well as the remarkable consistency of deficits observed in their short-term memory spans are two such findings. Both of these factors have important implications for deaf children's reading, writing, and cognitive abilities that merit further investigation.

There are also several areas in which the lack of research is surprising. We have little understanding of the need for achievement in deaf schoolchildren, for example, nor do we know much about the organization of their conceptual knowledge and its relation to language experience. Research on verbal and nonverbal problem solving by deaf children has largely been confined to analyses of IQ test results and early studies by Furth (1966) and others on the relation of problem solving to Piagetian stages of development. Given the current prevalence of manual communication in American deaf children, we probably know less about their cognitive and social problem-solving abilities now than we did 20 years ago.

The reviews presented here may have brought some coherence to diverse findings. Nevertheless, there is still a surprising amount of inconsistency and indeterminacy in literature pertaining to deaf children's reading skills, the possibility of their differing from hearing age-mates in neuropsychological organization, and their abilities to make use of strategies in memory tasks. The likely interaction of all of these areas with language ability, cognitive development, and early experience should be obvious, but the frequency with which investigators fail to control them (either through subject selection or statistically) suggests that the effects of these factors are frequently underestimated. This underestimation, I think, is a mistake.

Parenting: Integrating Research with Reality

As a nonparent and a nonclinician, it has been relatively easy to write portions of this book that would have been difficult otherwise. I know it is not easy for a hearing parent to have a deaf child; it is not easy to have any child who appears anything less than "normal" (raising relatively normal children is tough enough). Recognizing that deaf children are different from hearing children, however, is an important step for both researchers and parents. As much as we might want them to be like hearing children, forcing deaf children into that mold does them no service and may do them harm (Luterman, 1987). If deaf children are to receive help in areas in which they need it, they must be appreciated in their own right. Methods for understanding the competencies of hearing children might not always be appropriate for deaf children, and deaf children might need more and different educational experiences to derive the same benefits.

Identification of the differences between deaf and hearing children and of the relative deficiencies of deaf children is an essential precursor of education and remediation for those who are interested in such matters. Identifying these differences and deficiencies is also essential for those of us with scientific interests, either with regard to deaf children themselves or with the goal of better understanding normal development. The findings and conclusions described here, though, are also generalities based on averages across heterogeneous groups of children who are more variable than hearing peers in the first place. This generality means that there is no convenient mapping from these findings to any particular child, no matter how well that child seems to fit the prototype of membership of the group. The content of this book is descriptive not prescriptive—it is a manual for investigation and exploration, not for education and parenting.

The fact that this book is not a how-to manual does not mean that its implications are necessarily far removed from the day-to-day needs of individual deaf children. The focus here has been on considering the *whole child* while discerning and disentangling abilities that in some contexts are considered linguistic, in some contexts social, and in some contexts cognitive. Underlying all of these domains has been the assumption that deaf children (as well as hearing children) can make use of the heuristic principles described earlier in this chapter. Anything that facilitates the operation of those learning strategies should facilitate deaf children's abilities to interact with and learn from interactions with the world. Parental consistency, flexibility, patience, and communication are essential for any child. Deaf children may require a greater quantity of each of these, but the quality of these ingredients is essentially the same.

Notes

1. With all due apologies and respect to Dan Slobin.

2. It is now recognized that localization of language and visual-spatial abilities in the left and right hemispheres, respectively, is somewhat of an oversimplification (e.g., Kolb & Wishaw, 1990). The gross distinction still can be made, however, and is sufficient for the present purposes.

References

Abrahamsen, A., Cavallo, M. M., & McCluer, J. A. (1985). Is the sign advantage a robust phenomenon? From gesture to language in two modalities. *Merrill-Palmer Quarterly, 31*, 177–209.

Ackerman, J., Kyle, J., Woll, B., & Ezra, M. (1990). Lexical acquisition in sign and speech: Evidence from a longitudinal study of infants in deaf families. In C. Lucas (Ed.), *Sign language research: Theoretical issues* (pp. 337–345). Washington, DC: Gallaudet University Press.

Acredolo, L., & Goodwyn, S. (1988). Symbolic gesturing in normal infants. *Child Development, 59*, 450–466.

Acredolo, L. P., & Goodwyn, S. W. (1985). *Spontaneous signing in infants*. Paper presented at biennial meetings of the Society for Research in Child Development.

Ainsworth, M. D. (1973). The development of infant-mother attachment. In B. M. Caldwell & H. N. Ricciuti (Eds.), *Review of child development research* (pp. 1–94). Chicago: University of Chicago Press.

Allen, D. V. (1970). Acoustic interference in paired-associate learning as a function of hearing ability. *Psychonomic Science, 18*, 231–233.

Allen, D. V. (1971). Color-word interference in deaf and hearing children. *Psychonomic Science, 24*, 295–296.

Allen, T. E. (1986). Patterns of academic achievement among hearing impaired students: 1974–1983. In A. N. Shildroth & M. A. Karchmer (Eds.), *Deaf children in America* (pp. 161–206). San Diego, CA: College-Hill Press.

Als, H., Lester, B. M., & Brazelton, T. B. (1979). Dynamics of the behavioral organization of the premature infant: A theoretical perspective. In T. M. Field, A. M. Sostek, S. Goldberg, & H. H. Shuman (Eds.), *Infants born at risk* (pp. 173–192). New York: Spectrum Press.

Altshuler, K. Z. (1974). The social and psychological development of the deaf child: Problems and treatment. In P. J. Fine (Ed.), *Deafness in infancy and early childhood* (pp. 55–86). New York: Medcom Press.

Altshuler, K. Z., Deming, W. E., Vollenweider, J., Rainer, J. D., & Tendler, R. (1976). Impulsivity and profound early deafness: A crosscultural inquiry. *American Annals of the Deaf, 121*, 331–345.

Amabile, T. (1983). *The social psychology of creativity*. New York: Springer-Verlag.

Anderson, R. J., & Sisco, F. (1977). *Standardization of the WISC-R performance scale for deaf children* (Series T, No. 1). Washington, DC: Gallaudet University Office of Demographic Studies.

Arnold, P. & Walter, G. (1979). Communication and reasoning skills in deaf and hearing signers. *Perceptual and Motor Skills, 49*, 192–194.

Ashbrook, E. (1977). *Development of semantic relations in the acquisition of American Sign Language*. Unpublished Manuscript, University of Illinois, Urbana-Champaign.

Athey, I. (1985). Theories and models of human development: Their implications for the education of deaf adolescents. In D. S. Martin (Ed.), *Cognition, education, and deafness* (pp. 22–26). Washington, DC: Gallaudet College Press.

Bachara, G. H., Raphael, J., & Phelan, W. J., III. (1980). Empathy development in deaf preadolescents. *Americal Annals of the Deaf, 125*, 38–41.

Baddeley, A. (1986). *Working memory*. Cambridge: Cambridge University Press.

Baldwin, D. A., & Markman, E. M. (1989). Establishing word-object relations: A first step. *Child Development, 60*, 381–398.

Balogh, R. D., & Porter, R. H. (1986). Olfactory preferences resulting from mere exposure in human neonates. *Infant Behavior and Development, 9*, 395–401.

Balow, I. H., & Brill, R. G. (1975). An evalutaion of reading and academic achievement levels of 16 graduating classes of the California School for the Deaf, Riverside. *Volta Review, 77*, 255–266.

Banks, J., Gray, C., & Fyfe, R. (1990). The written recall of printed stories by severely deaf children. *British Journal of Educational Psychology, 60*, 192–206.

Barron, F., & Harrington, D. M. (1981). Creativity, intelligence, and personality. *Annual Review of Psychology, 32*, 439–476.

Bates, E. (1979). *The emergence of symbols: Cognition and communication in infancy*. New York: Academic Press.

Bates, E., Benigni, L., Bretherton, I., Camaioni, L., & Volterra, V. (1977). From gesture to the first word: On cognitive and social prerequisites. In M. Lewis & L. A. Rosenblum (Eds.), *Interaction, conversation, and the development of language* (pp. 247–308). New York: Academic Press.

Bates, E., Bretherton, I., Shore, C., & McNew, S. (1983). Names, gestures, and objects: The role of context in the emergence of symbols. In K. E. Nelson (Ed.), *Children's language* (Vol. 4, pp. 59–123). New York: Gardner Press.

Bates, E., Thal, D., Whitesell, K., Fenson, L., & Oakes, L. (1989). Integrating language and gesture in infancy. *Developmental Psychology, 25*, 1004–1019.

Battacchi, M. W. & Montanini-Manfredi, M. (1986). Recent research trends in Italy: Cognitive and communicative development of deaf children. *Sign Language Studies, 52*, 201–218.

Battison, R. (1974). Phonological deletion in American Sign Language. *Sign Language Studies, 5*, 1–19.

Bebko, J. M. (1984). Memory and rehearsal characteristics of profoundly deaf children. *Journal of Experimental Child Psychology, 38*, 415–428.

Bebko, J. M., & McKinnon, E. E. (1990). The language experience of deaf children: Its relation to spontaneous rehearsal in a memory task. *Child Development, 61*, 1744–1752.

Beck, K., Beck, C., & Gironella, O. (1977). Rehearsal and recall strategies of deaf and hearing individuals. *American Annals of the Deaf, 122*, 544–552.

Beech, J. R., & Harris, M. (1992). The prelingually deaf young reader: A case of logographic reading? Manuscript submitted for publication.

Bell, S. M., & Ainsworth, M. D. (1972). Infant crying and maternal responsiveness. *Child Development, 43*, 1171–1190.

Bellugi, U., Klima, E., & Siple, P. (1975). Remembering in sign. *Cognition, 3*, 93–125.

Belmont, J. M., & Karchmer, M. A. (1978). Deaf people's memory: There are problems testing special populations. In M. M. Gruneberg, P. E. Morris, & R. N. Sykes (Eds.), *Practical aspects of memory* (pp. 581–588). London: Academic Press.

Belmont, J. M., Karchmer, M. A., & Bourg, J. W. (1983). Structural influences on deaf and hearing children's recall of temporal/spatial incongruent letter strings. *Educational Psychology, 3*, 259–274.

Belsky, J. (1986). Infant day care: A cause for concern? *Zero to three, VI,* 1–7.

Bickerton, D. (1984). The language bioprogram hypothesis. *The Behavioral and Brain Sciences, 7,* 173–221.

Billow, R. A. (1975). A cognitive developmental study of metaphor comprehension. *Developmental Psychology, 11,* 415–423.

Bjorklund, D. F. (1985). The role of conceptual knowledge in the development of organization in children's memory. In C. J. Brainerd and M. Pressley (Eds.), *Basic processes in memory development* (pp. 103–142). New York: Springer-Verlag.

Blackwell, P., Engen, E., Fischgrund, J., & Zarcadoolas, C. (1978). *Sentences and other systems: A language and learning curriculum for hearing-impaired children.* Washington, DC: National Association of the Deaf.

Blair, F. X. (1957). A study of the visual memory of deaf and hearing children. *American Annals of the Deaf, 102,* 254–263.

Blanton, R. L., Nunnally, J. C., & Odom, P. B. (1967). Graphemic, phonetic, and associative factors in the verbal behavior of deaf and hearing subjects. *Journal of Speech and Hearing Disorders, 10,* 225–231.

Blennerhassett, L. (1984). Communicative styles of a 13-month old hearing-impaired child and her parents. *Volta Review, 86,* 217–228.

Boatner, M. T., & Gates, J. E. (1969). *A dictionary of idioms for the deaf.* Washington, DC: National Association for the Deaf.

Bolton, B. (1972). Factor analytic studies of communication skills, intelligence, and other psychological abilities of young deaf persons. *Rehabilitation Psychology, 19,* 71–79.

Bolton, B. (1978). Differential ability structure in deaf and hearing children. *Applied Psychological Measurement, 2,* 147–149.

Bonvillian, J. D. (1983). Effects of signability and imagery on word recall of deaf and hearing students. *Perceptual and Motor Skills, 56,* 775–791.

Bonvillian, J. D., & Folven, R. J. (1993). Sign language acquisition: Developmental aspects. In M. Marschark and M. D. Clark (Eds.), *Psychological perspectives on deafness* (pp. 229–265). Hillsdale, NJ: Lawrence Erlbaum Associates.

Bonvillian, J. D., Orlansky, M. D., & Garland, J. B. (1982). Handedness patterns in deaf persons. *Brain and Cognition, 1,* 141–157.

Bonvillian, J. D., Orlansky, M. D., & Novack, L. L. (1983a). Developmental milestones: Sign language acquisition and motor development. *Child Development, 54,* 1435–1445.

Bonvillian, J. D., Orlansky, M. D., Novack, L. L., & Folven, R. J. (1983b). Early sign language acquisition and cognitive development. In D. Rogers & J. A. Sloboda (Eds.), *The acquisition of symbolic skills* (pp. 207–214). Chicago: Plenum.

Braden, J. P. (1984). The factorial similarity of the WISC-R performance scale in deaf and hearing samples. *Personality and Individual Differences, 5,* 403–409.

Braden, J. P. (1985a). The structure of nonverbal intelligence in deaf and hearing subjects. *American Annals of the Deaf, 130,* 496–501.

Braden, J. P. (1985b). WISC-R deaf norms reconsidered. *Journal of School Psychology, 23,* 375–382.

Brasel, K., & Quigley, S. P. (1977). Influence of certain language and communicative environments in early childhood on the development of language in deaf individuals. *Journal of Speech and Hearing Research, 20,* 95–107.

Brazelton, T. B. (1982). Joint regulation of neonate-parent behavior. In E. Z. Tronick (Ed.), *Social interchange in infancy* (pp. 7–22). Baltimore, University Park Press.

Bronowski, J., & Bellugi, U. (1970). Language, name, and concept. *Science, 168*, 669–673.

Brown, R. (1973). *A first language*. Cambridge, MA: Harvard University Press.

Burnham, D. K. (1986). Developmental loss of speech perception: Exposure to and experience with a first language. *Applied Psycholinguistics, 7*, 207–240.

Caccamise, F., Hatfield, N., & Brewer, L. (1978). Manual/simultaneous communication research: Results and implications. *American Annals of the Deaf, 123*, 803–823.

Calderon, R., & Greenberg, M. T. (1993). Considerations in the adaptation of families with school-aged deaf children. In M. Marschark and D. Clark (Eds.), *Psychological perspectives on deafness* (pp. 27–47). Hillsdale, NJ: Lawrence Erlbaum.

Caselli, M. C., & Volterra, V. (1990). From communication to language in hearing and deaf children. In V. Volterra and C. J. Erting (Eds.), *From gesture to language in hearing and deaf children* (pp. 261–277). Berlin: Springer-Verlag.

Cates, D. S., & Shontz, F. C. (1990). Role-taking ability and social behavior in deaf school children. *American Annals of the Deaf, 135*, 217–221.

Cavedon, A., Cornoldi, C., & DeBeni, R. (1984). Structural vs. semantic coding in the reading of isolated words by deaf children. *Visible Language, 18*, 372–381.

Cazden, C. (1972). *Child language and education*. New York: Holt, Rinehart, Winston.

Center for Assessment and Demographic Studies. (1985). Today's hearing impaired children and youth: A demographic and academic profile. *GRI Newsletter*: Washington, DC: Gallaudet University.

Charrow, V. (1976). A psycholinguistic analysis of "deaf English". *Sign Language Studies, 1*, 139–150.

Charrow, V., & Fletcher, J. D. (1974). English as a second language of deaf children. *Developmental Psychology, 10*, 463–470.

Chen, K. (1976). Acoustic image in visual detection for deaf and hearing college students. *Journal of General Psychology, 94*, 243–246.

Chess, S., & Fernandez, P. (1980). Do deaf children have a typical personality? *Journal of the American Academy of Child Psychiatry, 19*, 654–664.

Chi, M. T. H., & Ceci, S. J. (1987). Content knowledge: Its role, representation, and restructuring in memory development. In H. W. Reese (Ed.), *Advances in child development and behavior* (pp. 91–142). New York: Academic Press.

Chomsky, N. (1957). *Syntactic structures*. The Hague: Mouton.

Chomsky, N. (1965). *Aspects of the theory of syntax*. Cambridge, MA: MIT Press.

Chomsky, N. (1986). *Barriers*. Cambridge, MA: MIT Press.

Chovan, J. D., Waldron, M. B., & Rose, S. (1988). Response latency measurements to visual cognitive tasks by normal hearing and deaf subjects. *Perceptual and Motor Skills, 67*, 179–184.

Church, R. B., & Goldin-Meadow, S. (1986). The mismatch between gesture and speech as an index of transitional knowledge. *Cognition, 23*, 43–71.

Cicourel, A., & Boese, R. J. (1972). Sign language acquisition and the teaching of deaf children. In C. B. Cazden, V. P. John, & D. Hymes (Eds.), *Functions of language in the classroom* (pp. 32–62). New York: Teachers College Press.

Cohen, E., Namir, L., & Schlesinger, I. M. (1977). *A new dictionary of sign language*. The Hague: Mouton.

Cohen, S. (1967). Predictability of deaf and hearing story paraphrasing. *Journal of Verbal Learning and Verbal Behavior, 6*, 916–921.

Conley, J. E. (1976). The role idiomatic expresions in the reading of deaf children. *American Annals of the Deaf, 121*, 381–385.

Conlin, D., & Paivio, A. (1975). The associative learning of the deaf: The effects of word imagery and signability. *Memory and Cognition, 3,* 333–340.

Conrad, R. (1970). Short-term memory processes in the deaf. *British Journal of Psychology, 61,* 179–195.

Conrad, R. (1972). Short-term memory in the deaf: A test for speech coding. *British Journal of Psychology, 63,* 173–180.

Conrad, R. (1973). Internal speech in the profoundly deaf child. *Teacher of the Deaf, 71,* 384–389.

Conrad, R. (1979). *The deaf school child.* London: Harper & Row.

Conrad, R., & Rush, M. (1965). On the nature of short-term memory encoding by the deaf. *Journal of Speech and Hearing Disorders, 30,* 336–343.

Conrad, R., & Weiskrantz, B. C. (1981). On cognitive ability of deaf children with deaf parents. *American Annals of the Deaf, 126,* 995–1003.

Cornelius, G., & Hornett, D. (1990). The play behavior of hearing-impaired kindergarten children. *American Annals of the Deaf, 135,* 316–321.

Cornoldi, C. (1974). Imagery values for 310 Italian nouns. *Italian Journal of Psychology, 1,* 211–225.

Cornoldi, C., & Sanavio, E. (1980). Imagery value and recall in deaf children. *Italian Journal of Psychology, 7,* 33–38.

Couch, C. G. (1985). *A test of Kohlberg's theory: The development of moral reasoning in deaf and hearing individuals.* Unpublished doctoral dissertation, University of North Carolina at Greensboro.

Craig, W., & Craig, H. (1986). Schools and classes for the deaf in the United States. *American Annals of the Deaf, 131,* 93–135.

Crittenden, J. B., Ritterman, S. I., & Wilcox, E. W. (1986). Communication mode as a factor in the performance of hearing-impaired children on a standardized receptive vocabulary test. *American Annals of the Deaf, 131,* 356–360.

Dale, P. S. (1976). *Language Development.* New York: Holt, Rinehart, Winston.

Day, P. S. (1986). Deaf children's expression of communicative intentions. *Journal of Communication Disorders, 19,* 367–385.

DeCaro, P., & Emerton, R. G. (1978). *A cognitive-developmental investigation of moral reasoning in a deaf population.* Paper presented to American Educational Research Association meetings.

DeCasper, A. J., & Fifer, W. P. (1980). Of human bonding: Newborns prefer their mothers' voices. *Science, 208,* 1174–1176.

DeCasper, A. J., & Prescott, P. A. (1984). Human newborns' perception of male vices: Preference, discrimination, and reinforcing value. *Developmental Psychobiology, 17,* 481–491.

DeCasper, A. J., & Sigafoos, A. D. (1983). The intrauterine heartbeat: A potent reinforcer for newborns. *Infant Behavior and Development, 6,* 19–25.

DeCasper, A. J., & Spence, M. J. (1986). Prenatal maternal speech influences newborns' perception of speech sounds. *Infant Behavior and Development, 9,* 133–150.

De Villiers, J. (1984). Limited input? Limited structure. *Society for Research on Child Development Monographs, 49,* 122–142.

De Villiers, J. H., & de Villiers, P. A. (1978). *Language acquisition.* Cambridge, MA: Harvard University Press.

DiFrancesca, S. (1972). *Academic achievement test results of a national testing program for hearing-impaired students—United States, Spring 1971.* Office for Demographic Studies, Gallaudet College.

Dobrich, W., & Scarborough, H. (1984). Form and function in early communication:

Language and pointing gestures. *Journal of Experimental Child Psychology, 38*, 475–490.

Dodd, B. (1980). The spelling abilities of profoundly pre-lingually deaf children. In U. Frith (Ed.), *Cognitive processes in spelling* (pp. 423–440). New York: Academic Press.

Dodd, B., Hobson, P., Brasher, J., & Campbell, R. (1983). Deaf children's short-term memory for lip-read, graphic and signed stimuli. *British Journal of Developmental Psychology, 1*, 353–364.

Dolman, D. (1983). A study of the relationship between syntactic development and concrete operations in deaf children. *American Annals of the Deaf, 128*, 813–819.

Eisenberg, R. B. (1976). *Auditory competence in early life.* Baltimore: University Park Press.

Eisenberg, R. B. (1978). Stimulus significance as a determinant of infant responses to sound. In S. Trotter & E. B. Thoman (Eds.), *Social responsiveness of infants. Pediatric Round Table: 2* (pp. 1–5). Skillman, NJ: Johnson & Johnson Baby Products.

Ellenberger, R. & Stayaert, M. (1978). A child's representation of action in American Sign Language. In P. Siple (Ed.), *Understanding language through sign language research* (pp. 261–270). Orlando, FL: Academic Press.

Engelkamp, J. (1990). Memory of action events: Some implications for memory theory and for imagery. In C. Cornoldi & M. A. McDaniel (Eds.), *Imagery and cognition* (pp. 183–220). New York: Springer-Verlag.

English, H. B., & English, A. C. (1958). *A comprehensive dictionary of psychological and psychonalytical terms.* New York: David McKay.

Erting, C. J. (1989, Fall). How deaf parents communicate with their deaf infants. *Research at Gallaudet.* Washington, DC: Gallaudet University Press.

Erting, C. J., Prezioso, C., & O'Grady Hynes, M. (1990). The interactional context of deaf mother-infant communication. In V. Volterra & C. J. Erting (Eds.), *From gesture to language in hearing and deaf children.* (pp. 97–106). Berlin: Springer-Verlag.

Evans, D. (1988). Strange bedfellows: Deafness, language, and the sociology of knowledge. *Symbolic Interaction, 11*, 235–255.

Everhart, V. S., & Lederberg, A. R. (1991). *The effect of mothers' visual communication use on deaf preschoolers' visual communication.* Paper presented at biennial meetings of the Society for Research in Child Development.

Everhart, V. S., & Marschark, M. (1988). Linguistic flexibility in the written and signed/oral language productions of deaf and hearing children. *Journal of Experimental Child Psychology, 46*, 174–193.

Ewoldt, C. (1981). A psycholinguistic description of selected deaf children reading in sign language. *Reading Research Quarterly, 17*, 58–89.

Feldman, H., Goldin-Meadow, S., & Gleitman, L. (1978). Beyond Herodotus: The creation of language by linguistically deprived deaf children. In A. Lock (Ed.), *Action, symbol, and gesture: The emergence of language* (pp. 351–414). New York: Academic Press.

Feyereisen, P., & de Lannoy, J. D. (1991). *Gestures and speech: Psychological investigations.* New York: Cambridge University Press.

Fischer, S. D. (1975). Influences on word-order change in American Sign Language. In C. N. Li (Ed.), *Word order and word order change* (pp. 1–25). Austin: University of Texas Press.

Fischer, S. D. (1978). Sign Language and creoles. In C. Siple (Ed.), *Understanding language through sign language research* (pp. 309–331). New York: Academic Press.

Fischler, I. (1985). Word recognition, use of context, and reading skill among deaf college students. *Reading Research Quarterly, 20*, 203–218.

Folven, R. J., & Bonvillian, J. D. (1985). *Nonlinguistic gestures and early sign language acquisition.* Paper presented at the biennial meetings of the Society for Research in Child Development.

Folven, R. J., & Bonvillian, J. D. (1987). *The onset of referential signing in children.* Paper presented at biennial meetings of the Society for Research in Child Development.

Fromkin, V. A., Krashen, S., Curtiss, S., Rigler, D., & Rigler, M. (1974). The development of language in Genie: A case of language acquisition beyond the "critical period." *Brain and Language, 1,* 81–107.

Fruchter, A., Wilbur, R. B., & Fraser, J. B. (1984). Comprehension of idioms by hearing-impaired students. *Volta Review, 86,* 7–19.

Frumkin, B., & Anisfeld, M. (1977). Semantic and surface codes in the memory of deaf children. *Cognitive Psychology, 9,* 475–493.

Furrow, D., Nelson, K., & Benedict, H. (1979). Mothers' speech to children and syntactic development: Some simple relationships. *Journal of Child Language, 6,* 423–442.

Furth, H. G. (1961a). Influence of language on the development of concept formation in deaf children. *Journal of Abnormal and Social Psychology, 63,* 386–389.

Furth, H. G. (1961b). Visual paired-associates task with deaf and hearing children. *Journal of Speech and Hearing Research, 4,* 172–177.

Furth, H. G. (1964). Reasearch with the deaf: Implications for language and cognition. *Psychological Bulletin, 62,* 145–164.

Furth, H. G. (1966). *Thinking without language.* New York: Free Press.

Furth, H. G. (1973). *Deafness and learning.* Belmont, CA: Wadsworth.

Furth, H., & Milgram, N. (1965). The influence of langauge on classification: Normal, retarded, and deaf. *Genetic Psychology Monograph, 72,* 317–351.

Furth, H. G., & Youniss, J. (1964). Color-object paired associates in deaf and hearing children with and without response condition. *Journal of Consulting Psychology, 28, 3,* 224–227.

Fusaro, J., & Slike, S. (1979). The effect of imagery on the ability of hearing-impaired children to identify words. *American Annals of the Deaf, 124,* 829–832.

Gaines, R., Mandler, J., & Bryant, P. (1981). Immediate and delayed story recall by hearing and deaf children. *Journal of Speech and Hearing Research, 24,* 463–469.

Gardner, H., Winner, E., Bechofer, R., & Wolf, D. (1978). The development of figurative language. In K. Nelson (Ed.), *Children's language* (Vol. 1). New York: Gardner.

Garrison, W. M., Tesch, S., & DeCara, F. (1978). Assessment of self concept levels amongst post-secondary deaf adolescents. *American Annals of the Deaf, 123,* 968–975.

Geers, A., Moog, J., & Schick, B. (1984). Acquisition of spoken and signed English by profoundly deaf children. *Journal of Speech and Hearing Disorders, 49,* 378–388.

Geers, A. E., & Schick, B. (1988). Acquisition of spoken and signed English by hearing-impaired children of hearing-impaired or hearing parents. *Journal of Speech and Hearing Disorders, 53,* 136–143.

Gibbs, K. W. (1989). Individual differences in cognitive skills related to reading ability in the deaf. *American Annals of the Deaf, 134,* 214–218.

Gilbert, J. H. V. (1982). Babbling and the deaf child: A commentary on Lenneberg *et al.* (1965) and Lenneberg (1967). *Journal of Child Language, 9,* 511–515.

Ginsburg, H., & Opper, S. (1979). *Piaget's theory of intellectual development.* Englewood Cliffs, NJ: Prentice Hall.

Glucksberg, S., & Krauss, R. M. (1967). What do people say after they have learned how to talk? Studies of the development of referential communication. *Merrill-Palmer Quarterly, 13,* 309–316.

Goetzinger, C. P., & Huber, T. G. (1964). A study of immediate and delayed visual retention with deaf and hearing adolescents. *American Annals of the Deaf, 109,* 297–305.

Goldin-Meadow, S., & Feldman, H. (1975). The creation of a communication system: A study of deaf children of hearing parents. *Sign Language Studies, 8,* 225–234.

Goldin-Meadow, S., & Morford, M. (1985). Gesture in early child language: Studies of deaf and hearing children. *Merrill-Palmer Quarterly, 31,* 145–176.

Goldin-Meadow, S., & Mylander, C. (1984). Gestural communication in deaf children: The effects and noneffects of parental input on early language development. *Society for Research in Child Development Monographs 49*(207).

Goodwyn, S. W., & Acredolo, L. P. (1991). *Symbolic gesture versus word: Is there a modality advantage for onset of symbol use?* Paper presented at biennial mettings of the Society for Research in Child Development.

Goss, R. N. (1970). Language used by mothers of deaf children and mothers of hearing children. *Americal Annals of the Deaf, 115*, 93–96.

Gottlieb, G. (1980). Development of species identification in ducklings: VII. Highly specific early experience fosters species-specific perception in wood ducklings. *Journal of Comparative and Physiological Psychology, 94*, 1019–1027.

Gottlieb, G., Doran, C., & Whitley, S. (1964). Cerebral dominance and speech acquisition in deaf children. *Journal of Abnormal and Social Psychology, 69*, 182–189.

Greenberg, M., Calderon, R., & Kusché, C. (1984). Early intervention using simultaneous communication with deaf infants: The effect on communication development. *Child Development, 55*, 607–616.

Greenberg, M. T., & Kusché, C. A. (1987). Cognitive, personal, and social development of deaf children and adolescents. In M. C. Wang, M. C. Reynolds, & H. J. Walberg (Eds.), *Handbook of special education: Research and practice. Vol. 3. Low incidence conditions* (pp. 95–129). New York: Pergamon Press.

Greenberg, M. T., & Marvin, R. S. (1979). Attachment patterns in profoundly deaf preschool children. *Merrill-Palmer Quarterly, 25*, 265–279.

Greenfield, P. M. (1991). Language, tools, and brain: The ontogeny and phylogeny of hierarchically organized sequential behavior. *Behavioral and Brain Sciences, 14*, 531–595.

Gregory, S. (1976). *The deaf child and his family*. New York: Halsted Press.

Gregory, S., & Mogford, K. (1981). Early language development in deaf children. In B. Woll, J. G. Kyle, & M. Deuchar (Eds.), *Perspectives on BSL and deafness* (pp. 218–237). London: Croom Helm.

Griffith, P. L., Ripich, D. N., & Dastoli, S. L. (1990). Narrative abilities in hearing-impaired children: Propositions and cohesion. *American Annals of the Deaf, 135*, 14–19.

Griswold, L. E., & Commings, J. (1974). The expressive vocabulary of preschool deaf children. *American Annals of the Deaf, 119*, 16–28.

Grossmann, K., Fremmer-Bombik, E., Rudolph, J., & Grossmann, K. E. (1988). Maternal attachment representations as related to patterns of infant-mother attachment and maternal care during the first year. In R. A. Hinde & J. Stevenson-Hinde (Eds.), *Relationships within families* (pp. 241–260). Oxford: Oxford Science.

Hairston, E., & Smith, L. (1983). *Black and deaf in America: Are we really that different?* Silver Spring, MD: T. J. Publishers.

Halliday, M. (1975). *Learning how to mean*. New York: Elsevier North-Holland.

Hanson, V. (1982). Short-term recall by deaf signers of American sign language: Implications of encoding strategy for order recall. *Journal of Experimental Psychology: Learning, Memory, and Cognition, 8*, 572–583.

Hanson, V. L. (1986). Access to spoken language and the acquisition of orthographic structure: Evidence from deaf readers. *Quarterly Journal of Experimental Psychology, 38A*, 193–212.

Hanson, V. L., & Fowler, C. A. (1987). Phonological coding in word reading: Evidence from hearing and deaf readers. *Memory & Cognition, 15*, 199–207.

Hanson, V. L., Goodell, E. W., & Perfetti, C. A. (1991). Tongue-twister effects in the silent reading of hearing and deaf college students. *Journal of Memory and Language, 30*, 319–330.

Hanson, V. L., Shankweiler, D., & Fischer, F. W. (1983). Determinants of spelling ability in deaf and hearing adults: Access to linguistic structure. *Cognition, 14,* 323–344.

Harmon, R. L., Jr. (1992). *The relationship of parental communication and acceptance to the behavioral problems of deaf children.* Unpublished master's thesis, University of North Carolina at Greensboro.

Harris, A. E. (1978). The development of the deaf individual and the deaf community. In L. Liben (Ed.), *Deaf children: Developmental perspectives* (pp. 217–234). New York: Academic Press.

Harris, M., & Arnold, P. (1984). Hearing-impaired and hearing pupils memory for lip. hand and letter shapes. *Journal of British Teachers of the Deaf, 8,* 65–68.

Harris, R. I. (1978). Impulse control in deaf children: Research and clinical issues. In L.S. Liben (Ed.), *Deaf children: Developmental perspectives* (pp. 137–156). Orlando, FL: Academic Press.

Hartman, J. S., & Elliot, L. L. (1965). Performance of deaf and hearing children on a short term memory task. *Psychonomic Science, 3,* 573–574.

Heider, F., & Heider, G. M. (1941). Studies in the psychology of the deaf. *Psychological Monographs 53*(242).

Henggeler, S. W., Watson, S. M., & Cooper, P. F. (1984). Verbal and nonverbal maternal controls in hearing mother-deaf child interaction. *Journal of Applied Developmental Psychology, 5,* 319–329.

Hermelin, B., & O'Connor, N. (1973). Ordering in recognition memory after ambiguous initial or recognition displays. *Canadian Journal of Psychology, 27,* 191–199.

Hermelin, B., & O'Connor, N. (1975). The recall of digits by normal, deaf, and autistic children. *British Journal of Psychology, 66,* 203–209.

Higgins, P. C. (1980). *Outsiders in a hearing world: A sociology of deafness.* Beverly Hills, CA: Sage Publications.

Higgins, P. C., & Nash, J. E. (1987). *Understanding deafness socially.* Springfield, IL: Charles C Thomas Publishers.

Hirshoren, A., Hurley, O. L., & Kavale, K. (1979). Psychometric characteristics of the WISC-R Performance Scale with deaf children. *Journal of Speech and Hearing Disorders, 44,* 73–79.

Hockett, C. F. (1963). The problem of universals in language. In J.H. Greenberg (Ed.), *Universals of language.* Cambridge, MA: MIT Press.

Hockett, C. F., & Altmann, S. A. (1968). A note on design features. In T. A. Sebeok (Ed.), *Animal communication* (pp. 61–72). Bloomington: Indiana University Press.

Hoemann, H., Andrews, C., & DeRosa, D. (1974). Categorical encoding in short-term memory by deaf and hearing children. *Journal of Speech and Hearing Research, 17,* 426–431.

Hofer, M. A. (1987). Early social relationships: A psychobiologist's view. *Child Development, 58,* 633–647.

Hoffmeister, R. J. (1982). Acquisition of signed languages by deaf children. In H. Hoeman & R. Wilbur (Eds.), *Communication in two societies.* Washington, DC: Gallaudet College Press.

Holmes, K. M., & Holmes, D. W. (1980). Signed and spoken language development in a hearing child of hearing parents. *Sign Language Studies, 28,* 239–254.

Hopkins, B. (1983). The development of early non-verbal communication: An evaluation of its meaning. *Journal of Child Psychology and Psychiatry, 24,* 131–144.

Hough, J. (1983). *Louder than words.* Cambridge: Great Ouse Press.

Hung, D. L., Tzeng, O. J. L., & Warren, D. H. (1981). A chronometric study of sentence processing in deaf children. *Cognitive Psychology, 13,* 583–610.

Iran-Nejad, A., Ortony, A., & Rittenhouse, R. K. (1981). The comprehension of metaphorical uses of English by deaf children. *Journal of Speech and Hearing Research, 24,* 551–556.

Itard, J. M. G. (1962). *The wild boy of Aveyron.* New York: Appleton-Century-Crofts.

Janos, P. M., & Robinson, N. M. (1985). Psychological development in intellectually gifted children. In F. D. Horowitz & M. O'Brien (Eds), *The gifted and talented.* Washington, DC: American Psychological Association.

Jacobs, L. M. (1988). *A deaf adult speaks out.* Washington, DC: Gallaudet University Press.

Jakobson, R. (1968). *Child language, aphasia, and general sound laws* (A. Keiler, Trans.). The Hague: Mouton.

Jarvella, R. (1971). Syntactic processing of connected speech. *Journal of Verbal Learning and Verbal Behavior, 10,* 409–416.

Jensema C. J., & Trybus, R. J. (1978). *Communicating patterns and educational achievements of hearing impaired students.* Washington, DC: Gallaudet College Office of Demographic Studies.

Johnson, R. A. (1977). Creative thinking in the absence of language: Deaf versus hearing adolescents. *Child Study Journal, 7,* 49–57.

Johnson, R. A., & Khatena, J. (1975). Comparative study of verbal originality in deaf and hearing children. *Perceptual and Motor Skills, 40,* 631–635.

Johnson, R. E., Liddell, S. K., & Erting, C. J. (1989). *Unlocking the curriculum: Principles for achieving access in deaf education.* Gallaudet Research Institute Working Paper 89-3. Washington, DC: Gallaudet University Press.

Jones, M. L., & Quigley, S. P. (1979). The acquisition of question formation in spoken English and American Sign Language by two hearing children of deaf parents. *Journal of Speech and Hearing Disorders, 44,* 196–208.

Jones, P. A. (1979). Negative interference of signed language in written English. *Sign Language Studies, 24,* 273–279.

Jordan, I. K. & Karchmer, M. A. (1986). Patterns of sign use among hearing impaired student. In A. N. Schildroth and M. A. Karchmer (Eds.), *Deaf children in America* (pp. 125–138). San Diego, CA: College-Hill Press.

Kail, R. (1990). *The development of memory in children.* New York: W. H. Freeman.

Kaltsounis, B. (1970). Differences in verbal creative thinking abilities between deaf and hearing children. *Psychological Reports, 26,* 727–733.

Kaltsounis, B. (1971). Differences in creative thinking of black and white deaf children. *Perceptual and Motor Skills, 32,* 243–248.

Kampfe, C. M. (1989). Reading comprehension of deaf adolescent residential school students and its relationship to hearing mothers' communication strategies and skills. *American Annals of the Deaf, 134,* 317–322.

Kantor, N. (1980). The acquisition of classifiers in American Sign Language. *Sign Language Studies, 28,* 193–208.

Kantor, R. (1982). Communicative interaction: Mother modification and child acquisition of American Sign Language. *Sign Language Studies, 36,* 233–278.

Karchmer, M. A. (1985). Demographics and deaf adolescence. In G. B. Anderson and D. Watson (Eds.), *The habilitation and rehabilitation of deaf adolescents* (pp. 28–47). Washington, DC: Gallaudet College Press.

Kelly, R. R., & Tomlinson-Keasey, C. (1977). Hemispheric laterality of deaf children for processing words and pictures visually presented to the hemifields. *American Annals of the Deaf, 122,* 525–533.

Kernohan, H. (1986). Visual memory for simultaneously presented data in hearing-impaired and normal hearing children. *Journal of British Teachers of the Deaf, 10,* 4–9.

Kimura, D. (1975). The neural basis of language qua gesture. In H. Avakian-Whitaker & H.

A. Whitaker (Eds.), *Studies in neurolinguistics* (pp.145–156). New York: Academic Press.

Kimura, D. (1981). Neural mechanisms in manual signing. *Sign Language Studies, 33,* 291–312.

King, C. M., & Quigley, S. P. (1985). *Reading and deafness.* San Diego, CA: College Hill Press.

Klima, E., & Bellugi, U. (1976). Poetry and song in a language without sound. *Cognition, 4,* 45–97.

Klima, E., & Bellugi, U. (1979). *The signs of language.* Cambridge, MA: Harvard University Press.

Koester, L. S., & Trimm, V. M. (1991). *Face-to-face interactions with deaf and hearing infants: Do maternal or infant behaviors differ?* Paper presented at biennial meetings of Society for Research in Child Development.

Koh, S. D., Vernon, M., & Bailey, W. (1971). Free-recall learning of word lists by prilingual deaf subjects. *Journal of Verbal Learning and Verbal Behavior, 10,* 542–547.

Kohlberg, L. (1969). Stage and sequence: The cognitive-development approach to socialization. In D. A. Goslin (Ed.), *Handbook of socialization theory and research* (pp. 347–480). Chicago: Rand McNally.

Kolb, B., & Wishaw, I. Q. (1990). *Fundamentals of human neuropsychology.* New York: W. H. Freeman.

Konigsmark, B. W. (1972). Genetic hearing loss with no associated abnormalities. *Journal of Speech and Hearing Disorders, 37,* 89–99.

Krakow, R. A., & Hanson, V. L. (1985). Deaf signers and serial recall in the visual modality: Memory for signs, fingerspelling, and print. *Memory & Cognition, 13,* 265–272.

Kramer, A., & Buck, L. A. (1976). Poetic creativity in deaf children. *American Annals of the Deaf, 121,* 31–37.

Kretschmer, R. R., & Kretschmer, L. W. (1978). *Language development and intervention in the hearing impaired.* Baltimore: University Park Press.

Kricos, P. B., & Aungst, H. L. (1984). Cognitive & communicative development in hearing-impaired preschool children. *Sign Language Studies, 43,* 121–139.

Krinsky, S. G. (1990). The feeling of knowing in deaf adolescents. *American Annals of the Deaf, 135,* 389–395.

Kusché, C. A., Garfield, T. S., & Greenberg, M. T. (1983). The understanding of emotional and social attributions in deaf adolescents. *Journal of Clinical Child Psychology, 12,* 153–160.

Kusché, C. A., & Greenberg, M. T. (1983). Evaluative understanding and role-taking ability: A comparison of deaf and hearing children. *Child Development, 54,* 141–147.

Kusché, C. A., Greenberg, M. T., & Garfield, T. S. (1983). Nonverbal intelligence and verbal achievement in deaf adolescents: An examination of heredity and environment. *American Annals of the Deaf, 128,* 458–466.

Kyle, J. (1980). Reading development of deaf children. *Journal of Research in Reading, 3,* 86–97.

Lamb, M., Thompson, R., Gardner, W., & Charnov, E. (1985). *Infant-mother attachment: The origins and developmental significance of individual differences in strange situation behavior.* Hillsdale, NJ: Lawrence Erlbaum.

Lamb, M. E., & Nash, A. (1989). Infant-mother attachment, sociability, and peer competence. In T.J. Berndt & G. W. Ladd (Eds.), *Peer relations in child development* (pp. 219–245). New York: John Wiley & Sons.

Lane, H., Boyes-Braem, P., & Bellugi, U. (1976). Preliminaries to a distinctive feature analysis of handshapes in American Sign Language. *Cognitive Psychology, 8,* 263–289.

Laughton, J. (1979). Nonlinguistic creative abilities and expressive syntactic abilities of hearing-impaired children. *Volta Review, 81*, 409–420.

Lederberg, A. R. (1991). Social interaction among deaf preschoolers: The effects of language ability and age. *American Annals of the Deaf, 136*, 35–59.

Lederberg, A. R. (1993). The impact of child deafness on social relationships. In M. Marschark & D. Clark (Eds.), *Psychological perspectives on deafness* (pp. 93–199). Hillsdale, NJ: Lawrence Erlbaum.

Lederberg, A. R., & Mobley, C. E. (1990). The effect of hearing impairment on the quality of attachment and mother-toddler interaction. *Child Development, 61*, 1596–1604.

Lederberg, A. R., Rosenblatt, V. R., & Vandell, D. L. (1987). Temporary and long-term friendships in hearing and deaf preschoolers. *Merrill-Palmer Quarterly, 33*, 513–533.

Lederberg, A. R., Ryan, H. B., & Robbins, B. L. (1986). Peer interaction in young deaf children: The effect of partner hearing status and familiarity. *Developmental Psychology, 22*, 691–700.

Lederberg, A. R., Willis, M. G., & Frankel, K. H. (1991). *A longitudinal study of the effects of deafness on the early mother-child relationship.* Paper presented at biennial meetings of the Society for Research in Child Development.

Leigh, I. W., Robins, C. J., Welkowitz, J., & Bond, R. N. (1989). Toward greater understanding of depression in deaf individuals. *American Annals of the Deaf, 134*, 249–254.

Lenneberg, E. (1967). *Biological foundations of language.* New York: John Wiley & Sons.

Lenneberg, E., Rebelsky, F. G., & Nichols, I. A. (1965). The vocalization of infants born to deaf and to hearing parents. *Human Development, 8*, 23–37.

Levine, E. S., & Wagner, E. E. (1974). Personality patterns of deaf persons: An interpretation based on research with the hand test. *Perceptual and Motor Skills Monograph Supplement, 39*, 23–44.

Leybaert, J., Algeria, J., & Fonck, E. (1983). Automaticity in word recognition and in word naming by the deaf. *Cahiers de Psychologie Cognitive, 3*, 255–272.

Leybaert, J., Algeria, J., & Morais, J. (1982). On automatic reading processes in the deaf. *Cahiers de Psychologie Cognitive, 2*, 185–192.

Leybaert, J., Content, A., & Alegria, J. (1987). *The development of written word processing: The case of deaf children.* Workshop presentation, ISPL Congress, University of Kassel.

Liben, L. S. (1978). Developmental perspectives on experiential deficiencies of deaf children. In L. Liben (Ed.), *Deaf children: Developmental perspectives* (pp. 195–215). New York: Academic Press.

Liben, L. S. (1979). Free recall by deaf and hearing children: Semantic clustering and recall in trained and untrained groups. *Journal of Experimental Child Psychology, 27*, 105–119.

Liben, L. S., & Drury, A. M. (1977). Short term memory in deaf and hearing children in relation to stimulus characteristics. *Journal of Experimental Child Psychology, 24*, 60–73.

Liben, L. S., Nowell, R. C., & Posnansky, C. J. (1978). Semantic and formational clustering in deaf and hearing subjects free recall of signs. *Memory & Cognition, 6*, 599–606.

Lichtenstein, E. (1985). Deaf working memory processes and English language skills. In D. S. Martin (Ed.), *Cognition, education, and deafness* (pp. 111–114). Washington, DC: Gallaudet College Press.

Lidell, S. (1980). *American Sign Language Syntax.* The Hague: Mouton.

Lillo-Martin, D. (1993). Deaf readers and universal grammar. In M. Marschark & D. Clark (Eds.), *Psychological perspectives on deafness* (pp. 311–337). Hillsdale, NJ: Lawrence Erlbaum.

Lister, C., Leach, C., & Wesencraft, K. (1988). Sequence in hearing impaired children's development of concepts. *British Journal of Educational Psychology*, *58*, 127–133.

Locke, J. L. (1978). Phonemic effects in the silent reading of hearing and deaf children. *Cognition*, *6*, 175–187.

Locke, J. L. (1983). *Phonological acquisition and change*. New York: Academic Press.

Locke, J. L., & Locke, V. L. (1971). Deaf children's phonetic, visual, and dactylic coding in a grapheme recall task. *Journal of Experimental Psychology*, *89*, 142–146.

Lowenbraun, S., & Thompson, M. (1987). Environments and strategies for learning and teaching. In M. C. Wang, M. C. Reynolds, & Walberg (Ed.), *Handbook of special education: Research and practice. Vol. 3: Low incidence conditions* (pp. 47–70). New York: Pergamon Press.

Lubin, E., & Sherrill, C. (1980). Motor creativity of preschool children. *American Annals of the Deaf*, *125*, 460–466.

Luetke-Stahlman, B., & Luckner, J. (1991). *Effectively educating students with hearing impairments*. New York: Longman Publishing.

Luterman, D. (1987). *Deafness in the family*. Boston: College-Hill Press.

MacDougall, J. (1979). The development of visual processing and short-term memory in deaf and hearing children. *American Annals of the Deaf*, *124*, 16–22.

MacDougall, J., & Rabinovitch, M. (1971). Imagery and learning in deaf and hearing children. *Psychonomic Science*, *22*, 347–349.

MacKay-Soroka, S., Trehub, S. E., & Thorpe, L. A. (1987). Referential communication between mothers and their deaf children. *Child Development*, *58*, 986–992.

MacKay-Soroka, S., Trehub, S. E., & Thorpe, L. A. (1988). Reception of mothers' referential messages by deaf and hearing children. *Developmental Psychology*, *24*, 277–285.

Macnamara, J. (1972). Cognitive basis of language learning in infants. *Psychological Review*, *79*, 1–13.

Maestas y Moores, J. (1980). Early linguistic environment: Interactions of deaf parents with their infants. *Sign Language Studies*, *26*, 1–13.

Main, M., Kaplan, K., & Cassidy, J. (1985). Security in infancy, childhood, and adulthood: A move to the level of representation. In I. Bretherton & E. Waters (Eds.), *Growing points of attachment: Theory and research. Monographs of the Society for Research in Child Development*. *50*(209), 66–104.

Markowicz, H. (1977). *American Sign Language: Fact and fancy*. Washington, DC: Gallaudet College Press.

Marmor, G., & Petitto, L. (1979). Simultaneous communication in the classroom: How well is English grammar represented? *Sign Language Studies*, *23*, 99–136.

Marschark, M. (1983). A code by any other name . . . *Behavioral and Brain Sciences*, *6*, 152–153.

Marschark, M. (1988a). Valutazione delle abilita linguistiche in bambini sordi: Lettura, scrittura, e linguaggio dei segni [Assessing language abilities of deaf children: Reading, writing, and sign language]. In R. Vianello & C. Cornoldi (Eds.), *Handicap linguaggio e communicazione* (pp. 69–79). Bergamo, Italy: Juvenilia Press.

Marschark, M. (1988b). Automaticity in word and sign recognition by deaf adults and children. *Sign Language Studies*, *58*, 1–19.

Marschark, M. (1989). Disturbi d'apprendimento e memoria in bambini sordi [Problems of learning and memory in deaf children]. In R. Vianello & C. Cornoldi (Eds.), *Handicap memoria e apprendimento* (pp. 37–48). Bergamo: Juvenilia.

Marschark, M. (1990). Lo sviluppo sociale dei bambini sordi [Social development in deaf children]. In C. Cornoldi and R. Vianello (Eds.), *Handicap autonomia e socializzazone* (pp. 112–125). Bergamo, Italy: Juvenilia.

Marschark, M. (1993). Origins and interactions in the social, cognitive, and language development of deaf children. In M. Marschark & D. Clark (Eds.), *Psychological perspectives on deafness* (pp. 7–26). Hillsdale, NJ: Lawrence Erlbaum.

Marschark, M. (1992). Gesture and sign. Manuscript submitted for publication.

Marschark, M., & Clark, D. (1987). Linguistic and nonlinguistic creativity of deaf children. *Developmental Review, 7*, 22–38.

Marschark, M., & Clark, D. (1993). *Psychological perspectives on deafness*. Hillsdale, NJ: Lawrence Erlbaum.

Marschark, M., De Beni, R., Polazzo, M. G., & Cornoldi, C. (1992). Relational and distinctive information in prose memory of deaf adolescents. Manuscript submitted for publication.

Marschark, M., Everhart, V. S., & Dempsey, P. R. (1991). Nonliteral content in the language of deaf, hearing, and bilingual mothers. *Merrill-Palmer Quarterly, 37*, 305–323.

Marschark, M., Everhart, V. S., Martin, J., & West, S. A. (1987). Identifying linguistic creativity in deaf and hearing children. *Metaphor and Symbolic Activity, 2*, 281–306.

Marschark, M., Mouradian, V., & Halas, M. (1992). The coherence of causal events in the signed and written stories of deaf children: A developmental study. Manuscript submitted for publication.

Marschark, M., & Nall, L. (1985). Metaphoric competence in cognitive and language development. In H. Reese (Ed.), *Advances in child development and behavior* (pp. 49–82). New York: Academic Press.

Marschark, M., & Shroyer, E. (1992). Hearing status and language fluency as predictors of automatic word and sign recognition. Manuscript submitted for publication.

Marschark, M., & Surian, L. (1989). Why does imagery improve memory?. *European Journal of Cognitive Psychology, 1*, 251–268.

Marschark, M., & West, S. A. (1985). Creative language abilities of deaf children. *Journal of Speech and Hearing Research, 28*, 73–78.

Marschark, M., West, S. A., Nall, L., & Everhart, V. (1986). Development of creative language devices in signed and oral production. *Journal of Experimental Child Psychology, 41*, 534–550.

Marshall, W. (1970). Contextual constraint on deaf and hearing children. *American Annals of the Deaf, 115*, 682–689.

Maskarinec, A. S., Cairns, G. F., Butterfield, E. C., & Weamer, D. K. (1981). Longitudinal observations of individual infants' vocalizations. *Journal of Speech and Hearing Disorders, 46*, 267–273.

Mateer, C., Rapport, R., & Kettrick, C. (1984). Cerebral organization of oral and signed language responses: Case study evidence from amytal and cortical stimulation studies. *Brain and Language, 21*, 123–135.

Mavilya, M. P. (1972). Spontaneous vocalization and babbling in hearing impaired infants. In G. Fant (Ed.), *International symposium on speech communication abilities and profound deafness* (pp. 163–171). Washington, DC: Alexander Graham Bell Association.

Mayberry, R. I., & Eichen, E. B. (1991). The long-lasting advantage of learning sign language in childhood: Another look at the critical period for language acquisition. *Journal of Memory and Language, 30*, 486–512.

McCune-Nicolich, L. (1981). Toward symbolic functioning: Structure of early pretend games and potential parrallels with language. *Child Development, 52*, 785–797.

McDaniel, E. (1980). Visual memory in the deaf. *American Annals of the Deaf, 125 (1)*, 17–20.

McGurk, H., & Saqi, S. (1986). Serial recall: A reply to the rejoinder by Dodd & Campbell. *British Journal of Developmental Psychology, 4*, 315–316.

McIntire, M. (1974). A modified model for the description of language acquisition in a deaf child. Unpublished master's thesis, California State University, Northridge.

McIntire, M. L. (1977). The acquisition of American Sign Language hand configurations. *Sign Language Studies, 16,* 247–266.

McNeill, D. (1966). Developmental psycholinguistics. In F. Smith & G. Miller (Eds.), *The genesis of language* (pp. 15–84). Cambridge, MA: MIT Press.

McNeill, D. (1985). So you think gestures are nonverbal? *Psychological Review, 92,* 350–371.

McNeill, D. (1992). *Hand and mind.* New York: Harper & Row.

McNeill, D. (1993). The circle from gesture to sign. In M. Marschark & D. Clark (Eds.), *Psychological perspectives on deafness* (pp. 153–183). Hillsdale, NJ: Lawrence Erlbaum.

McNeill, D., Levy, E. T., & Pedelty, L. L. (1990). Speech and gesture. In G. R. Hammond (Ed.), *Advances in psychology: Cerebral control of speech and limb movements* (pp. 171–224). Amsterdam: Elsevier/North Holland Publishers.

Meadow, K. (1968). Early manual communication in relation to the deaf child's intellectual, social and communicative functioning. *American Annals of the Deaf, 113,* 29–41.

Meadow, K. (1972). Sociolinguistics, sign language, and the deaf sub-culture; Psycholinguistics and total communication: the state of the art. *American Annals of the Deaf,* 19–33.

Meadow, K. P. (1976). Personality and social development of deaf people. *Journal of Rehabilitation of the Deaf, 9,* 1–12.

Meadow, K. P. (1980). *Deafness and child development.* Berkeley: University of California Press.

Meadow, K. P., Greenberg, M. T., Erting, C., & Carmichael, H. (1981). Interactions of deaf mothers and deaf preschool children: Comparisons with three other groups of deaf and hearing dyads. *American Annals of the Deaf, 126,* 454–468.

Meadow-Orlans, K. P. (1987). An analysis of the effectiveness if early intervention programs for hearing-impaired children. In M. J. Guralnick & F. C. Bennett (Eds.), *The effectiveness of early intervention for at-risk and handicapped children* (pp. 325–362). New York: Academic Press.

Meier, R. P., & Newport, E. L. (1990). Out of the hands of babes: On a possible sign advantage in language acquisition. *Language, 66,* 1–23.

Miyake, K., Chen, S-J., & Campos, J. J. (1985). Infant temperament, mother's mode of interaction, and attachment in Japan: An interim report. In I. Bretherton and E. Waters (Eds.), *Growing points of attachment theory and research. Society for Research in Child Development Monographs, 50*(209), 276–299.

Moerk, E. L. (1983). *The mother of eve—As a first language teacher.* Norwood, NJ: Ablex.

Moores, D. (1967). Applications of "cloze" procedures to the assessment of psycholinguistic abilities of the deaf. Unpublished doctoral dissertation, University of Illinois at Urbana-Champaign.

Moores, D., & Meadow-Orlans, K. P. (1990). *Education and developmental aspects of deafness.* Washington, DC: Gallaudet University Press.

Moores, D. F. (1990). *Old w(h)ine in new bottles.* Unpublished memorandum, Gallaudet University.

Moores, D. F., & Kluwin, T. N. (1986). Issues in school placement. In A. N. Schildroth & M. A. Karchmer (Eds.), *Deaf children in America* (pp. 105–123). San Diego, CA: College-Hill Press.

Moores, D. F., Weiss, K. L., & Goodwin, M. W. (1973). *Evaluation of programs for hearing impaired children: Report of 1972–1973.* University of Minnesota Research, Development, and Demonstration Center in Education of Handicapped Children.

Mott, A. (1899). A comparison of deaf and hearing children in their ninth year. *American Annals of the Deaf, 44*, 401–412.

Moulton, R. D., & Beasley, D. S. (1975). Verbal coding strategies used by hearing-impaired individuals. *Journal of Speech and Hearing Research, 18*, 559–570.

Myklebust, H. E. (1953). Towards a new understanding of the deaf child. *American Annals of the Deaf, 98*, 345–357.

Myklebust, H. E. (1960). *The psychology of deafness.* New York: Grune & Stratton.

Mylander, C., & Goldin-Meadow, S. (1991). The home sign systems in deaf children: The development of morphology without a conventional language model. In P. Siple & S. Fischer (Eds.), *Theoretical issues in sign language research.* Chicago: University of Chicago Press.

Nash, J. E., & Nash, A. (1981). *Deafness in society.* Lexington, MA: DC Heath.

Nass, M. L. (1964). The development of conscience: A comparison of moral judgments of deaf and hearing children. *Child Development, 35*, 1073–1080.

Neisser, U. (1976). *Cognition and reality.* San Francisco: W. H. Freeman.

Nelson, K. (1973). Structure and strategy in learning to talk, *Monographs of the Society for Research in Child Development, 38(149)*.

Neville, H., Kutas, M., & Schmidt, A. (1982). Event-related potential studies of cerebral specialization during reading: II. Studies of congentially deaf adults. *Brain and Language, 16*, 316–337.

Neville, H. J., & Lawson, D. (1987). Attention to central and peripheral visual space in a movement detection task: an event-related potential and behavioral study. II. Congenitally deaf adults. *Brain Research, 405*, 268–283.

Newport, E. L. (1977). Motherese: The speech of mothers to young children. In J. J. Castellan, D. B. Pisoni, & G. R. Potts (Eds.), *Cognitive theory* (pp. 177–210). Hillsdale, NJ: Lawrence Erlbaum.

Newport, E. L., (1981). Constraints on structure: Evidence from American sign language and language learning. In W. A. Collins (Ed.), *Minnesota symposium on child psychology* (pp. 93–124). Hillsdale, NJ: Lawrence Erlbaum.

Newport, E. L., & Ashbrook, E. F. (1977). The emergence of semantic relations in ASL. *Papers and Reports on Child Language Development, 13*.

Newton, L. (1985). Linguistic environment of the deaf child: A focus on teachers' use of nonliteral language. *Journal of Speech and Hearing Research, 28*, 336–344.

O'Connor, N., & Hermelin, B. (1972). Seeing and hearing and time and space. *Perception & Psychophysics, 11*, 46–48.

O'Connor, N., & Hermelin, B. M. (1973a). The spatial or temporal organization of short-term memory. *Quarterly Journal of Experimental Psychology, 25*, 335–343.

O'Connor, N., & Hermelin, B. M. (1973b). Short-term memory for the order of pictures and syllables by deaf and hearing children. *Neuropsychologia, 11*, 437–442.

O'Connor, N., & Hermelin, B. M. (1976). Backward and forward recall by deaf and hearing children. *Quarterly Journal of Experimental Psychology, 28*, 83–92.

Odom, P. B., Blanton, R. I., & Laukhuf, C. (1973). Facial expressions and interpretation of emotion-arousing situations in deaf and hearing children. *Journal of Abnormal Child Psychology, 1*, 139–151.

Odom, P. B., Blanton, R. L., & McIntyre, C. K. (1970). Coding medium and word recall by deaf and hearing subjects. *Journal of Speech and Hearing Research, 13*, 54–58.

Oléron, P. (1953). Conceptual thinking of the deaf. *American Annals of the Deaf, 98*, 304–310.

Oller, D. K. (1980). The emergence of the sounds of speech in infancy. In G. Yeni-

Komshian, J. F. Kavanagh, & C. A. Ferguson (Eds.), *Child phonology: Production* (pp. 93–112). Orlando, FL: Academic Press.

Oller, D. K., & Eilers, R. E. (1988). The role of audition in infant babbling. *Child Development, 59,* 441–449.

Oller, D. K., Filers, R. E., Bull, D. H., & Carney, A. E. (1985). Prespeech vocalizations of a deaf infant: A comparison with normal metaphonological development. *Journal of Speech and Hearing Research, 28,* 47–63.

Oller, D. K., Wieman, L. A., Doyle, W. S., & Ross, C. (1976). Infant babbling and speech. *Journal of Child Language, 3,* 1–11.

Olsson, J. E., & Furth, H. G. (1966). Visual memory span in the deaf. *American Journal of Psychology, 79,* 480–484.

Orlansky, M. D., & Bonvillian, J. D. (1984). The role of iconicity in early sign language acquisition. *Journal of Speech and Hearing Disorders, 49,* 287–292.

Orlansky, M. D., & Bonvillian, J. D. (1985). Sign language acquisition: Language development in children of deaf parents and implications for other populations. *Merrill-Palmer Quarterly, 31,* 127–143.

Ortony, A. (1975). Why metaphors are necessary and not just nice. *Educational Theory, 25,* 45–53.

Ottem, E. (1980). An analysis of cognitive studies with deaf subjects. *American Annals of the Deaf, 125,* 564–575.

Padden, C., & Humphries, T. (1988). *Deaf in America.* Cambridge, MA: Harvard University Press.

Page, J. L. (1985). Relative translucency of ASL signs representing three semantic classes. *Journal of Speech and Hearing Disorders, 50,* 241–247.

Paivio, A. (1971). *Imagery and verbal processes.* New York: Holt, Rinehart, Winston.

Paivio, A., & Begg, I. (1981). *Psychology of language.* Englewood Cliffs, NJ: Prentice-Hall.

Paivio, A., Yuille, J. C., & Madigan, S (1968). Concreteness, Imagery, and meaningfulness values for 925 nound. *Journal of Experimental Psychology Monographs, 76,* 1–25.

Pang, H., & Horrocks, C. (1968). An exploratory study of creativity in deaf children. *Perceptual and Motor Skills, 27,* 844–846.

Paquin, M., & Braden, J. P. (1990). The effect of residential school placement on deaf children's performance IQ. *School Psychology Review, 19,* 350–355.

Parasnis, I. (1983a). Effects of parental deafness and early exposure to manual communication on the cognitive skills, English language skill, and field independence of young deaf adults. *Journal of Speech and Hearing Research, 26,* 588–594.

Parasnis, I. (1983b). Visual perceptual skills and deafness: A research review. *Journal of the Academy of Rehabilitative Audiology, 16,* 161–181.

Parasnis, I., & Long, G. (1979). Relationships among spatial skills, communication skills, and field independence in deaf students. *Perceptual and Motor Skills, 49,* 879–887.

Perfetti, C. A., & Goldman, S. R. (1976). Discourse memory and reading comprehension skill. *Journal of Verbal Learning and Verbal Behavior, 15,* 33–42.

Petitto, L. A. (1987). On the autonomy of language and gesture: Evidence from the acquisition of personal pronouns in American Sign Language. *Cognition, 27,* 1–52.

Petitto, L. A. (1988). "Language" in the pre-linguistic child. In F. Kessel (Ed.), *The development of language and language researchers* (pp. 187–221). Hillsdale, NJ: Lawrence Erlbaum.

Petitto, L. A., & Charron, F. (1991). *The acquisition of Langue des Signes Quebecoise (LSQ): The first fifty signs.* Unpublished manuscript.

Petitto, L. A., & Marentette, P. F. (1991). Babbling in the manual mode: Evidence for the ontogeny of language. *Science, 251,* 1493–1496.

Petrie, H. G. (1979). Metaphor and learning. In A. Ortony (Ed.), *Metaphor and thought* (pp. 438–461). Cambridge: Cambridge University Press.

Piaget, J. (1932). *The moral judgment of the child*. London: Kegan, Paul, Trench, & Trubner.

Piaget, J. (1952). *The origins of intelligence in children*. New York: Basic Books.

Piaget, J. (1962). *Play, dreams, and imitation in childhood*. New York: W. W. Norton.

Pintner, R., & Patterson, D. (1917). A comparison of deaf and hearing children in visual memory for digits. *Journal of Experimental Psychology, 2*, 76–88.

Pizzuto, E., & Williams, M. (1979). *The acquisition of the possessive forms of American Sign Language*. Paper presented at NATO Advanced Study Institute on Sign Language Research. Copenhagen.

Poizner, H., Klima, E. S., & Bellugi, U. (1987). *What the hands reveal about the brain*. Cambridge, MA: MIT Press.

Pollio, M. R., & Pollio, H. (1974). The development of figurative language in children. *Journal of Psycholinguistic Research, 3*, 185–201.

Potter, M. C. (1979). Mundane symbolism: The relations among objects, names, and ideas. In N. R. Smith & M. B. Franklin (Eds.), *Symbolic functioning in childhood* (pp. 41–65). Hillside, NJ: Lawrence Erlbaum.

Power, D. J., Wood, D. J., & Wood, H. A. (1990). Conversational strategies of teachers using three methods of communication with deaf children. *American Annals of the Deaf, 135*, 9–13.

Powers, A., & Wilgus, S. (1983). Linguistic complexity in the written language of deaf children. *Volta Review, 85*, 201–210.

Prinz, P. M., & Prinz, E. A. (1979). Simultaneous acquisition of ASL and spoken English. *Sign Language Studies, 25*, 283–296.

Prytulak, L. (1971). Natural language mediators. *Cognitive Psychology, 2*, 1–56.

Putnam, V., Iscoe, I., & Young, R. K. (1962). Verbal learning in the deaf. *Journal of Comparative and Physiological Psychology, 55*, 843–846.

Pylyshyn, Z. (1977). What does it take to bootstrap a language? In J. Macnamara (Ed.), *Language, learning, and thought* (pp. 37–45). Orlando, FL: Academic Press.

Quigley, S. P., & Paul, P. V. (1984). *Language and deafness*. San Diego, CA: College Hill Press.

Quigley, S. P., Power, D., & Steinkamp, M. (1977). The language structure of deaf children. *Volta Review, 79*, 73–84.

Quigley, S. P., Wilbur, R., Power, D., Montanelli, D., & Steinkamp, M. (1976). *Syntactic structure in the language of deaf children*. Urbana-Champaign: University of Illinois, Institute for Child Behavior and Develelopment.

Rainer, J. D., Altshuler, K. Z., Kallman, F. J., & Deming, W. E. (1963). *Family and mental health problems in a deaf population*. New York: NY State Psychiatric Institute.

Rawlings, B. W., & Jensema, C. J. (1977). *Two studies of the familites of hearing impaired children*. Washington, DC: Office of Demographic Studies, Gallaudet College.

Rea, C. A., Bonvillian, J. D., & Richards, H. C. (1988). Mother-infant interactive behaviors: Impact of maternal deafness. *American Annals of the Deaf, 133*, 317–324.

Reynolds, R. N. (1986). Performance of deaf college students on a criterion-referenced modified cloze test of reading comprehension. *Amercan Annals of the Deaf, 131*, 361–364.

Ricks, M. H. (1985). The social transmission of parental behavior: Attachment across generations. In I. Bretherton & E. Waters (Eds.), *Growing points of attachment theory and research. Society for Research in Child Development Monographs, 50*(209), 211–227.

Ries, P. (1986). Characteristics of hearing impaired youth in the general population and of students in special educational programs for the hearing impaired. In A. N. Schildroth

& M. A. Karchmer (Eds.), *Deaf children in America* (pp. 1–31). San Diego, CA: College-Hill Press.

Rittenhouse, R. K., & Kenyon, P. L. (1991). Conservation and metaphor acquisition in hearing-impaired children. *American Annals of the Deaf, 136,* 313–320.

Rittenhouse, R. K., Morreau, L. E., & Iran-Nejad, A. (1981). Metaphor and conservation in deaf and hard-of-hearing children. *American Annals of the Deaf, 126,* 450–453.

Rittenhouse, R. K. & Spiro, R. J. (1979). Conservation performance in day and residential school deaf children. *Volta Review, 81,* 501–509.

Rodda, M. (1966). Social adjustment of deaf adolescents. In *Proceedings of a symposium on the psychological study of deafness and hearing impairment.* London: British Psychological Association.

Rodda, M., Cumming, C., & Fewer, D. (1993). Memory, learning, and language: Implications for deaf education. In M. Marschark & M. D. Clark (Eds.), *Psychological perspectives on deafness* (pp. 339–352). Hillsdale, NJ: Lawrence Erlbaum.

Rodda, M., & Grove, C. (1987). *Language, cognition, and deafness.* Hillsdale, NJ: Lawrence Erlbaum.

Sachs, J., Bard, B., & Johnson, M. (1981). Language learning with restricted input: Case studies of two hearing children of deaf parents. *Applied Psycholinguistics, 2,* 33–54.

Sachs, J., & Johnson, M. L. (1976). Language development in a hearing child of deaf parents. In W. von Raffler Engel & Y. Lebrun (Eds.), *Baby talk and infant speech* (pp. 246–252). Lisse, The Netherlands: Swets & Zeitlinger.

Sallop, M. B. (1980). Pantomime and gesture to signed English. In W. C. Stokoe (Ed.), *Sign and culture* (pp. 217–226). Silver Spring, MD: Linstock Press.

Sarachan-Deily, A. B., & Love, R. J. (1974). Underlying grammatical rule structure in the deaf. *Journal of Speech and Hearing Research, 17,* 689–699.

Schein, J. D., & Delk, M. T. (1974). *The deaf population of the United States.* Silver Springs, MD: National Association of the Deaf.

Schiff, N. B., & Ventry, I. M. (1976). Communication problems in hearing children of deaf parents. *Journal of Speech and Hearing Disorders, 41,* 348–358.

Schiff-Myers, N. B. (1982). Sign and oral language development of preschool hearing children of deaf parents in comparison with their mother's communication system. *American Annals of the Deaf, 127,* 322–330.

Schildroth, A. N. (1986). Residential schools for deaf students: A decade in review. In A. N. Schildroth & M. A. Karchmer (Eds.), *Deaf children in America* (pp. 83–104). San Diego, CA: College-Hill Press.

Schirmer, B. S. (1989). Relationship between imaginative play and language development in hearing-impaired children. *American Annals of the Deaf, 134,* 219–222.

Schlesinger, H. S. (1978). The effects of deafness on childhood development: An Eriksonian perspective. In L. S. Liben (Ed.), *Deaf children: Developmental perspectives* (pp. 157–172). New York: Academic Press.

Schlesinger, H. S., & Meadow, K. P. (1972a). *Sound and sign: Childhood deafness and mental health.* Berkeley: University of California Press.

Schlesinger, H. S., & Meadow, K. P. (1972b). Development of maturity in deaf children. *Exceptional Children, 38,* 461–467.

Schwam, E. (1980). "MORE" is "LESS": Sign language comprehension in deaf and hearing children. *Journal of Experimental Child Psychology, 29,* 249–263.

Sharpe, S. L. (1985). The primary mode of human communication and complex cognition. *American Annals of the Deaf, 130,* 39–46.

Shroyer, E., & Shroyer, S. P. (1985). *Signs across America.*. Washington, DC: Gallaudet College Press.

Siegel, L. S., & Brainerd, C. J. (1978). *Alternatives to Piaget: Critical essays on the theory.* New York: Academic Press.

Silver, R. A. (1967). *A demonstration project in art education for deaf and hard of hearing children and adults.* New York: New York Society for the Deaf.

Silver, R. A. (1977). The question of imagination, originality, and abstract thinking by deaf children. *American Annals of the Deaf, 122*(3), 349–354.

Singer, D. G., & Lenahan, M. L. (1976). Imagination content in dreams of deaf children. *American Annals of the Deaf, 12*, 44–48.

Sisco, F. H., & Anderson, R. J. (1980). Deaf children's performance on the WISC-R relative to hearing status of parents and child-rearing experiences. *American Annals of the Deaf, 125*, 923–930.

Slobin, D. I. (1973). Cognitive prerequisites for the development of grammar. In C. A. Ferguson & D. I. Slobin (Eds.), *Studies of child language development* (pp. 175–208). New York: Holt, Rinehart, Winston.

Snitzer Reilly, J., McIntire, M. L., & Bellugi, U. (1990). Faces: The relationship between language and affect. In V. Volterra & C. J. Erting (Eds.), *From gesture to language in hearing and deaf children* (pp. 128–141). Berlin: Springer-Verlag.

Spelke, E., & Cortelyou, A. (1981). Perceptual aspects of social knowing: Looking and listening in infancy. In M. E. Lamb & L. R. Sherrod (Eds.), *Infant social cognition: Empirical and theoretical considerations* (pp. 61–84). Hillsdale, NJ: Lawrence Erlbaum.

Spencer, P., & Delk, L. (1989). Hearing-impaired students' performance on tests of visual processing: Relationships with reading performance. *American Annals of the Deaf, 134*, 333–337.

Spencer, P.E. (1991). *Communicative behaviors of hearing mothers and their hearing-impaired and hearing infants.* Paper presented at the biennial meetings of the Society for Reserarch in Child Development.

Spencer, P. E., & Deyo, D. A. (1993). Cognitive and social aspects of deaf children's play. In M. Marschark and D. Clark (Eds.), *Psychological perspectives on deafness* (pp. 65–91). Hillsdale, NJ: Lawrence Erlbaum.

Spence-Sutton, R., & Woll, B. (1993). The status and functional significance of finger-spelling in BSL. In M. Marschark & D. Clark (Eds.), *Psychological perspectives on deafness* (pp. 185–208). Hillsdale, NJ: Lawrence Erlbaum.

Sroufe, A. (1983). Individual patterns of adaptation from infancy to preschool. In M. Perlmutter (Ed.), *Development and policy concerning children with special needs. Minnesota symposium on child psychology* (pp. 41–81). Hillsdale, NJ: Lawrence Erlbaum.

Sroufe, A. (1990). The role of training in attachment assessment. *SRCD Newsletter, Autumn*, 1–2.

Stafford, K. (1962). Problem-solving ability of deaf and hearing children. *Journal of Speech and Hearing Research, 5*, 169–172.

Stanovich, K. (1986). Matthew effects in reading: Some consequences of individual differences in the development of literacy. *Reading Research Quarterly, 4*, 360–406.

Stark, R. E. (1983). Phonatory development in young normally hearing and hearing-impaired children. In I. Hochberg, H. Levitt, & M. J. Osberger (Eds.), *Speech of the hearing impaired: Research, training, and personnel* (pp. 251–266). Baltimore: University Park Press.

Statistical Abstracts of the United States (1985). Washington, DC: Bureau of the Census.

Stoel-Gammon, C. (1988). Prelinguistic vocalizations of hearing-impaired and normally hearing subjects: A comparison of consonantal inventories. *Journal of Speech and Hearing Disorders, 53*, 302–315.

Stoel-Gammon, C., & Otomo, K. (1986). Babbling development of hearing-impaired and normally hearing subjects. *Journal of Speech and Hearing Disorders, 51*, 33–41.

Stokoe, W., & Battison, R. M. (1981). Sign language, mental health and satisfactory interaction. In L. M. Stein, E. D. Mindel, & T. Jabaley (Eds.), *Deafness and mental health* (pp. 179–194). Orlando, FL: Grune & Stratton.

Stokoe, W. C., Casterline, D. C., & Croneberg, C. G. (1965). *A dictionary of American Sign Language on linguistic principles.* Washington, DC: Gallaudet College Press.

Stoloff, L., & Dennis, Z. (1978). Matthew. *American Annals of the Deaf, 123*, 452–459.

Suty, K. A. (1986). Individual differences in the signed communication of deaf children. *American Annals of the Deaf, 131*, 298–304.

Suty, K. A., & Friel-Patti, S. (1982). Looking beyond signed English to describe the language of two deaf children. *Sign Language Studies, 35*, 153–168.

Swisher, M. V. (1984). Signed input of hearing mothers to deaf children. *Language Learning, 34*, 69–85.

Swisher, M. V. (1993). Perceptual and cognitive aspects of recognition of signs in peripheral vision. In M. Marschark and M. D. Clark (Eds.), *Psychological perspectives on deafness* (pp. 209–227). Hillsdale, NJ: Lawrence Erlbaum Associates.

Templin, M. C. (1950). *The development of reasoning in children with normal and defective hearing.* Minneapolis: University of Minnesota Press.

Tervoort, B. (1975). *Developmental features of visual communication.* Amsterdam: North Holland.

Todd, P. H. (1976). A case of structural interference across sensory modalities in second-language learning. *Word, 27*, 102–118.

Tomkins, W. (1969). *Indian sign language.* New York: Dover.

Tomlinson-Keasey, C., & Kelly, R. R. (1978). The deaf child's symbolic world. *American Annals of the Deaf, 123*, 432–458.

Torrance, E. P. (1966). *Torrance tests of creative thinking: Norms—technical manual.* Lexington, MA: Personal Press.

Torrance, E. P. (1974). *Torrance tests of creative thinking: Tests.* Lexington, MA: Ginn & Company.

Torrance, E. P., Khatena, J., & Cunningham, X. (1973). *Thinking creatively with sounds and words.* Lexington, MA: Personnel Press.

Treiman, R., & Hirsh-Pasek, K. (1983). Silent reading: Insights from second-generation deaf readers. *Cognitive Psychology, 15*, 39–65.

Trybus, R., & Karchmer, M. (1977). School achievement scores of hearing impaired children: National data on achievement status and growth patterns. *American Annals of the Deaf Directory of Programs and Services, 122*, 62–69.

Tweney, R. D., Hoemann, H. W., & Andrews, C. E. (1975). Semantic organization in deaf and hearing subjects. *Journal of Psycholinguistic Research, 4*, 61–73.

Tzeng, O. J. L., & Wang, W. (1984). Dearch for a common neurocognitive mechanism for language and movements. *American Journal of Physiology, 246*, R904-R911.

Ulissi, S. M., Brice, P. J., & Gibbins, S. (1990). Use of the Kaufman-Assessment Battery for Children with the hearing impaired. *American Annals of the Deaf, 135*, 283–287.

Vargha-Khadam, F. (1983). Visual field asymmetries in congenitally deaf and hearing children. *British Journal of Developmental Psychology, 1*, 375–387.

Vernon, M. (1967). Relationship of language to the thinking process. *Archives of General Psychiatry, 16*, 325–333.

Vernon, M. (1969). Sociological and psychological factors associated with hearing loss. *Journal of Speech and Hearing Research, 12*, 541–563.

Vernon, M. (1972). Mind over mouth: A rationale for total communication. *Volta Review, 74*, 529–540.

Vernon, M., & Andrews, J. F. (1990). *The psychology of deafness.* New York: Longman.

Vernon, M., & Koh, S. D. (1970). Effects of early manual communication on achievement of deaf children. *American Annals of the Deaf, 115*, 527–536.

Vernon, M., Westminster, M., & Koh, S. (1971). Effects of oral preschool compared to early manual communication on education and communication in deaf children. *American Annals of the Deaf, 116*, 569–574.

Volterra, V., & Erting, C. J. (1990). *From gesture to language in hearing and deaf children.* Berlin: Springer-Verlag.

Vosniadou, S. (1987). Children and metaphors. *Child Development, 58*, 870–885.

Wallace, G., & Corballis, M. C. (1973). Short-term memory and coding strategies in the deaf. *Journal of Experimental Psychology, 99*, 334–348.

Waters, G. S., & Doehring, D. G. (1990). Reading acquisition in congenitally deaf children who communicate orally: Insights from an analysis of component reading, language, and memory skills. In T. H. Carr & B. A. Levy (Eds.), *Reading and its development* (pp. 323–373). San Diego, CA: Academic Press.

Watts, W. J. (1979). The influence of language on the development of quantitative, spatial, and social thinking in deaf children. *American Annals of the Deaf, 12*, 45–56.

Webster, A. (1986). *Deafness, development and literacy.* London: Methuen.

Wedell-Monnig, J., & Lumley, J. M. (1980). Child deafness and mother-child interaction. *Child Development, 51*, 766–774.

Werner, H., & Kaplan, B. (1963). *Symbol formation.* New York: Wiley.

Whetnall, E., & Fry, D. B. (1964). *The deaf child.* London: Heinemann.

Whitehurst, G. J. & Valdez-Menchaca, M. C. (1988). What is the role of reinforcement in early language acquisition? *Child Development, 59*, 430–440.

Whorf, B. L. (1956). *Language, thought, and reality.* Cambridge, MA: MIT Press.

Wilbur, R. B. (1977). An explanation of deaf children's difficulty with certain syntactic structures in English. *Volta Review, 79*, 85–92.

Wilbur, R. B. (1987). *American Sign Language: linguistic and applied dimensions.* Boston: Little, Brown.

Wilbur, R. B., Goodhart, W., & Montandon, E. (1983). Comprehension of nine syntatic structures by hearing-impaired students. *Volta Review, 85*, 328–345.

Wilson, K. (1979). *Inference and language processing in hearing and deaf children.* Unpublished doctoral dissertation, Boston University.

Wood, D., Wood, H., Griffiths, A., Howaith, S., & Howaith, C. (1982). The structure of conversations with 6- to-10-year-old deaf children. *Journal of Child Psychology and Psychiatry, 23*, 295–308.

Woodward, J., & Allen, T. E. (1987). Classroom use of ASL by teachers. *Sign Language Studies, 54*, 1–10.

Yoshinaga-Itano, C., & Snyder, L. (1985). Form and meaning in the written language of hearing-impaired children. *Volta Review, 87*, 75–90.

Young, E. P. & Brown, S. L. (1981). *The development of social-cognition in deaf preschool children: A pilot study.* Paper presented at meetings of the Southeastern Psychological Association, Atlanta.

Youniss, J., & Furth, H. G. (1970). Prediction of causal events as a function of transitivity and perceptual congruency in hering and deaf children. *Child Development, 41*, 73–81.

Youniss, J., & Robertson, A. (1970). Projective visual imagery as a function of age and deafness. *Child Development, 41*, 215–224.

Zweibel, A. (1987). More on the effects of early manual communication on the cognitive development of deaf children. *American Annals of the Deaf, 132*, 16–20.

Zwiebel, A., & Mertens, D. M. (1985). A comparison of intellectual structure in deaf and hearing children. *American Annals of the Deaf, 130*, 27–32.

Author Index

Subject Index